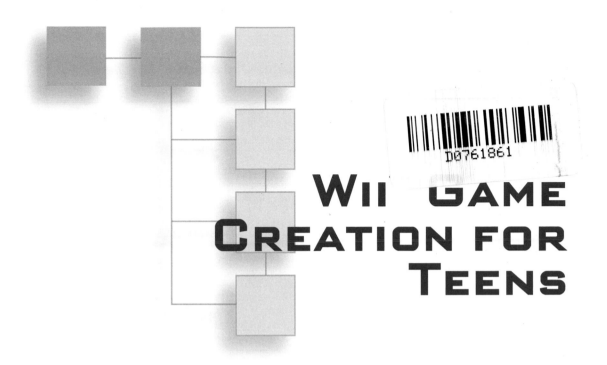

# WII GAME
# CREATION FOR
# TEENS

**MICHAEL DUGGAN**

**Course Technology PTR**

*A part of Cengage Learning*

COURSE TECHNOLOGY
CENGAGE Learning™

Australia • Brazil • Japan • Korea • Mexico • Singapore • Spain • United Kingdom • United States

## COURSE TECHNOLOGY
CENGAGE Learning

**Wii™ Game Creation for Teens**
Michael Duggan

**Publisher and General Manager, Course Technology PTR:** Stacy L. Hiquet

**Associate Director of Marketing:** Sarah Panella

**Manager of Editorial Services:** Heather Talbot

**Marketing Manager:** Jordan Castellani

**Senior Acquisitions Editor:** Emi Smith

**Project Editor:** Jenny Davidson

**Technical Reviewers:** Maneesh Sethi/Arlie Hartman

**Teen Reviewer:** J.T. Hiquet

**Interior Layout Tech:** MPS Limited, A Macmillan Company

**Cover Designer:** Mike Tanamachi

**CD-ROM Producer:** Brandon Penticuff

**Indexer:** Sharon Shock

**Proofreader:** Kim Benbow

For product information and technology assistance, contact us at **Cengage Learning Customer & Sales Support, 1-800-354-9706**

For permission to use material from this text or product, submit all requests online at **www.cengage.com/permissions**
Further permissions questions can be emailed to **permissionrequest@cengage.com**

Adobe Flash is the trademark of Adobe Systems, Inc. Flash Optimizer is the trademark of Eltima Software GmbH. Nintendo Wii is the trademark of Nintendo Co., Ltd. The WiiCade API is the product of WiiCade and redistributed by permission. Audacity is the trademark of Dominic Mazzoni and the members of the Audacity development team. Nvu is the trademark of Daniel Glazman. Audacity and Nvu are redistributed under the terms of the GNU General Public License as published by the Free Software Foundation. All other trademarks are the property of their respective owners.

All images © Cengage Learning unless otherwise noted.

Library of Congress Control Number: 2009941745

ISBN-13: 978-1-4354-5555-9

ISBN-10: 1-4354-5555-X

**Course Technology, a part of Cengage Learning**
20 Channel Center Street
Boston, MA 02210
USA

Cengage Learning is a leading provider of customized learning solutions with office locations around the globe, including Singapore, the United Kingdom, Australia, Mexico, Brazil, and Japan. Locate your local office at: **international.cengage.com/region**

Cengage Learning products are represented in Canada by Nelson Education, Ltd.

For your lifelong learning solutions, visit **courseptr.com**

Visit our corporate website at **cengage.com**

Printed by RR Donnelley, Owensville, MO. 1st Ptg. 01/2010

Printed in the United States of America
1 2 3 4 5 6 7 12 11 10

*To the people who have inspired me to become an artist: Don Bluth, Jim Davis, Walt Disney, Friz Freleng, Gary Goldman, Edward Gorey, Chuck Jones, Fred Moore, David Quesnelle, Charles M. Schulz, Jhonen Vasquez, and Michael Whelan. To my friends and family who always support me even when I'm going the wrong way. To Krystal, the love of my life. And to the child in all of us.*

# ACKNOWLEDGMENTS

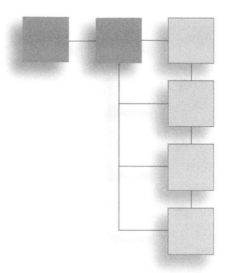

Thanks to my content editors at Cengage Learning: Jenny Davidson, Emi Smith, Maneesh Sethi, Arlie Hartman, and J.T. Hiquet. They make me better than I am. Thanks to the WiiCade team, Shigeru Miyamoto, and the fine people at Nintendo for making Wii for all of us. Thanks to my sweetheart, who turned my life around for the better and who put up with me spending long hours working on this book. And thanks to the animators and artists who inspire and improve our lives; if not for them, I never would have gotten into this field!

# About the Author

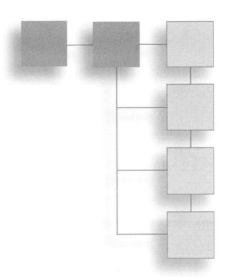

**Mike Duggan** is an author and illustrator by trade, in addition to being a college teacher in visual arts, graphic/web design, and game design. Duggan currently resides in northern Arkansas. He designed core curriculum for the gaming and robotics program at Bryan College (Springfield, Missouri) and the game development program at North Arkansas College (Harrison, Arkansas). He has been a guest speaker on the topic of game engine technology at several conferences and is the author and illustrator of *The Official Guide to 3D GameStudio, Torque for Teens, Web Comics for Teens,* and *2D Game Building for Teens.* Mike spends most of his free time drawing children's books and making cartoon animations and games. For more information about the author, go to http://mdduggan.com.

# Contents

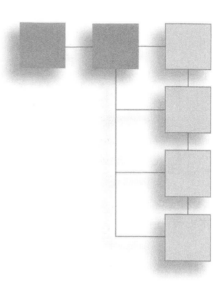

# INTRODUCTION

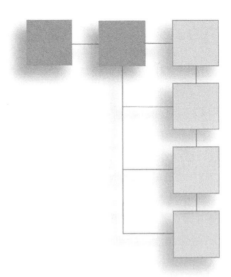

Games have come a long way since their inception far in our past. The tools we have used in our game play have changed, as well, from knuckle bones to cards to board games to early arcade games to today's spiffy video game consoles. The progression has been a lengthy one.

Now console games are even changing the way we play games with the latest hardware, such as the Wii Remote, the controlling device for Nintendo's breakthrough game system the Wii (pronounced like the pronoun "we"). As anyone who has tried it can tell you, the Wii has made games fun again, in a whole new way!

A seventh-generation home game console, the Wii competes primarily with Microsoft's Xbox 360 and Sony's PlayStation 3. The Wii Remote—which some have called a "magic wand"—stands out as one of the more distinctive features of the Wii game console. The Wii Remote is a wireless controller that can be used as a handheld pointer device and detect motion in three dimensions.

Like many next-generation home game systems, the Wii has allowed for independent content to be played through an Internet connection. With a strong Wii fanbase, independent game developers started creating Flash games to be played over the Wii. One World Wide Web portal and content creation site to emerge was WiiCade, which was launched the same day the Wii hit global markets. Using Adobe Flash and WiiCade, anyone with a little know-how can create electronic games to be played on the Nintendo Wii. That means that you, too, can make games for the Wii, no matter your age, income, or skill level.

# About This Book

Welcome to *Wii Game Creation for Teens*! This book will help you learn about the booming video game industry and the techniques it takes to make your electronic game ideas come to life.

This book is written in a tutorial format, so that as you read you don't just process information but you put it to immediate use and get hands-on learning to reinforce the knowledge. Through this book, you will start by learning how to draw on paper, then on the computer, and put your work into the Adobe Flash program. Using Flash, you will see what it takes to create animations and cartoons. Then you will learn ActionScript and how to design video games using Flash. Finally you will learn how to publish these games online for Nintendo Wii users to play.

It's hoped you will continue to use the skills you learn within these pages to springboard your  game development talents into making dozens of electronic games!

# What This Book Can Do for You

In *Wii Game Creation for Teens* you will learn about the electronic game industry, its history, the process by which video games are made, and how you can make your very own games for the Nintendo Wii using Adobe Flash and WiiCade.

The Wii is an uber-popular video game console from one of the industry titans, Nintendo, and WiiCade allows you to upload and share your Adobe Flash games for users of the Wii. This is not only a fantastic method for someone wanting to learn how to build electronic games, but *Wii Game Creation for Teens* will break it down for you in easy-to-understand techniques.

*Wii Game Creation for Teens* was written with three main aims:

- To supply you with an insight into the cartoon animation industry and how cartoons can be made through traditional means or on computers using animation software like Adobe Flash. The Flash cartoons you make can be published on the World Wide Web and for viewers using the Nintendo Wii.

- To provide an insight into game design; it's one of the biggest entertainment industries in the world. Globally, the video game market is worth billions of dollars. This book shows you how you can make games using Adobe Flash and publish them for use with the Nintendo Wii. There is also enough academic tutelage about game design to launch your career into that industry if you so wish.

- To endow you with practical exercises that require some of the skills and techniques required to become an animator or electronic game designer.

Each chapter in this book will give you an introduction to a topic and present you with some indispensable information you need to get started. When this is coupled with the associated practical exercises, you should begin to understand how to formulate your ideas and begin thinking like an animator and game developer.

Some of the lessons herein are based on material used in U.S. institutions at degree level. They are not a substitute for dedicated study or years of experience in the field, however.

The content of this book is intended to start you off on the long and exciting journey to becoming a professional in the animation or games industry.

## Who Should Read This Book

Anyone who is interested in working in the animation or games industry, who likes watching Flash cartoons or playing video games and would like to make his or her own, or someone who is interested in making games or cartoons as a hobby and doesn't know where to start, will find the contents of this book useful.

The following text goes over the specifics of creating games and cartoons with Adobe Flash, with the express intent of publishing them online via WiiCade for users of the Nintendo Wii to play, but it also covers the very real day-to-day responsibilities game developers have to deal with. This helps you to further understand and prepare yourself for the ever-growing game industry.

**Note**

Because this book is about designing computer games, you should have some experience with computers beforehand! It is not required that you be a computer nerd, but you need to know the difference between a file and a folder, how to drag-and-drop, and how to double-click.

## Why This Book Is a Starting Point

The electronics industry is a rapidly developing phenomenon. Technological innovation sees continual change in the devices people use, and as the market develops, users become more sophisticated and the types of materials used are ever-changing. This applies to changes in the animation and games industry.

Thanks to the Internet there is loads of fringe game development activity. With so many new and growing possibilities, this is an exciting time to get involved in the industry but also one where you have to keep on your toes if you want to stay fresh and ahead of the game (pardon the pun!).

A book like this could never hope to give utterly comprehensive coverage of such a dynamic subject. Rather like a guidebook to a big city, it provides you with a good grounding and indications of where to go, but specific locations and travel modes are bound to become outdated or ineffectual with time. Use this book as you would a guidebook to give yourself a heads-up on achieving your aspirations, and grow from there.

Every response this book provides is also a signboard for your ongoing discovery. Asking relevant questions is one of the key skills of being an artist or designer, especially "How can I make it better? " So keep pushing the boundaries and think (and work) outside the book.

## How This Book Is Organized

How you approach this book is up to you. Some readers like to methodically work through a book from start to finish, carefully digesting each piece. Others prefer to skim through the whole thing first and then go back to sections that interest them most. Either way has its own merits. Here are some specifics about the chapter breakdown for this book.

**Chapter 1: History of Games and Animation**—Before leaping into game production, this introductory chapter gives you a quick run-down on the video game industry, its progression, and the origins of digital animation that have made all this possible.

**Chapter 2: The Nintendo Wii**—This chapter shows you the name-brand history, hardware, and technical specifications of Nintendo's Wii console system.

**Chapter 3: Basics of Adobe Flash**—This chapter delves into the multimedia editing software you will be using to create your media.

**Chapter 4: Drawing Fundamentals**—A large part of digital media development is learning how to draw, and even if you're not an artist yourself, this chapter can teach you how to get the art you imagine onto your computer screen.

**Chapter 5: 2D Animation Principles**—This chapter educates you on the basic animation principles, both for traditional media and the computer, that you use in cartoon and game development.

**Chapter 6: Character and Story**—In this chapter, you'll learn how to conceive heroic characters and weave stories around them, to make your digital media more compelling and entertaining.

**Chapter 7: Building Scenes in Flash**—This chapter shows you how to design scenes and compose camera shots in Flash for your audience.

**Chapter 8: Sound FX**—This chapter covers sound recording, editing, composition, and the use of royalty-free sound effects libraries to bring life to your digital media.

**Chapter 9: Making a Short Cartoon**—This chapter tells you how to put everything you've learned together and make a quick Flash animation of your own. The cartoon is called *Wake Up Call for Count Stunkula*, about a vampire skunk.

**Chapter 10: Game Design Fundamentals**—Before getting down-and-dirty and creating your first electronic games, it's best to know some jargon and what *not* to do.

**Chapter 11: Players and Objectives**—This chapter enlightens you on why players play games and how to design missions for them to go on that will delight them.

**Chapter 12: Building Game Worlds**—Game worlds are as vastly dissimilar from one another as can be, and their manifestation exploratory in nature. Find out how to come up with interactive environments in this chapter.

**Chapter 13: Programming a Short Game**—This chapter tells you how to put it all together and make Flash games every bit your own, including a dress-up doll game, Fantasy Machine, shooting gallery, and tunnel maze game.

**Chapter 14: WiiCade Production**—This chapter shows you how to publish your digital media online and share your creations with Nintendo Wii users all around the globe.

**The Companion CD-ROM**—The companion CD for this book contains data files used in this book, as well as tools and resources you will need. You should find:

- **Adobe Flash CS4**: A link to the 30-day trial version of the Adobe Creative Suite 4 Flash program, which is used to create the animations and games within this book.

- **Any Audio Converter**: A free audio extractor and audio convertor software package.

- **Audacity**: An open-source sound-editing software package from SourceForge.

- **Eltima Flash Optimizer**: A free Flash compression program that shrinks your Flash files up to 70 percent.

- **Exercises**: Files that have been created by the author in demonstrating the practical exercises in this book.

- **Nvu**: A free website creation application.

- **WiiCade API**: The application programming interface that allows Flash apps to work with the Nintendo Wii.

## CD-ROM Downloads

If you purchased an ebook version of this book, and the book had a companion CD-ROM, we will mail you a copy of the disc. Please send ptrsupplements@ cengage.com the title of the book, the ISBN, your name, address, and phone number. Thank you.

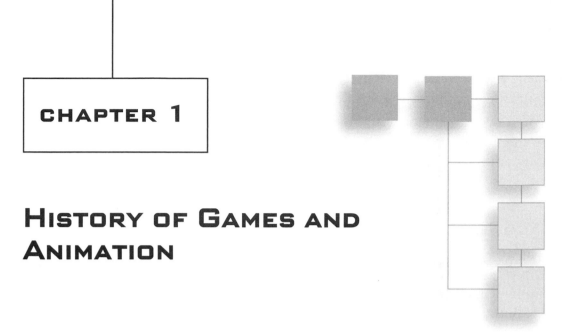

# CHAPTER 1

# HISTORY OF GAMES AND ANIMATION

In this chapter you will learn:

- How cartoons got started

- How to make a flipbook

- What traditional animation is and how it differs from digital animation

- How electronic games got their start

- How you can use Adobe Flash to make cartoons and video games

You might be thinking to yourself, "This book's title must be misleading. . . What does *history* have to do with making Wii games?" A proper teaching in the olden times of how games and cartoons came about will better prepare you, and perhaps provide you inspiration, for making your own Wii games. Or, as the proverb goes, you will know what has come before so as to be better equipped for what comes next. You may be more concerned about learning to do your own cartoons or video games, but if you don't know their history, how they got started, how do you expect to make your own mark?

Games and animation have been around for a while, 2D animation more than games, of course. This chapter will teach you where cartoons got their start and how electronic games came to be.

## Early Cartoon Making

Did you really think that Cartoon Network or Disney invented cartoons? Then you'd be wrong. Animation has been with us an awfully long time, and while Walt Disney and Cartoon Network have contributed to the look of our modern-day cartoons, they borrow on a long history and growth following moving pictures.

## Persistence of Vision Theory

The *Persistence of Vision theory* states that human beings (that is, you or I) compile flashes of images in time to create seamless perception in order to survive. In other words, flickering images can seem to be one continuous image in motion. This scientific theory forms the basis of moving pictures, including cartoon animation.

### Thaumatropes

This theory was beautifully illustrated by a clever optical contraption called a *thaumatrope*, which is shown for you in Figure 1.1. A thaumatrope is a disc held between two pieces of string or mounted on the end of a pencil that could be quickly twirled, making both sides of the disc blur together until they look like a faultless scene. Though originally a scientist's tool, the thaumatrope quickly became a cute toy kids got at Christmas. It was the highlight of fun at the time.

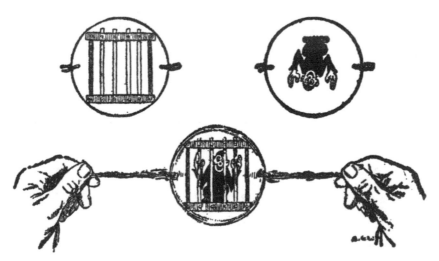

**Figure 1.1**
An early example of a thaumatrope.

*Flipbooks*

Similar to the thaumatrope was a novelty called a flipper book, or *flipbook*, which appeared worldwide in 1868. If you held the flipbook in one hand and used the other hand to flip the pages of the book, the drawings on the pages would create the illusion of continuous action.

**Creating a Flipbook**   One of the best ways to experiment with the Persistence of Vision theory is to create a flipbook yourself. Anyone can make a small flipbook. It's not that hard. You might have made something like it before in grade school. Here's how:

1. Plan your animation beforehand. Keep it short and sweet, because otherwise you will have more to draw, more paper to fill up, and more time spent than you might want to devote.

2. Find a blank notebook containing unlined paper. You can use a pad of tracing paper, which works faster, but if you are using unlined notebook paper or a sketchbook, here's what you do: Close the notebook and, using a Sharpie or pen, draw one or more black marks across the tops of all the pages in the book. These can be your placement guides.

3. Open the notebook and, on the first page, draw the picture you want to start with.

4. Trace the picture on the next page, this time making subtle changes to it as you do.

5. Repeat the last step, drawing page after page and adding subtle changes to the image each time, until you get to the end of your short animation.

6. Close the book now, and holding one end closed with one hand, flip the pages with the other, and notice how your illustration seems to be animated! That's all there is to it.

## Historic Moments in Animation History

A 4,000-year-old Egyptian mural showed wrestlers in battle, shown in Figure 1.2. The artist depicted the action by drawing a series of movements much like a modern-day comic strip, but since there was no way back then of viewing the pictures in motion it could not very well be called a cartoon.

**Figure 1.2**
An ancient Egyptian burial chamber mural.

In 1896, New York newspaper cartoonist James Stuart Blackton interviewed famed inventor Thomas Edison. Inventor of the light bulb and our modern system of electricity, Edison was then busy experimenting with moving pictures. During the discussion, Blackton did some quick sketches of Edison. Edison was so impressed by Blackton's speed and skill that he asked Blackton to do a whole series of them, which Edison then photographed. Later, in 1906, Edison and Blackton released *Humorous Phases of Funny Faces*, a short animated picture that used close to 3,000 "flickering drawings." The first of its kind, this picture was the forerunner of today's cartoons.

Winsor McCay, creator of the once-popular comic strip *Little Nemo in Slumberland*, subsequently played a crucial role in the development of cartoon animation into prodigious art form when, in 1911, he made his character Little Nemo move. In 1914 he stood before a projection screen as a giant cartoon dinosaur he named Gertie seemed to eat an apple from McCay's own hand (see the poster in Figure 1.3). This was long before cartoons had ever been established, and yet McCay did what *Who Framed Roger Rabbit?* wouldn't do until nearly 80 years later.

Among the first-ever beloved cartoon characters was Felix the Cat, a simply drawn black-and-white cartoon feline who, in the 1920s, became nearly as popular as the irrepressible Charlie Chaplin. Felix and another silent-film

**Figure 1.3**
Poster advertising Winsor McCay's Gertie the Dinosaur.

character, Betty Boop, whom you may have seen on some Hot Topic merchandise before, were really trendy animated characters back in the day before talkies.

In 1928 Mickey Mouse surpassed Felix in popularity as the first-ever animated cartoon to incorporate moving pictures and synchronized sound in *Steamboat Willie*, made by Walt Disney. Mickey was created by Walt Disney around a pet he'd adopted and kept in his Kansas City studio, and originally he called him Mortimer Mouse until Lillian Disney pointed out that "Mickey" sounded better.

Walt Disney had plans for a full-length feature film, which his family and friends dubbed "Disney's Folly" and tried unsuccessfully to persuade him to drop, because they felt it would drive him to bankruptcy. Disney astounded everybody in 1934 when his company released the first English-speaking full-length feature film. It involved drama, comedy, professional voice talents, and an orchestrated soundtrack and was an 83-minute-long masterpiece called *Snow White and the Seven Dwarfs*.

Nobody at that time could believe it. Disney animator Ward Kimball once recalled, "You can have no idea of the impact that having these drawings suddenly speak and make noises had on audiences at that time. People went crazy over it." The critical and financial success of *Snow White and the Seven Dwarfs* helped launch the Golden Age of Animation, during which Disney's company produced movies they are still known for today, including *Pinocchio*, *Bambi*, *Dumbo*, and *Fantasia*.

Indeed, some 80 years after the release of *Steamboat Willie*, Disney remains the most famous cartoon filmmaker of all time, even though he passed away in 1966. His corporation, The Walt Disney Company, today nets about $35 billion every year.

Walt Disney, known for experimenting until he found the right techniques to animate his cartoons, is credited for the standard 12 frames per second (fps) rate used in pictures today.

When *Snow White and the Seven Dwarfs* came out, critics warned that the fast moving pictures might cause optic nerve damage and other maladies. In reaction, Disney hired a professional optician to consult the matter. The medical specialist determined that viewing the animations would *not* result in eye damage. And although animation was then filmed at 24 frames per second, the specialist determined that the human eye could detect only about half of them, prompting Disney to conduct a quick study on the veracity of filming at 12 fps. The results: Removing half the frames in *Snow White* resulted in no discernible loss of quality. Future animations could be filmed with half the labor of their predecessors.

This is one of the reasons why Adobe Flash and many other animation programs default to a frame speed of 12 fps.

## Animation Techniques

Although equipment and materials have improved in the intervening years, the way animated cartoons are made has changed very little.

A motion picture is a sequence of tiny pictures called *frames*. The Persistence of Vision enables us to see continuous movement where there are actually multiple still images.

You make a film by taking photos of thousands of segments of action. These photos are combined into one extensive filmstrip, with each photo comprising a single frame. A projector shines light through each frame as the filmstrip rolls from beginning to end, magnifying the image on each frame onto a screen. Each frame is held still in front of the light just long enough to see it. Then a shutter comes down while the next frame is positioned. The frame rate change happens so quickly you don't even notice the individual frames or the shutter speed. Indeed, without the shutter between frames, the film would look like one long blur.

There are typically 24 to 30 frames for each second of film, with the average frames per second (fps) for television being 27. Although the perceptual difference between 12 and 24 fps is negligible, as mentioned above, most media producers believe that higher frame rates result in more fluid viewing and there are industry standards to keep up with.

Although digital filmmaking has since replaced the need for filmstrips and shutters with computer technology, thousands of individual frames still show action, but the speed and order in which they are shown are controlled by computer programs.

### *Traditional Animation*

The main difference between *traditional animation* and *digital animation* is the use of computers. Traditional animation does not use computers to effectively create 2D animation; instead, artists draw and paint each frame of the cartoons by hand. Today, most animators use a combination of traditional and digital animation, with a heavy emphasis on digital animation, but Walt Disney Animation Studios returned to traditional hand-drawn animation with *The Princess and the Frog* in 2009 and several companies have since followed suit. Traditional animation is the oldest and most historically fashionable form of animation.

The following is how traditional cartoon animation is fulfilled.

First, the cartoon animator breaks each scene down into different movements, as shown in Figure 1.4. Each animator works on drawing one movement at a time. Each picture drawn is called an *extreme*, and each extreme is numbered. The numbers on the extremes tell the other animators how many extra stages need to be drawn in between to complete the whole action.

The animator has a chart representing what will happen during each split second of film, including sound effects and voiceovers, and frame numbers to reveal the pacing speed. The movements drawn have to match up, or synch, to the recorded sound.

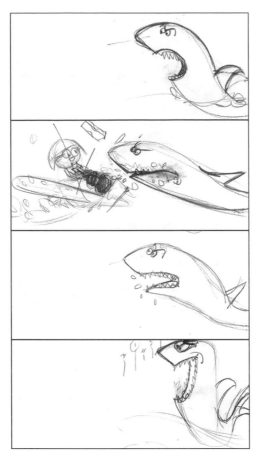

**Figure 1.4**
One example of motion break-down by Tissa David.

Once all the extremes are drawn by one bunch of animators, they are passed off to other members of the animating team to do all the drawings in between the extremes; these members are called *in-betweeners*. The numbers on the extremes show the in-betweeners how many pictures need to be drawn.

Animators, especially in-betweeners, work on a flat box with a glass surface called a light box to draw the frames of animation. See Figure 1.5. Light shining up through the glass surface of the light box allows the artist to stack several sheets of paper on top of one another and still see the papers underneath. This is an efficient way to trace over characters to make minute changes to demonstrate motion. It works more efficiently than using tracing paper or copying images roughly using guide lines like you would with flipbooks.

**Figure 1.5**
An animator using a light box.

**Figure 1.6**
A cel painting.

The finished drawings, the extremes and the in-betweens, are then traced onto transparent sheets called *cels*. Each cel, as shown in Figure 1.6, is turned over and painted on the back so the brush strokes would not be apparent from the front.

The cels, when dry, go to shooting, where they are photographed. The type of camera used to photograph cartoons is a special cartoon camera, which can take stop-motion pictures and combine them into one reel of film. Background scenery is painted on long rolls of paper and laid on the plate of the cartoon camera with the cels placed on top. The background scenery can be rolled to either side on rollers. As the camera takes pictures, this makes the character look as if it's moving across the background.

If you're paying careful attention to some classic *Scooby-Doo, Where Are You?* Episodes, you will see items in the background painted a slightly different shade from items on top that can or will be animated; that's because they are actually on separate cels.

This may sound tedious, and in many ways, it is. If you could go back in a time machine and watch a studio work to produce a single cartoon before the advent of computer technology, you would be mind-boggled. To get from simple hand drawings to animated features is often an extraneous labor process involving many animators and long months of effort.

### Digital Animation

Two-dimensional animation principles have changed little as the industry has switched from traditional to digital media, but today digital animation is aided by computer technology, making the need for cel painting and special cameras nearly obsolete.

Instead, figures are created and edited digitally using bitmap or vector graphics. This animation approach involves automated computer versions of such traditional animation techniques as in-betweening (now called *tweening*), morphing, onion-skinning, and rotoscoping.

Some very popular cartoons today are regularly created on computers and so never have to leave the digital environment. These shows are produced by skilled digital animators and include such programs as *Foster's Home for Imaginary Friends*, *The Powerpuff Girls*, *South Park*, *The Grim Adventures of Billy & Mandy*, and *El Tigre: The Adventures of Manny Rivera*.

Several 2D animation software applications are used to make cartoons today, probably the most popular being Adobe Flash. Other programs, like Toon Boom Studio (http://www.toonboom.com), Anime Studio (http://www.e-frontier.com), Bauhaus Mirage Studio (http://www.bauhaussoftware.com), and DigiCel Flipbook (http://www.digicelinc.com), can output files for the Web, television, or video with ease and many of them have a similar look and feel that allows you to acclimate to them quickly. See Figure 1.7.

**Adobe Flash Used in Digital Animation**   You might already be familiar with Adobe Flash, previously Macromedia Flash, because of the countless Flash animations you see on the World Wide Web. Many animators employ Flash to produce content for Internet distribution because Flash allows them to release

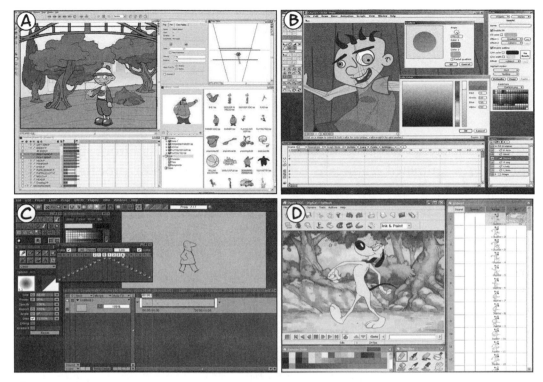

**Figure 1.7**
(A) Toon Boom Studio, (B) Anime Studio, (C) Bauhaus Mirage Studio, and (D) DigiCel Flipbook.

projects well under file size limitations. Look at the Flash interface shown in Figure 1.8.

When it comes to Flash animated cartoons, also called *webtoons*, the first noted use was in 1999 when *Ren & Stimpy* creator John Kricfalusi set out to bring cartoons to the World Wide Web. Soon after, webtoons began popping up everywhere.

Some webtoons became so trendy, due in part to programming networks like MTV or G4, that they have appeared on national television. These include *Happy Tree Friends* and the politically minded *Jib-Jab* shorts. Some webtoons, like James Farr's *Xombie* and Jonathan Ian Mathers' *Foamy the Squirrel*, became DVD productions with popular comic merchandise and toy lines.

You will learn more about Flash in Chapter 3, "Basics of Adobe Flash."

## Early Game Making

Animation laid the gravel for the road for graphical games that would come later, because electronic games using 2D graphics wouldn't be the same without those pretty animations.

**Figure 1.8**
The Adobe Flash interface.

Games have evolved from board and tabletop games to the tiny toy worlds of primitive 8-bit graphics to the high-quality next-generation landscapes of games that make even Hollywood directors envious. Electronic games, like cell phones, e-mail, digital cameras, and faux-hawk haircuts, are still very new to our society, although you might have grown up playing them and can't imagine a world without them. Yet electronic games haven't been around that long in the history of the world.

Even so, video games have quickly risen to a competent entertainment medium, peddling right alongside books, movies, music, and artwork. The game design industry, in fact, is the largest growing industry in America today. The ESA reports that the United States game industry made $9.5 billion in 2007 and $11 billion in 2008. Approximately $3 billion of the 2008 revenue was by Blizzard Entertainment for its *World of WarCraft* franchise.

Will Wright (shown in Figure 1.9), the creator of *The Sims* and *Spore*, said in an article for *WIRED Magazine* that "games have the potential to subsume almost

**Figure 1.9**
Will Wright, architect of *The Sims*, meets one of his characters.

all other forms of entertainment media. They can tell us stories, offer us music, give us challenges, allow us to communicate and interact with others, encourage us to make things, connect us to new communities, and let us play. Unlike most other forms of media, games are inherently malleable... And more than ever, games will be a visible, external amplification of the human imagination."

## Console Games

In 1961, Digital Equipment Corporation donated their latest computer to the Massachusetts Institute of Technology (MIT). It was called the Programmed Data Processor-1, or PDP-1. Compared to most computers at the time, the PDP-1 was comparatively modest in size, only as big as a large automobile!

Like most universities, MIT had several campus organizations, one of which was the Tech Model Railroad Club, or TMRC. TMRC appealed to students who liked to build things and see how they worked. They programmed for the PDP-1 for fun.

Steve Russell, nicknamed "Slug," was a typical science-fiction-loving nerd who joined TMRC. He put nearly six months and two hundred hours into completing an interactive game where two players controlled rocket ships. Using toggle switches built into the PDP-1, players controlled the speed and direction of their ships and fired torpedoes at each other. Russell called his game *Spacewar!* Thanks to "Slug," this game launched a whole new trend among programmers and became the predecessor for future arcade games.

Entrepreneur Nolan Bushnell saw *Spacewar!* and turned it into the first coin-op arcade game, called *Computer Space*, in 1971. *Pong* and *Asteroids* followed shortly thereafter.

*Pong*, some people argue, was the first game created, as it appeared in 1958 as a table tennis game on an oscilloscope built by Willy Higinbotham at the Brookhave National Labs in New York; it was later demonstrated on a console in 1972 by Magnavox and "appropriated" by Atari in the same year. But most tech historians agree that *Spacewar!* really started the video game industry. You can see an early arcade poster for *Pong* in Figure 1.10.

After the success of his *Computer Space* coin-op game, Nolan Bushnell went on to found the company Atari, which, roughly translated, means "Watch out, I win!" or "Check!" in the Japanese board game *Go*, along with Ted Dabney. Bushnell later left Atari to start a chain of pizza parlors with arcade games right inside

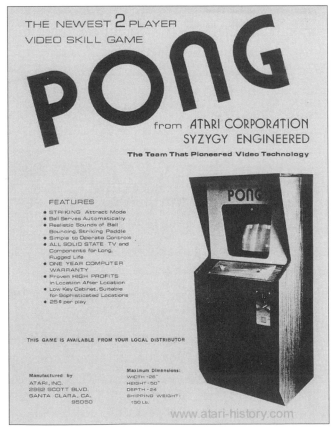

**Figure 1.10**
An early Atari poster advertising the arcade version of *Pong*.

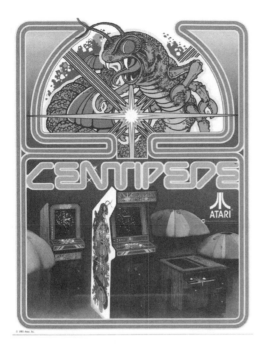

**Figure 1.11**
The game *Centipede* (created by Dona Bailey) featured a multi-segmented enemy like none before it.

them; he originally called his pizza arcade Pizza Time Theater, but the company eventually changed the name to Chuck E. Cheese.

Dona Bailey, one of the premiere female pioneers in the game industry and creator of the brightly-colored game *Centipede*, started working for Atari in 1980. She says that the work environment at that time was tough and competitive. Each employee was responsible for making a game by himself or herself, and all coding was done directly on the metal. If your game hit the arcades, you might see royalties (as long as you remained with Atari), but many games never saw release. Everybody remained persistently paranoid of somebody else stealing their program code and worked feverishly by themselves in cubicles, unlike today's crews of 40-some people working together cooperatively to turn out a top-name title.

Atari started with arcade games but eventually became better known for its console games, which they continued making, one right after the other, bringing video games into people's homes for the first time in history. You can see a stack of early Atari video game cartridges in Figure 1.12. Then a curious thing happened: Sales plummeted and the game industry slumped. Console sales bottomed out in 1983, causing everyone to question whether the industry could ever recover.

**Figure 1.12**
This pile of early Atari video game cartridges was similar to many in children's homes across America in the '80s.

Several theories for this slump have been supposed, one of which saying that with so much market saturation, development studios were pressured to crank out games quickly. This led to imitative, low-quality titles. One of the worst was the Atari game *E.T.* It was a rush job put out for Christmas to tie in to the Steven Spielberg movie and ended up with millions of units being sent back to the factories and later buried in a landfill, which if you've ever played the game is totally understandable. The game had lousy graphics, incomprehensible rules, and no storyline at all.

Thankfully, the video game industry recovered. The year 1985 marked the start of the video game "Golden Age." With the advent of tech innovations, and with Nintendo, SEGA, Sony, and Microsoft entering the console race, the bar was raised, to the delight of the player market. The substance and number of titles released with neat features quadrupled along with sales. Games went from being coded straight on the metal to being distributed on cartridges to being burnt on CD-ROM or DVDs, evolving along the way from chunky 8-bit graphics to the next-gen photo-real images we see today.

At the time of this writing the industry is dominated by three console giants: Microsoft (Xbox), Sony (PlayStation), and Nintendo (GameCube and Wii), who are all involved in the current console wars. The future of the console wars depends on the consumer, mainly kids and teenagers (see Figure 1.13).

One of the leading industry titans, Nintendo, started as a manufacturer of a playing card game called *Hanafuda* in 1889. That means Nintendo has been around for more than 120 years! Nintendo is the oldest console game publisher

**Figure 1.13**
A common sight to any parent.

in existence today, thanks in part to legend-in-his-own-time Shigeru Miyamoto. Miyamoto joined Nintendo in 1977 as a staff artist and helped Nintendo create its biggest-selling games, including *Donkey Kong*, *Super Mario Bros.*, and *Zelda*.

It was really Miyamoto who inspired me to create my personal formula for creating great games, the Four F's of Great Game Design, because he often was quoted as saying that all games had to be fun, and if you lost sight of the fun factor you had essentially doomed your product.

## Computer Games

Consoles aside, the first computer game was the text-based *Colossal Cave*, but it wasn't until Donald Woods expanded the idea and made Infocom's *Zork* game in 1979 that programmers everywhere were inspired to make their own computer games.

One of these developers was Roberta Williams, who, next to *Centipede* originator Dona Bailey, was one of the first female game designers. Roberta Williams launched the Sierra On-Line company with her husband. Back in the day, they'd package their computer games, distributed on floppy disks, in Ziploc baggies while sitting at their kitchen table.

Most of these early computer games were adventure games, also known as text-parser games, because players had to type in two-word combinations to interact with the game world, such as "walk north" or "get sword." Here was a typical, and rather sad, example of text adventure game play:

```
> kill monster
Be more specific?
> stab monster
Do not understand "stab"?
```

```
> hit monster
Hit monster with what?
> hit monster with sword
You are not currently equipped with "sword".
> run away
The monster's hideously long tentacles wrap around you, squeezing your torso
until you can no longer breathe. You have died. Your quest ends here.
```

As the level of graphics in computer games grew, mostly due to the invention of DirectX and Direct3D libraries, so did adventure games, replacing text choices with picture icons. LucasArts produced graphical point-and-click adventure games (sometimes not-so-lovingly referred to as "hunt-the-pixel" games) like *Maniac Mansion* and *Secret of Monkey Island* and set the standard for the genre. Look at Figure 1.14 for an example.

Networked computer games started when Rick Blomme made the very first multiplayer games at the University of Illinois in 1961. He used a software program popular even today for use with electronic-based education; it is called PLATO. His early games were mostly based on *Star Trek* or *Dungeons and Dragons*, but they were still not *true* online games because they were played over a network, such as a LAN, and not the Internet.

It wasn't until 1979 that some fellows in Essex in the United Kingdom created the first Multi-User Dungeon, or MUD, on Arpanet (the system that would later become the Internet). MUDs instantly became popular role-playing game communities on college campuses everywhere and the precedent for modern online games. MUDs, like the earliest adventure games, were text-based, and it wasn't until nearly twenty years later that they started incorporating graphics.

**Figure 1.14**
An archetypal vintage point-and-click adventure game.

Players today can immerse themselves in role-playing or strategy games played online, such as Blizzard Entertainment's *World of WarCraft*. With the sheer number of homes possessing computer technology and broadband or DSL connectivity, it's no surprise computer games are just as popular as ever. Many games have downloadable content that supplements and extends replay ability. There are map editors, mod communities, machinima, patches, wallpaper, desktop goodies, and loads more available on the Internet for these games.

Here is an interesting bit of trivia. According to a 2007 report from the market research NPD Group, among kids aged 2 to 17 who play games online, an average of 39 percent of their time is spent playing games online as opposed to offline. Kids ages 15 to 17 spend even *more* time than that and are considered super users, or players who spend 16 hours or more per week on gaming. That is as much time as most adults spend at a part-time job!

## Flash Games

Just as Adobe Flash became the predominant building environment for digital animations, a lot of Web-based games have started using Adobe Flash to make games, because of the ease of file publishing and online distribution. Strangely enough, the forerunners to use Flash to make games were advertisement companies making animated banners for commercial Web sites.

The types of Flash games now hitting the Internet closely imitate the older console games, the ones of the 1980s. There are several *Tetris* and *Pac-Man* clones, but these can be seen as rudimentary experiments testing the technology, since Flash's ActionScript coding language allows for endless versatility. Although Flash focuses primarily on two-dimensional bitmap and vector art, it has the potential for three-dimensional rooms and objects, and many users have had success making 2D/3D hybrid games with it.

Since Flash is an all-in-one kit for creating vector art, putting together raster art, audio, and video, and programming interactive functionality, it is ideal for game designers, especially when Flash ports to so many devices, including mobile and handheld devices and any hardware that has an Internet connection and browser interface.

Several multiplayer games built with Flash have become mainstream market games, such as Dofus (http://www.dofus.com), Habbo (http://www.habbo.com), Disney's Club Penguin (http://www.clubpenguin.com), The Continuum (http://www.thecontinuum.com), and Neopets (http://www.neopets.com).

You will read more about making games with Flash in Chapter 10, "Game Design Fundamentals."

## What's Next?

That was certainly a lot of information to take in at once, I know. So go get a drink, take a breather, and get ready to learn about Nintendo and its Wii console system.

## Review

At the end of reading this chapter, you should know:

■ The beginnings of cartoon animation and differences between traditional and digital animation

■ How to make a flipbook to test the Persistence of Vision theory

■ The starts and stops of arcade, console, and computer game evolution

■ How Adobe Flash is useful for creating digital animations and electronic games that can be shared via a browser

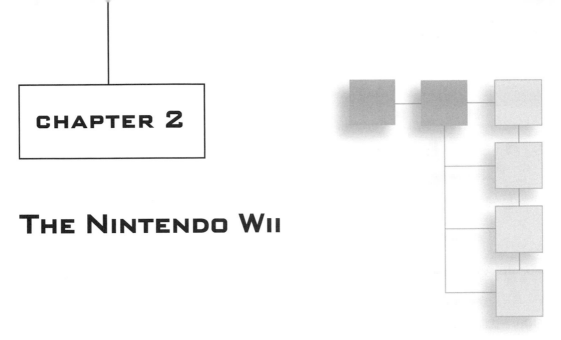

# CHAPTER 2

# THE NINTENDO WII

In this chapter you will learn:

- How Nintendo got its start

- What game systems Nintendo has released

- Where the Wii comes from

- How the Wii works

- How you can break into the Wii developer market

The Nintendo Wii, often referred to simply as the Wii (pronounced just like the pronoun "we") and also written in Japanese as ウィー?, is a home console system for playing video games, as shown in Figure 2.1. A seventh-generation console system, the Wii competes with Microsoft's Xbox 360 and Sony's PlayStation 3 (PS3). It also marginally competes with Nintendo's other console, the Game-Cube, although many see the Wii as a direct successor to the GameCube and therefore not in competition at all.

Starting at the first of 2009, Nintendo's Wii outsold the Xbox 360 and PlayStation 3, and Nintendo has repeatedly said their console attracts a much broader demographic than the others. Critics agree that Nintendo's Wii has launched itself onto the market as one of the trendiest consoles going.

**Figure 2.1**
The Nintendo Wii home console game system.

## Evolution of a Console

Before understanding how the Wii was birthed, it's important to know about the company that the Wii calls its mommy: Nintendo.

## History of Nintendo

Nintendo is a multinational corporation located in Kyoto, Japan. According to Nintendo's *Touch! Generations* website, the name "Nintendo" translated from Japanese to English means "Leave luck to Heaven."

As mentioned in Chapter 1, "History of Games and Animation," Nintendo was originally started in 1889 by a guy named Fusajiro Yamauchi to make handmade trading cards for the game Hanafuda (a modern version of which is shown in Figure 2.2). In 1956, Hiroshi Yamauchi, grandson of Fusajiro Yamauchi, visited the U.S. to talk with the United States Playing Card Company, the dominant playing card manufacturer in America, and found that the world's biggest company in his business was headquartered in a little office. This was a turning point, because Yamauchi realized the limitations of the playing card business and knew Nintendo needed to do "something different." He then gained access to Walt Disney's characters and put them on the playing cards to drive up sales.

By 1963 Yamauchi renamed Nintendo Playing Card Company Limited to Nintendo Company, Limited, and the company had been occupied in, or tried out, several other entrepreneurial ventures, including a taxi cab company, an

**Figure 2.2**
A modern deck of Hanafuda cards made by Nintendo.

instant rice manufacturer, a television network, and a love hotel. None of these panned out, and Nintendo's promise started to dwindle. Then in 1974, Nintendo secured the rights to distribute the Magnavox Odyssey home video game console in Japan. By 1977, Nintendo began producing its own Color TV Game home video game consoles.

A student product developer named Shigeru Miyamoto was hired by Nintendo at this time. Among his first tasks was to design the casing for several of the Color TV Game consoles. In 1981, Nintendo released Miyamoto's creation *Donkey Kong*, and changed the history of Nintendo forever. See Figure 2.3.

Eventually Nintendo became the software development company it is today, with a U.S. market value of over $85 billion, and is listed as the fifth largest software company in the world.

### Console Development

Before Nintendo came out with the Wii, it had released several other machines that shook the world in their time. Each built upon the development discoveries of the last one. They were, in order:

- 1977: Color TV Game

- 1985: Nintendo Entertainment System (NES)

- 1989: Game Boy (GB)

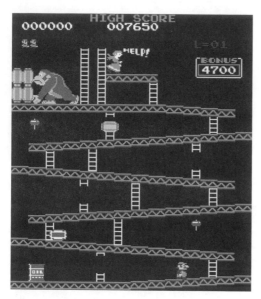

**Figure 2.3**
A vintage screen view of the *Donkey Kong* game made by Miyamoto.

- 1990: Super Nintendo Entertainment System (SNES)

- 1996: Nintendo 64 (N64)

- 2001: Nintendo GameCube (GCN)

- 2001: Game Boy Advanced (GBA)

- 2004: Nintendo DS (DS)

### Software Development

Nintendo has its own in-house game development unit, which has been responsible for the Mario, Zelda, and Pokémon franchises, but Nintendo also purchases contracts from outside game developers like Konami and Acclaim. Nintendo has strict licensing procedures and a firm no-emulation stance that make them more stalwart than looser organizations, but then consumers know when they are buying Nintendo exactly what they are getting, and that's often quality gaming merchandise.

**Nintendo Seal of Quality**    The Nintendo Seal of Quality (currently Official Nintendo Seal in NTSC regions) is a gold seal first used by Nintendo of America and later Nintendo of Europe. You can view an example of the seal in Figure 2.4. It is displayed on any game licensed for use on one of Nintendo's video game

**Figure 2.4**
The Nintendo Seal of Quality.

consoles. The seal tells buyers the game has been properly licensed by Nintendo (and, in theory, checked for quality). It is a golden starburst with the text "Original Nintendo Seal of Quality" or "Official Nintendo Seal."

Part of the reason for the Nintendo Seal was that gamers were understandably wary of game makers when the Nintendo Entertainment System (NES) came out in 1985. Publishers were encouraged to create high-quality titles in other ways, like only being allowed five releases per year (with certain exceptions). Currently, the seal makes no guarantee of quality software, instead referring to the truth that the game has been published or licensed by Nintendo.

**Nintendo's Family Image**    Nintendo has long been viewed as a "family company," because of its strict policy toward releasing only family-friendly titles. In 1994, when the ESRB video game ratings system came out, Nintendo chose to abolish those policies in favor of consumers making their own choices about the substance of the games they played. Today, since very few retail outlets sell games without an ESRB rating, all games Nintendo publishes have an ESRB rating. Most alterations to the content of games to fit within the ESRB guidelines are done primarily by the game's developer or, occasionally, at the request of Nintendo. The only clear-set rule is that ESRB Adults Only (AO) rated games will not be licensed on Nintendo consoles in North America, a practice also enforced by Sony and Microsoft.

Nintendo has since allowed several mature-content games, such as those rated M for Mature, to be published on its consoles, including: *Perfect Dark*, *Conker's Bad Fur Day*, *Doom*, the *Resident Evil* series, *Eternal Darkness: Sanity's Requiem*, and *BloodRayne*.

Certain games have continued to be modified, however. For example, Konami was forced to remove all references to cigarettes in their 2000 Game Boy Color game *Metal Gear Solid* (although the previous NES version of *Metal Gear* and the subsequent GameCube game *Metal Gear Solid: The Twin Snakes* both included cigarettes, as did the Wii title *MadWorld*), and maiming and gore were removed from the Nintendo 64 port of *Cruis'n USA*.

However, the release of the Wii has ensued in a quantity of even more contentious and mature titles, such as *Manhunt 2*, *No More Heroes*, *The House of the Dead: Overkill*, and *MadWorld*, the latter three of which are published exclusively for the console. And in recent press releases, Nintendo representatives have said that Nintendo is "growing up" and will offer more mature content in the future. At the same time, however, games like *Wii Fit* and *Pikmin* have proven that Nintendo is very conscious of its "family company" image and will retain that likeness for some time to come.

## Where Did Wii Come From?

The Wii console was conceived in 2001 just as the GameCube console was being launched. According to an interview with Nintendo's game designer Shigeru Miyamoto, the concept for the Wii involved focusing on a new form of human interaction. "The consensus was that power isn't everything for a console. Too many powerful consoles can't coexist. It's like having only ferocious dinosaurs. They might fight and hasten their own extinction," he was quoted as saying.

The Wii console is best known for its unique interface device, often referred to as a "magic wand." Of course, curious game controllers are no strangers to games.

A *game controller* is an input device used to control a video game; it is most often used to govern the movement or actions of an entity in a video or computer game. The type of entity controlled depends upon the game, but a typical entity controlled would be the player character's actions and movements. A controller is typically connected to a video game console or a personal computer. A game controller can be a keyboard, mouse, gamepad, joystick, paddle, or any other device designed for gaming that can receive input.

Special-purpose devices, such as steering wheels for driving games, light guns for shooting games, and fishing rods for fishing games, have also existed. Rhythm games like *Guitar Hero* and *Rock Band* have utilized controllers that are shaped and/or act like musical instruments, dance games like *Dance Dance Revolution* and *Pump It Up* use dance mats with sensors in them to detect foot motion, and some games, not just singing challenge ones, have used microphones and voice-recognition software.

In 2003, engineers and designers were brought together to develop the Wii concept further. By 2005, the controller interface had taken form. The console was known by the code name of "Revolution" until April 27, 2006, immediately prior to a proposed public showing at that year's Electronic Entertainment Expo (E3), one of the leading electronic games conferences in the world. Unfortunately, the E3 showing was withdrawn. Miyamoto explained that, "We had some troubleshooting to do. So we decided not to reveal the controller and instead we displayed just the console."

The handheld Nintendo DS, it is said, may have influenced the Wii design. Designer Ken'ichiro Ashida noted, "We had the DS on our minds as we worked on the Wii. We thought about copying the DS's touch-panel interface and even came up with a prototype." The idea was in due course rejected, with the notion that the two gaming systems would be too indistinguishable.

Nintendo has accredited the success of the Wii to the ideas originally presented in the business strategy book *Blue Ocean Strategy*. Within the context of the *Blue Ocean Strategy* analysis, what is termed the "Six Path Framework" described within the book were developed as key factors in the Wii. While Nintendo has not publicly released the factors used, it is believed that they include the following:

- Fun

- Game library

- Graphics

- Magic wand

- Movie playing

- Physics

- Price

They eliminated movie playing, reduced graphics and physics, raised the fun value and the game library, and eventually created their "magic wand": the Wii Remote, for which the game is best known.

## Who Came Up with That Name?

The console, as mentioned above, was called by its code name "Revolution" until 2006. The Nintendo Style Guide refers to the console as "simply Wii, not

Nintendo Wii," making it the first home console Nintendo has marketed outside Japan without the company name featured in its trademark.

Nintendo's spelling of "Wii" with two lowercase "i" characters is meant to resemble two people standing side by side, representing players gathering together, as well as to represent the Wii Remote and Nunchuk. Nintendo has given many reasons for this choice of name since the pronouncement, but the best known is, "Wii sounds like 'we,' which emphasizes that the console is for *everyone*. Wii can easily be remembered by people around the world, no matter what language they speak. No confusion. No need to abbreviate. Just Wii."

Despite Nintendo's justification for the name, some video game developers and members of the press reacted negatively toward the change. They favored "Revolution" over "Wii." Market analyst Forbes expressed fear "that the name would convey a continued sense of 'kidiness' [sic] to the console."

Nintendo of America's president Reggie Fils-Aime accepted the early reactions and further went on to explain: " 'Revolution' as a name is not ideal; it's long, and in some cultures, it's hard to pronounce. So we wanted something that was short, to the point, easy to pronounce, and distinctive. That's how 'Wii,' as a console name, was created." Nintendo of America's then-Vice President of Corporate Affairs Perrin Kaplan defended its choice of "Wii" over "Revolution" by saying, "Live with it, sleep with it, eat with it, move along with it, and hopefully they'll arrive at the same place."

While "Wiis" is a commonly used plural variation of the console's name, Nintendo has stated that the official plural form should be "Wii systems" or "Wii consoles."

## Who Would Play the Wii?

Game designer and *The Sims* creator Will Wright shared his thoughts on the Wii: "The only next-gen system I've seen is the Wii. The PS3 and the Xbox 360 feel like better versions of the last, but pretty much the same game with incremental improvement. But the Wii feels like a major jump—not that the graphics are more powerful, but that it hits a completely different demographic." *Demographic* means the target market, or audience, for a specific media.

Nintendo's plan is to target a wider demographic of player with its Wii console than that of other consoles released in the seventh generation, including the Xbox 360 and PS3.

At a press conference December 2006 for the upcoming Nintendo DS game *Dragon Quest IX*, Satoru Iwata insisted, "We're not thinking about fighting Sony, but about how many people we can get to play games. The thing we're thinking about most is not portable systems, consoles, and so forth, but that we want to get new people playing games."

This is reflected in Nintendo's series of television advertisements in North America, directed by Academy Award winner Stephen Gaghan, as well as multiple Internet ads. The ad slogans are "Wii would like to play" and "Experience a new way to play." These ads started running November 15, 2006 and had a total budget of over $200 million throughout the year. The production was Nintendo's first broad-based advertising scheme and included a two-minute video clip showing a varied assortment of people playing the Wii system, such as urban apartment-dwellers, country ranchers, grandparents, and parents with their children. The music in the ads is from the song "Kodo (Inside the Sun Remix)" by the Yoshida Brothers. See an early magazine ad for the Wii in Figure 2.5.

**Figure 2.5**
A magazine advertisement using the "Wii would like to play" slogan.

The marketing campaign has established itself to be really unbeaten: folks as old as 103 have been reported to be playing the Wii in the United Kingdom, and an account in the British newspaper *The People* said that Queen Elizabeth II of Great Britain has even been seen playing the Wii.

Ask anybody, and I'm sure you will find that either they or someone they know has played the Wii. You might even have one of the consoles in your home, or be an experienced Wii champion.

### Wii for Health

Using the Wii is often seen as being more physically demanding than other game consoles because of the way players must use the Wii Remote to interact with the games. Some Wii players have occasionally even experienced a form of tennis elbow referred to jokingly as "Wii-itis." See Figure 2.6.

A study published in the *British Medical Journal* says that Wii players use more energy than they do playing typical sedentary computer games. It is, however, indicated that while this energy increase may be beneficial to weight management, it is *not* an adequate replacement for regular exercise.

A case study published in the American Physical Therapy Association's journal *Physical Therapy* focused on use of the Wii for rehabilitating a teen with cerebral palsy. It is believed to be the first published research showing the physical therapy benefits resulting from use of the gaming system.

**Figure 2.6**
"Wii-itis" has become such a well-known phrase it has inspired T-shirt designs.

Researchers say the Wii complements traditional exercise techniques and is a vast improvement over earlier, more "couch potato" game systems.

## Wii's Dinky Yet Powerful Hardware Specs

The Wii is Nintendo's smallest home console to date, and in fact it is the lightest-weight console of all three major seventh-generation consoles. Shown in Figure 2.7, it is delicate even compared to Nintendo's other consoles.

### Wee Wittle Wii

Technically it measures 44 mm (1.73 in) wide, 157 mm (6.18 in) tall, and 215.4 mm (8.48 in) deep. This is the near-equivalent of three DVD cases stacked together. The stand included with the console measures 55.4 mm (2.18 in) wide, 44 mm (1.73 in) tall and 225.6 mm (8.88 in) deep. The console system weighs 1.2 kg (2.7 lb). The console can be set either horizontally or vertically.

**Figure 2.7**
The Wii (on top) compared in size to the GameCube, Nintendo 64, SNES, and NES.

The console features a recurring theme in design style: The console itself, its SD cards, the power supply, and all the sockets have one of their corners chipped off in a triangular fashion. Also, the prefix for the numbering scheme of the system and its parts or accessories is "RVL-" after its code name "Revolution."

## Wii's Components

The original Wii package includes the console, a stand that allows the console to be set vertically, one Wii Remote, one Nunchuk attachment, one Sensor Bar, one external main power adapter, two AA batteries, one composite AV cable with RCA connectors, operation manual, and, in all regions except Japan and South Korea, a copy of the game *Wii Sports*.

Although Nintendo has not ever released their full list of specs on the Wii, some key factors of the game system have leaked to the press. The following is the most accurate list of specs on the Wii you can find.

- CPU: PowerPC-based "Broadway" processor, made with a 90 nm SOI CMOS processor, reportedly clocked at 729 MHz

- GPU: ATI "Hollywood" GPU made with a 90 nm CMOS processor, reportedly clocked at 243 MHz

- 88 MB main memory (24 MB "internal" 1T-SRAM integrated into graphics package, 64 MB "external" GDDR3 SDRAM)

- 3 MB embedded GPU texture memory and frame buffer

- Up to four Wii Remote controllers (connected wirelessly via Bluetooth)

- 4 Nintendo GameCube controller ports

- 2 Nintendo GameCube Memory Card slots

- SD memory card slot (supports SDHC cards as of System Menu 4.0)

- 2 USB 2.0 ports

- Sensor Bar power port

- Accessory port on bottom of Wii Remote

- Optional USB keyboard input in message board, Wii Shop Channel, and the Internet Channel (as of 3.0 and 3.1 firmware update)

- DWM-W004 Wi-Fi 802.11b/g wireless module

- Compatible with optional USB 2.0 to Ethernet LAN adaptor

- Multi-AV output port for component, composite, S-Video, RGB SCART, and VGA

- 512 MB built-in NAND flash memory

- Expanded storage via SD and SDHC card memory (up to 32 GB)

- Nintendo GameCube Memory Card (required for GameCube game saves)

- Slot-loading disc drive compatible with 8 cm Nintendo GameCube Game Disc and 12 cm Wii Optical Disc

- Mask ROM by Macronix

- 480p (PAL/NTSC), 480i (NTSC) or 576i (PAL/SECAM), standard 4:3 and 16:9 anamorphic widescreen

- Stereo: Dolby Pro Logic II-capable

### Disc Reading

The front of the console features an illuminated slot-loading optical media drive that accepts both 12 cm Wii Optical Discs and Nintendo GameCube Game Discs. The blue light in the disc slot illuminates briefly when the console is turned on and pulsates when new data is received through WiiConnect24. After the update that includes System Menu 3.0, the disc slot light activates whenever a Wii disc is inserted or ejected. When there is no WiiConnect24 information, the light stays off. The disc slot light remains off while the player is playing a game or when using other features. An SD card slot hides behind the cover on the front of the console, and two USB ports are located at its rear.

The disc reader of the Wii does not play DVD-Video or DVD-Audio discs. A 2006 announcement had stated a new version of the Wii capable of DVD-Video playback would be released in 2007, but Nintendo delayed its release to focus on producing the original console to meet with popular demand. Nintendo's initial announcement stated that it "requires more than a firmware upgrade" to implement, although third parties have used Wii homebrew to attach DVD playback to the original unmodified Wii units.

The Wii also can be hacked to smooth the progress of an owner to use the console for other activities than those intended by Nintendo.

### Memory Storage

The Wii console contains 512 megabytes of internal flash memory and features an SD card slot for external storage. An SD card can be used for uploading photos as well as backing up saved game data and downloaded Virtual Console and WiiWare games. To use the SD slot for transferring game saves, an update must be installed. An installation can be initiated from the Wii options menu through an Internet connection, or by inserting a game disc containing the update. Virtual Console data cannot be restored to any system except the unit of origin. An SD card can also be used to create customized in-game music from stored MP3 files, as well as music for the slideshow feature of the Photo Channel. Version 1.1 of the Photo Channel removed MP3 playback in favor of AAC support.

Nintendo released an update March 25, 2009 that gave Wii owners the option to download WiiWare and Virtual Console content directly onto an SD card. The option offered an alternative to "address the console's insufficient memory storage." In addition to the previously announced functionality, this update lets the player load Virtual Console and WiiWare games directly from the SD card. The update allows the use of SDHC cards, increasing the limit on SD card size from 2 GB to 32 GB.

### Wii Remote

The Wii Remote, colloquially referred to as the Wiimote, is the primary controller for the console system. You can see it in Figure 2.8. It uses a combination

**Figure 2.8**
The Wii Remote.

of built-in accelerometers and infrared detection to sense its position in 3D space when pointed at the LEDs within the Sensor Bar that also comes with the system. This design allows users to control the game using physical gestures as well as traditional button presses.

The controller connects to the console using Bluetooth and features a rumble function (for feel) as well as an internal speaker. The Wii Remote can connect to expansion devices through a proprietary port at the base of the controller.

The device bundled with the Wii retail package is the Nunchuk unit, which features an accelerometer and a traditional analog stick with two trigger buttons. In addition, an attachable wrist strap can prevent the player from unintentionally dropping or throwing the Wii Remote. Nintendo has also since offered a stronger strap and the Wii Remote Jacket to provide extra grip and protection.

Two new devices have been showcased that will improve the functionality of the Wii. The Wii MotionPlus was announced as a device that connects to the Wii Remote to supplement the accelerometer and Sensor Bar capabilities and enable actions to be rendered identically on the screen in real time. This would make onscreen interaction faster and more receptive. Nintendo also revealed the Wii Vitality Sensor, a fingertip pulse oximeter sensor that connects through the Wii Remote, which will gauge your physical response to game stimuli, such as during workout routines in the game *Wii Fit*.

### Wii Balance Board

Nintendo revealed the Wii Balance Board at E3 2007 along with their game *Wii Fit*. The Wii Balance Board is a wireless balance board accessory for the Wii that contains multiple pressure sensors used to measure the user's center of balance. Namco Bandai produced a mat controller, a simpler, less sophisticated competitor to the balance board, which connects to the GameCube controller port.

### You Mean There Are Other Colors Besides White?

Before it was launched, Nintendo showed the Wii console and the Wii Remote in white, black, silver, lime green, and red, but so far it has only been available in white for its first two and half years of sales. Black Wii systems were made available in Japan in August 2009 and in Europe in November 2009. Future sales will probably involve more color choices, or so it is hoped.

**Figure 2.9**
The Wii Menu interface.

## Wii Features

The console system contains a number of standard features available from its firmware. The firmware receives regular updates via the WiiConnect24 service. The following is a brief look at these features.

## Wii Menu Interface

The Wii Menu interface (shown in Figure 2.9) is designed to represent television channels. Separate channels are graphically displayed in a grid and are navigated using the pointer capability of the Wii Remote. It is possible to change their arrangement by holding down the A and B buttons to grab channels and move them around.

There are six primary channels: the Disc Channel, Mii Channel, Photo Channel, Wii Shop Channel, Forecast Channel, and News Channel. The latter two were initially unavailable at launch, but activated through updates. Additional channels are available for download from the Wii Shop Channel through WiiWare and also appear with each Virtual Console title. These include the Everybody Votes Channel, Internet Channel, Check Mii Out Channel, and the Nintendo Channel.

## Backward Compatibility

The Wii console is backward compatible with all official Nintendo GameCube software, as well as Nintendo GameCube Memory Cards and controllers. Compatibility with software is achieved with the slot-loading drive's ability to accept Nintendo GameCube Game Discs, as shown in Figure 2.10. Peripherals

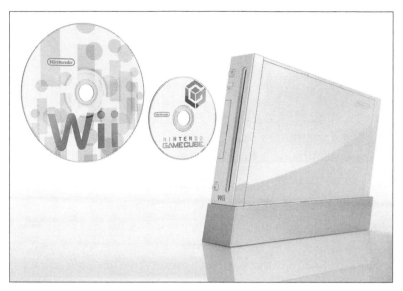

**Figure 2.10**
The Wii can accept Wii Optical Discs and Nintendo GameCube Game Discs.

can be connected via a set of four GameCube controller ports and two Memory Card slots concealed by removable flip-open panels.

The console retains connectivity with the Game Boy Advance and e-Reader through the Game Boy Advance Cable, which is used in the same manner as it was used with the GameCube. This feature can only be accessed on those select GameCube titles that previously utilized it. For whatever reason, the Wii released in South Korea lacks GameCube backward compatibility.

A Wii console running a GameCube disc is restricted to GameCube functionality. As such, a GameCube controller is required to play GameCube titles, as neither the Wii Remote nor the Classic Controller functions in this capacity. A Nintendo GameCube Memory Card is also necessary to save game progress and content, as the Wii internal flash memory will not save GameCube games.

The Wii system supports wireless connectivity with the Nintendo DS without any additional accessories. This connectivity allows the player to use the Nintendo DS microphone and touch screen as inputs for Wii games. The first example Nintendo has given of a game using Nintendo DS-Wii connectivity is that of *Pokémon Battle Revolution*.

Nintendo later released the Nintendo Channel, which allows Wii owners to download game demos or additional data to their Nintendo DS in a process similar to that of a DS Download Station. The console is also able to expand Nintendo DS games.

## Online Connectivity

The Wii console can connect to the Internet through its built-in 802.11b/g Wi-Fi or through a USB-to-Ethernet adapter, with both methods allowing players to access the established Nintendo Wi-Fi Connection service.

Just as for the Nintendo DS, Nintendo does not charge fees for playing via the service and the 12-digit Friend Code system controls how players connect to one another. Each Wii also has its own unique 16-digit Wii Code for use with Wii's non-game features. This system also implements console-based software, including the Wii Message Board. You can also connect to the Internet with third-party devices.

The service has several features for the console, including the Virtual Console, WiiConnect24, Internet Channel, Forecast Channel, Everybody Votes Channel, News Channel, and the Check Mii Out Channel.

The console can also communicate and connect with other Wii systems through a self-generated wireless LAN, enabling local wireless multiplayer on different television sets. *Battalion Wars 2* first demonstrated this feature for non-split screen multiplayer between two or more televisions.

## Parental Controls

I'm sure this section isn't all that important to you, but it is something you may have had to deal with if you have overzealous parents who want to curb your game play by censoring what you have access to.

The Wii console features parental controls, which can be used to prohibit younger users from playing games with content that would be considered unsuitable for their age level. When you attempt to play a Wii or Virtual Console game, the console reads the content rating encoded in the game data; if this rating is greater than the system's set age level, the game will not load *without* a correct override password.

The parental controls can also restrict Internet access, which blocks the Internet Channel and system update features. Since the console is restricted to Nintendo GameCube functionality when playing Nintendo GameCube Game Discs,

GameCube software is unaffected by Wii parental control settings. Parents can, however, block all GameCube software through the parental controls. This prevents all GameCube discs from being played, regardless of rating.

European units mainly use the PEGI rating system, whereas North American units use the ESRB rating system. The Wii unit supports the native rating systems of many countries, including CERO in Japan, USK in Germany, both the PEGI and BBFC in the United Kingdom, and the OFLC in Australia and New Zealand.

## Games for the Wii

Retail copies of games are supplied on proprietary Wii Optical Discs packaged in a case along with instruction information. On European releases, these retail boxes have a triangle printed at the bottom corner of the paper insert sleeve side. The hue of the triangle is used to identify which region the particular title is intended for and which manual languages are included.

More than 353 million Wii games were sold worldwide as of March 2009. The most successful game is *Wii Sports*, which comes bundled with the console in most regions, and sold 45.71 million copies worldwide as of March 2009, and surpassed *Super Mario Bros.* as the best-selling game of all time. The best-selling unbundled game is *Wii Play*, with 22.98 million units.

New games representing Nintendo's flagship franchises, including *The Legend of Zelda*, *Super Mario*, *Pokémon*, and *Metroid*, have been released or are in development for the Wii, in addition to many original titles and third-party developed games. Nintendo has received strong third-party support from outstanding companies like Ubisoft, Sega, Square Enix, Activision Blizzard, Electronic Arts, and Capcom, with more games being developed exclusively for the Wii than for the PlayStation 3 or Xbox 360.

The Virtual Console service allows Wii owners to play games originally released for the Nintendo Entertainment System, Super Nintendo Entertainment System, and Nintendo 64, as well as Sega's Mega Drive/Genesis and SG-1000 Mark III/ Sega Master System, NEC's TurboGrafx-16/PC Engine, SNK's Neo Geo console, the Commodore 64, and a selection of vintage arcade games. Virtual Console games are distributed over broadband Internet via the Wii Shop Channel, and are saved to the Wii internal flash memory or to a removable SD card. Once downloaded, Virtual Console games can be accessed from the Wii Menu as individual channels, or directly from an SD card via the SD Card Menu.

There is also a wide Wii homebrew community dedicated to creating and playing content that does not receive Nintendo endorsement. This area is what you, future game developer for the Wii, are looking to settle in as your niche after reading this book.

The game development suite Unity can be used to create official Wii games, but unfortunately the developer using Unity must be authorized by Nintendo to develop games for the console and all games must be submitted to and accepted by Nintendo in order to be released. So this book *won't* teach you about using Unity.

Instead, we will use Adobe Flash and the API from WiiCade to produce our very own electronic games for the Wii console.

## What's Next?

Now that you are prepared a little bit better for designing games for Nintendo's Wii, it's time to look at the Adobe Flash software application you will use to make your very own Wii games.

## Review

At the end of reading this chapter, you should know:

- The beginnings of Nintendo, its struggles and successes, and the game systems it has released in the past

- The creation of Nintendo's Wii console and how it works

- All about the Internet connectivity, compatibility, and downloadable content available for the Wii

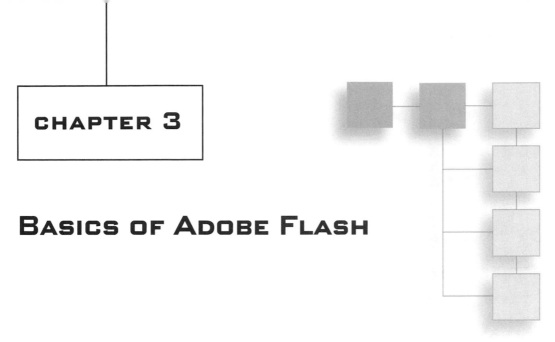

# CHAPTER 3

# BASICS OF ADOBE FLASH

In this chapter you will learn:

- What makes Flash such a versatile tool for you to use

- How to find your way around the Flash application

- How to draw, color, and modify vector art objects on the Stage

- How to use layers, layer folders, and text in your Flash document

- How to import bitmap graphics from outside sources to use in your movie

The Adobe Flash program is the one you will learn to use to make animations and games for the Nintendo Wii. Adobe Flash is a multimedia program designed specifically for the Web. Flash began as FutureSplash, which Macromedia acquired in 1997. Adobe obtained Flash from Macromedia a decade later. Flash (seen in Figure 3.1) combines motion, graphics, sound, and interactive functionality in a format proficient for a Web page.

Flash has long been a popular method for making cartoons and games, and what you learn through the course of this book will serve you in developing Flash games and animations for the World Wide Web and multiple platforms just as much as making games for the Wii.

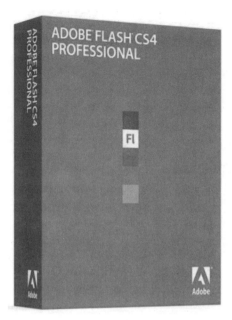

**Figure 3.1**
Adobe Flash.

## Flash on the Web

Since its introduction in 1996, Flash technology has become the premier method of adding animation and interactivity to Web pages.

The earliest Web pages were incredibly bare: just text with Web links on a gray background. That was all the original Web browsers could show. There were no images, special typefaces, or colors. As Web artists saw the prospect to do more, from file sharing to e-commerce to entertainment to games, they bellowed for more tools. Static images (ones that didn't move), colors, and typefaces were implemented first. Later, motion rolled out in the form of animated GIF images and Shockwave files.

Early Shockwave files appeared groundbreaking, though rarely seen because the program used to make them (Macromedia Director) was too complex for everyone to master and because the files produced were too hefty to be sensible on most Web pages. Today, Flash is the popular program for creating rich multimedia experiences, in part because it is so versatile and easy to use. Flash also creates small enough Shockwave files to be useful on a Web page.

There are various ways Flash can enrich a Web site. Its biggest strength lies in entertainment.

**Figure 3.2**
Updated daily, http://www.newgrounds.com is a host site for loads of Flash content.

There is simply no better tool for creating an animated Web cartoon. It has also been used to make cartoons you may have seen on the television, such as *Mucha Lucha!, Foster's Home For Imaginary Friends, Atomic Betty*, and more.

More advanced users of the software can create compelling games. Places like http://www.newgrounds.com showcase both (as seen in Figure 3.2). You can use Flash to create buttons to navigate around a site or make an entire Web site. Several software products, hardware devices, and systems can display Flash.

Flash sounds tempting to use for just about everything, doesn't it? Unfortunately, Flash makes a lot of sense for an entertainment or game site, but for a more mainstream site such as http://www.msn.com or http://news.bbc.co.uk—or for an informative site such as http://www.behindthename.com or http://www.aaa-math.com—simple text and static graphics would work better. Visitors to these sites prefer the more direct experience of a conventional HTML Web page.

A number of other software packages are available that can create output in the Shockwave file format. Among these are Toon Boom, Toufee, KoolMoves,

Express Animator, and Anime Studio. These front-ends often provide additional support for creating cartoons, with tools more tailored to traditionally trained animators. Flash is still the most versatile, as it creates not only animated cartoons but also interactive media and electronic games due to its scripting language *ActionScript*.

We are going to be using Flash in this book to develop games for the Nintendo Wii. How you do that is create your content in Flash and then use the WiiCade API to prepare your Flash content to be compatible with the Nintendo Wii console system (something we will cover in Chapter 14).

## The Flash Player

To exhibit Flash content a Web user must have installed a particular piece of software called a *plug-in*. The necessary Flash plug-in is called Flash Player. Flash Player is free, and approximately 98% of all Web users already have some version of it installed on their computer. Flash is an integrated development environment, or IDE, whereas Flash Player is a virtual machine used to run Flash files over a Web browser.

If you have ever surfed the Web on a slower browser, you might have noted how some pages took longer to download than others. File size has a huge influence on how fast Web pages display. Used well, Flash can create relatively small files that are both easy to download and rich with animation, sound, and interactivity.

## Vector Versus Bitmap

Vector graphics are one reason why Flash files are so small. Flash is a vector-based graphics program. You can create two basic types of graphics on a computer: *bitmap* or *vector*. Most Web pages display bitmap graphics in either JPEG or GIF formats, but with vector format there are several advantages.

A bitmap (often called *raster*) image file is composed of tiny squares (or *pixels*) of color information, which when viewed together create an illusion that we perceive as a photograph or other piece of artwork (see Figure 3.3). You may have seen pixels if you've ever zoomed in on an image in a graphics program such as Photoshop. Generally, one GIF or JPEG image is composed of thousands of pixels.

Graphics come with instructions, and the instructions a GIF or JPEG image tell your computer is, "Make this pixel that color, that pixel that color, and so on. . . ." A vector image tells your computer, "Make this geometric shape, and make it this

**Figure 3.3**
A close-up look at a bitmap image.

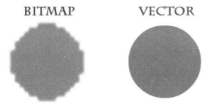

**Figure 3.4**
The comparison between bitmap and vector graphics.

color, and make it good." By "make it good," I mean that vector images are unique in their display quality. A vector shape will always look snappy whether resized smaller or bigger—even if it's resized to the dimensions of a billboard. A bitmap can look pretty good, but it almost certainly won't look so good enlarged like a billboard. See Figure 3.4 for a comparison.

Flash highlights vector graphics but supports bitmap graphics too. Bitmaps are still better at reproducing photographs, while vectors have the digital edge in rendering type and shapes.

## File Extensions

While using Flash, you'll be creating two kinds of files. Each can be identified by its three-letter suffix, called its *extension*. The work document or file (something like thisismyfile.fla) is where you do your work. FLA files can be opened only by the Flash program. From there you create and publish a second kind of file, the Shockwave file (something like thisismyfile.swf). SWF files play in your Web browser. SWF is pronounced "swiff." Windows (and Macintosh OS X) may hide these extensions from you, but they are still there.

The SWF file is going to be your end product, or the exported movie you make with Flash. SWF files are unique because they have relatively small file sizes (increasing portability), the vector format draws quickly on slower computers (increasing speed), no external resources are required (no need to import other files or fonts), and they are compatible with all major operating systems, allowing them to be cross-platform capable.

When developing content, it's best to reveal these extensions. These settings are outside the Flash program in the computer's operating system. In Windows, open the Folder Options control panel and uncheck Hide File Extensions for Known File Types. In Macintosh OS X, choose Finder > Preferences and check Always Show File Extensions.

## Tour the Flash Program

If you are familiar with other graphics programs, such as Adobe Photoshop, Adobe Illustrator, Corel Draw, or Paint, you are way ahead of most of us in learning Flash. To use Flash, all you need is a personal computer, the Flash software, and a Web browser with the latest version of the Flash Player installed. If you can't get a copy of Flash and aren't sure you want to buy it yet, Adobe provides a free 30-day trial version, which you can find at http://www.adobe.com/downloads. Once you've installed Flash, you should have everything you need. Open the Flash program and go to File > New to start a new document from scratch. If prompted by a window to choose what kind of document you want to create, choose a new Flash document using ActionScript 2.0. ActionScript 2.0 is the scripting language version we will be using later in this book to program games.

There are four main parts to the Flash program: the Stage, the Timeline, the Menu Bar, and panels. See Figure 3.5 as you read about each of them.

### The Stage

First, there's the *Stage* where you assemble everything that will be seen in your Flash movie. The Stage is your main workspace in Flash. You can draw, select, and reposition artwork here. The Stage represents what you will see in the final Flash movie. Although it's not a perfect preview of your finished movie, it does display where objects are placed and how they change according to the Timeline.

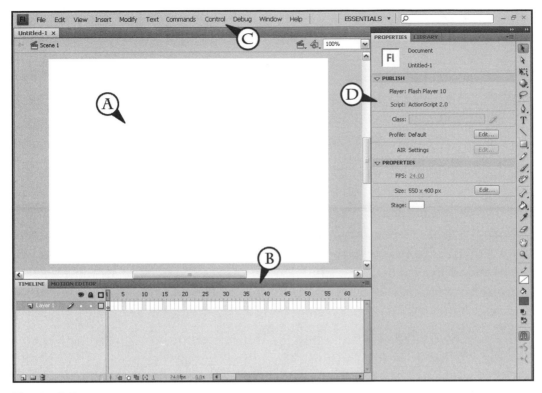

**Figure 3.5**
(A) The Stage, (B) Timeline, (C) Menu Bar, and (D) Panels.

Flash provides you a workspace around the Stage to place stuff on while you are working.

## Timeline

Accompanying the Stage is the *Timeline*, which is where you determine what happens when. The Timeline, as the name implies, shows you a scale of time when events can take place within your movie. It is like nothing you will find in your analog studio, unless you have a time machine that allows you to move forward and backward in time and up and down between dimensions. This may seem like a far-fetched analogy, but it's true. You would have to borrow Doctor Who's TARDIS, in other words, to accomplish the same feats you will in a time-based application.

The Timeline window is comprised of two sections: the Layer section where content is stacked according to virtual depth, and the Timeline/Frames section where content is planned in frames. In the Layer section of the Timeline, you can

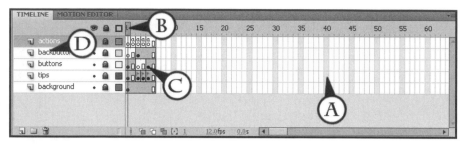

**Figure 3.6**
(A) Frames, (B) Playhead, (C) Keyframe, and (D) Layer Names.

label and organize your stacks of frame rows. You can also lock or hide individual layers. Each *frame* on the Timeline, indicated by cells from left to right, represents an increment of time. The moveable red frame indicator, also called the *playhead*, determines what frame is currently shown on the Stage. Special frames called *keyframes* mark changed views on the Stage. Dots, arrows, comments, and other markings indicate what is happening from frame to frame. See Figure 3.6.

At the underside of the Timeline are a few important buttons. The first will center the current frame in the Timeline. The others are for the onion skin feature, which allows you to view/edit multiple frames at once. The numbers to the right of these indicate the current frame number, the frame rate (how fast the movie is set to flow), and how much time has elapsed up to the current frame number.

## Menu Bar

The *Menu Bar*—which you may be familiar with in other programs—appears at the top of the program window and displays categories of commands. The Menu Bar gives you access to many of the program's features. Click on a top category and pull down a menu to select from a list of commands.

For instance, to open a new document in the Flash program you can go to File > New. At many times during the course of this text, I will tell you to select a command from the Menu Bar in this fashion. The command will start with the main menu's names (in this case, File) and may be followed by a submenu, ending with the command itself (in this case, New).

Most menu items have *keyboard shortcuts*. Shortcuts save you time for commands you use frequently. Usually, they are displayed alongside the menu commands so you can easily remember the ones you want. Not every command, however, has a shortcut.

# Panels

Most of the controls you need to change elements on the Stage and Timeline are located in the last part of Flash, the panels. *Panels* are small windows that float in the Flash workspace. Each panel has controls dedicated to specific tasks such as selecting tools, changing colors, or writing actions for selected objects. You can open new panels from the Windows category on the Menu Bar.

The upper-right corner of most panels has a minus-sign symbol used to minimize or collapse the panel and an X symbol to close the panel. Directly under those is an arrow symbol you click on to bring up the panel options list specific to that panel. Several panels have white boxes for input where you designate object properties like color code or line thickness. Most of these input boxes are accompanied by sliders or drop-down menus, so you don't have to remember what to type.

You can group panels in Flash to suit the way you work. To do this, just drag a panel's tab and release it over the top of another panel's name tab. To separate them, or to undock a panel, simply drag one panel's tab away from those of the other panels. Once you have opened several panels the way you prefer them, you can save that arrangement by selecting Window > Workspace > Save Current. Any time after that, you can select your workspace from the Window > Workspace submenu to instantly rearrange the panels to the saved arrangement.

The panel you use most often will be the *Properties Inspector* panel, shown in Figure 3.7. This context-sensitive panel shows up automatically in most default workspaces, and you can use it to alter the properties of the movie or individual objects selected on the Stage.

**Note**

Never be afraid to try something you haven't before in Flash. Anything you draw, erase, delete, change, or otherwise modify can be undone with a single command. Choose Edit > Undo (Ctrl+Z for Windows or Command+Z for Macintosh), and the last thing you did in Flash will be undone as if it never happened. You can repeat this command, too, thereby undoing more than one successive modification.

# Visibility

While working, you may need to zoom in to see some detail or zoom out to see "the big picture." Various tools in Flash allow you to alter the view of the Stage.

You probably won't be content to always view the entire Stage at its widest view. There are two tools for this on the Tools panel (shown in Figure 3.8).

**Figure 3.7**
The Properties Inspector panel.

**Figure 3.8**
The Zoom tool and Hand tool.

### *The Zoom Tool*

The Zoom tool, allows you to enlarge the view of the Stage area. It looks like a magnifying glass. Select the Zoom tool and click it anywhere on the Stage to zoom in for a closer look at the area you click. Click more than once to enlarge the view even more. Click-drag to define a rectangular marquee and release, and the view will zoom to cover the area you selected with the marquee. In order to zoom back out again, or reduce the view, hold down the Alt (Option) key on your keyboard before you click with the Zoom tool.

### The Hand Tool

To move your view around the Stage, you can click on the scroll bars and sliders on the edges of the Stage, or select and use the Hand tool. Select the Hand tool and the cursor becomes a hand. Just as you would with artwork on your desk, click-drag the hand on the Stage to reposition your view of the work area.

### Magnification

Current *magnification* is displayed in the bottom-left corner of the Stage. 100% is the size that the published movie will normally be displayed at in a Web browser window. Anything less than 100% gives you a wider, less detailed view. A value greater than 100% gives you a larger, close-up view. To zoom to an exact percentage, type the number in right there and then press the Enter (or Return) key on your keyboard. Pull down the menu right next to the percentage box for preset magnification values.

### Rulers and Guides

In most cases, you might feel comfortable aligning objects on the Stage by eye, but other times you may want more exactness than that. When that is the case, you can use rulers, guides, or a grid (shown in Figure 3.9). Select View > Rulers, and two rulers will appear at the top and left side of the Stage. These rulers are a reference for positioning and aligning objects on the Stage. Click on either ruler, and drag a blue guide onto the Stage. Drag an existing guide to reposition it; or drag it back into the ruler to remove it. *Guides* are light-colored guidelines to help you align objects vertically or horizontally. They do not show up in your published movie. Once you have placed any guides you want, you can hide or lock them under the View > Guides submenu.

The *grid* works a lot like guides, except it covers the entire Stage, looking much like graph paper. You can show or hide the grid, and turn its Snap To feature On or Off. The Snap To feature will help you magnetically align objects to your grid or guides, even if they are hidden.

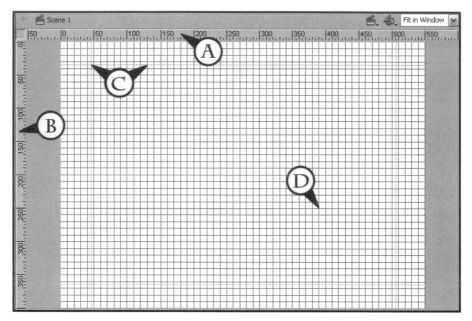

**Figure 3.9**
(A) Top Ruler, (B) Left Ruler, (C) Guidelines, and (D) Grid.

## Drawing in Flash

Drawing in Flash is reasonably straightforward. For simple drawing, use the Pencil, Brush, or Pen tools. Choose one of them and start clicking and dragging around on the Stage. That's fundamentally all you need to do to draw in Flash by hand.

## Drawing Tools

Every shape created in Flash is vector and can have a fill or stroke, or both (see Figure 3.10). The fill refers to the solid area inside a shape. The stroke outlines a shape or acts like the border of the shape. The Brush tool creates fill-only shapes, and the Pencil tool creates stroke-only shapes. The Pen tool creates shapes with

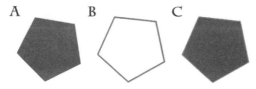

**Figure 3.10**
(A) Fill, (B) Stroke, and (C) Fill and Stroke.

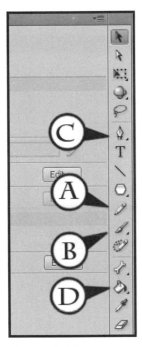

**Figure 3.11**
(A) Pencil tool, (B) Brush tool, (C) Pen tool, and (D) Paint Bucket tool.

both fill and stroke. The Paint Bucket tool can add or modify the fill of a shape. Refer to Figure 3.11 to see where the tools are positioned on the Tools panel.

### Pencil Tool

Use the *Pencil tool* to depict straight and curved lines. Click and shift the mouse in any direction on the Stage. Your line doesn't have to be straight unless you want it that way. Can you draw a perfect circle or straight line? Don't worry; most people can't. The Pencil tool can help. Underneath the Options section of the Tools panel, you can tell your drawing to Straighten or Smooth.

You don't have to draw an entire line in one motion, either. You can extend a line with the Pencil tool. Starting from one end of an existing line segment, draw where you want to extend it.

### Brush Tool

The Pencil tool creates a line with a steady thickness, a stroke. Use the *Brush tool* to make a solid shape, or fill. Just click down the mouse and draw in the Stage. As you paint with the Brush tool, all touching or overlapping shapes of the same color will merge into a single shape.

### Pen Tool

If you are familiar with another vector-based program from Adobe called Illustrator (also part of the Adobe Creative Suite), you may recognize the *Pen tool*. Sometimes it is called the Bezier tool, which is the name of the paths it creates with points and handles. Use this tool to draw lines and shapes by clicking and dragging from point to point.

If you are satisfied with the work you make with the Pencil and Brush tools, you don't need to use the Pen tool. But if you draw a lot, and want to make perfect reproductions or commercial artwork, it will be worth it to you to practice and learn how to use the Pen tool. The Pen tool lets you draw paths to create your shape's anchor point by interconnected anchor points. It gives you more control over the minute details of every curve and angle by adjusting using each point's *handles.*

When you draw with the Pen tool, you generate points with either curved or straight lines between them, depending on what type of point you create. Refer to Figure 3.12 to see what kinds of points you can have.

To create a *corner anchor point,* simply click with your mouse and a new point will appear. This point will have no handles, because any line coming out from it will be straight and therefore need no adjustment. You can move it about by using the *Subselection tool* (the white arrow icon on the Tools panel) to select and move an anchor point.

To create a *curve anchor point,* when you click your mouse on the location of your anchor point, don't immediately let go; drag a little, until you see the connecting

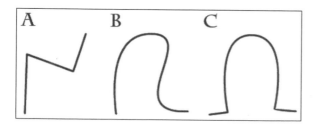

**Figure 3.12**
(A) Corner Anchor Point, (B) Curve Anchor Point, and (C) Bezier Corner Point.

lines between your points begin to curve and two antennae-like handles appear on either side of the point. You can use the Subselection tool to grab these handles and drag them about to control the size and angle of the curves to either side of the point.

There's also a combination of the two called a *Bezier corner point*, which is an anchor point that has a straight line to one side and a curve to the other side. To create one of these, you need to first have an anchor point that is corner-only; a Bezier point created immediately adjacent to that one will automatically be a Bezier corner with only one handle and a curve to only one side, because one side of it connects to a corner point.

Any lines drawn, whether in a closed shape or just an open path, will be stroked with your selected stroke color.

When you close a path (by clicking on your starting point; you'll know you're about to close your path because a small circle will appear to the right of your Pen tool mouse cursor), it will automatically fill with whatever fill you have set in your options. You can use the Paint Bucket tool to change this, or just select it and change the fill options in the Properties Inspector panel.

### Paint Bucket Tool

The *Paint Bucket tool* can add a fill shape inside an empty stroke or change the color of an existing fill. The Paint Bucket tool works with both solid fills and gradients.

The options for the Paint Bucket tool control just how tolerant the flood fills are. If you set it to Don't Close Gaps, then the Paint Bucket tool will only work to fill completely enclosed areas of a shape (that is, shapes that are completely bounded by a line with no broken spaces). But if you set it to Close Small Gaps, it will ignore small breaks in the bounding lines to fill the enclosed area. Close Medium Gaps and Close Large Gaps will cause the Paint Bucket tool to ignore larger and larger spaces in the bounding lines to treat them as enclosed areas.

### Other Drawing Tools

The *Oval* and *Rectangle tools* are fairly straightforward. Click and drag them on the Stage to create a circular or rectangular shape. These tools create shapes with both a fill and a stroke. Hold down the Shift key on your keyboard while dragging to constrain the shapes to a perfect circle or square.

The *Eraser tool* is the opposite of the Brush tool. It removes, or erases, anything you drag it over, both fills and strokes. From this tool's options, the Eraser Shape offers different sizes and shapes for the Eraser. Double-click on the Eraser tool to clear everything on the Stage.

**Note**

Flash has the option to take any line or stroke you've drawn and convert it to a fill instead, affecting its behavior and how various Flash drawing tools and their settings operate on them. To do this, select the fill you want to convert, and click Modify > Shape > Convert Lines to Fills.

## Selection Tools

To alter an object in Flash you need to first let the program know you want to modify it specifically by selecting it. Selecting an object makes it active and allows you to move or transform it in a number of different ways.

### Selection Tool

The *Selection tool*, also called the Arrow tool (because it looks like a little black arrow), is active by default whenever you first launch Flash. It's used for selecting, reshaping, moving, and deleting objects. Select an object on the Stage with the Arrow tool before applying an effect to it. For some objects, you can simply click on some objects to select them.

If you click on a fill, the fill itself will become selected (which is displayed by a pattern of tiny white overlaid dots). If you click on a stroke, the stroke by itself will become selected. If you double-click on the fill, the nearest or connecting stroke will also become selected, or vice versa. Hold down the Shift key before you click on objects to select multiple objects at once. You can also click down and drag diagonally to define a rectangular *marquee* that selects an area. A marquee is a dotted preview of the area that will be selected when you release the mouse button.

### Subselection Tool

Flash lets you manipulate lines and shapes in two different ways. Remember the Pen tool? It's different from the other drawing tools in that it uses anchor points and handles to define its shape. The *Subselection tool* allows you to reshape any object, but with the points and handles of the Pen tool.

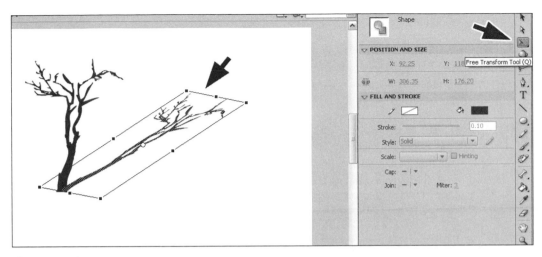

**Figure 3.13**
Using the Free Transform tool.

### Lasso Tool

Not everything you want to select fits in a rectangular marquee. The *Lasso tool* allows you to make an irregular selection. Just click and drag in any path and it will select the area you describe. You can move or delete what you select or modify it with another tool.

### Free Transform Tool

Click the *Free Transform tool* on an object and that object will sprout a frame with handles at the corners and sides (see Figure 3.13). You can resize, rotate, and distort an object by moving the various handles and sides of the frame. Watch your mouse cursor carefully, because it will indicate what transformation will occur to your object when you start clicking-and-dragging from the current cursor position.

**Note**

> Even if you start with the Selection tool and switch to using the Lasso tool, you can combine these selections. You can add to a current selection by pressing the Shift key before clicking on an unselected object to add it to the selection. Shift-click again on a selected object to drop it from the current selection.

## Color in Flash

Up to now we've just looked at drawing in Flash with little regard to color. You can choose colors before drawing new objects, or change the colors of existing objects. There are several ways to select colors.

**Figure 3.14**
Color swatches for both the stroke and fill can be found on the Tools panel.

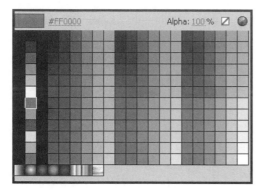

**Figure 3.15**
The color grid pop-up window helps you choose colors.

### Colors on the Tools Panel

Every object in Flash, as mentioned, can have either or both a stroke and a fill. The stroke has its own color, and so does the fill. From the Colors section of the Tools panel, shown in Figure 3.14, click on the fill or stroke *swatch* (sample square of color) and a color grid will pop up, like the one in Figure 3.15, allowing you to select a color. The preferred color will apply to whichever tool, such as Pencil, Brush, or Pen, you have active, or if you have an object selected, it will change to this color.

### Color Panels

You can also choose colors with the *Mixer* and *Swatches panels* (found under the Window category on the Menu Bar) as you would from the Tools panel, but with a few more options. To specify colors from the Mixer panel, enter numeric values or click in the color bar rainbow. Select a color from the grid of color swatches on the Swatches panel just as you would from the pop-up color grid accessed from the Tools panel.

**Note**

Flash uses only Web-safe colors, which means a color palette that displays well on most media, but especially over the Web. These colors each have a corresponding alphanumeric representation, called a *hexadecimal*; for instance, the color black is #000000, red is #FF0000, and blue is #0000FF.

### Dropper Tool

After you have created an object, it is unlikely that you would commit to memory its exact colors, when you might just want to use those same colors somewhere else for a new object. Use the *Dropper tool* (it looks like an eyedropper) to select a color from an existing object on the Stage, and it will apply it to whatever tool or object you might have selected.

### Gradient Fills

A *gradient fill* is a gradual change in tone or color, including at least two different colors. Gradients add dimension and depth to your 2D artwork when used appropriately—and since Flash is a vector-based application, you can use a few smart gradients for shading while still retaining a relatively small file size for your published movie.

You apply a gradient fill just as you would a solid color fill. Choose an existing gradient, a blue, red, or green one, from the color grid or Swatches panel and use the Paint Bucket tool to add it to an existing object you have on the Stage to see what a gradient fill is and what it does.

To adjust the positioning and shape of the gradient, choose the Gradient Transform tool, hidden behind the Free Transform tool, shown in Figure 3.16. Then select a gradient-filled object with your tool, and it will sprout controls for adjusting the position and shape of the gradient's shading.

## Manipulating Multiple Objects

Once you've created an object in Flash, you can draw over it to change it. Any tool does the job. Use the same color to add a shape, or use a different color to create a second adjacent shape. You could also select an object, copy it (going through Edit > Copy on the Menu Bar), and paste a duplicate of it (going through Edit > Paste on the Menu Bar). Note that to copy-and-paste quicker you can use the shortcut keys Ctrl+C and Ctrl+V (for Windows users) or Cmd+C and Cmd+V (for Mac users).

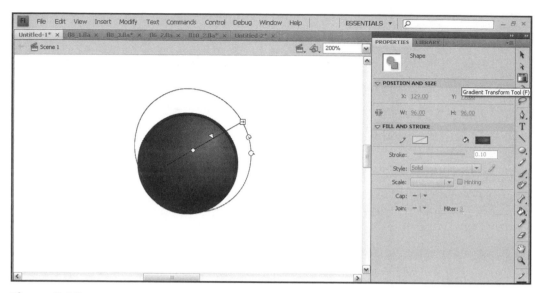

**Figure 3.16**
Finding and using the Gradient Transform tool option.

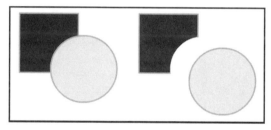

**Figure 3.17**
Combining unlike objects cut into and away from each other.

If you place a new object over a same-color object, they merge into a single shape. Place a shape of a different color over an object, and it will cut into the other shape—as shown in Figure 3.17.

## Layers in Flash

*Layers* work like overlays and are an important organizational tool in Flash. They are based on the concept of overlays in classic graphic design. Overlays are clear sheets of plastic laid over one another, creating a composite. Each sheet contains a graphic object, allowing other layers below to show through outside of that object.

If you have used another graphics program, such as Photoshop, you may be familiar with the use of layers. You can create one layer for an imported bitmap image and another for a cartoon character you want to show in front of that bitmap image. So if you want a side-view of a rabbit walking in front of some trees but want a bush passing by in front of his bouncy stride, you would put the bush on the top-most layer, the rabbit in the middle, and the trees in the bottom-most, or farthest, layer.

Here are some reasons for adding layers:

- To be sure one object appears in front, or on top, of another.

- To distinguish between different elements on the Stage.

- To animate an object on the Stage (animations should be on separate layers).

- To prevent one graphic from merging into another or accidentally editing one object when working with another.

- To systematize all your elements for easier editing, especially if another Flash artist is planning to come behind you or you are working on a project with someone else.

- To separate frame actions, labels, or sound from other elements in the same movie.

Layers are found on the Timeline. The left side of the Timeline lists the layer names with the corresponding frames to the right. Each layer on a Timeline corresponds to a layer appearing on the Stage. The contents of layers at the top of the list appear in front of the layers lower on the list.

Choose Insert > Layer to add a layer to the Timeline. Conveniently, below the layer names are a few buttons that make it easy for you to add or remove layers. Create as many layers as you need. There's no limit, but the more layers you create, the more you will have to manage as you edit the Flash file.

You can also organize your layers into *layer folders*. Add a layer folder to the Timeline as you would a standard layer. Add other layers to it by dragging their names over the folder. You cannot add frames to layer folders, just other layers.

By default Flash names new layers with numbers (Layer 1, Layer 2, Layer 3, and so on). If you are only using two or three layers, those default names will do fine. When you start working with lots of layers, that's when you might want to consider naming them something specific so you will remember what goes on each layer. Identifying the contents of a layer by the use of a specific layer name

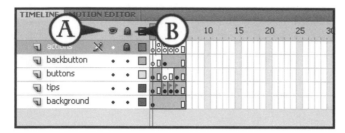

**Figure 3.18**
(A) Show/Hide icon and (B) Lock/Unlock icon.

goes a long way to improve organization. To rename a layer, first double-click the current name to select it, and when you see the text highlight or a typing cursor appear, type in the new name you want the layer to have.

The order of the layers determines what appears on top or behind. The top-most layer in the Timeline will appear on top of everything else on the Stage, while the bottom-most layer in the Timeline will appear behind everything else on the Stage. To change the order of a layer, click and drag it up or down in the list.

You can also show or hide layers, and lock or unlock layers; these buttons are found just to the right of the layer names, as shown in Figure 3.18. The show/hide icon looks like an eyeball, and the lock/unlock icon looks like a key lock. Hide layers to uncover what lies beneath, and click again to reveal that layer again. Lock a layer and it will still be visible, but you cannot inadvertently move or edit anything on that layer. When you want to edit a locked layer, click the icon to unlock it.

## Text Blocks in Flash

You can use text for just one word, a caption, a block of information, a business logo, or for several paragraphs. Flash can create text much richer than what it appears on standard HTML pages, because Flash uses vector type. Flash does not limit you in choice of fonts (typefaces), either, so you can use any font found on your computer while building your movie.

To add or edit text in a Flash movie, choose the Text tool from the Tools panel. Click it anywhere on the Stage, then type from your keyboard, and you will see what you type appear right there on the Stage. Click down, drag, and release with the Text tool to automatically constrain the text to a specific text box width. Otherwise, the text will continue on a straight line until you press the Return or Enter key. See Figure 3.19 for an example of each. When you have completed

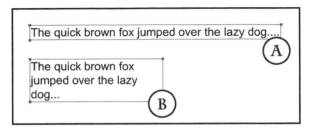

**Figure 3.19**
(A) Text running in a straight line, and (B) Text set within a fixed text box.

typing, you will have a new text box, which you can position anywhere you like with the Selection tool just like any other object on the Stage.

With the Text tool, you can select individual words or characters in a text block and use the Text options that appear in the Properties Inspector panel to modify them (shown in Figure 3.20). You can change the font to whatever is available on your computer and make it big or small. You can change the color of the text here as well. The text color is considered the same as the fill color in Flash, so you can change the fill color on any panel to affect the selected text.

Other text options are available in the Properties Inspector panel for more advanced dynamic text features. Three options are here: Static Text, Dynamic

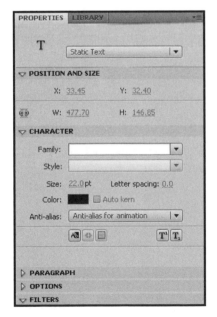

**Figure 3.20**
The Text options in the Properties Inspector panel.

Text, and Input Text. Use Static Text unless you need to implement dynamic behavior through ActionScript code or user input boxes.

Lastly, you can choose Modify > Break Apart to convert a text block into vector shapes that can be reshaped, painted, and modified just like other Flash vector art. However, once you convert a text block into a vector shape, you will not be able to edit it as text again.

## Bitmap Graphics in Flash

Through subtle experimentation you should have learned by now the benefits of vector graphics. Sometimes, however, only a bitmap graphic will work. Flash accepts several varieties of bitmap graphics.

Assuming you have first saved an image, you would choose File > Import to Stage and a dialog box will pop up. You would navigate through that window until you locate and select the desired image file. Then click the Open button and the desired image will appear on the Stage. To import artwork of this nature, an unlocked layer must currently be active. Upon import, the artwork will be placed on the Stage in the active layer. You can resize, rotate, or move your bitmap image as you would any other object on the Stage. If you choose Modify > Break Apart, you will be able to select, remove, or recolor any part of the bitmap image.

Another way to get bitmap graphics onto your Stage is to copy-and-paste them from another graphics editing program, like Photoshop, or to drag-and-drop them from your Desktop or another window into your open Flash program window. These are handy shortcuts to know, but they don't work every time. So just for starters use the Import to Stage command.

On some rare occasions you might want to apply vector attributes to a bitmap image. After you have imported a bitmap image into Flash, convert it into a vector image by choosing Modify > Bitmap > Trace Bitmap. A window will pop up with various settings. You can experiment with these values here. Depending on the bitmap image you are converting, this may help improve file size or the appearance of the artwork. You may also use it to create an interesting effect.

## What's Next?

Next you will learn how to draw your own images and scan them into the computer to use them in Flash.

## Review

At the end of reading this chapter, you should know:

- Why Flash is so popular as a multimedia creation program

- How to navigate your way around the Flash program

- How to draw, color, and transform art objects in Flash

- How to import bitmap graphics from outside Flash to use in your movie

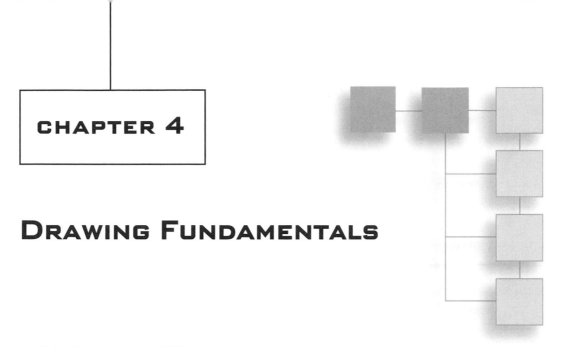

# CHAPTER 4

# DRAWING FUNDAMENTALS

In this chapter you will learn:

- What kind of drawing tools you will need

- How to draw basic shapes

- How to make those shapes look like something

- What perspective is and how to use it

- How to scan your artwork into your computer

When I was in high school I went to summer arts camp, and there the students were admitted based on their talents. I was accepted into the drawing department. The other students in that department and I came up with a running gag—whenever someone would ask what we were, we would tell them, "I am a drawer—just don't try and put socks in me!"

We didn't consider ourselves "artists"—partly because that term is so general and partly because we knew we were grungy dirty drawers; we tromped in the woods all day long, our sketchbooks in hand, covering ourselves head to toe in charcoal smudges. We drew nature as we saw it, and we did not care what others thought of us. That freedom and feeling of creative self-confidence followed me into college.

There are finer books that will teach you how to be an actual artist. This book teaches you the ins and outs of being a drawer. Your drawings may not be pretty, but they will be yours, and people will notice them. In the music industry, there are concert pianists and fine musicians—and then there are rock stars. You are going to learn to become a rock star of the art world.

## You, Too, Can Be an Artist

Somewhere along the way from crayons to pubescence we stop drawing. Perhaps you are muttering right now, "I just can't draw." That is pure nonsense. Anyone can learn to draw. Everyone is born with at least some ability to draw. There are lots of reasons you might have abandoned drawing (you had a bad art teacher who harped on you all the time in class, maybe other kids ridiculed your drawings, or perhaps you simply lost the urge to draw because you saw other kids who seemed to draw so effortlessly); whatever the reason, the ability rests within you, and we have to bring it out.

On occasion when someone says, "I just can't draw," they really mean "I just can't draw as well as the other guy!" Are you a defeatist just because you really like someone else's work and don't think yours could ever measure up? I'll let you in on a little secret: Every artist feels that way! There are hundreds of other artists I admire and wish I could draw like—but I have never let that inability hold me back, because I know that my own style is distinctly unique, and being unique is what gets you noticed and what sells.

There are almost as many styles of drawing as there are artists. Everyone's style of handwriting differs and so do styles of drawing (see Figure 4.1). One artist may use a few quick lines to encapsulate the subject, another may use many lines. You

**Figure 4.1**
Many of these artists have obviously different drawing styles.

may be attracted by the style of one artist and not another, but think how boring life would be if all drawings looked the same. Explore your own natural style and see what works best for you.

## Art Supplies

Almost anything you can make a mark with can be used to draw with. The early cave painters of France and Spain produced dramatic images of hunters chasing animals with the very basic materials they found around them in their environment. There was no prehistoric art shop along the road where they could stop and buy art supplies. They had to improvise in the creation of their own drawing materials. So they used berry juice and rock dust as pigments and dyes. We are fortunate to have a superb selection of art materials conveniently available from art shops in almost every town and city. The materials we buy today have been created based on the need, skill, and experience of artists across the globe.

All you really need to start drawing is a pencil and sheet of paper. If you look around your home you will most likely be able to find suitable materials for drawing, including ballpoint pens, pencils, felt-tipped and nylon-tipped pens, colored markers, and plain ruled notebook paper or typing paper. It is possible to draw in a wide range of other mediums, too.

Let us look at some of the most versatile tools you can find at your local art shop. Many of these should eventually find their way into your personal art studio, if you desire to become an artist.

- **Drawing table or desk**. You need a proper place to draw. You could draw on a sketchpad you set in your lap or draw laying stretched out on the floor, but you will quickly learn that you don't have the proper range of motion in your drawing arm when you do either of those things. Any kind of flat, sturdy surface should do, but try to find an equilibrium between comfort and proper range of motion.

- **Pencils**. If you successfully completed kindergarten, you know what a pencil is and what it is good for. But not all pencils are made for drawing. A standard No. 2 pencil can work in a pinch, but you should try to get real art pencils. All pencils are made from a mixture of graphite and china clay. The more graphite there is in a pencil, the softer and darker the mark it will make. Art pencils come in varying degrees of hardness. Soft pencils are known as B, harder pencils as H. They are also numbered 2, 3, 4, 5, 6, 7, 8, and 9. You will find that the higher the number, the softer, or harder, the pencil lead. Basically, it's like a sliding scale with HB in the middle, at "0," and B being the negative numbers and H being the positive numbers. So 5H is harder than 2H but 5B is softer than 2B. 2B and 3B are medium soft and ideal for sketching. My favorite number pencil to sketch with is the 2B, and I remember it as "2B or *not* 2B, that is the question!" The H pencils are too hard for most artwork, being preferred tools for technical or engineering diagrams.

- **Blue color pencils**. These are used by several industry pros to make soft-tone guidelines and preliminary sketches, which they then can ink over. The reason is that blue won't show up when you make copies of your inked pages on a copying machine. Prismacolor/Col-Erase makes the best blue color pencils.

- **Graphite sticks**. These are sticks of graphite not bound by wood casing but varnished or wrapped in paper to stop the graphite from dirtying your fingers. The main advantage to using graphite sticks is that the tip can serve as well as a pencil, but the wide side of the sharpened end can be used for bold sweeps of pencil marks and for shading large areas.

- **Erasers**. The Pentel Clic eraser is a refillable eraser pen that is great for detail work. You will also need larger erasers for covering larger areas. The one eraser preferred by most artists is the kneadable rubber eraser because it can be molded with your fingers into all sorts of shapes for rubbing out, modifying, or lifting out passages or work. Also, it is unique in that it does not create lots of loose pieces of paper and eraser shavings, so the work does not have to be dusted off by hand, which in turn reduces the risk of smudging.

- **Pens**. The antique dip-in, sketching, or mapping pens are the most common art tool. These all have a metallic nib in a wooden or plastic holder. The pen can be dipped into ink to load the nib of the pen. You have to be careful about cleaning off the nib before storing, so the ink does not dry on it and form a crust. India ink is black and won't fade. It comes in waterproof and non-waterproof forms, but I recommend the waterproof version for sketching. Colored inks are also available, but the main problem with them is that they do fade with time in the sunlight. You can also use a regular fountain or ballpoint pen to sketch with. Some manufacturers have a whole range of fountain pens for drawing, such as the technical but expensive refillable Rapidograph ones. I personally prefer Faber-Castell's PITT artist pens, because they come in sizes adequate for line artwork. The ones I use time and again are their Black, Fineliner Set of 4, as they use India ink, are waterproof, and smudge-proof, and they ranges in sizes S, M, and F, and have an extra brush-type for getting really cool line variations. Although these pens can be expensive, they do improve the quality of your work. You can find out more about the Faber-Castell PITT artist pens on DickBlick.com (http://www.dickblick.com/products/faber-castell-pitt-artist-pens).

- **Sharpie pens.** Sharpies are a standard for making thick, strong, permanent lines or filling in vast areas of a black-and-white illustration with shadow. Many black magic markers are smelly and slow-drying, or they bleed across paper, but Sharpie pens are practically quick-dry and don't fade. You can now get Sharpies in fine or fat tips and in a wide range of colors.

- **White-out**. Inking can be very messy sometimes, especially if you draw a lot, so you will want to use some corrective white-out liquid for making immediate fixes. Carefully dab it where you need to and wait for it to dry thoroughly before attempting to draw over it.

- **Contés Carres crayons.** These are square sticks of extra-firm pastel. The most common colors are black, gray, white, sanguine, and sepia. They offer beautiful results, especially on tinted paper.

- **Charcoal**. Black, burnt wood, often made in a kiln from willow wood. Charcoal can be reduced to fine powder for fine smudging on paper. Otherwise, using charcoal is very close to using graphite sticks. However, you must use some kind of fixative spray to get the charcoal to stay on the paper.

- **Fixative spray.** Pencils, graphite, and especially charcoal drawings need "fixing" to prevent them from smudging. Clear fixative is widely available in spray can form. If you cannot find it in stores, most generic forms of hairspray work just as well.

- **Paper.** Bristol board is too expensive (about $10 U.S. currency for 20 sheets), bond paper is too thin, and animation paper is too large. Cartridge paper is the most popular and can be obtained by the sheet or in a pad. Popular sizes are 4″ × 6″, 6″ × 8″, 9″ × 12″, 14″ × 17″, and 18″ × 24″.

Sketching paper can be obtained in different weights and thicknesses, as well, but 50-lb bleached white paper is ideal for most drawing work.

- **Pencil sharpeners, craft knives, and sandpaper**. You can use any of these tools to bring your pencil point to the shape you desire to use for the drawing you are going to make.

- **Drawing boards, pins, clips, and masking tape**. You can use a clipboard for smaller works, or a sturdy piece of cardboard for larger works. Or you can buy a secure easel or other physical support for your paper. Try not to use drawing pins as they make marks in the board that can show through in other work if shading or drawing over holes. Drawing board clips hold the paper to the board just fine, but I prefer securing paper to the board with masking tape.

- **Rulers**. An all-purpose 12-inch mid-sized hypotenuse triangle will work best for most drawing needs, but it should have an inking lip or edge to prevent smearing. I also use a straight ruler composed of bendy plastic so it always lays flat to the paper, even if I get a crinkle in the paper.

- **Computer hardware and software**. You should definitely get a computer, flat-bed scanner, color printer (or preferably an all-in-one printer), and image-editing software. I prefer working with the Adobe Creative Suite, which includes Photoshop, Illustrator, and Flash. You could also use Corel Painter, Corel Paint Shop Pro, or an open-source application such as GIMP or Paint.NET. For a complete list of raster image editing software, check out http://en.wikipedia.org/wiki/List_of_raster_graphics_editors#List.

In case you need to pack all your gear and be ready to take your art on the road, you will need a box or some similar container to put your art supplies in. Most of my teen years I used a grungy tackle box that I found in a thrift store to put my art supplies in. Tackle boxes or makeup kits work well, because they have these partitioned slots for you to put your pens, pencils, white-out, crayons, markers, erasers, and more in.

## Drawing Techniques

This section is targeted at those readers who are beginning artists or who have difficulty drawing cartoons. Toward that end, I will show you the basic sketching and inking techniques that will allow you to wow your friends and family and get

Web visitors to notice you. These techniques work capably in any medium and are a great place to start.

Before we get to those techniques, I will first point out that the world all around you, this book, the chair on which you sit, your computer, are in three dimensions (3D). When you sit with pencil and paper, you are going to create a two-dimensional reflection of your 3D world. You render 3D objects and people in 2D through the use of lines and values, counting on your audience's eyes to interpret what you draw. This may sound tantamount to magic, but really it is not. Whenever you draw two dots and a curvy line under them, anyone looking at your image will assume you've drawn a smiley face. This perceptive filter will be your closest ally as an artist.

## Holding Your Pencil or Pen

When first holding a pencil for drawing, most people adopt the writing position. They rest their hand on the paper and hold the pencil tightly in their fingers. This gives a small controlled area and allows for sketching lines and curves of very short length. This is fine for writing notes but not practical for sketching or painting.

By lifting the hand off the page, you can work from your wrist as well as your fingers. A single line or curve drawn from the wrist can be two to three times longer than a line drawn from the fingers when the hand is resting on the table.

Sit back in your chair with your hand still off the page. Try drawing a line from your elbow joint. This will give you more freedom to draw longer, free-flowing lines. You will have a much larger area for your hand and arm to sweep curved and straight lines.

Finally, with your sketchpad on an easel or table top, stand up and draw a line using your entire arm and shoulder, as shown in Figure 4.2. This gives you the largest possible area for your arm and hand to sweep and work with.

Try sketching lines on your sketchpad in the ways described above, working alternately from your fingers, wrist, elbow, and shoulder. Note how each way has its advantages and disadvantages.

## Drawing Basic Shapes

Everything you ever draw or paint will be based on one or more basic shapes: circles, ovals, squares, rectangles, triangles, and cylinders. By taking things step by

**Figure 4.2**
Use your entire arm to draw with for sweeping results.

step and building on a sound foundation, you will soon find that you can begin to sketch successfully. Rather than drawing your subject from the top and working downward, I recommend you use a slightly different approach. Squint at the subject and see what its underlying basic shapes are, and sketch those first before adding the details of the subject over the initial outline.

For instance, an apple is really a simple circle. And a coffee mug could start as a vertical cylinder with a handle sticking off of it. You can use simple shapes you already know how to draw and turn them into recognizable characters. It has been proven to work for thousands of people. For now, I don't want you to worry about making perfect pictures. You are just going to begin drawing.

### Two Basic Shapes

There are two flat shapes you will draw over and over in the construction of subjects you are drawing. They are the circle and the square. Try drawing these two basic shapes, shown in Figure 4.3. The circle can be one of the hardest for beginners to draw; just remember that it is like the square but with the corners whittled off. Plus, you are *not* an android, so your circle doesn't have to be perfect.

Keep your grip on your pencil loose, and try to draw from your shoulder or your elbow. Lightly drawing the basic shape, or shapes, of your subject will ensure it is

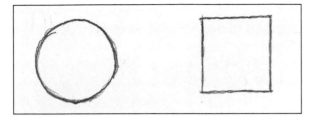

**Figure 4.3**
The two most basic shapes: circle and square.

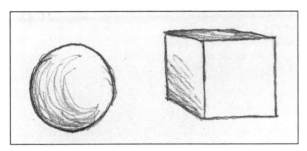

**Figure 4.4**
Make the basic shapes seem real.

going to sit in the right place on your sketchpad and be of the right proportions. The subject should sit neither too high nor too low on the page, nor be too wide, too thin, too tall, nor too short. Look around your home for objects based on basic shapes, and sketch them so as to build drawings on them.

### Making Shapes Look Real

These are still flat geometric shapes. Your next step is to stretch your imagination and draw them as they would look in three dimensions. The easiest way to add depth is to imagine multiple sides to the same shape, some of which you can't see from your viewing angle. The circle becomes a sphere, egg, or cylinder; the square becomes a cube or rectangular box, shown in Figure 4.4.

You might have seen other artists draw cubes as shown in Figure 4.5. What they are really doing is drawing two squares and then connecting them with lines, making a transparent cube, much like an ice cube, so you can see all sides. If you want to make the cube appear opaque, you simply erase the lines making up the back side of the cube.

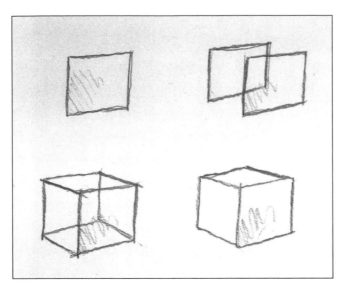

**Figure 4.5**
The quick I-see-through-you way of drawing a basic cube.

### Shading

The easiest way to make shapes appear even more three-dimensional is to add values, such as highlights and shadows. All you need are three values: one for the basic color of the object, one for the highlighted area, and one for the shaded area. Later, depending on your artistic style, you can add graduated tones, which will make the object appear more realistic and less like a cartoon.

To decide the placement of highlights and shadows on an object, you must determine the direction from which the light source in a given scene is coming. Most artists choose a light source off to the left or right of the scene. Highlights appear on objects on the sides and edges nearest to and facing the light source, while shadows appear on the same objects on the opposite sides, facing away from the light source. Try adding lights and darks to your shapes.

Pencils vary in degree of softness and hardness. Copy the image in Figure 4.6. Vary the strength of shading by varying the pressure of your hand on the pencil.

After you complete tonal experimentation using your pencil, switch to your pen. You use a variety of ink lines to create many other shading effects. These come under four headings:

- **Hatching.** Hatching is the use of parallel lines. The closer together the lines, the darker the area will look; the farther apart, the lighter the area.

**Figure 4.6**
A lot of tonal variation can come about when pencil shading.

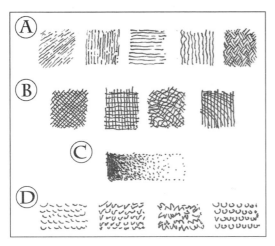

**Figure 4.7**
(A) Hatching, (B) Crosshatching, (C) Stippling, and (D) Random Lines.

- **Crosshatching**. This is where one set of hatching lines is placed over another set, making an area look even darker.

- **Stippling**. Stippling uses dots. The closer the dots are, the darker the area; the farther apart, the lighter the area.

- **Random lines**. Marks, semicircles, ticks, and wiggly lines do not fall under the other three headings but can be very useful.

Draw the chart in Figure 4.7 in your sketchbook. Invent several types of hatching, crosshatching, and random lines all your own.

You can also start to simulate volume for your objects by placing shadows on the ground beneath them. The placement of the light source in your picture will

**Figure 4.8**
Light casts shadow.

affect the shadow cast by the subject. See Figure 4.8. Look at these rules of thumb when drawing your shadows:

- The higher the source of light, the shorter the shadow should be.

- The lower the source of light, the longer the shadow should be.

- The stronger the light, the darker the shadow should be.

- The softer the light, the gentler the shadow should be.

### Tactile Values

Any piece of artwork consists of three main parts: the outline of the subject, the coloring and value study of it, and the ability to show, or at least suggest, the material the subject is made from. As artists, what we are trying to do is to trick the eye of the onlooker into believing that a few marks of a pencil on paper is nothing of the sort, but is wood, silk, metal, hair, fur, flesh, or whatever it is you are drawing.

You can use traditional shading, hatching, crosshatching, stippling, and random lines to gain an insight into the art of rendering textures, often referred to in the

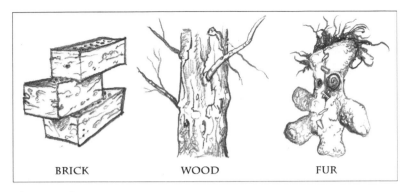

**Figure 4.9**
Tactile values of different subjects.

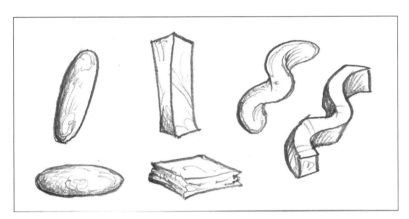

**Figure 4.10**
Twist, stretch, and squash your shapes.

industry as tactile values. Find and sketch two very different types of materials, reflecting in your artwork the material's surface type through the use of these techniques. Look at Figure 4.9 for an example.

### Manipulating Shapes

Now attempt to twist these shapes. Stretch and squash them in your mind. Imagine that each is made of putty and can be manipulated in many different ways. Remember, however, that all objects have volume and an object cannot show a loss of volume. So even if you show a rubber sphere squashed flat against the ground, the sphere flattens out at the sides as it becomes thinner in the center, but it doesn't lose its overall volume. Try manipulating your shapes like those in Figure 4.10.

### Perspective

Perspective is another word used to mean "point of view" or "view angle" and in art it is crucial to showing objects the way they should look in relationship to their environment and objects next to them. To create a sense of depth or distance in your pictures you must use perspective. Applying the rules of perspective will help you in everything you draw. So when working, make it a habit to sketch guidelines lightly on your paper to make sure all the lines in your picture are properly in perspective.

Unfortunately, perspective is the one area of drawing in which most people experience some degree of difficulty. When people hear perspective mentioned, they often go to the library, obtain a book on the subject, flip through it, see lines shooting about all over the place, and usually end up more confused than they were before they opened the book. The secret is to keep the whole business of perspective as simple as you can, to bear in mind a few basics, and to bear in mind that perspective is not something you can master in one, two, or three lessons. Learning perspective is an ongoing process.

**Horizon Line**   The first basic trick to perspective is this: The farther away something is, the smaller it looks. In your field of view, objects closer to you will look bigger, and they shrink as they get closer to the horizon line. The *horizon line* is an imaginary line across your field of vision when you look straight on; not up or down, but straight ahead.

In Figure 4.11 you see how the horizon line stays directly in front of the subject regardless if he is sitting down, standing level, or standing on a crate. To determine the horizon line when looking at a real subject you are drawing, try holding a ruler by its thin side, horizontally in front of your eyes. If outdoors in relatively flat terrain, you might notice the horizon line coincides to where the sky and earth meet each other in the far distance, from your viewpoint. This is where your horizon line should be in your composition.

Generally, I draw my subject lightly first, then apply the horizon line to my sketch. The horizon line is then used to apply perspective to the rest of your work and to check and corroborate your subject.

**Vanishing Point**   When you have parallel lines running alongside each other, like edges of a sidewalk or rooftops, note that the parallel lines appear to get closer together the farther away they are. In fact, they will almost seem to meet on the horizon line. The point where they do meet is called the *vanishing point*. We know that the lines don't really merge, but by having them vanish

E.L. = EYE LINE

**Figure 4.11**
The horizon line remains at eye level to the viewer.

on the horizon line we create the illusion that they are getting farther away and that the scene has more depth. Notice this in Figure 4.12.

**Putting Objects in Perspective**    There are multiple points of view you can use that are considered very dynamic. Figure 4.13 shows examples of these. The standard view is straight on, which is how we normally see objects. Then there's the bird's-eye view, which is from a higher elevation looking down on the subject. Last there's the mouse-eye view, from the elevation of the ground level looking up. These last two lead to foreshortening, which is making parts of a single object look smaller as they recede, or go back, from the viewer. Foreshortening uses perspective, even though the horizon line has been rotated up or down, respectively.

Look at Figure 4.12 again. This is the front view of a fishing dock, from a bird's-eye-view. With this view there is just one vanishing point on the horizon line for the sides of the pier.

In Figure 4.14 the building is set at an angle. We now have two vanishing points, one for each side. Guidelines will often want to converge at vanishing points off the page. This is normal. When it does, lay scrap paper at the sides and tape them on from behind, then extend the guidelines onto it, so you can stretch your lines to the proper vanishing points. Never assume that your perspective is correct or guess at it; always try to prove it.

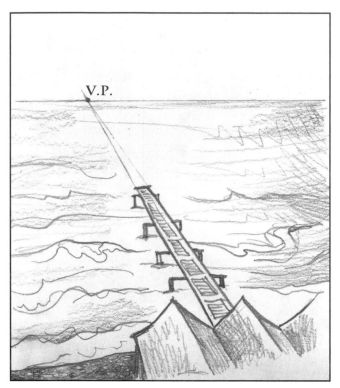

**Figure 4.12**
Parallel lines run off to apparently merge at the vanishing point (VP).

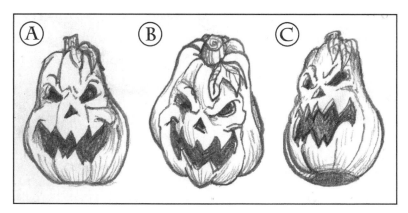

**Figure 4.13**
(A) Standard View, (B) Bird's-Eye View, and (C) Mouse-Eye View.

Most newbie artists don't realize that perspective like I showed for drawing a building can be used to make ovals and cylinders. Lightly draw squares enclosing the circles you are using, and then apply the one-or-two-point perspective, as exhibited in Figure 4.15. Check to make sure that four edges

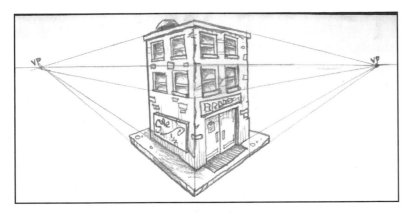

**Figure 4.14**
A building shown in two-point perspective.

**Figure 4.15**
Use perspective to put ovals in proper places.

of the circle touch the sides of the lightly sketched squares enclosing them. The squares and guidelines can be gently rubbed out before you shade your picture.

Objects are not the only thing you will want to put into perspective. People and animals classify, too. If two people are the same size and one is standing behind the other, the one in back will appear smaller than the one in front, because of perspective. If you draw a person's face, and they are turned slightly to the side, the eye farthest away from you will appear smaller in contrast to the one closer to you. Keep perspective in mind whenever you draw, because everything must be in perspective. And when in doubt, draw your guidelines to know just where objects should be and what they should look like.

## Scanning Your Artwork

To get your finished drawings off your sketchpad and into your computer, you will need to use a flatbed scanner. How you do so is up to the model scanner you are utilizing, the computer programs you have on your computer, and your computer skills. What follows are answers to the most often queried issues with scanning pictures.

## Resolution and Pixels Per Inch

There are two very different ways to use images, printing or video screens. We scan for the capability of our output device. We choose the scan resolution based strictly on the needs of the output device that will process that image. At home, that output device is normally a printer or a video monitor.

Printer ink dots and image pixels are very different concepts, but both use the term *DPI (dots per inch)* in their own way. Inkjet printer DPI ratings refer to printer ink dots (the four colors of ink), which is *not* the same thing as image pixels. These are such different concepts that some people think we should reserve the term DPI for inkjet ink dots, and reserve use of *PPI (pixels per inch)* only for image pixels.

You may hear scanning resolution called SPI (samples per inch), and that is indeed what it is. You often hear image resolution called PPI (pixels per inch), and that is indeed what it is. The SPI and PPI terms are correct. But historical and common usage has always used DPI for image resolution, meaning pixels per inch, and fully interchangeable with PPI. Pixels are conceptually a kind of colored dot, too, and resolution has always been called DPI—for years before we had inkjet printers. Scanners and scanner ratings say DPI, too, meaning pixels per inch. What you need to get out of this is that the idea of printing digital images is always about pixels per inch, so when the context pertains to images instead of printers, all of these terms—SPI, PPI, and DPI—are exactly the same equivalent concept: they all mean pixels per inch.

For images viewed on computer screens, scan resolution merely determines image size. If you scan 6 inches at 100 DPI (or 1 inch at 600 DPI), you will create 600 pixels, which will display on any screen as 600 pixels in size.

You might think greater resolution means showing more detail, and while that's generally true (within reasonable limits), it's because greater resolution makes the image larger. But you are always limited by your output device, and often cannot take advantage of maximum resolution. The images are huge, and our screens are simply not large enough.

If you don't know your screen size, then the Windows Start > Settings > Control Panel > Display > Settings tab will show or change it. On the Macintosh, you can do the same at the Apple Monitor Control Panel.

Popular video screen size settings are:

- 640×480 or 800×600 pixels for 14-inch monitors

- 800×600 or 1024×768 pixels for 15-inch monitors

- 1024×768 or 1152×864 pixels for 17-inch monitors

- 1152×864 or 1280×1024 pixels for 19-inch monitors

Inches simply have no meaning on the computer screen; we all see something different. Inches are not defined in the video system. The way video works is that when you set your video settings to say 1024 × 768 pixels, then that 1024 × 768 pixels of memory on your video board defines your video system. The programs you use will copy your pixels directly into that 1024 × 768 pixel video memory. One image pixel goes into one video board pixel memory location, one for one. A 100 × 50 pixel image fills 100 × 50 of those 1024 × 768 pixels. Those 1024 × 768 pixels are output to your screen, regardless of the size of the glass tube attached. Video is only about those 1024 × 768 pixels (or whatever the current setting is).

You might hear how 72 DPI or 96 DPI images are somehow important for the video screen, but that's totally wrong. Video simply doesn't work that way. Video systems have no concept of inches or DPI. No matter what DPI value may be stored in your image file (like 300 DPI for printing), your video system totally ignores it, and always just shows the pixels directly.

As a general rule of thumb, scan your pictures at 300 DPI if you want to print your work, but if you are making a Flash animation or game you can settle for less detail, so 72, 96, or 100 will work fine.

## Using an All-In-One Printer

The following are steps for scanning your images if you use an all-in-one printer that has a scanner built in. This is the type of scanner bed used by most professionals.

1. Blow the dust from your scanner and printing area with canned air. Clean the scanner bed and the underside of the document lid with a damp, lint-free cloth before scanning. This removes dust and fingerprints.

2. Get your computer and all-in-one printer turned on and talking to each other. Open the scanning software on your computer if needed. If not, you can use the controls on your printer to run the show.

3. Lay the picture to be scanned face-down on the glass. Square up the photo using the guides that are usually located along the edges of the scanning bed. Close the lid.

4. Go for a higher DPI count if you plan to display the scanned image at larger-than-life size. Otherwise, you can select a lower resolution.

5. Click the Scan button on your computer's scanning software window. Some all-in-one printers need you to press the Scan button on the printer itself, so check the manual before using.

6. Get a preview of the scanned image up on your computer monitor. This might happen automatically depending on your software settings; if not, prompt your computer to display one.

7. Accept the scan and save to your hard drive. Remember to put your picture away.

A few last words.

Make sure your picture is clean and dry before scanning; remove any dust, hair, or fingerprints from the surface of the picture. Exercise caution when cleaning your artwork so as not to smear the image.

Use the scanner bed even if your all-in-one printer has a document feeder. The feed process can do horrible things to your picture. Trust me.

JPEG (pronounced "jay-peg") files can compress the image to a smaller size for ease of storage, but the higher you set the compression factor, the more the picture quality will suffer. TIFF files do not significantly compress the information and preserve quality, but their file size can be 10 or more times bigger than JPEGs.

## Review

At the end of reading this chapter, you should know:

- What art tools you must own in order to draw

- How to draw basic shapes and make them look real

- How to use perspective to add depth and dimension to your art

- How to scan in your artwork so that you can manipulate it on a computer

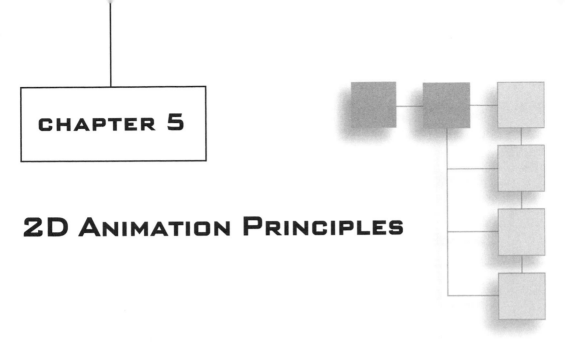

# CHAPTER 5

# 2D ANIMATION PRINCIPLES

In this chapter you will learn:

- To create visual humor

- The Disney principles of animation

- Traditional animation and Flash animation techniques

- How to make characters walk, talk, and "come alive" onscreen

Reality TV, just like real life, can be pretty boring. Who wants to see a bunch of whiny people sitting around their apartment or in a backyard just like your own, griping to each other or to the camera about how life is so unfair? I would much rather escape to a mock reality, preferably a wonderland of strangeness, involving wisecracking androids, sexy pixies, intergalactic cowboys, smooth-talking lizards, ill-tempered ogres, or carnivorous man-eating plants.

If any of those things interest you, too, or if you feel like coming up with your own cartoons for viewing online or on the Wii, instead of vegging out on a couch watching more mindless television, then this chapter will help you get started!

This chapter will show you how to take your computer and prepare to make Flash animations with it.

## Computer Animation

I remember, when I was a kid (and I hope I don't start sounding old at this point!) we only had cartoons on Saturday mornings. Animated films were few and far between and often produced by Disney. Today, cartoons are so commonplace, they even have their own channels (Cartoon Network, Disney Channel, Nickelodeon, and more) and new animated motion pictures come out just about every other week.

Part of the reason animations are more commonplace is because the kids that grew up sitting glued to their tubes Saturday mornings, like me, are in charge of their production. And because technology has advanced significantly, it's made animation more convenient, if not easier.

Simulating real life in 2D isn't easy. Animation is all about bringing characters to life in a vivid imaginary world. Some people have two misconceptions: (a) that drawing and animating are easier on computers, and (b) that moving stuff around onscreen counts as animation. Neither could be further from the truth!

First of all, computers don't do the dirty work for you. Computers may make some tasks easier, but they make others harder. Creating digital art and animations is deliberately slow and tedious whether you choose to do it by hand or with a software application. You have to own a lot of patience to work in animation.

Secondly, making an animated character look good is never going to be quick or super easy just because you are using a computer to do your work. Simply moving objects around on your screen *does not* make an animation. It may entertain a Neanderthal, but real animation is about simulating actions in an artificial environment, and doing so in a way that is both stylish and cool enough to keep the viewer's attention fixed to the screen.

Therefore, you need some fundamental understanding of animation before you start simulating action.

## Creating Visual Humor

**Tip**

"Comedy is simply a funny way of being serious."

—Peter Ustinov

Of course, you might have other designs for your cartoon animation, but if you are creating cute or comical animations, here are a few basic suggestions for keeping your audience in stitches.

Some folks believe drawing is some kind of unique talent, given only to a lucky few, and can't be learned. I hope I have shown you how wrong that is. Likewise, there are those who believe humor is fickle, that joke writing is impossible if a person was not born a comedian. Let me tell you: I've met several cartoonists, and they can appear meek, quiet, and demure, the same as anybody. They aren't born comedians. They aren't always clowning around, either. But they *have* learned how to draw really funny gags.

### What's So Funny?

Nobody laughs at the same jokes. This is true. You must recognize that just as there are many different drawing styles, there are also many styles of humor. Some of them may appeal more to you than others. Some jokes may have you rolling on the floor, while your friends and family scratch their heads, trying to figure out what's so funny.

Pick a few cartoons that you know make you laugh. Then try to work out what makes them seem so funny to you. Is it because they have a weird twist at the end that you did not expect? Is it because they exaggerate somebody or some event from real life? Does something disastrous or embarrassing happen to someone in the joke that makes you laugh because you are glad it's them and not you?

Most humor breaks down into several well-used comical themes. You see these used over and over. The following are just a few examples of these themes.

### Escher Effect

**Tip**

"Consistency is the last refuge of the unimaginative."

—Oscar Wilde

Whenever something happens that you did not expect, like the cream pie in the face that comes from out of nowhere, it's funny.

As a classic example, consider Warner Brothers' Wile E. Coyote in any number of the *Looney Tunes* episodes he appeared in. Look at Figure 5.1. While chasing the ever-escaping Road Runner, the cunning and adorable scoundrel runs off a cliff.

**Figure 5.1**
A common sight in cartoon animations is the defiance of gravity.

You expect him to fall to his death, but first he stops running, looks down, realizes his terrible plight, stares meekly at the camera for a few seconds, and sometimes even holds up a letter sign he pulls from his hidden back pocket. After the cartoonist allows viewers to read the sign, which says "Whoops!" gravity takes over and the poor coyote falls to the canyon floor far below. He doesn't die, however. Instead, he makes a coyote-shaped hole in the ground and crawls back out alive.

We not only delight in his pain, we also giggle over the unexpected humor in this situation. The laws of physics are clearly defied in order to gag us. This is known as the *Escher effect*, a special effect in cartoons where the natural order of life is not adhered to—as long as the results are funny!

**Schadenfreude Effect**   When pain happens to you, it's not funny. When pain happens to someone else, especially if it's someone we think "deserves" it, or we know there will be no social repercussions from laughing at it, it *is* funny.

Look at *Tom & Jerry* cartoons, where Tom, the cat, is always trying to teach Jerry, the mouse, a lesson. But it never works out the way Tom plans it. Just when he thinks he's caught the clever little mouse and is going to bite down on "him," he realizes the mouse has switched places with the cat's own tail, and now Tom is howling in pain after chomping his poor tail!

Most cartoons would not be as amusing if all the daring pain-filled antics were taken out of them. However, the violence doesn't last long; it's for comedy's sake, and nobody actually is harmed, because, as in the Escher effect, cartoon characters get right back up afterward, defying logic.

Violence without consequence is pure comic genius, and it's called the *schadenfreude effect*, borrowing a word from the German that means "taking pleasure from someone else's misfortune." Experiences that are normally stressful, unpleasant, or even tragic can be treated with a grain of laughter in cartoons.

**Doolittle Effect**    Remember Doctor Doolittle, who could talk to animals and they would talk back? I don't know why, but there has always been something really funny about making animals walk on two legs, talk just like people do, and behave in similar manners to us ungainly bipeds. Anthropomorphic animals are nothing new. They framed the heart of tales written by Beatrix Potter and capitalized in the media by Disney.

This anthropomorphizing of animals is known as the *Doolittle effect*, but it does not just apply to animals. You can also personify objects, as long as you keep the basic look of them realistic. Imagine what one trash can might say to another: "I think I've got something between my teeth!"

Animal characters that dress, talk, and walk like us are fun to draw and come with a slew of facial and body elements that work really well when drawing expressions, including whiskers, tails, hair, scales, feathers, beaks, muzzles, snouts, claws, talons, and so on. Study the animal you want to draw before putting it in a T-shirt or jacket, and then do more sketches of it in anthropomorphized poses. Make your animals look expressive without appearing too human. You want to capture the essence of intelligence without supplanting the animal's nature completely.

For more examples, look at the motion picture *The Secret of NIMH* from Don Bluth Productions (see Figure 5.2).

**Screen Actors Guild Effect**    Acting is not relegated to Hollywood types with snazzy smiles. Your animated characters are essentially actors, too. The following tricks are all part of the *Screen Actors Guild effect*.

*Acting in Character*    People who act in-character can appear really funny given the current circumstance, especially when they do so at inopportune times or when situations would normally call for other types of action. Think of a spaceship hurtling closer and closer to the sun, with no way for the ship's

**Figure 5.2**
Character model sheet designed by Don Bluth for his movie *The Secret of NIMH*.

crew to pull out of the fatal nosedive. If the space cowboy pilot were to smile his usual smile and slip on his sunshades, *that* would be funny!

*Acting Out of Character*   Characters can also act out of character for humorous effect. An especially well-known character that does so is always good for a laugh. For instance, what if you had the monosyllabic Tarzan of the Apes decide to become a brain surgeon? Or Captain Hook from *Peter Pan* became a corporate financial advisor?

*Overacting and the Take*   Overacting can be funny, too. Jim Carrey, who has done some very funny movies, like *The Mask* and *Ace Ventura*, is well-known for his comic genius at overacting. He exaggerates the emotions he portrays in front of the camera and goes over the top whenever he does anything, acting like a human cartoon.

Look at some of the classic cartoons. In them, most characters do what is called in the industry a *take*: If a wolf sees a pretty girl at a nightclub, he not only acts lusty, but steam comes out of his ears, his jaw drops to the floor, his tongue unfolds to hit the carpet, and his eyes roll back in his head and come out his mouth. Or when an old lady sees Casper the Friendly Ghost, seen in Figure 5.3, she screams "Ah! Ghost!" and her wig pops off the top of her head, she drops her cane, and before she dashes off stage, leaving a woman-sized puff of dust in her wake, her dentures jump out of her head, chatter, and then leap back between her gums.

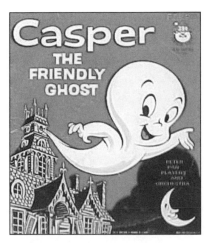

**Figure 5.3**
Cover for a book starring iconic character Casper the Friendly Ghost.

The *take* is one way that cartoon characters break all natural laws to take a singular emotion over the top for a laugh.

*Straight Guy/Gal*    Being serious is also a vital part of being frivolous. Seriousness and frivolity are akin to good and evil or yin and yang: One cannot exist without the other. If you include a total lunatic in your animation, not just a comic relief agent, then you should also include a *straight guy/gal*.

Graham Chapman plays the best deadpan roles in the Monty Python bunch, including the completely serious King Arthur in *Monty Python and the Holy Grail*. Likewise, Dean Martin was Jerry Lewis's straight man, and Marge Simpson always sees the saner side of things, as opposed to her hubby Homer, in the television show *The Simpsons*.

Have the straight guy/gal help the joker tell the jokes in your animation and further the story.

### Things to Watch Out For

Before you rush off to draw your own cartoons, dribbling your ink all over the place and making a mess, you should watch out for some things. These are pitfalls that can ruin a would-be joke, and if you aren't careful, you could even make enemies.

- #@%&*!: Being crass or tasteless will not make your jokes funny. Only in rare situations does scatological, or "toilet," humor make a cartoon really funny, and even then it's usually funny only because of the temporary shock value and wears off after a while.

- **In-jokes**: Just because your jokes are funny to you and your closest friends does not mean the whole world will laugh with you. Most in-jokes are just that: meant to be shared by a few select people, an in-crowd, and are based on "had to be there" moments.

- **Personal bias/sarcasm**: While sharing your point of view about certain topics is acceptable, especially through the use of satire or sarcasm, often exposing a personal bias—or worse, a prejudice!—is not. Being sassy can be funny, but being pretentious or bitter just won't do.

### Jokes Without Words

If you have a talent for visual humor, that is, telling jokes in pictures without words, you will have a hidden ace up your sleeve when it comes to drawing funnies. Two of the greatest comic artists at this sort of humor were Gary Larson, creator of *The Far Side* comic, and Charles Addams, frequently featured in *The New Yorker*, who is well-known for his darlings, *The Addams Family*. They could tell knee-slapping stories just by their drawings alone.

Try turning the soundtrack off to your cartoon, and if you can still follow the action onscreen and enjoy it, you are halfway there. If you find yourself splitting up with laughter, sound or not, then you know you have made a great cartoon! See Figure 5.4.

**Figure 5.4**
One example of a joke that needs no dialogue to get laughs.

## Prominent Animators of Note

### Chuck Jones

Charles Martin "Chuck" Jones (see Figure 5.5) started out as a cel washer and worked his way up to animator and then director at the animation division of Warner Brothers Studios. He is renowned for creating such beloved cartoon characters as Wile E. Coyote, Pepé Le Pew, Marvin the Martian, Road Runner, among others, as well as adding to the development of *Looney Tunes* favorites such as Bugs Bunny, Daffy Duck, Porky Pig, and myriad others.

When talking about one of his most adored creations, Wile E. Coyote, Chuck had this to say: "I think he's a heroic character. I admire him because he keeps trying all the time. Also, it's legitimate—he is just trying to get something to eat. Evidence of logic is vital to comedy. You must believe it or you can't laugh at it. The Coyote and the Road Runner are the only two alive out there. There was a drought or famine. The Road Runner, who lives on insects, probably didn't have to leave during the drought. The coyote starts out after him because there's nothing left and by the time that others return the coyote has become a fanatic. That fanaticism is more vital to him—and us—than any present need. We all pursue hopeless goals at times, don't we?"

And on the subject of animation in general, he said, "I don't think it has to be realistic. It just has to be believable," which if you have ever watched this master's works, you can definitely believe!

### Fred Moore

Often regarded as having made the largest impact at the Disney animation studios, Fred Moore, shown in Figure 5.6, was posthumously honored as a Disney Legend in 1995. Moore worked as an animator at Disney during the 1930s and 1940s and is best known for creating the most

**Figure 5.5**
Chuck Jones.

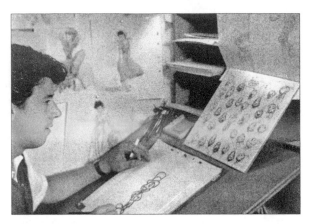

**Figure 5.6**
Fred Moore.

endearing look of Mickey Mouse today and having started most of the animation precedents at the studios.

Moore's look and actions for Mickey started in 1938 with the short *Brave Little Tailor* and cemented by the acclaimed *Fantasia* shortly thereafter. Moore continued his animation tradition with *Snow White and the Seven Dwarfs, Pinocchio, Dumbo, Alice in Wonderland,* and *Peter Pan*. The hallmark of Fred's drawing style was his uncanny ability to give emotion, charm, and appeal to his characters, while making their actions seem more convincing.

Moore created a list of important items to check your animation against. Here is Fred's 14 Points of Animation:

1. Appeal in drawing

2. Staging

3. Most interesting way [to depict action]? (Would anyone other than your mother like to see it?)

4. Is it the most entertaining way?

5. Are you in character?

6. Are you advancing the character?

7. Is this the simplest statement of the main idea of the scene?

8. Is the story point clear?

9. Are the secondary actions working with the main action?

10. Is the presentation best for the medium?

11. Does it have two-dimensional clarity?

12. Does it have three-dimensional solidity?

13. Does it have four-dimensional drawing? (Drag and follow-through)

14. Are you trying to do something that shouldn't be attempted? (Like trying to show the top of Mickey's head)

### James Farr

James Farr is an artist and writer working for television and film as well as comics. He is the creator of *Xombie* (see Figure 5.7), an online cartoon and printed comic book series called *Xombie: Reanimated* centered on Dirge, an intelligent and friendly zombie, and young ward Zoe, in an apocalyptic setting where ravenous zombie hordes and crazy folk are the norm. Appealing to viewers of all ages, tastes, and backgrounds, Xombie episodes have been downloaded and viewed more than 13 million times! You can see them, and more, on http://www.xombified.com.

James says, "As long as I can remember, I've been drawing, writing stories, or both. I can't really remember a time when I wasn't trying to create a character, or make one move."

When asked for any beginner tips, he states, "Always finish what you start. I think a lot of genuinely creative people have trouble finding the focus to complete a project. In other words, it's easy to get distracted, and doubly so for creative types. Half the battle is having a great idea. The other half is having the self-discipline to push it out into the world as a fully realized product. Seeing your ideas through to the end builds a great deal of focus over time, and helps save you from a house (and mind) full of abandoned ideas."

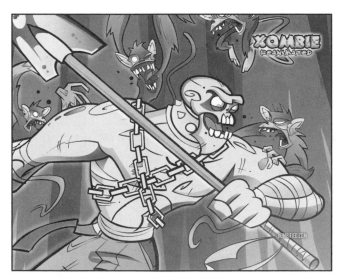

**Figure 5.7**
James Farr's cartoon *Xombie*.

On the subject of what he found most rewarding about his job, he replied, "Being able to create worlds and characters that people genuinely want to visit again and again. That and getting to work from home, of course."

## The Disney Principles

Frank Thomas and Ollie Johnston wrote a book called *The Illusion of Life: Disney Animation*, which was ratified in the 1930s by Disney Studios. In it, they classified 12 essential principles of animation, which are still used by industry experts today:

1. Anticipation

2. Appeal

3. Arcs

4. Exaggeration

5. Follow-Through

6. Secondary Motion

7. Slow-In and Slow-Out

8. Solid Drawing (or Weight)

9. Squash and Stretch

10. Staging

11. Straight-Ahead and Pose-to-Pose

12. Timing

To read more about Frank and Ollie's tips, go to http://www.frankanollie.com. Let's look at some of the more important animation principles Frank and Ollie wrote about.

### Anticipation

*Anticipation* is declaring to the viewer what is about to happen before it happens. It sets up the probable action and lets the viewer's eyes drink in what comes next.

In the wood-chopper example in Figure 5.8, his exaggerated swing does not start when the axe falls. The action begins with the anticipation as he brings the axe

**Figure 5.8**
This wood chopper scenario demonstrates multiple animation principles.

back over his head and builds the momentum that will result in his downward swing. We time it just right, and the viewer will have no problem imagining what is about to happen.

This also adds drama, which a clever animator can use to manipulate his audience by getting them to anticipate one thing about to happen and delivering them another (like in horror movies where the intrepid young girl looks in the cabinet, thoroughly expecting a monster to jump out at her, and when she does it's only her pet cat, but it makes the viewers jump anyway!).

### Appeal

Frank and Ollie said in their book, "While a living actor has charisma, the animated character has appeal." What they were talking about was that live actors are living beings that come across mostly through their raw magnetism, but you cannot emulate raw magnetism in doodles, so you have to count on your animated characters oozing *appeal*.

Your audience must not mind looking at your drawings and must have a definite psychological connection to them as the action progresses. I am not suggesting that every female character has to have the curves and bust line of Lara Croft in *Tomb Raider* or that all your alien critters be cute and furry with big eyes like Ratchet from *Ratchet & Clank*, either. Use your best judgment when drawing to give your characters adequate appeal.

Appeal can often come out of exhibiting personality that the audience identifies with. As Irish artist J.B. Yeats once said, "Personality is born out of pain. It is the fire shut up in the flint." If your pen or mouse strokes can breathe that fire to life on the screen, you will have it made.

### Exaggeration

*Exaggeration* is the process of slowing down and over-emphasizing the action you want to show in order for audiences to keep up with and understand exactly what is going on. Exaggeration also makes for more exciting animation. Indeed, it is arguably the core of truly great cartoons.

For example, when a wood chopper chops wood in real life, he moves quickly and decisively, and sometimes his axe may appear to blur by. In a cartoon, however, you don't want that, so you exaggerate his motion. For example, notice in Figure 5.8 how the wood chopper's arms go back, his chest heaves out, and his legs strain. Then, in the forward swing, the axe whirs by, leaving whiz lines, and goes right through the wood being chopped, and the wood chopper's feet actually leave the ground.

### Follow-Through

Just as the baseball batter does not quit swinging the bat as soon as it hits the baseball and knocks the hide-covered sphere into orbit, the wood chopper in our illustration does not stop his forward momentum after his axe taps the wood. Instead, he goes right through the wood, the axe embedding itself in the stump on which he's chopping, and his feet fly off the ground and he nearly loses his hat.

Depending on the severity of the blow, the axe might stop so suddenly when it *thunks* into the tree stump that it sends reverberations up his arms and causes his shoulders and head to shake!

*Follow-through* is about avoiding stopping everything all at once, because that would be unnatural. Related to Newton's law of physics, all things have mass and all objects with mass have momentum. If energy is applied in any given direction, the object will continue in motion until another object repels it or the object exhausts its energy. There should always be some obvious continuation of motion, like cause and effect; otherwise, your animation will look wooden or robotic.

### Secondary Motion

*Secondary motions* are smaller, more detailed actions that take place during the main action to support it. They are also called overlapping actions. Secondary

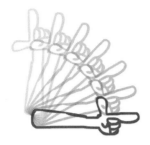

**Figure 5.9**
A simple motion tween showing a finger pointing.

motions should never override or appear more important than the main action, or else they'll confuse the viewer.

Think of the wood chopper, again, and how his hair, clothes, and body parts react to his swing. When he comes for the down-swing, his feet actually leave the ground and his eyes scrunch shut to show much force he's put into the action. These are secondary motions, because they are subtle reinforcements of the primary motion.

Great character animation should clearly communicate to your audience what is going on onscreen.

### Slow-In and Slow-Out

If you have a character's arm moving from straight up to straight out, and you want it to move at a smooth, uniform speed in the space of five frames, you will need a series of in-betweens, created in Flash by using a motion tween. You set two keyframes with five frames in-between (see Figure 5.9).

All this works fine if you are working with a mechanical robot. But how often do people move like robots in the real world? Most often, people and other creatures have a strong tendency to speed up or slow down as we move, thanks in part to the laws of physics that guide us along. It's what is referred to in animation as *slow-in* and *slow-out*.

You have the same number of drawings, practically, but you can see in the top of Figure 5.10 that the arm starts out faster and slows into the stop at the bottom. Consequently, the other part of that illustration shows slowing out, or speeding up as the arm gains momentum.

To do this, all you would have to do is change the motion tween's Ease property (found in the Properties Inspector panel when the motion tween is selected). The

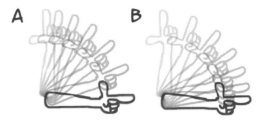

**Figure 5.10**
A motion tween with (A) slow-in and (B) slow-out applied.

left of Figure 5.11 has an Ease value of -50 (in), and the right of that figure has an Ease value of +50 (out). Play around with each tween you create and find a better balance that looks more natural.

### Solid Drawing (or Weight)

Every existing object shares space, volume, and mass. Keep this in mind, even when drawing and animating comical characters like Wile E. Coyote. Notice that when he is riding an Acme brand rocket and runs into a boulder, his body doesn't scrunch up as skinny as he looks; instead, he flattens out like a pancake or folds up like an accordion.

When the rubber ball bounces, in the principle of squash and stretch, it flattens out when it hits the ground and stretches when it leaps through the air. This is because of weight distribution through the object due to vertical mass.

You want to make your 2D images appear to carry definite weight because they will appear more solid to your viewer, and the world in which they reside, while never truly real, will appear more convincing a place.

### Squash and Stretch

Twinkle animation studio co-founder Gary Leib says, "This isn't rocket science, folks. It's more like rubber ball science," and he's right!

When something like a rubber ball hits the ground, it squashes flat. When it bounces back up again, it stretches out. It goes back to normal, turning perfectly spherical again, before starting back toward the ground, in which case it elongates for a second time. Then it will hit the ground and go flat once more. It repeats this cycle until the rubber ball loses forward inertia or it strikes another object, like a wall. The repeated process of *squash and stretch* results in the flexible, fluid, and bouncy objects and characters you see in all cartoons.

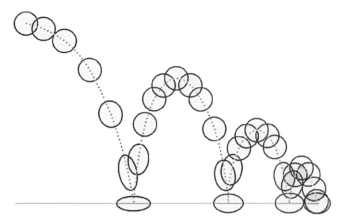

**Figure 5.11**
Rubber ball animation.

Even Disney characters act like rubber balls when they walk, their shoes squashing a bit and their knees bending with each step they take, reflecting their elastic nature.

Practice the bouncing ball exercise shown in Figure 5.11 to get squash and stretch down-pat.

1. Open a new Flash file (ActionScript 2.0). The Publish Settings must be set to ActionScript 2.0.

2. Work within the Essentials workspace, with the Library panel docked with the Properties panel.

3. On the stage, create a perfect circle using the Oval tool. First, select the Oval tool. It is hidden behind the Rectangle tool and is hotkeyed to the letter "O." Then, pick black for your Stroke color (in the Properties panel) by clicking on the color swatch beside Stroke. A pop-up color swatch palette will appear, and black is on the left-hand side of the palette. Pick "none" for your Fill color. "None" looks like a white square with a red slash through it in the pop-up color swatch palette. Now, draw the oval on the stage by click-dragging. To make it a perfect circle, hold down the Shift key while you draw.

4. Look at the bottom of your screen for the Timeline panel. Right-click on Frame 1 of Layer 1 in your Timeline panel, and choose to Create Classic

Tween from the pop-up options list. Note that a blue border will appear around your circle.

5. Grab the Selection tool and click-drag your circle to the bottom left of your stage.

6. On your Timeline panel, right-click on Frame 30 and choose to Insert Keyframe. Note how the frames between 1 and 30 turn purple or blue in color and have a bold arrow running between them. This indicates your tweened animation.

7. With your circle selected on Frame 30, use Shift + Right Arrow Key to nudge the circle to the right-hand side of the Stage, but still on the Stage. When you have the circle positioned where you want it, scrub through your animation to preview it. To scrub through your animation, click-drag the red handle above the frames on the Timeline panel. Drag the handle to the left to the start of your animation, then press Enter (Windows) or Return (Mac) to play your animation. Note how the circle moves from left to right.

8. Right-click on Frame 15 of Layer 1 on your Timeline and choose to Insert Keyframe. Select your circle and use Shift + Up Arrow Key to move the circle up close to the top of your Stage. This will make it look like your circle goes straight up and then straight down, forming an "A" shape.

9. Right-click on Frame 7 and choose to Insert Keyframe. Select your circle and drag it slightly to the left, imagining where an invisible arc would be before the circle reaches the peak. The arc could be done much better using a guided motion tween, but we will get to that later. For now, we will create the illusion of an arc with what we have.

10. With your circle still selected, use your Free Transform tool to reshape it as you see the object stretched in Figure 5.11. You will need to drag the sides in to make it appear thinner, and drag the top and bottom out to make it appear longer. Then go up to the main Menu Bar and choose Modify, Transform, Rotate, and Skew. Now all you can do to your circle is rotate or skew it. Skewing an object makes it lean one way or the other, and the cursor icon will look like a double set of arrows when it is set to skew. Skew your circle to the right, to lean into the arc of its jump.

11. Right-click on Frame 22 and choose to Insert Keyframe. Select your circle and drag it slightly to the right, along the invisible arc again.

12. Use the Free Transform tool to reshape the circle again, as you did in step 10, except this time you will skew your circle so that it looks like it is leaning to the left.

13. Right-click on Frame 33 and Insert Keyframe. This seems redundant, I know, but trust me. Go back to Frame 30 and use the Free Transform tool to squash your circle. Make it seem shorter and wider, which will squash it, and then make sure that its bottom line is the same as the bottom line of the circle in Frame 33.

14. The last thing to do is to add some slow-in and slow-out as mentioned previously. Select Frame 9 and look in the Properties panel. Set the Ease to -20. Select Frame 18 and set the Ease to 20. This will make the ball appear to speed up as it reaches its peak height and then hurriedly leave, heading back to earth.

15. Click on Frame 1 and press Enter (Win) or Return (Mac) to play your animation. It's a little rough, which a guided motion tween would help to fix, but it still looks like a ball that is bouncing from left to right, with the appropriate squash and stretch applied. Compare your work to Figure 5.11.

### Timing

As mentioned, cartoonists of yore drew extremes and then put a number beside them to show how many in-betweens there needed to be between them. All this came from exposure sheets, which broke down the animation to the exact screen time each frame would be shown. The number of frames for each pose affects the overall feel of animation, meaning you must strike the right balance between allowing the action to register with the viewer and creeping along so slowly you bore your audience.

I will take a moment to point out that *timing* has long been an issue of live action filmmaking, as well, and some cinematography and directors have become well-known for their use of timing in their movies. For example, directors M. Night Shyamalan, Roman Polanski, and Stanley Kubrick are well-known to the American public for their quirky, slow, and emotionally laden scenes. They use slower timing to lend more weight to each scene.

**Figure 5.12**
Line of action.

Generally speaking, however, when it comes to cartoons, faster is better, but because computers can make images go by more quickly than the human eye can track them, you run the risk of making your scenes blur past too fast and nauseating your audience. Find a happy medium when it comes to timing your scenes.

## Other Animation Principles

What follows next are some other industry principles not specifically written in Frank and Ollie's book.

### Line of Action

A *line of action* is an imaginary line running through the figure doing the acting. It is one of the key ingredients to producing dynamic, clear, and action-based animations. Look at Figure 5.12.

Lines of action are special guidelines that show the general direction and flow of the character's movement, and they usually follow the character's spine and reaching, although this is not always the case. A line of action gives a drawing direction, and just like rays of lines or pointing to the center of focus, a line of action can subtly lead the viewer's eye where you want it to go.

### Silhouettes

The creator of *Earthworm Jim* and *Messiah* said that creating a character with a strong silhouette was important; this is imminently visible in *Earthworm Jim*, as no other character possibly shares the side profile that Earthworm Jim, the titular character, does (shown in Figure 5.13).

If you can "read" what is going on in a silhouette, chances are it's a successful animation drawing, even if you don't display the silhouette to the viewer but show the fully drawn detailed version. Silhouettes are best previewed and

**Figure 5.13**
Earthworm Jim's silhouette is irregular and noticeable.

developed in the thumbnail stage of a drawing: When sketching the look of your characters in a scene, think about just their character outline, as well as their line of action, to determine how to make a successful scene animation.

### Do Your Homework

There's an old saying in animation: "When in doubt, act it out." This is just as easily true for game design, as well, and in fact a lot of 3D games use mo-cap, or motion capture technology, to do just that!

If you are having troubles coming up with a character pose, then act it out yourself. And don't just act it out with your face or hands, but use your whole body. Find a full-length mirror, if you don't already own one, to pose in front of, or prepare your camcorder or web-cam to record your actions. You can then use your posing as a reference guide when you are drawing.

If all else fails, don't forget the three Rs of drawing anything: *research*, *reference*, and *resource*.

**Tip**

"There is nothing like looking, if you want to find something. You certainly usually find something, if you look, but it is not always quite the something you were after."

—J.R.R. Tolkien

**Research**    Investigate what it is you are animating. If you are animating some characters dancing in a Renaissance ballroom, look up waltzes and other old-fashioned dance moves, Renaissance costumes, and ballroom architecture you might want to include in your drawings.

**Reference**   Look up similar poses on the World Wide Web, browse through fashion magazines, or put together your own morgue file of character poses. A *morgue file* is a quick and handy collection of images you have found and keep in a folder or Desktop folder, even, for reference use. Every artist should keep a morgue file handy, because no one, not even Picasso, can draw in a vacuum!

**Resources**   The Internet can be a great place to start, but like most technology, the Web offers way too many dangerous distractions and the temptation to succumb to a tangent is too great, leading you to procrastination and not getting anything productive done.

Instead, try your local library, where the nice people working there can help you find just about any information you want for free. Just about any topic you can think of has a book written about it, often a book with pictures, and if your local library does not have a copy of that book, they can usually order it for you for little or no fee.

## Animating in Flash

Flash has strengths and weaknesses, making Flash better for some things than it is for others. As with most software applications, if you cannot get what you want done with one tool, seek out another. Toon Boom Studio and some of the other 2D applications are technically more compatible with pen-tablet drawing and cel painting, for instance.

For the animation exercises in this book, I will be using Adobe Flash CS4, but most of these principles and steps are general enough to carry over into whatever animation software you prefer using.

### Symbols

Flash has unique reusable content in the form of its Library. This Library not only stores graphic images, sound effects, music files, and movie clips, it can also store symbols.

A *symbol* is any reusable object created inside Flash. A symbol can be reused throughout your movie or be imported and used in other movies you make.

A copy of a symbol used within your movie is called an *instance*. Instances can have their own individual settings, such as color, size, function, and alpha transparency.

All the symbols you can use in your movie are stored in the Flash Library, which appears as a long list from which you can drag-and-drop instances onto your work stage. If you decide you need to edit a symbol, all instances of that symbol within your movie are automatically edited as well, which can save you a lot of time and worry.

Using symbols correctly in your Flash movie is absolutely crucial. A movie's file size depends on the size and number of graphics and sounds used in your Flash movie. Reusing symbols rather than importing new graphics all the time reduces the file size of your Flash movie, better enabling people to download and view it on the Web or on their Wii.

That's because a symbol's contents are taken into account and drawn only once in your movie, even if your movie contains thousands of instances of that symbol!

Flash has three major types of symbols you can use (see Figure 5.14). They are:

- **Graphics**: *Graphic symbols* are reusable graphic images that are used mainly for drawing and animation. These symbols can be bitmap/raster images or vector art. They can be large or miniscule, and can be a combination of separate images grouped together for ease of manipulation.

- **Buttons**: *Button symbols* are used for timeline navigation and interactivity. They respond to mouse clicks, rollovers and rollouts, and key presses. Each button has different graphic states, such as Up, Over, Down, and Hit, for which you can define different looks. Button symbols are not typically used

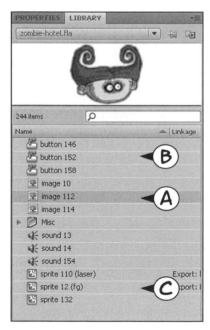

**Figure 5.14**
(A) Graphics symbol, (B) button symbol, and (C) movie-clip symbol.

in cartoons, except to click Play, but they are used in more interactive media, such as websites and video games.

- **Movie clips**: *Movie-clip symbols* are reusable Flash movies with their own timelines, and can be made up of multiple images. Placing a movie clip on your stage is like playing a movie within a movie. The great thing about movie clips is that you can also use the ActionScript to control their settings.

*ActionScript*, by the way, enables you to make Flash interactive and gives you the tools you need to make Flash games and applications. For more information, you should visit http://www.senocular.com or http://www.flashkit.com. We will cover ActionScript in further depth later.

**Note**

Make it a habit to give your symbols clever and identifiable names from the start, and use folders to group like symbols. This will help you a lot. It is easy to wind up with dozens or even hundreds of symbols in a single Flash project, which makes it next to impossible to find or edit the one you want. I typically put all the movie clips in one set, all the buttons in another, and all the graphics in yet another, and I take the time to name each one so I will know what the symbol contains without having to click on it to preview it.

### Flash Animation Sequences

When working in Flash, you will find it necessary to create shorter animation sequences within the larger whole. Often this is done by placing a blank keyframe in each of your layers on the timeline, reflecting the start of a new sequence, or by creating a new Scene in your Scene list (which you can view by going to Window > Scene in the main Menu Bar). The use of Scenes is largely discouraged, though, because it can sometimes cause problems animating later on.

Evaluate the sequence you need to animate based on what is being animated, how it should look as it's animating, and what would be the most efficient animation method.

## Methods of Animation

**Tip**

"Animation is not the art of drawings that move but the art of movements that are drawn."

—Norman McLaren

When you come down to it, there are roughly three different methods of animation, as shown in Richard Williams' book *The Animator's Survival Kit*, where he goes into the advantages and disadvantages of each method in detail. Here are the main highlights of each method, although it would probably behoove you to purchase his book at some point in the future, if you decide to further your education in the animation field. Along with the highlights, I will discuss how you can make each in Flash.

### *Straight-Ahead Animation > Frame-by-Frame Animation*

This is probably the earliest way to animate, and the way that you animated when you put together your little flipbook. In straight-ahead animation, you do all your drawings consecutively from start to finish. You make drawing number one, drawing number two, and so on, illustrating each frame of the animation on paper.

The primary advantage to straight-ahead animation is (a) it gets the job done, and (b) it looks good and can sometimes surprise you with its spontaneity.

The disadvantage stems from the last part. Things unexpected start occurring that get in your way. For instance, the scene may go on too long, the size or proportion of your character might change, or she might not "hit her mark" on the stage at the right time, causing lots of edits later on.

In Flash, the straight-ahead animation method is best used with frame-by-frame animation, where each frame in an object layer's timeline is a keyframe with a new image on it (shown in Figure 5.15). Frame-by-frame animation is lengthy, laborious, and resource-consuming, as it takes up more room in the file's memory, but it definitely can look very professional. Traditional animators call this "shooting on ones" because you are basically using each shot of motion on camera as one frame of action in Flash.

### *Pose-to-Pose > Tweened Animation*

The pose-to-pose method introduces a term you are probably familiar with now in Flash: keyframes. You do drawings that are key drawings, placed in keyframes, and then you (or somebody else on the animation team) do the in-betweens.

The key drawings are important poses the viewer needs to "read" what's going on, so they are often held on-camera for a whole second or more, allowing the audience time for the visual information to sink in before the story proceeds.

**Figure 5.15**
Frame-by-frame animation.

Think of a comic book. Although close to animation, a comic book is made up of 2D still images. Each panel in a comic book, however, reveals a key pose of the characters. It's what is not shown, the frames that would come between each of the panels (indicating true animation) that make up pose-to-pose animation sequences.

In Flash, you create a keyframe for each key pose and then develop motion or shape tween animation for your in-betweens. Flash's tweened animation saves you a lot of long, laborious efforts drawing all the in-betweens yourself or having someone else do it. Flash makes pose-to-pose animations much easier with tweened animation, seen in Figure 5.16.

The advantages to using pose-to-pose or tweened animation should be obvious: They save you a lot of time drawing each and every frame. Another advantage is that it is easier to edit the key poses or length of time for in-betweens, and less frustrating when you have to do edits.

The main disadvantage is the fact that real life is practically frame by frame, so doing frame-by-frame or straight-ahead animation looks more realistic and is therefore more interesting to watch, while pose-by-pose or tweened animation

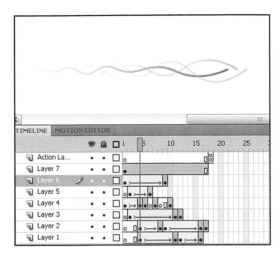

**Figure 5.16**
Tweened animation.

can look less real, more robotic, and therefore any animation primarily done as such will look like cheating to your audience.

Flash offers three types of tweening:

- **Motion tweening**: The *motion tweening* technique involves placing a symbol somewhere on the stage, creating a keyframe on the timeline there, and then moving along the timeline to a point sometime later and adding another keyframe in which the symbol's position or other setting has been changed. You then apply a motion tween to the intervening frames, enabling Flash to interpolate the action that occurs between the keyframes for you. You created a motion tween on the rubber ball exercise.

- **Shape tweening**: *Shape tweening* is similar to motion tweening, except you use separate symbols, usually vector art, in their own keyframes and add a shape tween between them. The shape tween then attempts to gradually shift the look of one symbol into the shape of the other over the course of the intervening frames. This can be a fast and ready way to animate a character's mouth or to show the character's eyes blinking.

- **Guided motion tweening**: *Guided motion tweening* uses an invisible guideline, or path, to carry the symbol from one keyframe to the next. In the intervening frames, Flash pushes the symbol a little farther along the path until it gets to the end. This is excellent if you want to animate, say, the arc of a baseball soaring through the air or the zigzag of a UFO in flight.

### The Best Method

Remember that I said there are three methods for animating? Well, by this point, I am sure you have wondered to yourself, "What if we took the best of both of these methods and somehow combined the two methods into one?" Thus, you get the third animation method: the best method!

You can use straight-ahead or frame-by-frame animation where you think it calls for it, that is, where you need to show something moment by moment that would be too hard to do pose by pose or tweened. And when there are times in the animation where it would be easier to tween the animation, or carry it pose by pose, you do that instead. Alternating between the first two methods creates a syncopated harmony that looks really good and helps tell your story.

### Basic Walk Cycle

The most basic animation you will do is the walk cycle. Animated characters are expected to both walk and talk. We will get to the talking part in just a sec, but right now let's look at the walking part.

A bipedal character has two legs. That's what "biped" means: two feet. There will be times that you must animate characters with four legs, but first it is imperative to work out how to get a character walking on two legs. To do so, use the walk cycle of the normal human being from real life as reference.

Taking a look at yourself while walking would be very difficult. You can look at friends or family members as they walk, but *The Animator's Reference Book* by Les Pardew and Ross S. Wolfley will do you one better. Not only does this reference book show you still-frame images of people walking, but also bending, jumping, running, and more.

Look at Figure 5.17 for one example of a bipedal character's side profile walk cycle.

### Lip Synching

*Lip synching* is quite simply the act of matching up a character's mouth and lip positions with the spoken lines of dialogue. If you have ever chuckled in derision at one of those old karate movies with poor dubbing, where the mouths don't match the words you hear, then you know just how important lip synching can be.

Figure 5.18 shows you that there are a number of mouth positions to make your lip synching easier, as this is what most people generally look like when sounding out the letters. This is just a helpful suggestion, as everyone sounds out words

**Figure 5.17**
A basic walk cycle animation shown from a side profile.

differently, which anyone who has ever tried to learn lip reading can tell you, but Figure 5.18 shows you the basic ones.

Just as nobody enunciates each and every word they speak just right, you don't have to draw each and every vowel or syllable in Flash. It would look just silly. Look for special emphasis on certain words within the dialogue, and place emphasis in the scene by having your character linger on that vowel or syllable, or show the character giving a grand facial or hand gesture, in accompaniment of the dialogue.

A really good example of this can be seen in Disney's movie *The Rescuers*. I can't repeat how important a learning tool it is to watch the older hand-drawn animated movies, especially the Disney ones, as they were some of the greatest masterpieces of cartoon animation ever.

There's a scene done by artist Milt Kahl where the villainess Madame Medusa is taking off her makeup and scoots the chair she's sitting on across the room while she speaks. She bounces her chair on the emphasized words in her dialogue. In other words, she hits each and every accented word. This might seem like over-acting, but as a cartoonist, you have license to overact!

## What's Next?

You have learned about the artwork and the animation, but they cannot exist by themselves. What they need is a story to connect them. The next chapter shows you some great ways to make up stories and write a narrative.

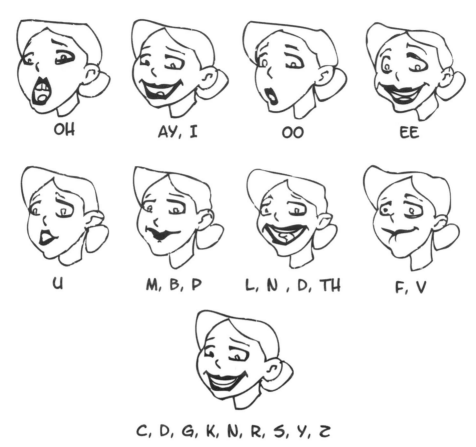

**Figure 5.18**
Mouth movements in synch with vowels and consonants.

## Review

At the end of reading this chapter, you should know:

- How to create visual humor

- What the Disney principles of animation are

- Both traditional animation and Flash animation techniques

- How to make characters walk, talk, and "come alive" onscreen

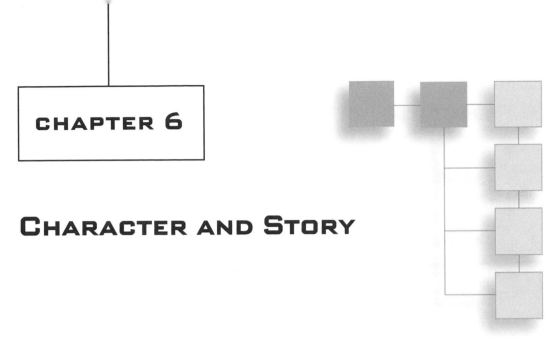

# CHAPTER 6

# CHARACTER AND STORY

In this chapter you will learn:

- How you can create compelling characters for your stories

- Methods for drawing your characters to place into your movies

- How to develop a story outline

- Storytelling techniques, such as the monomyth and ABDCE

Whether you are reading a comic, watching a cartoon, or playing a video game, the two things you really are paying close attention to are characters and the story line. These are part of two totally separate but related disciplines. Characters, in part, are outlined by writers, developed by artists, and tested by the way they relate to the story. The story is outlined by the writer, conveyed to the audience by actions on-screen, and understood on a subliminal level by that audience, who may partake in the story.

As an artist, you must be able to draw great characters. As a writer, your characters have to be immediately compelling and keep your audience's attention. And when it comes to story, as a writer, you must make it feel immersive and entertaining to your audience.

What follows are tried-but-true methods of character development, drawing characters for animations and game concept art, and storytelling.

## Character Development

Conan, Sherlock Holmes, Doctor Who, Indiana Jones, Darth Vader, Spongebob Squarepants... their names evoke memories and feelings, don't they? All these characters, plus many more, have become memorable in their own right. They exist beyond the stories they were originally a part of or the line drawings and color compositions they were imparted to their audiences by; they have become cultural icons. Sometimes a character becomes a legend overnight, but in fact, it is the struggle, creative vision, and luck of its creators that lead to a character's ultimate success, on and off the page. No characters start fully formed.

First, a writer will generate a character idea, add details to that initial character concept, and top off the details with a cool-sounding name. Then, artists sit down and brainstorm character ideas. Character concept sketches are drawn (see Figure 6.1 for one such sketch). Amid countless variations, a single sketch will be chosen and launched into a full-fledged character. Digital artists then perform color compositions, editing, and (when necessary) 3D modeling. Finally, a character for a comic, cartoon, or electronic game is born.

**Figure 6.1**
An example of character concept artwork. Image from *PrisonTale II* used courtesy of Key To Play.

Before you go gallivanting off into the wonderful world of make-believe character generation, we need to take a look at the concepts that form the substrate of what makes a truly stupendous character. What are the common attributes of the making of an icon? Let's look at the work that goes into making a memorable character.

## Personality

Creating a memorable character that audiences will feel for and desire to know the outcome of conflicts the character might face is definitely rewarding, from the commercial end as well as the artistic and technical end. One of the most important elements of a character's particular appeal is personality.

Character traits are important, not only because they influence the audience's reactions, but also because they can shape the character's looks, behavior, and dialogue. All the most successful characters ever have well-defined personalities. Some may even appear as caricatures of ordinary personalities. Spongebob Squarepants, for example, is a nerdier-than-life fry cook who is so perky he is almost unbelievable; but then again, his environment and the circumstances he finds himself in are equally unbelievable, so he fits.

So before you make up a character, you have to make sure you know some of its primary character traits and what skills it might possess. Some designers take the old-school approach to this and use character sheets full of information about each character, much like the paraphernalia used for tabletop role-playing games such as *Dungeons & Dragons*. You can also use the Traits Triangle popularized by David Freeman. Let's look at both.

### Old-School Approach

Get yourself a piece of notebook paper, and get ready to fill in some blanks. Using the old-school approach to character generation, you have to make up details about your character to write down, as if you were interviewing that character about his most intimate particulars, or getting an ID at the Department of Motor Vehicles (see Figure 6.2). Details you will want to know about your character include, but are not limited to:

- Name
- Age
- Gender
- Height/Weight

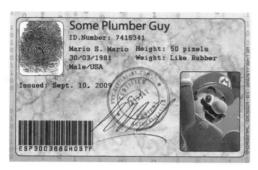

**Figure 6.2**
Character ID.

- Eye and Hair Color

- Profession

- Income Level

- Education

- Skills

- Residence

- Family/Friends

- Place and Date of Birth

- Pets

- Hobbies

- Pet Peeves

- Likes/Dislikes

- Background

- Equipment

### Traits Triangle

Giving your character three foremost traits, displayed as three sides of a triangle (Freeman calls it a *Traits Triangle*) as shown in Figure 6.3, you can straight away see how the traits would interrelate to shape the character's behavior and the choices he or she would make. Whatever you do, don't choose dull or agreeable traits.

**Figure 6.3**
Traits Triangle.

Making your character strong, loyal, and stalwart is fine and dandy if you are tailoring a stereotypical Prince Valiant, but stereotypes are boring and predictable in any story.

Mix it up more. Try making your character heroic, ugly, and clumsy, like Shrek, and you instantly have a winner on your hands. Trust the process.

### Nested Personalities

There is another theory, born of the modern science of psychology, that says people are complex constructions of multiple personalities and that we all have different sides we show to different people or to no one but ourselves. Here is how it breaks down:

- **Ego:** The character's core identity/personality, which must be protected at all costs.

- **Superego:** The character's parental inner voice or higher self. Imagine this as the angel sitting on one shoulder, telling the character what not to do.

- **Id**: The character's childlike inner voice and whimsy. Imagine this as the devil sitting on the character's other shoulder, telling the character what to do.

- **World mask/demeanor:** How the character appears to the rest of the world, which can change depending on the setting and circumstance just like donning an outfit.

### Idiosyncrasies

Identify at least three, preferably more, idiosyncrasies in the character's makeup. An *idiosyncrasy* is defined as a personal peculiarity of mind, habit, or behavior; a singular quirk. These quirks can be totally useless skills or absurd qualities that stand out.

For instance, a character might have a complex physical system where he cannot drink anything with caffeine or it may kill him, but he can, and does, imbibe in super-hot jalapenos all day long. The same character might also have a passion for picking up stray bits of metal he finds on the ground whenever he goes for a walk, and keeps them in a shoebox at home. These sorts of things make a character different, interesting, unpredictable, and identifiable.

### Personal Growth

In traditional film and literature, the worth of the plot is measured by the *personal growth*, or how far the character has to go to get what he wants most. Characters such as Nick (*Nick and Norah's Infinite Playlist*) and Napoleon Dynamite reveal humanity's ever-present desire to rise above the contented state and reach for something better.

What are the challenges that define such characters? What approach to these challenges best exemplify their personality? How does what happens to the character change him into a different person?

On the reverse side of the fence are those stories where events happen, but the character doesn't seem to change or grow at all; he merely survives. Doctor Who, James Bond, and Conan are all perfect examples of characters that we can count on to be the way they are, no matter what story we watch or read with them as central figures. It is even true that considering characters like these, if they were to change dramatically, we would actually be offended beyond belief (see Figure 6.4).

### Slacker Heroes

Biographer John E. Mack wrote in his *A Prince of Our Disorder*, "A vital ingredient in hero-making is the resonance that the follower finds between the conflicts and aspirations of his own and those he perceives in the person he chooses to idealize. . . ." In other words, try to find problems that we all share as individuals in the struggle of life, and let your audience fantasize through your hero character about the ways we can actually solve them, real or not. This is one

WHAT YOU A' LOOKIN' AT?
POUNDING GOOMBAS JUST WASN'T PAYIN' OFF.
MAMA MIA, JUST LOOK AT THIS CLOG!

**Figure 6.4**
Would we be as fond of some of our favorite characters if they tried to change?

reason why *Rolling Stone Magazine* has said that we are living in the age of the *slacker hero*: People like to root for the underdogs that reflect the underdog in all of us. This has been one of the key ingredients to the ghetto background in the *Grant Theft Auto* series.

## Appearance

Designers find the greatest challenge to making a character is evincing a strong reflection of the character's personality in a single visage that can be glorified through words or in 2D/3D art. Heroic characters are expected to look cute, handsome, winsome, clever, beautiful, elegant, grungy, powerful, tough, lithe, bouncy, dashing, and a string of other adjectives that put them above the stratosphere of ordinary.

What are some dramatic and telling features that will draw and hold your audience's attention? What if your character was portrayed in film or appeared larger than life, billboard-sized? What would attract your attention to the character then?

Take a look at the Traits Triangle or the old-school method for creating characters I showed you. How would each of those character traits show up or be represented in the character's physical appearance? If you wrote down "slovenly," what visual cues could you use to reveal that he or she is slovenly? Create a crafted visual hook by selecting one or more of these specific traits about your character and accentuating them.

Indiana Jones has his fedora and bullwhip; Ash Ketchum (*Pokemon*) has his blue vest, green gloves, and cap; Mario has his black mustache, red cap, and overalls; Link (*Zelda*) has his pointy ears, green cap, and green tunic; Spock (*Star Trek*) has neatly trimmed Beatles-style hair and large pointy ears, not to mention his upraised eyebrows that always made him appear to be questioning what he was being told.

Many characters have a distinct costume that sets them apart. Color schemes and noticeable familiar details should remain consistent, endearing your character to your audience. Set your character apart from the rest by developing habitual stances, looks, and visual traits.

The appearance of the character must be thought out at conception, the same way personality is, but the appearance will further be developed by sketch artists and rendered for the cartoon or game. The first impression audiences have of a character is its appearance, and often this impression is formed before the audience ever starts watching the animation or picking up the game controls, likely in a trailer or demo or box art the developer has released. The character's first impression must encompass personality, voice, expression, vitality, and flair.

## Name

Another element of character appeal that you should concentrate on is the character's name. Your character's name is really important, as it reflects the character, gives the audience something to identify him or her with, and can be oft-spoken of once the character reaches iconic status.

The choice of name should not be lightly made. It influences the audience's perceptions of that character. If you name a character Grunt Masterson, you would automatically assume just by the name that the character is tough or surly; it's a good name for a thug, but not for a romantic hero. Whereas someone named Guybrush Threepwood sounds like, and should act like, a total dweeb. A character's name should fit the character. It should also fit the story you are telling, and it should be short enough that the player can become instantly familiar with it.

Avoid making too many characters' names similar to one another or homonyms in a story. You run the risk of confusing the audience or causing her undo frustration if she has to remember some character based solely on name alone. For instance, you should never have two characters, one named Quentis and one named Quint, because they run together when you hear them out loud.

Use a baby name book, which you can find at your local library or bookstore—or go online to http://www.kabalarians.com to find help picking out a really good name. Some of these sources even have unique names included. Make sure to pick names that fit your characters' personalities.

## Voice

Finding your character's voice should not be an arduous task, but can end up a costly one. Most all animation or game characters to date are given recorded voices that are played during the cartoon or video game; quality voice talents are hired from studios in Hollywood. You can find some friends to supply you with voiceovers for free for starters. All you would need is a computer, microphone, and recording/editing software.

Regardless of how you do the vocals, the words with which your character speaks tell volumes about his/her personality. Dialogue gives tremendous insight into what sort of character this is, what accent or education the character might possess, and what respect the character shows for the people he/she is busy talking to. Consider the writing of dialogue carefully. Keep dialogue short because of space constraints, but keep dialogue filled with cues as to the impression of the character speaking.

## Just Say No to Stereotypes!

One lesson that should be learned in creating memorable characters is never to go in for stereotypes. A *stereotype* is originally a one-piece printing plate cast in type metal from a mold taken of a printing surface, as a page of set type; it has come to mean an unvarying form or pattern, specifically, a fixed or conventional notion or conception, held by a number of people, and allowing for no individuality. Stereotypes are flat character types with no originality. In other words, stereotypes are clichés that have been done to death.

The Crooked Policeman, the Mysterious Stranger, the Brunette Bombshell, the Cute Kid. . . these are all examples of stereotypes used over and over again, and part of the lack of originality in stereotypes is the fact that they have been used over and over, until audiences are bored of them. Don't use them, unless you are intentionally poking fun at yourself or the media industry (see Figure 6.5).

## You Can Say Yes to Archetypes

An *archetype* is an original model of a person, ideal example, or a prototype after which others are copied, patterned, or emulated. Archetypes sound a lot like

**Figure 6.5**
Stereotypes are not recommended unless you are poking fun at them.

stereotypes, but trust me, they're not. An archetype isn't clichéd, for one thing, and decent archetypes can help you by providing a jumping-off point to developing characters. What follows are some of the most often used archetypes in fiction.

- **Best friend** (male): decent regular Mister Nice Guy.

- **Boss** (female): a take-charge kind of woman.

- **Chief** (male): quintessential alpha hero, someone used to giving orders.

- **Free spirit** (female): playful fun-loving hippy/artsy type.

- **Librarian** (female): prim and proper but repressed spirit, brainy but insightful.

- **Lost soul** (male): tortured brooding loner type.

- **Nurturer** (female): capable and comforting caretaker or mothering type.

- **Professor** (male): logical introverted bookworm or genius.

- **Rebel** (male): the bad boy image, who is a bit of an idealist.

- **Smooth operator** (male): fun irresistible charmer.

- **Spunky kid** (female): the mousy girl with moxie or all-American girl next door.

- **Survivor** (female): mysterious manipulative cynic.

- **Swashbuckler** (male): physically daring and daredevil explorer.

- **Waif** (female): the typical damsel in distress.

- **Warrior** (female): thoroughly modern heroine, tough-as-nails fighter.

- **Warrior** (male): the weary white knight or reluctant protector of the weak.

Mythic archetypes are listed in a later section of this chapter, titled "Monomyth."

## Drawing Characters

You can focus, first, on how the character will look. Do several thumbnails of your character before you make the final decision on what he/she will look like. *Thumbnails* are smaller sketches that cover the salient points concisely without any real details. Fill one or more pages with thumbnails; then squint at them to see which one leaps off the page at you. If squinting doesn't help, put the thumbnails away for a day or two; when you look at them again, one of the images may call to you more than the rest.

Choose the strongest most impressionable image for your character, and sit down and get busy drawing. First do a full-featured drawing; after that, draw a model sheet. *Model sheets* depict the same character from multiple angles, in multiple poses, and with multiple expressions—in other words, in as many varieties as possible. See Figure 6.6 for an example of one model sheet. Model sheets help not only you when you are drawing, but also when other artists work with you to complete a project.

## Organic Construction

Using just basic shapes, you can doodle any character you can dream up. The following techniques show you how to make lines on paper look like something, or preferably somebody.

The simple shapes I show you here are just a framework on which to build your characters. After you've mastered the basic skeleton of character creation, you

**Figure 6.6**
Model sheet.

can create endless varieties of people. After all, most humans have the same basic shape, although no two of us are exactly alike. As your confidence grows as an artist, you will be able to modify the shapes and add all kinds of stylistic details that really bring characters to life.

### Note

When you look at an artist's work, you are really seeing the final polished product they came up with. There is no telling how much preliminary work it took for the artist to get to that stage. So you shouldn't worry if it takes you time to get from a basic character to a fully realized character.

### *Physical Proportion*

Learning the proportions and developing a practical technique are the keys to sketching figures successfully. There are 8 heads in the length of an adult male figure, 7 ½ heads in the length of the adult female figure, and 4 ½ heads in the

**Figure 6.7**
The basic proportions.

young child figure; by "head" I mean the length of someone's head. Look at Figure 6.7 to imprint these proportions in your mind.

Body shape can let a person know a lot about character, especially gender, age, strength, how much they work out, and more. Men have a larger rib cage and torso, while women have larger pelvises. People know what people look like, so if the body you draw looks odd, chances are people will notice. Take a look at Figure 6.8 for a typical hero and heroine body shape.

You can morph this organic construction setup in many different ways to create a cast of thousands. For instance, you can elongate the torso and limbs to make a taller character and give him a square head, or you can squash the torso and make the limbs shorter, as shown in Figure 6.9. These endless variations, when placed in your other drawings, will make your characters more identifiable and compelling.

### Making Faces

This demonstration is intended to be a quick guide. Drawing faces is a subject deserving an entire book and a lot of practice to master; however, there are a few

**Figure 6.8**
A typical hero and heroine body shape.

**Figure 6.9**
Morphing the typical body shapes into something new.

fast rules that if followed correctly can help you to sketch faces more successfully. Look at Figure 6.10 as you read on.

1. The head is an egg shape.

2. Use halfway lines. The centers of the eyes are on a line halfway between the top of the skull and the bottom of the chin. The bottom of the nose is on a

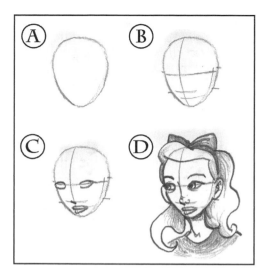

**Figure 6.10**
Drawing a character's head starts with a wobbly egg shape, some guidelines, and features on top of those.

line halfway between the center of the eye line and the bottom of the chin. The middle of the mouth is on a line halfway between the bottom of the nose and the bottom of the chin. The top of the ears are just slightly above the center of the eye line, and the bottoms of the ears are on the bottom of the nose line.

3. A vertical line down the center of the face sees the eyes, nose, mouth, and ears divided equally on either side of it. The eyes are kept one eye length apart.

4. Turn the halfway guidelines into ellipses and place features on them. This starts to bring the face into circular perspective and helps with any fore-shortening of the face. We can now use another head, rotated to the side, to overcome all sorts of positional problems. The contours of the face, hair, and features can be built upon the foundation of the guidelines of the head, no matter what its incline or pose.

## *Facial Features*

An age-old adage says that eyes are the windows to the soul. Indeed, eyes and eyebrows are among the most genuinely expressive features people have, and they can set one character's appearance apart from another's. Eyes are just as diverse as fingerprints, and just as much so in drawings. Good guys and girls, small children, and cute fuzzy things tend to have large eyes with wide pupils and thin eyebrows, whereas bad guys and shifty characters often have much narrower eyes and big bushy eyebrows.

The size, slope, and contour of the eyes add a lot of character to people, as do the size and thickness of the brows. For instance, eyebrows that rise up in the middle, just above the bridge of the nose, could indicate confusion, surprise, shock, sadness, or interest, while if they slope down into a sharp V over the bridge of the nose they could indicate rage or disgust.

As a structure made of cartilage that can and does come in all shapes, the nose can be insufferably difficult to draw. Some artists opt to use a dot, dash, or single line to indicate a nose, while others draw long sweeping vertical lines ending in more realistic nasal depressions. Still others, using the old-school Saturday-morning-comic-strip style, use bulbous ovals for noses.

You have just as much freedom, if not more, with mouths. Keep in mind the other half of expressions, besides eyes, is found in a person's lips, from an O of fright to a sideways D of joy. You can draw mouths simply as a set of lines or more detailed and realistic; it is really up to you. Men's lips tend to be thinner than women's, and the bottom lip is generally larger than the upper lip. When the mouth is open, some teeth typically show. You can draw teeth as just a white space, you can add lines to separate individual teeth, or you can attempt some style in between these two.

People's faces stop growing as they mature, except for the nose and ears, which continue to grow for the rest of your life; the older a person, the larger the nose and ears will look in comparison to the remainder of their face. People get wrinkles, too, mostly from demonstrating the same facial expressions over and over again. Common areas for wrinkles are at the corners of the eyes, around the mouth, and along the forehead.

Little children are different-looking, too, in that they have big round heads relative to the size of their bodies, and their bodies are rounded all over by what is referred to as "baby fat," which goes away as they grow older. Kids have small unformed lips, button noses, and missing teeth, all of which helps shape their facial structure.

Look at Figure 6.11 to see some varieties of facial features.

**Figure 6.11**
A wide variety of different faces.

### Extremities

Arms and legs are jointed cylinders that come off of the torso or pelvis. They appear thicker, generally, the closer they are to the body, and taper out to the end of the wrists or ankles.

You can cheat when sketching hands and feet. Feet you can make out of single flattened ovals or joined spheres. Try making hands by drawing long ovals and sticking thumbs onto them. Don't worry about individual fingers for now. If you hadn't noticed before, most cartoon drawings of hands show fewer fingers than human beings have, and this is no mistake; this convention came about because it is easier for artists to paint and animate only a few fingers, if any, and it also helps prevent drawers from making their characters' hands look like bunches of bananas.

### Hair and Fashion

Hair and clothing are extensions of the character's personality. Just as we humans fuss with our own hair and outfits on a nearly daily basis, in part to show our individuality and to look good when we go out, you can make the best impression of your character by dressing them for the right part or fixing them with a wonderful hairdo.

Hair and clothes are rarely plastered to the skin. Instead, they have volume and life all their own. People arrange their hair in countless ways, including cut, dyed, permed, and styled. Block in hair when sketching, and then draw hair in clumps or shapes. Look at a beauty magazine if you have trouble imagining hairstyles.

Although clothing is worn primarily for protection, modesty, and warmth, another primary reason people wear clothes is for individual expression. Characters can show their personality in the clothes they wear and the way they wear them. Clothing can alter perceptions of a person, instantly giving away clues about his or her personality, tastes, socio-economic status, profession, beliefs, and whether he or she belongs to a specific group (see Figure 6.12). It can also be used to determine time period and convey visual interest. Peruse costume books, fashion magazines, and even your own wardrobe for inspiration. Placing different outfits on your character can be lots of fun in and of itself.

### Poses and Line of Action

If you get stuck when trying to draw a character in a specific pose, try sketching a stick figure in that pose and build a model over that skeletal framework (see Figure 6.13). Alternatively, you could ask a friend to pose for you or use a mirror and pose yourself. What you really are after are the base proportions of shapes in the character's pose, and what body parts overlay or are in front of or behind other body parts when the body is in that specific pose. This process can take a while to learn, and you might need to take figure-drawing classes at an art school to get really good at it.

In cartoons and games, it is crucial that poses not appear static or flat. Characters must always be in motion and should appear animated even when they are not. One trick is to draw special guidelines for the entire body of the character called *lines of action*; these show the general direction and flow of the character's

**Figure 6.12**
A wide variety of hairstyles and costumes.

**Figure 6.13**
Use a rough skeleton to sketch in where body parts go in any pose.

**Figure 6.14**
Line of action.

movement. Lines of action usually follow the character's spine, but this is not always the case. Look at Figure 6.14 to see an example of a line of action used.

### Facial Expressions and Body Language

Drawing facial expressions can be a terrifying challenge. We look at faces every day of our lives, and faces are what we focus on when trying to understand another person's emotions or reactions. Despite this obvious familiarity, we find drawing facial expressions a challenging task. However, making very simple changes to a basic face, you can portray a wide range of expressions.

Most expressions are universal. If you were to fly from San Diego, California, to Russia, and step off the plane there, you would still understand when a native smiled at you that he probably was being friendly. If you know the facial expression you are trying to draw, chances are good your audience will recognize it, because many expressions are universal in nature. For example, a down-turned mouth and eyebrows drawn together in a sharp V over the bridge of the nose are pretty universal indicators that the character is furious.

To get better at drawing expressions, set up a mirror in front of your workstation and model for yourself any time you need to see how a facial expression should look. Because you are drawing for cartoons or games, you are not hampered by drawing realistic facial expressions, either. Chris Hart, best-selling author of art instruction books covering Manga, cartoons, and comics, says, "Don't settle for the ordinary. By tweaking, or *pushing*, a character's facial expression, you get that extra energy and vitality that can make a memorable moment." See Figure 6.15 for an example of different facial expressions pushed to the edge.

Of course, people don't just express themselves with their faces; their bodies can convey a lot of feeling and even help them communicate without words. To see

ORDINARY        PUSHED TO THE EDGE

**Figure 6.15**
Pushing expressions to the edge.

what I mean, go to a crowded place and sit and draw passersby for a while. Notice how people carry themselves and use gestures and body movements to communicate. For example, a guy with hunched shoulders, hands in pockets, staring at his feet while he walks, is obviously not a happy camper. Also, when you do this exercise, be on the lookout for interesting or unusual physical quirks or habits you can give your characters.

As with facial expressions, you can exaggerate a character's posturing, as well. One of the most notable examples of this is the cartoon *take*, where a character overreacts to something unexpected; different artists have played around with takes, but usually the character leaps off his feet, his eyes jump out of his skull, and his mouth drops to the floor. Depending on your art style, and the needs of the story, you can try all kinds of expressions with your characters.

## Drawing Creatures

You can draw animals and other nonhumans in a similar way to drawing people, using simple shapes and guidelines and adding features afterward

**Figure 6.16**
Creatures can be sketched just like humans.

(see Figure 6.16). Creatures make good characters, too, because you can use their natural physical characteristics, such as tails, ears, snouts, and claws, to great effect. Use a photograph of the original animal as reference when drawing so as to get proportions and anatomy correct. If you are drawing a mythical or imaginary beast, you should use a combination of artist renderings of that type of creature and photographs of animals that are pretty close to the creature you are drawing; for instance, when drawing dragons, you can look at paintings by Keith Parkinson, a well-known dragon painter, and photos of crocodiles, iguanas, and bats.

## Storytelling

Whether scripting an animated movie or writing the outline for an electronic game that will have a narrative, you should know at least the basics of telling decent stories. We as a species have been telling stories since our earliest caveman days, surrounding a campfire after a long day of hunting, weaving tales of our hunts and "the one that got away." Today's stories are more complex, of course, and may fit specific genres: Westerns, fantasy, science fiction, mystery, horror, romance, and much more. But the essence of storytelling hasn't changed; stories still entertain us and connect us on a baser, almost subconscious level.

## Story Terms

Following are some of the terms that will invariably crop up over and over again while developing game narrative.

### Characters

These are actors in your story. The main character, also called *protagonist*, is the hero of the story, while secondary characters, such as monsters, enemies, villains, allies, and henchmen, are supporting the story through their interactions with your main character.

Every character in your story has a *motivation*; to understand a character's motivation, ask yourself, "Why does the character do this, and is it consistent with his/her beliefs?" Distinguish between internal and external motivations: External motivations (also called universally-held wants) include things like survival, safety, comfort, pleasure, power, success, and mastery; internal motivations (also called individual wants) include things like acceptance, love, revenge, guilt, ego, surcease (conflict avoidance), and vindication. A character acts out of their motivation every single time, even if their actions appear mysterious. (It's not a mystery; the audience just doesn't understand their motivation yet.)

**Note**

Motivation is the past, goal is the future, and conflict is the present.

### Story

Story is what happens during your narrative. You can generally sum up your whole story in a fast blurb, also called a *high concept*. For instance, Stephen King wrote a creepy book, later turned into a movie, called *The Shining*, and you could sum it up as, "Jack Torrance and his family go to be caretakers at a haunted resort lodge, and Jack goes crazy and tries to kill his family."

### Setting

This is the world the story takes place in and that the characters share as actors on a stage. A setting can be as small as a single apartment or as large as a galaxy,

**Figure 6.17**
An example of setting.

depending on the scope of the story you are crafting. Settings for most stories determine the underlying mechanics of the story; setting defines the reality, character professions and races, the physical laws, and metaphysical laws (for example, magic spells, spaceships, laser blasters, and so on). If you look at Figure 6.17 you can tell that this setting is medieval in nature.

I know it sounds contradictory, but you shouldn't overburden your audience with too much description of your setting, because that is dull and will wear them out; yet you should know as many intimate details of your setting as possible, almost as if you yourself live there. If the place you are using as a setting is a real place, see if you can't visit it for a time; or write about what you know, using your personal surroundings as a setting. If the place you are using is a fantasy place out of your make-believe, draw a map of it (at least a mental one) and include as many details as possible, but remember that this is just for your information, not to bore the audience with.

## Plot

The driving storyline of the game, or the path that the story takes, is called *plot*. Don't confuse plot with bits of land set aside to dig graves in! Plot takes many guises in stories. Fiction stories usually have a major linear plot line, with several engaging subplots to keep the reader guessing.

## Theme

Probably the most dubious term in storytelling is *theme*. Theme is meant to reflect the story's main idea, moral, or meaning. You can see the morals behind most of Aesop's Fables, and they, in their way, are themes, but often it is more difficult to pierce your own story's heart and bleed its meaning out in a single descriptive sentence, especially if it's an idea you just came up with.

## Backstory

The history of all the events that have led up to the current action in the story is what we refer to when we say *backstory*. This can be far-reaching as the creation myth of the world composing the setting, or the abduction of the perilous princess the night before the handsome prince wakes up and sets off on his quest. Backstory is sometimes referred to by the characters in bits of expository dialogue or shown in *flashbacks*.

## Conflict and Suspense

*Suspense* is the core ingredient of a good story; allow your reader some unfulfillment, some fear or unknown element. Suspense calls for a deep emotional response in the reader, which compels them to stay engaged to see how your story will be resolved. For suspense to work, remember to use characters the reader will care for and worry about. You might have to make the characters even more identifiable for a wider target audience to do so, as long as your audience is sympathetic toward your characters' desires. Use plot twists and unexpected turns to escalate suspense; you can also use life's essential weirdness (coincidences, synchronicity, déjà vu, and so on) to increase the unknown element.

"Thou shalt have conflict on every page," say the Wee Gods of Storytelling. *Conflict* is a challenge that the hero faces that must be overcome. For instance, the princess is kidnapped by an evil warlock, and the prince must rescue her. The conflict that arises out of this is that the evil warlock lives in a dark castle on the other side of a haunted forest, and the prince has obstacle after obstacle to face before he can get there. Conflicts can be internal (within us) or external (with others).

Are things becoming too complacent? Invent a new crisis or bring an old one back. *Complications* add stumbling blocks and obstacles for the hero to overcome. Complications must:

- Arise out of the story (no throwing whipped cream pies at a funeral!).

- Make some real sense.

- Be significantly challenging without being overwhelmingly hopeless.

Allow the hero several failed attempts before overcoming conflict; this builds suspense and audience identification. Don't delay conflict resolutions just thinking it will build more suspense; it will usually only frustrate the audience.

### Story Arc

The *story arc* is a description of the curve of action within the story, often the transformation of the main character but also of the minor changes in difficulty and danger. A proper arc rises in tension throughout the course of the story, and finally at the end there is a major climax followed by a *denouement*, which is a series of events that take place after the climax as part of catharsis. Appropriate pacing is essential in capturing the arc.

### Climax

*Climax* is the final showdown, the last battle between the hero and the force of darkness, or whatever your story has in equivalence. Fiction reaches climax when the main challenge is answered and the hero reaches the conclusion of all his/her desires. The climax is always anticipated and perceived by the audience, and if it comes too early or does not fulfill their hopes, then it becomes a bungle, or *anti-climax*. A proper climax thrills and surprises us.

The number one no-no in developing plots is to have a predictable story. Symptoms include your audience figuring out plot twists before he/she is expected to. If these symptoms crop up, then you've just lost your audience completely. She might become so bored with your animation/game that she might never watch or play it again. Make sure your audience is constantly on the edge of their seat, and place well-crafted twists and turns designed to surprise and delight throughout your story. Never let your story get dull. See Figure 6.18.

**Figure 6.18**
Never leave a dull moment.

## Storytelling Methods

A lot of people make the mistaken assumption that coming up with story ideas is a talent that only a small fraction of people are born with and cannot be taught. For ages, these same people have thought the same about art. However, coming up with ideas is not all that hard. Once you begin making up stories, you will see inspiration is all around you.

As a writer, the yarns you spin through your narratives have the power to change people's moods and affect the experience they have, whether watching an animation or playing a video game. If you are having trouble with structure or outlining your narrative, there are three main storytelling methods you need to know. One is Elmer Rice's Greek drama set-up, the second is the monomyth popularized by Joseph Campbell, and the last is the ABDCE method for short-story construction. Let's take a look at these three.

### Elmer Rice's Three-Act Method

When talking about early Greek dramas, American playwright Elmer Rice, best known for winning the Pulitzer Prize for his 1929 play *Street Scene*, said there was a definitive method. Greek dramas were always told in three acts, and each of these acts framed a particular part of the story. Here was his breakdown:

- **Act I**: Get a man up a tree

- **Act II**: Throw rocks at the man

- **Act III**: Get him down out of the tree

Essentially what Rice is saying here is that at the start of your story you describe the setting, introduce the character, and give hints as to the main conflict coming. Then in the middle of your story, you deliver all the complications you can think of and really test the character. Lastly, you climax and provide a believable ending to your story to leave your audience satisfied.

### Monomyth

Mythology holds a wealth of possibilities. The film *O Brother, Where Art Thou?*, if you didn't already know, was based on the Greek myth of Ulysses. Of course, if you really watch the film, it doesn't seem anything like the original myth it was based on, and rightly so; metaphors remained the same but details were changed to another era. The underlying structure of the story remains a warped mirror image of Ulysses.

Hercules, Cinderella, Robin Hood, and Red Riding Hood have been plumbed to their depths in recent times, but thousands of other myths, fairy tales, legends, and religious stories can still be mined for ideas.

The world's leading mythologist, Jospeph Campbell, has a book *The Hero with a Thousand Faces* that is a great resource for understanding the relationships between these stories. When considering the story you are telling, be sure to get a copy, and while you are at it, read Christopher Vogler's *The Writer's Journey*. Vogler takes an authoritative look at some mythic archetypes set forth by Joseph Campbell and how they relate to books and film. The material in *The Writer's Journey* applies to electronic games and cartoons as much as it does cinema. These mythic archetypes are powerful symbols that go directly to the audience's subconscious, meaning that the audience reacts immediately to such metaphors, without having to take a lot of time drawing conclusions why it is so.

**Mythic Archetypes**    For instance, some of the character archetypes that have the all-entrenched mythic connotation are the Hero and the Shadow, who represent the ever-enduring battle between good and evil. There are five character

**Figure 6.19**
Typical heroes.

archetypes you must remember: the Hero, the Shadow, the Mentor, the Trickster, and the Guardian.

*Hero*    The *Hero* is the protagonist of the story, and classically he has the courage to do what he thinks is right, even against his own best judgment, the cleverness to get out of trouble time and again, and a strong code of ethics. The Hero is often resourceful and good at what he or she does. See Figure 6.19.

*Shadow*    The *Shadow*, also referred to as the villain, is the Hero's archenemy, the total opposite of everything the Hero is and stands for. The Shadow (shown in Figure 6.20) is a projection of the Hero's baser dark side, and therefore also has some of the same characteristics as the Hero, except for the Hero's code of ethics. The Hero and Shadow will always stand valiantly opposed, as these are the most primal archetypes.

*Mentor*    The *Mentor* comes across the Hero's Journey in the Supernatural Aid stage; ideally the Mentor is an older, wiser version of the Hero himself, but debilitated in some way so that he doesn't do any active heroism. The Mentor provides tips and help along the Hero's path, and he may even sacrifice himself to help the Hero's cause.

*Trickster*    The *Trickster* is not always present in the Hero's Journey but when he does appear he is a prankster who may trick, ambush, or trap the Hero, either to get the Hero to open his eyes and see the big picture or to aid the

**Figure 6.20**
Typical villains.

Shadow in leading the Hero down a dead end. The Trickster, shown in Figure 6.21, appears even more frequently in ancient myths, as the Norse god Loki, the Native American Coyote, and the African Anansi, where his actions are chaoticly neutral at best, aiding as well as pranking humans, never forthright or predictable.

*Guardian*    Another mythic archetype is the *Guardian*. Guardians are not the Hero's allies; a Guardian shares some relationship with the Shadow (like being a henchman or evil accomplice) and stands as an obstacle or trial along the Hero's Journey. The Guardian tests the Hero's abilities, and if the Hero perseveres, the Guardian gives the Hero new items or powers to stand up to the Shadow with.

**Figure 6.21**
The Trickster archetype.

**Hero's Journey**   The *monomyth*, as described by mythologist Joseph Campbell in his *The Hero with a Thousand Faces*, is filled with many steps, more like story suggestions, that naturally follow one another in a chain of events common to legends, fairy tales, books, and more. These steps are as follows, in proper sequence:

- **The Common Day World.** This is the "fish out of water" concept, where you see the Hero is taken out of his ordinary space and time and lands in a strange, more challenging world or predicament he never imagined existing.

- **The Call to Adventure.** The Hero is presented with a problem, challenge, or quest, which will take him further away from everything ordinary he used to know. Often, he refuses the call until the ante is raised and the Hero is further motivated to accept; if this happens, it is usually a self-sacrificing acceptance. (Not only has the Shadow taken over the kingdom, but now he's kidnapped the Hero's girlfriend, too, and the Hero isn't going to stand for that!)

■ **Supernatural Aid**. The Hero encounters aid in the persona of an advisor (the Mentor) or supernatural force. It is here that the Hero often finds a map, where to get a weapon that will smite the Shadow, or other useful tool to aid him in his quest.

■ **Into the Woods**. Prepared for adventure, the Hero crosses a threshold into a new and dangerous part of the imaginary world. His journey truly begins in earnest. Fraught with peril, this strange new world will test the Hero's nerve.

■ **Trials and Tribulations**. Once our Hero has escaped the ordinary and advanced down a dangerous path on a noble goal, he will face many obstacles and tests. Some of these may be in the form of Guardians or Tricksters. Along the way, the Hero will gain new allies, artifacts, weapons, or knowledge to help him face the Shadow.

■ **The Greatest Trial**. At the heart of the big nasty woods, the Hero reaches the lair of the Shadow. Here he must face his own fears, deal with his own lingering doubts, and overcome adversity through a galvanizing ordeal that will lay his soul bare.

■ **The Sword in the Stone**. The Hero has beaten death, risen from the ashes a transformed, more heroic Hero, smiting all enemies, and now gains that which he has sought so long—the pretty damsel, the golden chalice, the cure for a vile plague, or whatever the goal was in the first place—but is this The End?

■ **The Return Trip**. Danger is not out of the way yet, as the Hero must now try to reenter the ordinary world. He may have more foes to beat, traps to escape, or death to outrace. Campbell likens this scene to rebirth and transformation, where the Hero—like a phoenix—dies and is resurrected an avenging angel.

### ABDCE

So you've doled your story out into three acts, like Rice said, you've looked to myth and fairy tale for examples and even applied Campbell's monomyth, and you still have plot problems? Can't seem to structure your story? Try using the ABDCE method, then.

This tried-and-true abbreviation, invented by the Greek playwright Aeschylus—who also invented the Greek tragedy—can be seen as the apparatus in many short stories and can work equally well for games or animations. Here is what ABDCE stands for:

- **A is for action**. Begin your story with a bang. The Greeks called this starting *en medias res*, or in the middle of the thick of it. You should just dive right in, and don't worry about the audience getting lost or needing more information at first, because what you want to do is hook them. Your beginning doesn't have to be Jackie Chan–style, but anything with plenty of movement and dynamism will do.

- **B is for background**. Now that you've gotten your audience excited and eating up the world of your story, step outside the immediate action for a moment and provide a flashback or other expository background information about your characters, grounding your audience further in the story.

- **D is for development**. Now that you have set the ball rolling and provided some crucial background information, your story premise has been set. You've wound up your story, and it's time to let it go. Allow characters to clash and further the story.

- **C is for climax**. Eventually it's time for the critical point, the point the story has been building toward all along. This is the instant that changes the course of all events in your story. Every story needs a central moment that carries the emotion to its peak. After all, this is what the audience has been waiting on the edge of their seat for.

- **E is for ending**. Now it's time to wind down the story. No one likes a story to linger like month-old leftovers, so let your story fade swiftly and gracefully out the door after the climax has passed.

Whenever you find yourself struggling to space out your story, give the ABDCE method a try as a series of ladder steps to hang your material on.

## Review

At the end of reading this chapter, you should know:

- How to conceptualize your fictional characters

- How to draw the human body

- How to draw faces and use expressions to convey feeling

- What stories are composed of, and how to make up compelling stories

# CHAPTER 7

# BUILDING SCENES IN FLASH

In this chapter you will learn:

- Why a storyboard helps animators plan an animation

- To compose scenes using the rule of thirds, rays, hiatus, and details

- What the different camera shots arc that you can use

- To control, or change the position, of a camera

- To transition in-between shots

- To draw and scan in your artwork for backgrounds

- To make backgrounds out of photos using Trace Bitmap

- To use multiple Flash layers to add more depth to a scene

You can draw 2D images and animate them in Flash now, but there's a lot more to making a movie than putting objects in motion.

First, you need to know how to plan your animation better, which is done through the use of storyboards. Then, you should gather all the filmmaking secrets, including camera shots and transitions, because the manner in which you show your objects in motion will greatly affect your viewer's entertainment. Lastly, this chapter will show you how to put together backgrounds (and foregrounds) in Flash, because your characters can't float in blank space forever!

## Storyboards

*Storyboards* are a series of illustrations or images displayed in sequence for the purpose of pre-visualizing a motion graphic media sequence. Although "motion graphic media sequence" is a long term, it can mean cartoon animations.

If you draw an animation, you should start by drawing a storyboard. Storyboards, as exhibited in Figure 7.1, are loosely sketched or roughed in so the artist knows what direction to take. Don't be overly critical or concerned with the quality of art in a storyboard. You can even get away with sloppy thumbnails to sketch your storyboards. Concentrate instead on determining the best camera shots and proper composition in each shot to help the story flow.

**Note**

If you have trouble visualizing a script for cartoons, visit writer Jeffrey Scott's Web site at http://www.jeffreyscott.tv, and you will find several sample scripts that artists base storyboards and animatics off of, including some he has done for *Teenage Mutant Ninja Turtles*, *Muppet Babies*, and *Dragon Tales*.

## Composition

**Tip**

"Good composition is like a suspension bridge. Each line adds strength and takes none away."

—Robert Henri

**Figure 7.1**
A storyboard.

In addition to layout and visual design matters, the composition of your camera shots can convey a lot of information about the perspective and emotion of your scene.

### Rule of Thirds

Divide your computer or TV screen (your blank canvas) horizontally and vertically into thirds. The linear intersections provide key focal areas in which you ought to place items and/or characters.

Also note how the upper-right intersection has the most dominant focal point, while the lower-left intersection has the weakest. You can use this to create a mood within a composition. For instance, in Figure 7.2, notice that the illustration is given a wide open, almost bleak atmosphere just by the placement of objects along the rule of thirds.

### Point Things Out

Rays of lines can draw the human eye into or out from a piece. When Maurice Noble drew Wile E. Coyote cartoons, he used these rays to heighten suspense whenever he showed the Coyote falling from cliff tops. The rays were subtle,

**Figure 7.2**
Use of the rule of thirds to give a scene a bleak look.

because they were natural landscape lines surrounding the plummeting villain, but they were very effective at pointing to where the Coyote was inevitably heading, which pulls a lot of kids to the edges of their seats in anticipation (see Figure 7.3).

You don't have to be subtle, either. You can use arrows, blades, pointing fingers, sunrays, or other lines of direction within your composition to point your viewer's eye where you want them to look. It's not good advice to do this for every single frame of action, as that would get tedious and lose its effectiveness, but doing so for one or two key dramatic scenes wouldn't hurt.

### Take It on Hiatus

Sometimes, the center of interest in a compositional shot is given prominence by a *hiatus*. That is where there is a clear space around the object of attention separating it from the rest of its environment. Or you could draw thicker lines around the subject to single it out.

**Figure 7.3**
The fall is accompanied with lines arrowing toward the critter's inevitable target.

You can also create a center of interest by giving it a very different tone or color separating it from its background. Imagine a television cold commercial that shows a woman who has a runny nose, and everything in the shot is black and white. After she pops some cold medicine, her boots and jacket turn bright red, and she pulls out a brilliant red umbrella and starts skipping through the puddles, happy to have kicked her cold. The fact that the clothes she has on are the only colorful thing in the shot draws immediate attention to her by arresting the viewer's eye.

## Planned Reduction

Really, this only applies to animation and not so much to live action.

Setting a scene just right in order to progress the story involves some analytical work. You must encapsulate a lot of information for your viewer in every frame you draw in order to tell your story in a limited space. These space restrictions mean that any character or object you decide to include in a shot must serve a specific purpose. Indeed, every prop you include must be carefully considered as to its relevance in the composition.

If you look at the work of other cartoonists, you will see right off that scenes can be reduced to an essential minimum. Precedents have already been established in this, so audiences are not dismayed. For example, you can determine a character's profession or socioeconomic status with just a few wardrobe accessories or handheld props.

Not only are objects refined to essential representations of the whole, but details and textures are, too. You will notice that most cartoonists don't draw every detail in a picture. Instead, they give enough to allow the reader to fill in the blanks for themselves. When a cartoonist draws a field of grass, for example, he or she seldom draws every single blade of grass, but instead draws three or four blades of grass sporadically spread out to indicate the whole. Likewise, when drawing a brick wall, artists don't have to draw each and every brick. Instead, he or she can draw four or five evenly spaced bricks and let the viewer's imagination do the rest. Look at Figure 7.4 for some examples.

You can apply this method of planned reduction to your artwork. Just remember: You have a limited space to convey an entire story, so the items you choose to draw must enhance rather than detract from that story. Think of the scene as visual real estate.

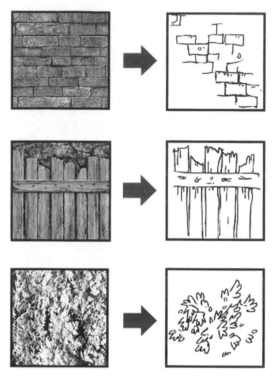

**Figure 7.4**
Artists often use a shortcut method by minimizing real details.

## Camera Shots

The most basic camera shots include the wide shot, the full shot, the medium shot, the close-up, and the extreme close-up. Take a look at Figure 7.5 for examples of each. In Flash, the camera's eye is the Flash Stage, so anything you place on the Stage will appear in the camera shot.

These have been used in film and animation for generations, and there's no reason they can't apply to your Flash cartoon or game.

### The Wide Shot

Before you see the action going on onscreen, there is often some kind of shot that establishes for the viewer where the action is taking place. The *wide shot* is the best place to begin. As with most scene setups, your camera shot is going to be determined by the action taking place in it. In this case, what you want to do is establish the locale, so you start with a wide shot that includes the locale.

**Figure 7.5**
(A) Wide shot, (B) full shot, (C) medium shot, (D) close-up shot, and (E) extreme close-up shot.

### The Full Shot

We know where our characters are, but who are our characters? It is time to cut to a full shot. A *full shot* is pretty much what it sounds like: You show a good view of the full character or characters, from head to toe, so that the viewer can see what they look like and tell what they are doing.

### The Medium Shot

Whenever showing the entire character, or the character's feet, for instance, would be pointless to carrying the action of the narrative, we use a *medium shot*. Most medium shots show the character's upper body and head but nothing else. Medium shots are often used in movies, TV shows, and comics when two or more characters are talking. To indicate a character's personal expression, facial expressions and hand gestures are used.

### The Close-Up

In the *close-up*, we focus on a character's face, particularly in a dramatic scene to show facial expression. A close-up may even show a bit of the shoulders, but the central concentration is on the face.

### The Extreme Close-Up

The most overused shot in horror film movies has to be the *extreme close-up*. The primary difference between the close-up and the extreme close-up is that the close-up shows a character's face, but an extreme close-up focuses more on the eyes. Eyes are the windows of the soul, as they say, and close-ups have a special liking of showing eyes so they can show you into the character's soul.

Occasionally, an extreme close-up can focus on other body parts. It can also be used to show the viewer important details about the action in-scene they shouldn't miss, such as the broken piece of glass a character is about to step on, a car tire deflating after running over a tack, or a fist about to smash through a plate glass window.

### Other Useful Camera Shots

Notice that animators who do a lot of cartoons get tired of drawing facial expressions and mouths moving in sync to the voiceovers. A lot of times, they will do these a little bit before cutting away. In this case, you don't even see a lot of animation going on, as the artist shows you the look on the fellow's face the guy is talking to, or a breeze ruffling the tree branches over the characters' heads, all while the voiceover continues, overlapping the scene. These tricks effectively conceal the fact that less animation is happening during long periods of exposition, and they also keep the audience from getting bored.

**The Cutaway Shot**    The *cutaway* is a shot that shows something else, it doesn't matter what, other than the main action, before returning back to the main action. Like the example given above, you could start one character giving a long-winded speech and then cutaway to something else going on in the background that has nothing to do with the current action, which has slowed to a crawl.

**The Cut-In Shot**    Similar to a cutaway is a *cut-in shot*, where you cutaway to another shot, but whatever the new shot is, it gives something more to the current action. For instance, you could show a woman searching produce aisles in a grocery store for oranges. You could cut-in a shot of the oranges, hidden behind some apples or melons, then go back to the woman. You effectively draw the viewer's attention to some element of the scene that has direct impact on the main action.

**Over-the-Shoulder Shot**    An *over-the-shoulder*, or OTS, shot is seen exactly as the name implies. The camera we are viewing all the action through appears to be positioned over someone's shoulder. This is often used in film and TV during dialogue scenes, as the person talking will be the shoulder the camera is mounted on and you can see the reaction on the other person's face to what the first person is saying.

**Point-of-View Shot**    A *point-of-view*, or POV, shot has the camera positioned where the main character is standing, as though the viewer is looking through the eyes of that character. This is similar to the first-person view you see in shooter games like *Doom*, and, in fact, the 2005 movie adaptation of *Doom* featuring Dwayne Johnson ("The Rock") used a POV shot for more than three minutes, where the action switches to the main character's sight and the viewer feels like they are really there, going on a rampage and killing an array of horrifying mutants.

**Noddy Shot**    A particular shot common to news story interviews is the *noddy shot*. In the noddy shot, to help break up long-winded dialogue without a lot of action to keep the eyes busy, the camera will sometimes switch to a medium close-up of the interviewer or a person listening, who nods or otherwise indicates they are listening. The noddy shot has been helpful in live action when you have to edit a nine-minute speech down to three minutes, because you can cut-in the noddy shot to conceal your edits.

## Changes in Camera

Even with all these camera shots, the camera itself is not an immobile lump of lead, even when shooting live action. Cameras can move, rotate, dip, and dance to capture any angle of the scene you want. In animation and video games, cameras are virtual, meaning they don't have a physical form and can literally be taken anywhere.

In Flash, the Stage is the camera's eye, so any time you want it to look like the camera is moving, you must grab and rearrange the items on the Flash Stage to give the illusion of the camera in motion.

### Zoom In/Out

The most widely heard bit of terminology in the industry, and often the most misused, is the *zoom in* or *zoom out*. If you zoom in on a particular scene, it does not mean the camera moves closer to the scene but that the camera lens focuses in on a particular object, making it appear dominant in the scene. When you zoom out, you are giving the impression of backing off or taking your focus off of the subject.

### Truck In/Out

Also referred to as pushing in or pulling out, because you are referring to physically pushing the camera closer to the subject or pulling it back, farther away from the subject, is the *truck in* or *truck out*.

### Tilt Up/Down

You *tilt* the camera up to get a better look at a subject just over your head, and you tilt down to get a better look at a subject on the ground. This is a great way to get shots of objects from dramatic angles, rather than looking at them straight on.

### Pan Left/Right

You swivel the camera to your left or right when you say you are panning left or right. You can *pan* the camera left to right to show a car entering a scene, passing you, and leaving the scene again.

### Diagonals and Foreshortening

From a graphic standpoint, it is always recommended to show diagonals in your compositions, such as in Figure 7.6. This happens naturally whenever you use a low- or high-angle camera for a scene, but can also be achieved by rotating the camera so that the horizon line is at a slight diagonal. When you use foreshortening, the perspective adds diagonals to the scene naturally.

## Ways to Cut

Up until now I have mentioned that you can cut from one view of a scene to the next, or to a view of a different scene altogether. A *cut* is a term taken from the old days of filming, because when the film editor came to the last frame in a scene, he

**Figure 7.6**
Use of diagonal lines, given naturally in perspective views, makes for more dramatic looks.

would literally cut the roll of film with a pair of scissors and attach the film to the next frame from a different roll with film paste.

The way to make a cut in Flash is to overlap one scene with another, and when it comes time, establish keyframes in each of the different Flash layers, and have one scene disappear while the other appears. Or you could use separate Flash elements called *scenes*, and switch between scenes, but Flash scenes are not generally recommended. I will show you how to do both in Chapter 9, "Making a Short Cartoon."

Whether you think about your cuts or not, a cut is used between every new shot within a scene. You can also do special things between cuts to add dramatic impact.

### Fade-In/Out

First, you can *fade-in* to a scene, meaning that you start out with a completely black or white screen and gently ease in to the shot. Doing the opposite is called a *fade-out*, where you go from an established shot and ease the picture out to completely black or white. This can be used to make a room look like the sun's going down outside, turning everything dark, or that the characters are outside becoming lost in a white blur of a blizzard.

### Dissolve

A *dissolve* is what happens when one scene becomes more and more transparent, slowly revealing another scene beneath it that comes into clearer and clearer focus. Dissolves are old hat in Hollywood, but they are still used on occasion to show the passing of time or like the story is going into a flashback.

### Blur/Zip Pan

Another nice way to transition between two scenes is with a *blur* or *zip pan*. The two are separated only by their look: A blur pan shows a brief blurry motion frame, while a zip pan shows quick lines of action. They are usually horizontal, diagonal, or radial (in a swirl).

A blur or zip pan, whether in live action or animation, offers us a quick and cheap way to transition between two drastically different scenes or settings, and can be used to imply traveling. You don't have to look any further than the old live-action TV series *Batman* with Adam West and Burt Ward, where they frequently used these types of pans to show Batman and Robin racing from one place to the next: "Quick, Robin, to the Bat Cave!" (See Figure 7.7.)

**Figure 7.7**
A transition pan like they used in *Batman*.

# Backgrounds

Setting is just as important as character in a good story. Really, setting can be another type of character, albeit limited in the form of interactions it can provide the viewer. Some people like stories that are set in far-off lands and places they would like to visit if they went on vacation. Other people like stories set some place welcoming and familiar, like their own backyard.

## Designing Backgrounds

When you design a *background* for your Flash, you need to keep it clear in your mind that the action does not take place in a vacuum. There has to be some indication of the setting, that is, where the action is taking place, for the viewer to immerse herself in it.

Charles Schulz, creator of *Peanuts* and the lovable Snoopy, often did not draw in backgrounds to his comic strips. Instead, he added a simple horizon line or a few tufts of grass that would cement the setting conceptually and let the rest fade to white or some off-white color. He did this intentionally. Indeed, he made his characters just as simple looking as his backgrounds, with very few illuminating details about what they looked like.

On the other end of the spectrum you see artists like the ones who do the *Batman* comics, who create endless amounts of realistic detail and sweeping vistas of Gotham, and blend it all with dark impenetrable shadows. The only problem with this mode of illustration is that, if you are not careful, you can obscure or lose your characters completely by making the background seem more interesting and dominant. You will find you might have to create a hiatus around your characters or find other ways for them to "pop out" from the background in that case.

See Figure 7.8 for examples of each.

This visual choice is really the artist's decision. What do you want to convey, and how do you want to convey it? Consider this carefully before you draw backgrounds for your Flash.

### Scanned Artwork

You can use your own artwork that you have scanned in to your computer for backgrounds. In this method, you have total control over how the artwork will look when in the scene before you even place it there. You could draw or paint your backgrounds, use colored pencils or pastels, or any other version of traditional art media you can think of or feel comfortable using.

**Figure 7.8**
(A) A simple background versus (B) a more complex background.

It also does not matter if you use an art media that you don't use with your characters, because a background shouldn't have to compete with the main action onscreen, and having a background made entirely of pastels and vector art characters on top will serve you best by making the characters "pop" out into focus.

1. When you get through with scanning your background in, import it to your Flash project Library.

2. Create a new Flash layer and call it something distinctive, like "background." I usually call my background layer "BG" for short.

3. Move your new background layer to the very bottom of your layer stack, under all your other layers.

4. Make sure the background layer is selected, then drag an instance of your background graphic from your Library to the Stage.

5. Use the Align options now to help you align the background graphic correctly on the stage. It can help to make sure the Align/Distribute to Stage button is highlighted, or active, and then click the Align to Horizontal Center and Align to Vertical Center buttons to center the background image to the center of the Flash Stage. If this looks okay to you, use Edit, Undo to remove it.

### Using Photographs

You could also use photographs for your backgrounds. One Flash artist well known for this method is Jon Mathers, creator of *Foamy the Squirrel* at http://illwillpress.com, who uses photographs as the basis for many of his outdoor backgrounds. He brings the photographs into Flash, uses the Trace Bitmap function to reduce the photos to vector artwork, as seen in Figure 7.9, and arranges them to cover the background in a logical way.

Trace Bitmap basically sends a tiny robotic tracer around every line in your artwork or photograph, modifying each of these pixel-based shapes into vector-based shapes.

Nowadays Adobe Illustrator has a built-in image vectorization program that does this, too, but back when I first experimented with Flash (it was still Macromedia-owned then), I was pleasantly shocked to find this program a natural part of Flash.

Trace Bitmap can make any bitmap image you import into a super-smooth vector art image, and like Mathers, this can be very handy for turning raw photos into vector art backgrounds.

You can do this, too.

1. When you find your photograph and have it on your computer, import it to your Flash project Library.

2. Create a new Flash layer for your background.

3. Move your background layer to the bottom of your layer stack.

4. Make sure the background layer is selected, then drag an instance of your background graphic from your Library to the Stage. Arrange it how you would like it to look. You might want it to fill up the entire scene or only one

**Figure 7.9**
You can use Trace Bitmap to reduce an image to vector art to use as a background.

part of it. You can use the Align panel (look under Window on the main menu for Align) or go to Modify > Align on the main menu.

5. With your graphic selected, go to Modify > Bitmap > Trace Bitmap on the main Menu Bar. You will have several options available to you, including Color Threshold, Curve Fit, and Corner Threshold. Although I rarely adjust Color Threshold, Curve Fit is something you will more than likely want to fiddle with. To prepare an image for the World Wide Web, you will probably want to set your curves to Smooth, because the more corner points you have in your image, the more memory it takes and more unwieldy it will be trying to distribute over the Internet. When ready, click OK to process your changes. It will take some time for the Trace Bitmap process, so don't worry if Flash is nonresponsive for a while.

6. You should see a grid of tiny dots covering your entire image when it is done. This shows that it has been traced. Move your image to the center of the Stage, and if you need to resize it (which is easier done before you use Trace Bitmap), you can use the Free Transform tool.

### Multilayered Backgrounds

Many backgrounds will require characters to walk behind or over objects that exist as part of the background. Characters may have to walk through doorways, stoop behind boulders, or cross in front of a chair in a living room. If they do not, if they walk over the top of a chair that is obviously supposed to be out in front of them, the audience will receive a minor shock and get distracted from the narrative.

When you need to show the characters moving behind other scene items, you can either make the objects separate to start with or trace a copy of the objects. Either way, you will have to place them on a Flash layer higher than the rest in the timeline hierarchy. This makes those items part of the *foreground*, or the area supposed to be visually in front of the subjects of viewer focus.

A more advanced Flash user could also use layer masks, but we won't get into that in this book, as it is a slightly more complicated though equally effective technique.

Layering your background in this way (see Figure 7.10) breathes more depth to your settings and makes them seem more believable. It is really easy to do with Flash, so taking the time to add a few minor foreground items will pay off in the end product.

## LAYERED CEL ANIMATION

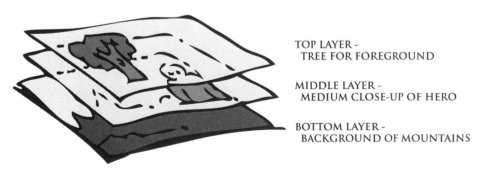

TOP LAYER -
TREE FOR FOREGROUND

MIDDLE LAYER -
MEDIUM CLOSE-UP OF HERO

BOTTOM LAYER -
BACKGROUND OF MOUNTAINS

**Figure 7.10**
Use a foreground layer in front of characters, and characters in front of a background layer.

## What's Next?

Now you can draw, make animations, and set up backgrounds for your scenes in Flash, plus you know the best ways to transition between scenes in Flash and make a composite movie. But what makes a movie more engaging goes beyond visuals into the aural experience. Before we put together our short cartoon, it's vital you know how sound is used in Flash, because movies and games wouldn't be the same without sound!

## Review

At the end of reading this chapter, you should know:

- Why storyboards help animators plan out their animations

- How to compose scenes using the rule of thirds, rays, hiatus, and details

- The different types of camera shots (wide, full, medium, close-up, and extreme close-up)

- How to zoom, truck, tilt, and pan your camera for better shots

- How to transition cuts between shots

- How to draw and scan in your artwork for backgrounds

- How to make backgrounds out of photos in Flash

- How several Flash layers can add more depth to a scene

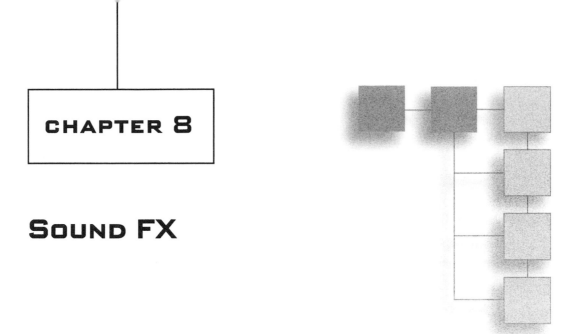

# CHAPTER 8

# Sound FX

In this chapter you will learn:

- How sound has been used in TV and film to support narrative

- What the difference between real and hyper-real sound is

- What that sound jargon about Hertz and decibels is all about

- What influences sound FX, such as space, time, and events

- To soundproof and set up your own recording studio

- What to remember when recording yourself

- What the differences are in compressed and uncompressed file types

- To use Audacity to record, edit, and export audio files

- To use Flash to plug in your own custom sound effects

Humans can perceive auditory signals coming from many different directions at once and singularly separate the sounds based on where they come from. Sound forms at least a full fifth of the way we perceive our environment, and we innately use sound as a means of survival. Being capable of telling when a noisy ambush predator like a cougar snuck up behind our ancestors helped our ancestors stay alive—and today we use sound to listen to the latest music hits on our MP3 players.

Sound makes everything come more alive. It stamps the heartbeat for our culture and provides us with an aural experience. It can support the story of a game and shape the soundtrack. Try playing a video game with the TV or the computer speakers on mute. Watch a YouTube video without headphones or a speaker and realize just how disappointing the experience quickly becomes.

We are going to look at how you create sound for use with Flash, and you'll learn how to edit sound using Audacity.

## Sound Used in TV and Film

Electronic games follow the cinematic wake of the TV and movie industry, so game designers can learn a lot from the way those industries use sound. Sound can support a narrative, documentary, or commercial film or program, telling the story directly or indirectly and enhancing the overall experience.

### A Short History Lesson

The movie industry started seriously using sound in the 1920s, but the process was incredibly difficult back then. Because of limitations to the sound cameras, actors often had to be experienced theatrical performers and practically shout to be heard on the final recording. A good deal of silent film actors lost their jobs at this time, because audiences discovered many of them had poor speaking voices or foreign accents.

Today's recording processes are a lot better, and most of the work goes straight to digital tracks. Actors can act naturally and underplay their roles if they wish, even so much as whispering, and still be heard in the final edit. Unfortunately, directors are becoming more and more *laissez faire* now that the technology has caught up to demand that they put a lot of technical problems on the sound engineers, who are expected to make actors' voices sound clear in post-production even if the directors can't hear them on set.

The people working on the production of a film or TV show think of sound every step of the way. Screenplay writers make suggestions for noises that may be heard and lines of dialogue to be spoken by paid actors. Location scouts consider noise conditions of prospective shooting sites. Although directors can frame a shot to effectively remove a sign or offensive place from being seen on camera, they have no control over random noises such as airplanes flying overhead or construction workers off-camera.

Sound delivery has also improved vastly over the years. Sound delivery started out mono and only as recently as the 1970s went to stereo. Today's modern audiences, including you, not only expect to hear their TV shows, movies, and games in stereo, they expect to be rocked by Dolby surround sound and amplified bass. The increased resolution of HDTV images requires a similarly improved high-definition sound track. A 5.1 high-fidelity surround-sound system, which literally surrounds you with the best sound, provides the most balanced aesthetic energy between picture and sound.

The technology has advanced, and even the game industry must stop and think about sound critically during development.

## Hyper-Real Sound

You may not realize it, but most film and TV sound for your entertainment pleasure does not come from the original recorded sound. Sounds you hear in the cinema are rarely accurate representations of real sounds.

Instead, engineers construct the sound in post-production utilizing many pieces of sound they mix together in software programs to create a seamless whole. These professionals often take separate pieces from sound effects libraries and from custom recordings done in studios, what's called *Foley sound*. Foley artists record custom sound effects that emphasize sounds that should be heard in context. For instance, a Foley artist might shake a sheet of metal to record thunder, or squash melons to represent a character getting squished by a falling anvil. Foley sound is named after Jack Foley, one of the earliest and best-known Hollywood practitioners of the art. Foley began his career in the industry as a stand-in and screenwriter during the silent era, and later helped Universal Studios make the transition from silent movies to talkies.

When creating a game, every piece of sound has to be manipulated by the game programmer and the piece of sound used can be hyper-real, placing emphasis that subtly influences the game's players.

## Sound Fundamentals

The Greek mathematician Pythagoras not only delivered us a triangle, but also discovered the octave and came up with numeric ratios connected to harmony.

Galileo formed many of the scientific laws of sound.

Since the 1600s there have been numerous advances in the study of sound, some of them coming from such great individuals as Heinrich Hertz (where we get our "hertz" from) and Alexander Graham Bell (where we get our "decibel" from).

It has been discovered that sound comes in the shape of vibration waves. Some sound waves can actually travel at frequencies so high or low that humans cannot hear them, but some animals can (such as the dog hearing a dog whistle).

Here are some of the most basic laws of sound:

- A *sound wave* moves pretty much in a straight-forward fashion.

- *Pitch* refers to how fast the sound wave vibrates, also known as *frequency*. Humans can discern sound frequencies by a 2:1 difference, so many of our music notes are on a scale of 2.

- The term *hertz* (Hz) comes from a unit of frequency equaling one vibration per second.

- *Intensity* is how loud the sound comes across, also called amplitude or volume. Intensity can be measured by the decibel, or dB. The increasing intensity of a sound wave is known as *gain*.

- *Timbre* is the waveform or accuracy of the sound frequency. Timbre is different for every instrument and every voice, and it reflects a change in quality that is not dependent on intensity or frequency.

## Influencing Factors

The outside factors that influence sound include space, time, situation, and outside events. As with many of the other elements of media aesthetics, these factors can overlap.

### Space

Location defines many sounds. Stereo sound makes it possible to hear sound relative to onscreen positioning. For instance, most of the player character's dialogue will come from the front forward-facing speaker in 5.1 Dolby surround sound, but if you show a comrade yelling for the player to catch up and you show him slightly off-screen over on the right, you better make sure the sound comes out of the right-side speakers.

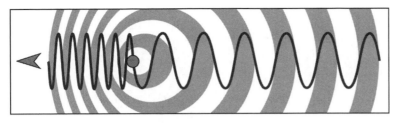

**Figure 8.1**
An illustration of the Doppler Effect.

Sound perspective means that you must also match close-up video images with "near" sounds, and long shots with sounds that come from far away. Close sounds take the spotlight, often sharing more presence than the softer background noises.

The same principle takes the Doppler Effect (see Figure 8.1) from physics to media: as a loud sound source comes closer to the listener, the higher the sound gains; the farther away the sound source moves from the listener, the softer the sound gets until it fades completely. Positioning themselves in a virtual world, 3D sounds take advantage of the Doppler Effect. In most 3D game engines, this is handled for you.

### Time

Different times of the day and different climates are reflected in sound. If you are creating a summer glen, you will want to use noises such as chirping birds, breezes blowing, or tree branches rustling. On the other hand, a scene that takes place at night might have owls hooting, crickets chirping, or coyotes barking in the distance.

There are two special uses of sound that have to do with time: (a) predictive sound and (b) *leitmotiv*.

**Predictive Sound**   *Predictive sound* involves the placement of certain sounds before an event actually takes place. An example of a predictive sound would be letting the player of a game hear battle sounds coming from over a hill before showing them that there is a fight taking place or letting the player hear a rumbling noise right before an earthquake shakes the streets their character is walking down.

**Leitmotiv**   The other special use of sound dealing with time is the *leitmotiv* (German for "leading motif"). The *leitmotiv* is similar to Pavlov's bell (if you have studied psychology, you know what I mean). Some games play a short

**Figure 8.2**
As seen but not heard, combat often ramps up the sound in games.

music piece every time a specific boss monster or enemy shows up, letting the player know that she has to prepare to fight.

Many next-generation games use soft-key music in the background and as soon as the player enters combat, tenser hard-edged music starts playing, which is another form of *leitmotiv*. See Figure 8.2. The *leitmotiv* most often heard in the popular survival horror games under the *Resident Evil* title is the moaning of zombies. If the player enters a room or new area, he or she doesn't even have to see a shambling corpse; if she can hear a shuffling noise or a low moan, she knows she's about to have to face off against the undead.

### Situations and Outside Events

Sounds can describe a specific situation or (used cleverly) be effected by outside events that help put the listener into the scene.

Here is one example: A lonely geezer leaves the front door of his wooden shack high in the snow-capped mountains to chop wood. He crunches through snow with every step, and occasionally the forest is disturbed by the cries of hawks, but otherwise the sound stays very much muted. Why, you might ask? Snow acts as a sort of natural sound dampener, absorbing noises. So the scene would be a hushed one.

## Soundtracks

After compiling your artwork and putting together the layout of your scenes for Flash, you are still left with a really fun part of making a Flash cartoon: adding the soundtrack. By now you should have written a storyline to your first efforts, so you have a pretty good idea about what dialogue is needed, as well as the sound effects and music you want to include.

## The Dialogue Track

Many animators start with the *dialogue track*, as it is the most difficult to align the animation to. The dialogue track is where you hear the voices of all the characters talking. This is also called a *voiceover*, because the voices overlay the animation taking place onstage.

I started out when I was ten years old with one of those old clunky tape recorders. I would carry that recorder around with me everywhere, taping my thoughts or sound bytes off the television. One day I got a copy of Douglas Adams' *The Hitchhiker's Guide to the Galaxy* radio screenplay. I decided to put on my own radio play, using that screenplay as the basis. Being only ten and not having a slew of friends to help, I did all the voices by myself by making lousy impressions of famous actors and actresses at the time. By the time I was done and showing what I had created to my mother, I had just about decided that theater was the life for me.

You, too, can do all your own voiceovers for your dialogue track. There are plenty of animators who have done their own voices. Walt Disney, as the story goes, was so tired of demonstrating to voice actors how they should do the voice of Mickey Mouse that one of them finally suggested, "Why don't you just do it yourself?" And he did. Walt Disney was Mickey's first voiceover, up until the late 1940s. John Kricfalusi, creator of *Ren and Stimpy*, performed the voice of his lead character Ren Hoek, the skinny asthmatic Chihuahua. Again, nobody he interviewed could give Ren the sort of intensity John wanted, so he did the voiceover himself.

If you are at a loss for inspiration for a "voice," just look around you. There are lots of voices you can do for your recordings.

One tip is to pick an actor or actress and do your own impression of them. I remember when I was in speech and drama classes at my high school, we had a student who was fall-down funny when it came time to do humorous interpretations. He would pick the most outlandish clashing voices he could think to imitate and do them. For example, he once did a classic scene from *Robin Hood* starring the voices of Peter Lorre (the creepy short guy they poked fun at a lot in *Looney Tunes*), Darkwing Duck, Darth Vader, and Barbra Streisand. He got a lot of laughs, but even if he was being serious instead of being over the top he would still be entertaining.

So choose voices at random that are so different from each other to sound like different people, and practice them before getting in front of the mic.

If you feel uncomfortable doing voiceovers of the opposite gender, or if you're afraid your voice is just as bad as scratching nails on a chalkboard, you might consider talking a friend into helping you. If you have the wherewithal, you could even bribe them. Tell them you will help make them a star! If you can afford to hire professional voice talent, that would be even better, but don't sweat it if you can't. Everyone has to start somewhere!

## The Music or Sound FX Track

You probably already know this, but you can get in some serious trouble for using music or sound effects intended for private home use in a for-profit production, even if it's a cartoon or video game. If you pay special attention at the beginning of movies there is usually a message warning that comes up saying, "unauthorized duplication or presentation, even without monetary gain is punishable by law." That means that even though you might be legit and not intending to make a few bucks, even if you own an original copy of the product, or you are just making an unauthorized copy for your own personal use, you can still get fined or thrown in jail!

For educational or private usage, it might be fine to use an MP3 of your favorite band, be it Snoop Dogg or Paramore, but you won't be able to show it to anyone without special permission or a usage license from the artist.

### Permissions and Licensing

You can attempt to write to your favorite band and tell them what the music is for and ask if it's okay to use it, and if you get signed written permission from them, then you are in the clear.

Whether it is sound FX, music, 3D models, artwork, or anything else going into my creative pipeline, I try to keep it as clean as possible. If I ever use anything that is not my own original piece or something I have purchased to be royalty-free, I write to the piece's creator and ask them for permission to use it. I don't lie; I tell them exactly what I'm using their piece for and who might see or hear it.

Gaining permissions has helped me countless times in the past, covering my rear, and I have often been amazed at how helpful other artists have been. For instance, when I started my first game, I contacted three rock bands to see if I could use their music in my game, and two out of the three eagerly agreed, sent me free CDs, and joined my close acquaintances! This shows it never hurts to try.

Most often, however, artists will have their lawyers draw up a single-user license and charge you a fee or percentage in royalties for using any of their creations.

### Royalty-Free

On the other hand, you could use royalty-free music or sound FX. *Royalty-free* means that once you pay a set price for a CD or download, you're done paying for it and can use it in any productions you want to make.

Be sure, if you go this route, to carefully read your licensing agreement with the creators of the royalty-free tunes or sound FX, because there will occasionally be stipulations written into the fine print. For instance, some royalty-free places want you to advertise or credit them in your finished product, which is only fair as they are still saving you money and time having to make all that stuff yourself.

Some popular sites you might look at that have royalty-free music or sound FX include:

- **Bbm.net**: http://www.bbm.net

- **DeusX.com**: http://www.deusx.com/studio.html

- **Flashsound.com**: http://www.flashsound.com

- **Flashkit.com**: http://www.flashkit.com

- **Partners in Rhyme**: http://www.partnersinrhyme.com

- **Shockwave-Sound.com**: http://www.shockwave-sound.com

- **Sound-Ideas.com**: http://www.sound-ideas.com

- **MusicBakery.com**: http://musicbakery.com

- **Soundrangers.com**: http://www.soundrangers.com

A number of these even have 100% free sound sources, and most incorporate directly into Flash. Check them out!

If you truly do not want to use anybody else's sound work, then you are going to have to make some of your own. To do that, you will have to set up a sound recording studio in your home.

## Starting Your Own Sound Studio

You must keep in mind some serious fundamentals to starting a home studio space. You will probably set up your recording studio around your computer desk, in your bedroom or garage. The garage might be best, simply because of the sound isolation there.

We will discuss the two most important aspects to remember when setting up your own sound studio: soundproofing and setup—and then we'll look at what it takes to start recording.

## Soundproofing

Make sure the room you use does not have serious leaks for sound to invade, such as door cracks and windows. You will want to keep noise from the outside from filtering in, and you want to stop short of being a nuisance to your parents and neighbors. Sound absorption and isolation will be your primary goals.

Short of going out and buying expensive commercial eggshell panels to cover the walls and ceiling in your room or garage, you can drape wool blankets over the windows and door or add bookshelves filled with books to your walls. This will limit the amount of reflective sound (or echoing) while improving the sound quality when you record.

You might also make sure that your parents, siblings, or pets know you are recording before you start, so they won't walk in and disturb you in the middle of a complicated recording session.

## Setup

You will need an easy-to-use sound editing software program to do audio mixes with, and if the program you choose does not include a recording or micro-phone-line-in system, you might have to use Microsoft's built-in sound recorder or other inexpensive software to initially record your audio. The following programs are the most widely used sound-mixing packages available:

- Audacity (found on the companion CD-ROM)

- Broadcast

- Cool Edit Pro

- Pro-Logic

- Slab

- SONAR

- Sound Forge

Before using a sound editing program, you should check to make sure that your computer has a suitable sound card and peripheral speakers for playback.

### Microphones

Besides having the right computer software and hardware, you must also have a microphone (as shown in Figure 8.3). There are fundamentally two different types of microphones to choose from: (a) dynamic and (b) condenser microphones.

**Figure 8.3**
An example of a condenser microphone.

**Dynamic Microphones**   Dynamic microphones use a wire coil over a magnet to catch sound waves, producing an electronic voltage in response to sound. These microphones reproduce sound pretty well, but their actual accuracy is based on voltage rather than the sound source.

**Condenser Microphones**   For killer vocal recording, you should consider a condenser microphone. Condenser microphones use an electronically charged stretched diaphragm over a thin plate, and fluctuations caused by sound waves passing over the diaphragm cause changes in the electronic current, producing output signals.

Condenser microphones tend to be more accurate than dynamic microphones, particularly in mid and high frequencies. Unfortunately, they are more fragile and less likely to handle abuse.

**Practice at the Mic**   Practice will show you whether or not you have chosen the right sound editing setup for you. Practice with your microphone to see what its sound range is like and if you pick up any background noise. If your microphone is sensitive enough to pick up the fan motor on your computer, you might have to replace the fan motor on your computer or tone it down a notch. Practice with recording techniques until you find the right setup that works for you.

## Sound Recording

If you plan to record your own voice, you must stop and think about your voice, how you place the microphone, and how to mix digital audio files on the computer.

### Listen to Yourself

Evaluate how you sound on the mic. The human voice is a complex topic in and of itself.

Don't fret if you freak out the first time you hear your own voice recorded and played back, as it probably doesn't even sound like you think you sound. This is because we hear ourselves muffled through our inner ear and can never accurately hear the timbre of our own voice unless recorded. Although you may sound different, it by no means reflects poorly on you. Your voice will do just fine for most recording efforts, unless you want to talk your friends into helping out.

There are many tricks to make you sound better. The majority of these tricks to consider are as follows.

**Use Proper Posture**    Stand or sit up straight. Let your muscles in your body relax. Don't let tension build up or it will tighten your vocal cords. Don't slump down in your chair or lean way over when talking.

**Remember to Breathe**    Breathing is critical to enunciation. Unless you practice breathing correctly, you can develop poor habits that make your speech pattern erratic, soft, or breathless. You should take deep breaths in, letting them out slowly, to practice proper breathing. Don't take up smoking or hollering your lungs out when you have a chest cold, because you can actually hurt your organs.

**Don't Crack Up**    If you talk so loud or so fast that your voice actually cracks, you are "cracking up" and it won't sound good. Breaks—or noticeable pauses or transitions in your speech—will maintain a more consistent sound. Knowing when to take breaks will increase your overall performance and if you time them well, will actually cause your listeners more pleasure listening to you.

**Say It, Don't Spray It**    Your unique tone, the speed with which you speak, how clearly you speak, and the interplay of your expression with the words you are reading from—these are the elements that have the most critical role in making you an effective speaker.

Part of your delivery comes from the words you are speaking, and part of your delivery comes from how you speak them. You have a unique vibe all your own. Strive to be yourself, but do so in a way that others can understand your message.

### Digital Sound

It is important before we get started mixing and calling digital audio files in Flash to understand what digital sound files are called, what compression of these files is all about, and some of the most basic keywords in digital sound mixing.

**Sound File Formats**    Computer-based sound editing generally involves one of three digital audio file formats. These file formats are as follows: WAV files, MP3 files, and OGG files. WAV files are uncompressed, while MP3 and OGG files are compressed.

*WAV Files*    WAV files are usually uncompressed audio files. This means that they can be quite large and sound pretty good. The quality of a WAV file is determined by how well it was originally recorded or converted. Generally, you will want to work with WAV files for some sounds, but they can take up quite a lot of memory.

*Compressed Files*   Compression restricts the range of sound by attenuating signals exceeding a threshold. By attenuating louder signals, you limit the dynamic range of sound to existing signals.

Imagine that the audio file is a piece of paper with sheet notes on it. Compressing it is literally wadding up the piece of paper into a tiny ball. To listen to the music in its compressed state, you have to use a device like an MP3 player to un-wad and smooth out the piece of paper.

There are two types of compressed audio files that bear mentioning: (a) MP3s and (b) OGG files.

**MP3s**   The most popular compressed audio file on the market right now (mostly due to the popularity of iPods and other MP3 players) is the MP3.

MP3 stands for Moving Pictures Expert Group, Audio Layer 3. It started in the 1980s by the German Fraunhofer Institut. In 1997 the first commercially acceptable MP3 player was created, called the AMP MP3 Playback Engine, which was later cloned into the more popular Winamp software by college students Justin Frankel and Dmitry Boldyrev.

Napster and its gangbuster follow-up MP3 file-sharing services blew the lid off the MP3 boom, making it the number one most-recognized audio file on the Internet.

**OGG Files**   For other systems, Ogg Vorbis is probably the format of choice on Linux and AIFF for Macintosh. OGG files use a different (and some say better) encoding process to compress the audio. If you've never heard of OGG files before, check out www.vorbis.com for more information.

## Audacity

A great open-source program (meaning it doesn't cost you anything under the GNU General Public License) is Audacity, and it's the program suggested for you to use and is enclosed on the accompanying CD-ROM.

Go ahead and install your free Audacity on your machine, if you haven't already, and we'll look at how you use it.

### Recording Sound

Let's record some sound. Open up Audacity and click the Record button, as shown in Figure 8.4. The program is now recording from your microphone, so

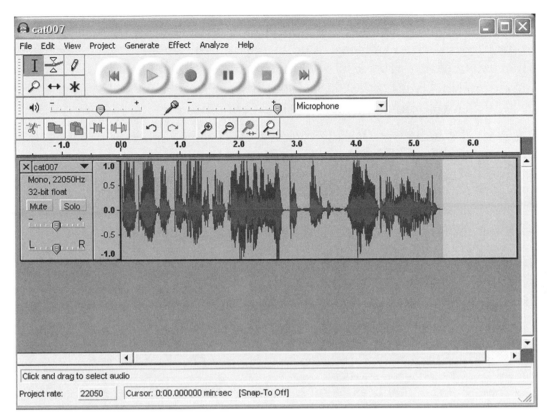

**Figure 8.4**
The Audacity interface.

you better say something. You can see the progress and the waveforms of the sounds in the Audacity window as you speak.

When you're done talking, click the Stop button. Play back your recording by clicking the Play button.

If you can't hear anything coming out, but you see a waveform in Audacity, make sure you have the volume turned up on your computer and your speakers. If everything looks good, but you still can't hear any sound, check the microphone level in the Mixer Control in Audacity, and you might raise it a notch.

## Editing Sound

Now, if you didn't start speaking into the mic right away, you will probably have a long period of "dead air" before the sound wave you made and another chunk of "dead air" after. This is typical, but it's certainly not optimal for a sound you're recording for a cartoon or game. You have to edit your sound.

Place your cursor at one side of the portion of the waveform you wish to get rid of, and drag it across to the other side, highlighting the area you want eliminated. Then go to Edit > Delete. The selected portion will be removed from the waveform. Notice under the Edit menu that you also have the option to Cut and Paste, which will come in handy when you are mixing multiple sound tracks.

Play back the audio to make sure you didn't remove too much or not enough of the waveform. Eventually, you'll have it finished.

### Effects

I suggest you highlight the entire waveform and experiment with the effects that Audacity ships with. Go up to Effect on the menu and drop the list down. You can select and play around with any of these effects, and play back the sound to hear how each effect changes the recording. When you find an effect you don't like, you can click Edit > Undo to remove it.

- **Repeat**: Repeats the last effect command.

- **Amplify**: Increases or decreases the volume of your track.

- **Bass Boost**: Amplifies the lower frequencies, leaving the other frequencies untouched.

- **Change Pitch**: Changes the audio pitch without affecting the tempo.

- **Change Speed**: Resamples and changes the speed, thereby changing the pitch.

- **Change Tempo**: Changes the tempo (speed) of the audio without affecting the pitch.

- **Click Removal**: Removes clicks, pops, and other artifact noises.

- **Compressor**: Compresses the range of the audio so the louder parts are quieter.

- **Echo**: Repeats the audio again and again, softer each time, like an echo.

- **Equalization**: Amplifies or diminishes specified frequencies using curves.

- **Fade In/Out**: Fades audio in or out.

- **FFT Filter**: Applies a Fast Fourier Transform using a curve on a linear scale.

- **Invert**: Flips the audio upside down.

- **Noise Removal**: Removes constant background noise, such as the wind, fans, tape noise, or humming.

- **Normalize**: Corrects for vertical (DC) offset of the signal.

- **Nyquist Prompt**: Uses a programming language to massage the audio.

- **Phaser**: Combines phase-shifted signals with the original.

- **Repeat**: Repeats the audio a given number of times.

- **Reverse**: Makes the audio run backward, which is really cool!

- **Wahwah**: Uses a moving bandpass filter to create a "wah-wah" sound over the existing signal.

## Exporting Sounds

Lastly, you need to save the bit of dialogue or sound effect as a file so you can use it in Flash. Click File > Export as WAV, and name your file trialrun.wav, putting it somewhere convenient for the moment such as your Desktop. Browse to your Desktop or wherever you placed the file, and double-click (Win) or single-click (Mac) to open it in your operating system's default media player. Listen to your sound as it exists.

**Note**

You have to find a special plug-in to export your recordings as compressed MP3 files. It is called an Audacity LAME Encoder. This is not really necessary for our current game project, so the MP3 encoder is not found on the CD, but you can do a brief Web search to discover it.

## Importing Sounds into Flash

Adding sound FX to Flash projects is fast and easy.

Sound files are imported by choosing File, Import, Import to Library from the Menu Bar and browsing for the sound file. You can import WAV or MP3 or AIF files, among others.

WAV or AIF files are the best option if you have them, since they are uncompressed coming into Flash. You can then select the compression to apply in the Publish Settings of Flash. MP3 files already have some compression applied, which can only be left as is. Also, MP3 files may have a pause at the end when looping, which WAV or AIF files do not. Since I showed you how to export WAV files from Audacity, we will just use that file type for now.

Selecting the file you want to use once it is located will import the file into your project's Library, and a new audio icon will appear with your other files. I am importing a file named "trialrun.wav." If you do not see your Library, just go to Window in the menu options at the top of the screen and select Library, and it should appear.

Audio files in the Library are distinct from other files, besides having an audio icon beside them. You can see the *waveforms*, or the two spiky lines, which indicate the levels of the left and right audio channels, along with Play and Stop buttons in the Library preview window when the new audio file is selected in the Library. See Figure 8.5.

When your audio file is ready and rests within the Library for your project, it is best to add each of your sound FX to a separate layer within Flash, as shown in Figure 8.6. In Flash, go to the main menu bar and choose Insert, Timeline, Layer. To rename it, go to Modify, Timeline, Layer Properties and in the Layer Properties dialog window, there is a place to name your new layer. I usually name the layer I have sound on "audio."

This naming system is, of course, merely a suggestion, but having clear names will help you locate yourself within your project as it expands with more layers.

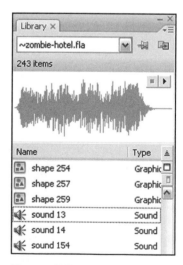

**Figure 8.5**
This is what the Library preview window looks like when an audio file is selected.

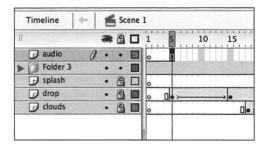

**Figure 8.6**
Add a layer just for your audio files to be placed on.

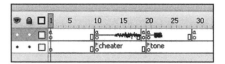

**Figure 8.7**
The waveform's appearance on the audio layer.

Make sure there is a blank keyframe where you want the audio to start, and at least a few blank frames (if not more) after that keyframe. The more blank keyframes you have, the better Flash will allow you to see the audio file once it is on the layer.

After the audio file has been imported into the Library and a layer created to sport it, select the audio layer in your Timeline, and drag your file from the Library directly onto the work area of your main Stage. You should see a thin waveform appear in those few frames in the audio layer of your Timeline. Now select the end frame and drag it further down the Timeline. This should reveal the rest of the waveform in the audio layer. See Figure 8.7.

The waveform spikes can assist you in timing your audio to your animation, something that is also known as *synching*. If you want to move the beginning of the audio around in the layer, you can select the first frame, and drag it to the frame where you would like the audio to begin. Then just grab the last frame and drag it to where you want your audio to end.

It's important to know that the audio file on the layer cannot have a keyframe anywhere between the beginning and the end of the waveform. If you insert a keyframe, it will stop the audio at that point and clear any audio after it. You can still move the frame at the end of the audio to reveal the waveform again,

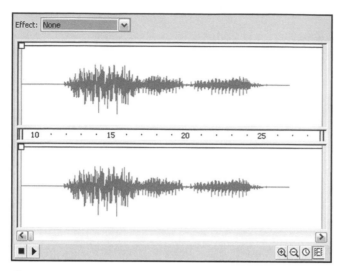

**Figure 8.8**
The Edit Envelope panel.

however. Also it would likely make it easier if you reserve this layer only for the audio you have applied to it.

If you are importing a longer audio file that requires a fade out, you will need to do that manually. If you do not cut your audio down, your Flash file will get to the end of the animation and repeat while the previous audio continues to play. This will result in multiple layers of audio playing at once, and can distort the SFX. To fade out the sound, simply select it in the audio layer, and you will notice the Properties Inspector panel displays the audio file name and properties. Select Fade Out from the Effect drop-down list, or click Edit to open the waveform's Edit Envelope panel, as shown in Figure 8.8, where you can directly edit the sound's fade.

After adding audio to a project in this manner, all you need do next is save your project and test your movie to see what it sounds like.

## What's Next?

Now that you know all about adding sound FX to your Flash, it is time to put together the pictures and sound and make a complete animation using everything you've learned.

# Review

At the end of reading this chapter, you should know:

- That sound has played an important role in the development of film and TV

- What hyper-real sound is and how it's different from regular sound

- All the fancy sound engineering jargon

- How space, time, and situations influence sound

- How to set up your own sound recording studio at home

- Some basic tips for recording your own voice

- The differences between various digital sound files

- How to use Audacity to record, edit, and export audio files

- How to use Flash to plug in your own sound effects

# CHAPTER 9

# MAKING A SHORT CARTOON

In this chapter you will learn:

- How to spring off a storyboard

- How to create a title and credits screen with music

- How to create movie clips and buttons and manage imported media

- How to make motion tweens, shape tweens, and guided motion tweens

- How to put together a Flash puppet, or fluppet, for animation purposes

- How to lip synch in Flash

- How to create a preloader in Flash

In this chapter, you will take your art and animation skills to the next level. You will put everything I have mentioned so far to the test and create a short cartoon using Flash. This prepares you for digital animation and how to manipulate the Flash program in the best way to make 2D images spring to life.

Sure, you might want to jump right into game making. But to make Flash games, it's good to know how to make Flash animations, because you can include animation in your games to make them cooler or draw people in. Plus, the Wii and Opera browser can surf the whole of the Internet, and WiiCade as well as other prominent Wii fan sites, include Flash cartoons as well as games.

You might find you have a knack for digital animation and want to focus your energies there.

Or you might discover that you really hate drawing and animating characters and that you only want to come up with game designs, for which the second half of this book will prepare you.

So, without further ado, let's make a cartoon!

## Wake Up Call for Count Stunkula

Since the world is your oyster, so to speak, you have all kinds of options open to you when you think about making a cartoon. You could make a serious drama in anime style, all about demon slayers or witch girls—or a whacked-out cartoon about junior scientists who accidentally transform their brother into a troll—or a sci-fi Western opera where sterling silver cowboys fly rocket ships to herd cosmic cattle in space! The choices are only limited by your imagination.

The *rendition*, or how you make your idea come to life, is only limited to your skill with the software.

I will show you some basic tricks with Flash as we go along, but it is up to you to continue your training. If you're serious about wanting to learn Flash animation, you should read the helpful Adobe tutorials that come with the software, Eric Grebler's *Flash Animation for Teens*, or James E. Shuman's *Adobe Flash CS4 Revealed*.

## Draft a Plan

As the type of cartoon you could make in Flash is near infinitely open-ended, I will come up with a storyline, show you how to make it, even provide you with some starter tools, and then let you go. After this chapter, you should be competent enough to create your own cartoons. Even if you never plan to distribute them for the Wii, you should still upload them to YouTube to amaze your friends.

I have a short cartoon for you to make called *Wake Up Call for Count Stunkula*.

**Figure 9.1**
Storyboard for *Wake Up Call for Count Stunkula.*

Here is the plot: "An alarm clock goes off and wakes up Count Stunkula, our skunk vampire. He gets out of his coffin, decides he's going 'out for breakfast,' and heads to the door. When he opens the door, we see it's still daylight, and Stunkula is reduced to ash. The joke's on Stunkula, as he set his alarm clock for AM, not PM!" This is short enough to complete in one chapter, yet you will learn a lot about digital animation in one fell swoop.

Look at the storyboard in Figure 9.1.

I have created a lot of media elements already for you. You can find them on the companion CD-ROM in the Exercises folder. Whenever I mention one of these files in a step in the exercise you are reading, go to your disc and find the correct file and import it to your current Flash project Library if you have not already done so. You could also copy the files from the Exercises folder on the disc to your computer, to save yourself time trying to find them. It's up to you.

## Create a Title Screen

No matter whether you are making a video game or animated film in Flash, you will need to make a title/intro screen. This is the first thing the viewer will see when the Flash .SWF file opens up. It is exceedingly easy to make one, but with a little extra keyboard grease you can make yours special.

1. Open a new Flash file (ActionScript 2.0).

2. I prefer to work within the Essentials workspace, but with the Library panel open and docked with the Properties panel. To do this, go to Window > Workspace > Essentials on the main Menu Bar (if you are not already in the Essentials workspace). Then, if your Library panel is not already open, go to Window > Library (or Ctrl + L in Windows, Command + L on Macs) to open it. If it opens as a floating panel, click-drag it to the Properties panel (in the Essentials workspace, this is found on the right) and let go when you see the blue border surround that other panel, docking Library with Properties.

3. In your Properties panel, look under the subsection Properties. Currently your Flash file is set to run at 24 fps, or frames per second. This may appear fast, but it will look really nice in the end, so leave it at 24.

4. Make sure, also, that your file is set to 550 × 400 px, or pixels. Standard screen size for older model PCs is 800 × 600. Typical ones today are 1024 × 768 or 1280 × 1024, but you have to make reservation for the borders, scrollbars, and other content a Web browser might have, so something around 550 × 400 is decent without being overbearing. If you plan to publish your movie for things other than webtoons, you might have to adjust the screen size. For instance, TV media needs to be larger, and mobile devices need to be smaller.

5. You will need to change the background color of your movie. Look in the Properties subsection of the Properties panel for Stage. Beside it is a small color swatch or chip. This square filled with color demonstrates the current background color, which can be any hexadecimal color you can imagine. *Hexadecimal colors* are number sequences representing Web-safe colors and are used in HTML, XHTML, CSS, SVG, and other programs. They display color combinations of red, green, and blue. Click on the swatch beside Stage to open the color swatch palette. This includes several hex color samples you might want to pick from. Whenever you become unsatisfied

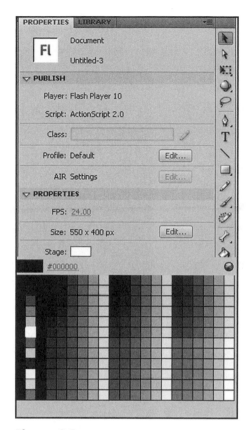

**Figure 9.2**
Color palette used to change the Stage color.

with the palette samples, you can click the color wheel icon in the upper right-most corner of the palette (see Figure 9.2) to open the Color window, where you can define your own custom color. For now, pick the color black as your background color. Black's hex color is #000000.

6. To insert a new layer, right-click on the current layer, Layer 1, and choose to Insert Layer from the pop-up options list. Rename Layer 1 "Background" by double-clicking on the layer title in the Timeline until it blinks and the title is highlighted, then type directly in the new title. Rename Layer 2 (your new layer) "Title," as this is the layer we'll put our title screen items on.

7. Insert a new layer above the Title layer and name it "Actions." Although we will not focus on programming overmuch in this chapter (that will come in Chapter 13, "Programming a Short Game"), we do have a little programming to do here.

8. Open the Actions panel by going to Window > Actions on the main menu. Since we won't do a whole lot of scripting right now, there is no need to dock the Actions panel or keep it open for long. Click on Frame 1 of your Actions layer in the Timeline, and then look at your Actions panel, on the left-hand side of that panel. If your Global Functions is not expanded yet, click on it once to expand it, and then click on Timeline Control once to expand it as well. Make sure that, on the right-hand side of the panel, the tab at the bottom under the white input field says "Actions: 1." This means that you have Frame 1 of the Actions layer selected. Double-click on the "stop" function under Global Functions, Timeline Control, and you should see "stop();" appear in the white input field to the right (as shown in Figure 9.3). This function tells your Flash movie to stop on this frame, or freeze, and go no further. A little lower-case letter A will appear in Frame 1 of your Actions layer on the Timeline to show you that an action has been placed there. Close your Actions panel for now.

9. Click on Frame 1 of the Title layer. Get your Text tool from the toolbox. Click and drag to create a textbox on the Stage. The textbox should be smaller than the Stage, so that the text can be read. Then type the following: "Wake Up Call for Count Stunkula by. . ." and your name. As you can see in Figure 9.4, I used a creepy-looking font. You can change the font you use for your text in the Properties panel. There you can also change the font size,

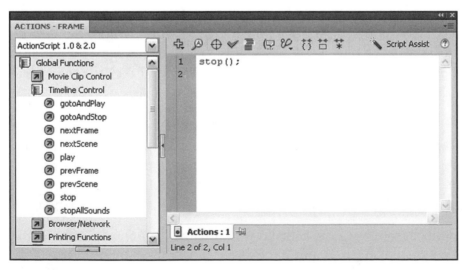

**Figure 9.3**
Add a "stop();" function to Frame 1 of your Actions layer.

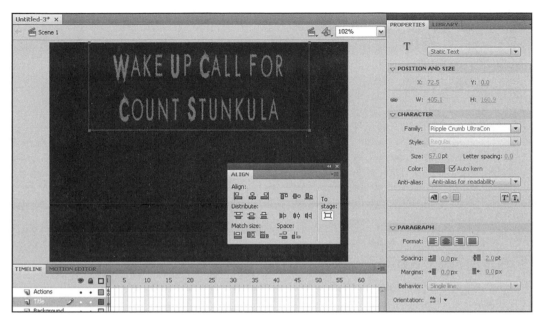

**Figure 9.4**
Add a title to your Stage and align it so that it looks nice.

paragraph formatting, and more. Because we are using a black background color, you will want to pick a vibrant font color. I chose primary red (#FF0000). I also center-aligned my text, which you can do in the Paragraph subsection of the Properties panel.

**Tip**

Flash uses whatever fonts are currently stored on your computer to generate a font list. If you want to add more fonts from such great Websites as 1001 Free Fonts (http://www.1001freefonts .com), Urban Fonts (http://www.urbanfonts.com), or Font Space (http://www.fontspace.com), feel free to do so. After adding them to your system's font folder (in Windows, this is typically found in C:\WINDOWS\Fonts), you will need to restart the Flash program so that it can reinitialize your font list.

10. Open the Align panel (Window > Align on the main menu). The Align panel is great for aligning your objects to your Stage in unique ways. First, make sure that the To Stage button is highlighted, meaning that it is active. Then, click the Distribute Horizontal Center and the Align Top Edge buttons to move your title text to the center of your Stage and flush with the top edge of your Stage. Close your Align panel when you are done.

11. The movie will stop on this title until the viewer decides he wants to watch the show. When he does so, he will click a button that reads, "Play." Let's add that button now. Use your Text tool to make another text object—this time that reads, "Play." You can use the same or a different font.

**Tip**

Here's a quick design tip for you: Stick with just a few similar-appearing fonts in each of your Flash movies. This lends a certain "look" and consistency to your project. If you get carried away and use a bunch of different fonts in a single project, your movie can look too busy or even gaudy.

12. Right-click on your Play text and choose to Convert to Symbol from the pop-up options list. In the Convert to Symbol window (see Figure 9.5), make your symbol a button symbol named "btn_play." This will make a symbol out of your text that you can put ActionScript to.

13. Button symbols have their own timeline. Double-click on the button instance on Stage to see what I mean. Buttons have an Up, Over, Down, and Hit frame. The Up frame is what the button looks like when left alone. The Over frame is what the button looks like when you mouse over it. The Down frame is what the button looks like when you click it with your

**Figure 9.5**
Make a Play button for your movie.

mouse. And the Hit frame defines the parameter of the clickable area for the button. If you do not add a keyframe to the Over, Down, or Hit frames, then Flash automatically uses the Up frame for them by default. So, technically, after making your Play text a button, you don't need to edit it any further, but we will just to make it look better.

14. Add a keyframe to the Over frame by right-clicking that frame and choosing Insert Keyframe from the pop-up options list. Deselect everything on your Stage by clicking once off the Stage. Then select the Play text again. Look in the Properties panel, and change the size (make the text slightly bigger) and the color (make it duller). This will alter the look of the Play button when you mouse over it.

15. Add a keyframe to the Down frame by right-clicking that frame and choosing Insert Keyframe. Deselect everything, again, and then select your Play text. In the Properties panel, change the color of your text (make it brighter). This will alter the look of the Play button when you click it.

16. Compare your work to Figure 9.6.

17. Double-click off your Stage to exit the symbol editing mode and return to the main project. Test your Play button. Go to Control > Enable Simple Buttons on the main menu. This will allow you to interact with your new button just as if it were in the final published file. You can see how it behaves when you mouse over and click on it, but it will not react even if it had ActionScript attached to it. Go to Control > Enable Simple Buttons again to turn this testing function off.

**Figure 9.6**
Design a look to your button by changing its appearance through the Timeline.

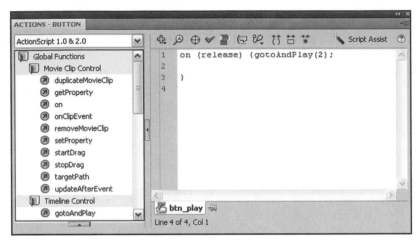

**Figure 9.7**
Add a script to your Play button.

18. With your Play button selected, open your Actions panel. Under Global
Functions, expand Movie Clip Control. Double-click "on" under Movie
Clip Control. The pop-up tips help guide you through the scripting phase.
Here, you will want to pick "release" because this means when the button is
pressed, the mouse is released. Move your cursor between the open brackets
to the right of the script. This is where the instructions will go that tells the
Flash Player what to do when the button is pressed and the mouse
is released. Choose "gotoAndPlay" from the Timeline Control in the
Global Functions on the left. All you have to do is type in the number 2,
which tells the computer you want to move to Frame 2 when the button is
clicked. Your screen should appear like the one in Figure 9.7.

## Create a Movie Clip Bat

The last thing we need to add to our title screen is some graphic or animation to
make it interesting to look at. Text on a blank screen does not make a very
interesting opening to our movie, does it?

Think of your title screen as your audience's first impression. Right now, they
have nothing besides the font choices you've made to go on when it comes to first
impressions. So let's add some animation!

To make an animation on a still frame, as we are doing here (remember, Frame 1
has been frozen by the "stop();" action we added to it), we will need to make a

movie-clip, which is a little like having a mini Flash movie embedded in our bigger Flash movie.

1. Go to File > Import > Import to Library on the main menu. Find the folder marked Exercises in the companion CD-ROM. Select all of the files within the Chapter 9 folder. To select all, you can hold down the Shift key while clicking on the first and final files, or click-drag a marquee to select all file icons within the window. Import all files to your current project Library. Once imported, these files will appear in your current project's Library. In that panel, you will be able to see a preview of them in the upper window area, and you can see what they will look like against the background color of our movie. It is smart to organize your files by putting all the sounds in a Sounds layer folder, all the graphics in a Graphics layer folder, all Stunky's body parts in a separate layer folder, and so on. That way you stay organized, and (with so many files to have to sort through) you can find the files you need faster. For now, find Bat.png. Most bats are black, but this one is purple to make it stand out against the black Stage color.

2. Drag and drop the Bat.png graphic to the Stage. Yes, this is only a head for now; we will add the wings soon. First, we need to shrink the head, as it is awfully large for our Stage. Use the Free Transform tool to resize it. Hold down the Shift key on your keyboard as you drag one of the corner handles to resize the bat head proportionally, because we don't want him looking all squished. See Figure 9.8.

3. Right-click on your bat and choose to Convert to Symbol, this time making it a movie clip called "mc_bat." You might notice how I am labeling my

**Figure 9.8**
Place and size your bat graphic accordingly.

symbols. First, there was the button symbol I had you call "btn_play," and now there is this movie clip symbol I have you call "mc_bat." Part of the reason I do this is to keep types of symbols apart, but since Flash shows you a different kind of icon in the Library for each, that's sort of redundant. I also do it because otherwise Flash likes to sort objects in the Library alphabetically, and I often organize my objects into different folders: one for movie clips, one for buttons, and another for graphics. By adding "mc_" or "btn_" or "img_" to the start of my symbols, I can keep them apart alphabetically to sort them into folders easier later.

4. Double-click on your new mc_bat symbol to enter its editing mode. See how movie clips are given their own timeline? It's identical to a regular Flash movie, only embedded inside another Flash movie.

5. Create a new layer above Layer 1. Here, we will create a shape tween. Choose the Brush tool and pick a purple Fill color. To get an exact purple that matches your bat head, do this: Click on the swatch beside Fill in the Properties panel when your Brush tool is selected. When you move your mouse away from the color swatch palette, see how your cursor becomes an eyedropper. Move your eyedropper tip over the center of the bat head, over the purple part, and click once. Your chosen hex color should switch to #B885BB.

6. On Frame 1 of Layer 2, draw wings on your bat with your Brush tool, being sure to fill in so there are no empty spaces (see Figure 9.9).

**Figure 9.9**
Add wings to your bat.

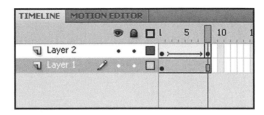

**Figure 9.10**
Add a shape tween to your bat wings.

7. Right-click on Frame 1 of Layer 2 and choose to Create Shape Tween. Right-click again and choose to Copy Frames. Go to Frame 8 of Layer 2, right-click, and choose to Paste Frames. You should see that you have two black dots (keyframes) and a solid arrow between them (your tween) and that the frames are colored green (shape tween). See Figure 9.10. Nothing is happening, because the start and end keyframes are the same, which we'll fix in a jiff.

8. However, first, our bat head has disappeared after Frame 1. We have to change that. Right-click on Frame 8 of Layer 1 and choose to Insert Frame. There! That was easy enough.

9. Right-click on Frame 4 of Layer 2 and choose to Insert Blank Keyframe. There are no wings here, so draw them. Use the Brush tool and draw a pair of wings as if in their full swoop down, like in Figure 9.11. If you scrub through your Timeline (meaning, if you grab the red bar above the frames in

**Figure 9.11**
Draw the downward swoop of your bat's flight.

the Timeline and click-drag it left and right to preview your animation), you will see a disturbing thing: Your shape tweening goes wonky! To fix this, we will need to add some shape hints. *Shape hints* are tiny markers that can smooth shape tweening.

10. Deselect everything. Click on Frame 1 of Layer 1 on your Timeline. Go to Modify > Shape > Add Shape Hint to insert a shape hint to your Stage. Note that the hotkey for this is Ctrl + Shift + H (Win) or Command + Shift + H (Mac). Click-drag your shape hint to the side of the left wing that touches the bat head. Go to Frame 4 and move the same shape hint to the same place. Go back to Frame 1 and add another shape hint, moving it to the tip of the left wing. Return to Frame 4 and move the same shape hint to the tip of the left wing here, too. Now scrub your animation back and forth between Frame 1 and 4 and see the difference. Do the same thing to the right wing. Compare your Frames 1 and 4 to Figure 9.12.

11. Now add shape hints for Frames 4 and 8, to help connect those two. This will mean that Frame 4 will show shape hints for both shape tweening from Frames 1 to 4 and Frames 4 to 8. If you get lost which shape hint is supposed to be which, take a look at their designations. Each one has a lower-case letter of the alphabet attached to it, starting with the letter A. A goes with A, B goes with B, and so on.

12. When you have your wings animation the way you want it to look, lock that layer by clicking the lock icon. Now we need to add a body wiggle on the bat head layer (Layer 1). Right-click on Frame 1 of Layer 1 and Create Classic Tween. Right-click on Frame 8 of Layer 1 and Insert Keyframe. The reason I have started both tweens this way, with a start and end keyframe the same, is because I am making a looping cycle. A looping cycle

**Figure 9.12**
Use shape hints to fix your wings' shape tween.

means that this animation can go on forever, because when it gets to the end it starts all over again. So I want the start and end frames to appear exactly the same, so there's no blip.

13. Insert a keyframe on Frame 4 of Layer 1. Use the Selection tool and/or the up arrow key on your keyboard to move the bat head up a bit, but not far enough that you break him away from his wings. Scrub through your animation, or if you like, press Enter (Win) or Return (Mac) to see the playback of your animation. He should look as though he's flapping his wings and bobbing in the air slightly. You're done! Now it is time to start the movie.

14. Exit the symbol editing mode and return to your main project (Scene 1). Save your file (if you have not done so already) as Wakeup.fla.

## Create a Movie Clip Clock and a Tweened Animation

The first part of our movie will show Count Stunkula getting out of his coffin after his alarm goes off. The second part (demonstrated in the next section) will have his walk cycle. The last part is him opening the door and getting a face full of sunrays, turning him into a pile of ash. Let's begin.

1. Insert a new layer called "Clock" above the others. Insert a new keyframe on Frame 2 of the Clock layer. Drag the Clock_body.png image to the Stage. Right-click on the graphic and convert it to a movie clip symbol called "mc_alarmclock." Double-click on the clock instance on Stage to enter its editing mode.

2. Insert a new layer above Layer 1. Drag the Clock_bells.png image from your Library to the Stage on Layer 2 of your Timeline. Position the clock bells image above the clock body image, as you see in Figure 9.13.

3. Right-click on Frame 2 of Layer 2 and insert a new keyframe there. Rotate the bells slightly to the left. Right-click on Frame 3 of Layer 2 and insert a new keyframe there, where you will rotate the bells the opposite direction. Right-click on Frame 1 and choose to Copy Frames, then go to Frame 4 and Paste Frames.

4. Now add a new keyframe on Frames 2 and 3 of Layer 1, and use the Free Transform tool to slightly squash the clock body on 2 and stretch it out on 3. Then copy Frame 1 to Frame 4. This completes the alarm clock animation.

**Figure 9.13**
Position the clock and table just so.

5. Insert a new layer above Layer 2. Drag the Alarm-clock.wav file from your Library to the Stage when you have Layer 3 selected.

6. Return to Scene 1. Add a new layer just underneath the Clock layer in the stacking order, and call your new layer "Table." Insert a keyframe on Frame 2 of the Table layer's Timeline. Drag the Castle_table.png image to the Stage on Frame 2 of the Table layer. Arrange the table to be under the alarm clock (see Figure 9.13).

7. Insert a new layer folder (Insert > Timeline > Layer Folder on the main menu). Name the layer folder "Stunky." All the layers with corresponding parts making up our leading character will go in this layer folder. Go ahead and create several layers inside the Stunky folder. In descending stacking order, they should be mouth, eyes, head, body, neck, leg2, leg1, arm2, arm1, and tail (see Figure 9.14).

8. Don't worry about what we are going to do with these layers. For now, select Stunky's arm1 layer, and place a blank keyframe on Frame 2. With this frame selected, you can drag-and-drop the Stunky_arm1.png image from the Library to the Stage.

9. Note how the hand of Stunky_arm1.png seems to disappear, because the hand is black and our Stage color is black. For this reason, and for appearances, we need to add some color to our background. Select the Background layer and insert a blank keyframe on Frame 2. In this frame, use the Brush tool to paint a swab of color in the background. It's okay if you

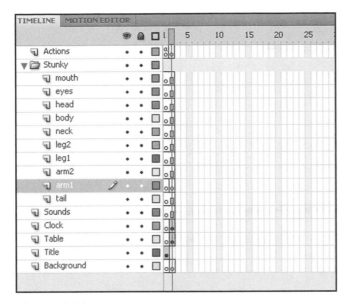

**Figure 9.14**
Create a layer folder just for Stunky's parts.

paint outside the borders of the Stage, too. As you paint, it might look as though you are painting over the top of your other objects, but when you let up on your mouse you should see the paint stays in the Background layer. Compare your work to Figure 9.15.

10. Create a classic tween on the arm you placed on the arm1 layer. In Frame 2, you want it to be completely off the Stage somewhere to the left. Also, rotate

**Figure 9.15**
Paint a swab of contrasting background color.

it so the fingers are reaching up to the sky. Create a keyframe on Frames 65, 68, 70, and 75. On Frame 65, the arm needs to be rotated down, back in the scene, and on top of the clock. On Frame 68, the arm should be moving up, rotated slightly. You can also make use of the Free Transform tool to skew and resize the arm slightly on both 68 and 70. On Frame 70, the hand comes back down, as if it finally found the "off" switch on the alarm clock. On Frame 75, the arm leaves the scene quickly, rotated down where the fingers are reaching the ground and the arm is taken off the bottom of the Stage, out of sight.

11. It might be easier to see what you are doing, because after leaving Frame 2 all the other objects disappear. They existed only on Frame 2. To extend the appearance of a layer, go to Frame 75 and insert a frame. The objects should pop into view.

12. Click somewhere between Frames 2 and 65 on the arm1 layer. In the Properties panel, add an Ease of -100, so that the arm descends slowly but gets quicker when it gets closer to the clock (called a *slow-in*).

13. On Frame 70 of the Clock layer, insert a keyframe, and then select the clock object in that frame. Right-click on it and choose to Break Apart. This reduces the movie clip symbol to its basic components, without changing their size and relationship to the Stage. In effect, we have stopped the alarm clock from shaking.

14. However, the sound effect of the alarm clock will keep going. It looks pretty funny that our alarm clock has stopped moving, but the alarm keeps on going! Let's fix that. Go to Frame 70 on the Actions layer and insert a keyframe. With this new frame selected, open the Actions panel. Under Timeline Control you will find an action called "stopAllSounds." Double-click on this action to add "stopAllSounds();" to the input field for Frame 70.

**Tip**

Occasionally you will find it difficult to access the object you are trying to click on the Stage. When this happens, decide what layer the object exists on. Lock all the other layers by clicking on the Lock All button at the top of the layers in the Timeline, and then unlock just the layer you want to work in. You can also set the visibility of all the other layers, in case you need to see behind objects to get your work done. Just remember to unhide or unlock the layers when you are through!

## Create Your First Fluppet

Jon Kuramoto, Gary Leib, and Daniel Gray wrote a book in 2001 called *The Art of Cartooning with Flash: The Twinkle Guide to Flash Character Animation* (Sybex). In it, they describe what they call "the Twinkle method," which is, more or less, creating a digital Flash puppet and animating it.

Flash puppets, or *fluppets* as Gary Leib calls them, are animated characters constructed from smaller individual parts.

A fluppet typically is made from separate symbols, like two eyes, one mouth, a head, hair, a torso, clothes, two arms, and two legs. These symbols are given their own layers in Flash and can then be manipulated to create the illusion of movement. For example, imagine a character like a Powerpuff Girl. You can rotate her legs to make her look like she is kicking or walking down a street, and you can rotate her arms to make her appear to be swinging or punching with them. You can resize her eyes to make them widen in surprise or shrink in suspicion. You can do all this by repositioning her parts and setting up keyframe animation. As an added bonus, using symbols in this way leads to shorter file sizes and increases upload/download speeds.

We are going to make Count Stunkula a fluppet. Here is how.

1. Insert a blank keyframe on Frame 76 of the Background layer. Drag the CastleBG.png to the Stage. Scale it with the Free Transform tool so that it fits the Stage, as shown in Figure 9.16.

2. Add the Coffin.png image, Castle_table.png image, Clock_body.png image, and Clock_bells.png image to your Stage. Resize them as you see in Figure 9.17, and use Modify > Arrange from the main menu to sort them so that the coffin looks like it is in front of the table, the clock is on top of the table, and the clock bells are on top of the clock.

3. Create a new layer called "Stunky_bat" with a keyframe on Frame 76. Shrink the bat so that he is about the size of the pillow in the coffin and positioned inside that coffin. Add a classic motion tween to that frame. Create a keyframe on Frame 130 on the same layer, and move the bat from left to right and nearer the floor. You will have to extend the frames for the Background layer to be able to see the floor. For now, this will animate our bat to travel in a direct line from the coffin to the floor. We will change that!

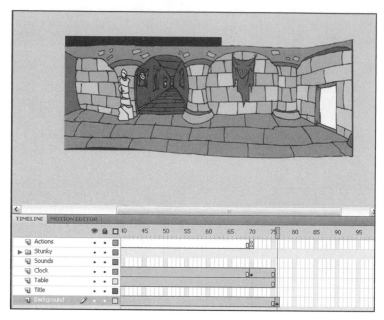

**Figure 9.16**
Add the CastleBG.png image to the Stage like so.

**Figure 9.17**
Decorate your castle.

4. Create a layer above the Stunky_bat one, and call it "Guide." Right-click on it and choose Properties from the pop-up options list to open the Properties window. Here, you will want to set the Guide layer to Guide by clicking that radio button before clicking OK. See Figure 9.18.

5. On the Guide layer, use the Pencil tool to draw a squiggly line from the coffin to the floor. You can see my squiggly line in Figure 9.19. I turned the

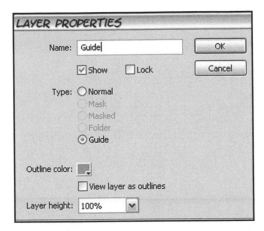

**Figure 9.18**
Convert the Guide layer to a *real* Guide layer!

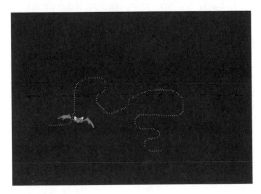

**Figure 9.19**
Draw a squiggly guide line.

visibility of the Background layer off, so you could see the line better, and then I turned it back on after the screenshot.

6. Click and drag your Stunky_bat layer under the Guide layer, until you see the dark line appear like in Figure 9.20. When you let go, you should see the layer icon for your Guide layer change: It should show an arc. If you were to open the layer properties for your Stunky_bat layer, you would see that it has become a Guided layer.

7. When you publish the movie later, the Guide layer will become invisible, but (as you can see by scrubbing through the animation) the bat will follow the pencil line on the Guide layer, giving it an erratic flight pattern as it moves from the coffin to the floor.

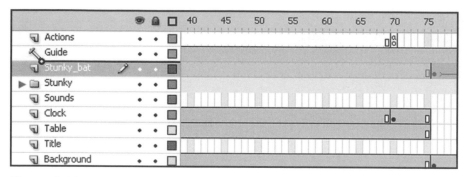

**Figure 9.20**
Make the Stunky_bat layer a Guided layer.

8. We want to add a transformation cloud for when Count Stunkula turns into the bat in his coffin, and when he changes from a bat to himself on the floor. Create a new layer above the Guide layer. Call it "Poof." Insert a keyframe on Frame 76. Use the Brush tool set to a gray Fill color to draw a puff cloud that covers up the bat. Create a classic tween here with a keyframe on Frame 85. Deselect everything, and then click on the cloud on Frame 85. In the Properties panel, set the Color Effect to Alpha 0% (completely transparent). This makes the cloud seem to disappear in 9 frames.

9. Insert a keyframe on Frame 128 of the Poof layer. Move the cloud to the floor, where the bat will come to rest. Create another keyframe on Frame 130, where the Alpha should be set to 100% (completely visible) and resized so it's bigger.

10. Insert another keyframe on Frame 140, making the cloud stretched even bigger, and then another keyframe on Frame 145 where it's smaller and its Alpha is again at 0%, or transparent.

11. Insert a blank keyframe on Frame 140 on the Stunky layers. Drag to the Stage, resize, and arrange the following files (use Figure 9.21 as a guide):
    - Stunky_mouthMBP.png > Mouth
    - Stunky_eyes1.png > Eyes
    - Stunky_head1.png > Head
    - Stunky_arm2.png > Arm1
    - Stunky_body1.png > Body
    - Stunky_tail1.png > Tail

12. Before adding the arm to the Arm1 layer, there's something you have to do first! Scroll back up the Timeline to where we had our previous arm. Create a

**Figure 9.21**
Assemble Stunky's various body parts.

blank keyframe on Frame 76. Then add another blank keyframe on Frame 140 to add the arm image. The frames in between Frames 76 and 140 should appear white, indicating they are blank and do not have any residual tweens on them.

13. Copy the Stunky_arm2.png image file on the Arm1 layer on Frame 140. Create a blank keyframe on Frame 140 on the Arm2 layer, right-click the Stage, and choose to Paste In Place. Go to Modify > Transform > Flip Horizontal, and then move the arm to the right side of Stunky so that he has two arms, as you see in Figure 9.22.

14. Create a classic tween on the mouth layer and make the mouth rotate, or slide up to the right slightly, between Frames 140 and 160, then return to the same position it was in Frame 140 on Frame 175.

15. Create a classic tween on both the arm1 and arm2 layers to show them rise up in the air, rotating from his shoulders, between Frames 140 and 160, then dropping to his sides in Frame 175. Add a slow-in by experimenting with the Ease factor.

16. Create a classic tween on the Body layer to show the body gently rising up between Frames 140 and 160, then going back to its original position on Frame 175.

**Figure 9.22**
Add Stunky's other arm by duplicating the one.

17. Create a classic tween on the Tail layer to show the tail slide gently side to side from Frames 140 to 175 (I used a keyframe on 155, but you can put them where you see fit). Add a slow-out by experimenting with the Ease factor.

18. Extend the Timelines of the Eyes layer, Head layer, and Background layer to Frame 175. Save your file.

## Create a Lip Synch

Count Stunkula has awoken from his coffin! After a brief stretch, before he gets going, we need him to say a few words. First, you need to record a voiceover for Count Stunkula. Then, you are going to take that recording and use the mouth symbols given for you in the Exercise files to create lip synching on Stage.

1. Use Audacity to create a .WAV file. Record yourself or one of your friends saying something similar to the following: "Night again! Great Scott, I'm terribly thirsty. Don't feel like I slept very long, either. Ah well. . . time for a sip from some young maiden!" Finish your recording with an evil laugh.

2. Import your .WAV file into your Flash Library.

3. Create a blank keyframe on Frame 176 of a new layer called Sounds. With your new frame selected, drag-and-drop your .WAV file to the Stage. You should see the waveform appear in the Sounds layer, but since you are only

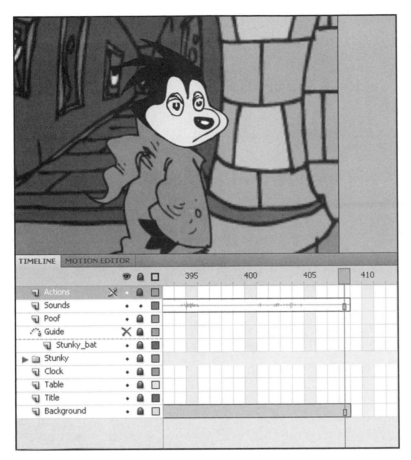

**Figure 9.23**
Extend your Sounds layer until the waveform stops.

seeing a single frame there isn't much to look at. Right-click on Frame 185 of the Sounds layer and insert a frame. Still, you can't see the end of the waveform. Click-and-drag the frame on Frame 185 to the right. Where you let go it will rest, and you will see the waveform unfold. Keep going until the waveform stops. Mine did on Frame 408, as you can see in Figure 9.23.

4. Now go back and add a blank keyframe on Frame 176 on Stunky's Head layer. Drag-and-drop the Stunky_head3.png image to the Stage. On Frame 176 of Stunky's Body layer, add a blank keyframe and remove the tween that's there. Add Stunky_body2.png to the Stage. Add a blank keyframe to Frame 176 of the Background layer and place a super-enlarged instance of CastleBG.png to the Stage. Arrange your pictures so they look like

**Figure 9.24**
Set up your medium close-up shot of Stunky as so.

Figure 9.24. You might extend the frames on these three layers out to your final frame number for your voiceover.

5. Go to Stunky's Mouth layer. Use the Brush tool to draw a line for the closed Stunky mouth on Frame 176 of the Mouth layer. Then with the Selection tool, click on the mouth to select it. Go to Modify > Convert to Symbol (hotkey F8) on the main menu. Make this a movie clip symbol named "mc_mouthtalking." Double-click on your new symbol when you get done to enter the editing mode for that symbol.

6. Create a shape tween starting on Frame 1. On Frame 4, insert a blank keyframe where you will use the Brush tool to draw an open mouth. On Frame 8, insert another blank keyframe showing the mouth open as wide as it will get (I also painted a red tongue inside mine). On Frame 12, insert another blank keyframe and draw the mouth open a little ways, as it will be shutting now. Copy and paste Frame 1 to Frame 15, to end the loop. Look at what I did in Figure 9.25. When done with your mc_mouthtalking clip, exit the editing mode and return to Scene 1, Frame 176. Copy your new movie clip to the Clipboard by selecting it and pressing Ctrl + C (Win) or Command + C (Mac).

**Tip**

To see your sound's waveform better as you do lip synching in Flash, you will probably want to change how you see the individual frames in the Timeline. You can do this by clicking on the list options button at the top-right of the Timeline panel; here you will see options such as Tiny, Small, Normal, Medium, Large, Preview, and Preview in Context. I found it easiest to see my waveform in Preview in Context, but when I encountered problems seeing my frames I had to switch back to Normal. Play around until you find the easiest viewing mode for what you are doing.

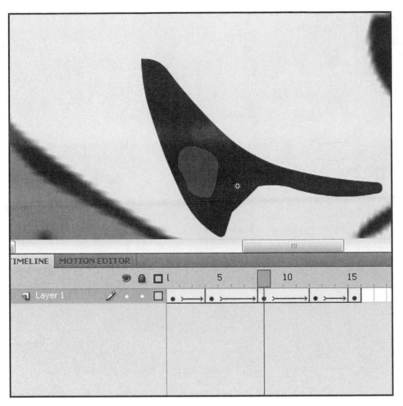

**Figure 9.25**
Set up a shape tween for your character's mouth when talking.

7. Depending on your version of Flash and how you have it set up, you can sometimes hear the sound on the Sounds layer as you scrub through your animation. This can be a boon to you when testing your lip synching! Regardless, you should, along the waveform, see bouncing spikes where there is a rise in pitch and straight lines where there is none. Along the Mouth layer, insert blank keyframes on the frames right before the rise in pitch starts and paste a copy of your new movie clip. Insert blank keyframes right after a wave, before it turns into a straight line, and leave it blank for now. Do this until you have filled the Mouth layer from beginning of the recorded sound to the end. Where you left blanks along the Mouth layer, you will paste a copy of a closed mouth, which you can draw with your Brush tool or copy from the first of the mc_mouthtalking movie clip.

8. When you get done with the mouth, it is time to work on the Eyes layer. There are several Stunky eyes to choose from in your Library. Occasionally, a skunk has to blink, so I am going to make Stunky a blinking eyes movie clip.

**Figure 9.26**
Add Stunky's eyes.

You can, too, if you like. Drag Stunky_eyes2.png to the Stage and position it how you like on Frame 176 of the Eyes layer. Then convert these eyes into a movie clip called "mc_blinkingeyes," and enter its editing mode by double-clicking it on the Stage. On Frame 1 of Layer 1 add a classic tween. On Frame 4 insert a new keyframe and use the Free Transform tool to squash the eyes. Insert a blank keyframe on Frame 5 and remove the tween from it. Drag an instance of Stunky_eyes1.png to his face on the Stage and resize/position it as you like. Then copy Frame 4 to Frame 6, add a classic tween to it, and copy Frame 1 to Frame 9. That's all you need for a simple eye blink! Look at my example in Figure 9.26.

9. Exit the editing mode. You will have to alternate between a normal pair of eyes (I used Stunky_eyes4.png) and your mc_blinkingeyes symbol. Fill your frames first with the normal pair of eyes you want to use, and then place pairs of keyframes where you want the blinks to start and to end. In total, in my Flash movie, I have Stunky blink four times during this intercourse.

**Tip**

When it comes to animating eyes, it is better in the long run if you use Flash's drawing tools to draw them in separate oval parts: one large oval for the eyeball and one smaller oval for the pupil. That way, you can animate the pupil separate from the eyeball, like when you need characters to look to the left or to the right, or when you want the pupil to dilate (become smaller) because the character is afraid or angry. I have not elected to do this in this short demonstration, but you should try out the technique in your own projects afterward.

## Create a Walk Cycle

His little spiel concluded, Count Stunkula must walk to the door and open it as if going out. The easiest way to get him walking is to animate his fluppet doing a walk cycle. I have a very basic walk cycle in mind.

1. In the Background layer, copy and paste Frame 76 to the final frame, after Stunky's lip synch. There are several graphic images that I have given you in the Chapter 9 folder for decorating the castle. There's a suit of armor, a cobweb and spider, an open book, and much more. Go ahead and add any of these you like to the area off Stage to become a part of the background at this time. Arrange them where you like.

2. When you are through, add a classic tween starting this frame, go 100 frames to the right of it, and insert another keyframe. On your final keyframe, use the Selection tool to select the background (which is now a single tween symbol) and drag it to the left, until the yellow doorway can be seen and the edge of the castle background touches the furthest right edge of the Stage.

3. Add blank keyframes to all of your Stunky body parts layers on the same frame where you start the tween for the background moving. On Arm1, Arm2, and Tail, you might have to remove a tween from the new keyframes, back up a few frames, and remove a tween from there, and delete the symbols apparent on Stage on those earlier frames, too. Otherwise, when you run your movie you'll see arms and tails floating over the top of Stunky talking.

4. Add the following graphic images to their layers (leaving Mouth, Arm1, and Arm2 blank). Arrange them as you see in Figure 9.27.
   - Stunky_eyes7.png > Eyes
   - Stunky_head2.png > Head
   - Stunky_body2.png > Body
   - Stunky_neck.png > Neck
   - Stunky_foot.png > Leg1, Leg2
   - Stunky_tail2.png > Tail

5. Create a classic tween for the Leg1 layer and a new keyframe every 15 to 20 frames, rotating up in the air to the right, then back down again, then

**Figure 9.27**
Put Stunky together to prepare him for walking.

rotating up behind him to the left, and back down again. It might be best, before you start, to set the transformation point of the foot symbol in the upper left-hand corner of the image, near the top of the leg, so that you rotate from the top of the leg rather than the center of the image. After you finish a short cycle, you can probably copy-and-paste these frames until you reach the end of the background layer's tween.

6. Repeat this with the Leg2 layer, but take it in the opposite direction. Where Leg1 may go to the right, take Leg2 to the left, and so on.

7. Create a classic tween on the Tail layer. Every 40 or so frames move the tail so that it looks like it is dipping up and down. You can move the transformation point of the tail symbol to the bottom right, where the tail would connect with Stunky's body, for more realistic rotation, just as you did in the legs. Stop the tail's animation when Stunky comes to a rest at the door.

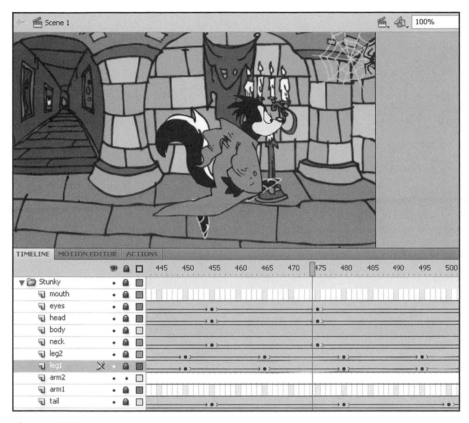

**Figure 9.28**
When through, scrub through your walk cycle to see how it looks.

8. Do the same thing with the head, eyes, and neck layer. You can nudge the head down and to the right for a better bob, and rotate the neck to follow the head. The eyes need to keep up with the head, so where the head goes the eyes should go, too.

9. Compare your walk cycle to Figure 9.28.

## Finish Him!

Now Count Stunkula is at the door! He opens it, discovers sunshine, and falls to pieces. Here is what I have in store for him.

1. Insert a new layer you call "Door." Go to the same frame number on the Door layer that the background image starts its tween on, insert a keyframe, and drag an instance of Castle_door1.png to the Stage. Use the Free

Transform tool to position, scale, and skew the door so that it covers up the yellow doorway at the end of the castle background.

2. Create a classic tween on the Door layer, because the door must move with the background into view. Put a stop after 100 frames just like you did with the Background layer, and you should be good.

3. Once in place, add a keyframe to the very next frame for the Stunky parts you used at the end of the walk cycle, the castle background, and the door. Did you know you can do a similar operation to more than one frame at once, even on different layers? Holding the Ctrl (Win) or Command (Mac) key down, you can select more than one frame at a time. They darken as they are selected. Then right-click on one of them to insert a new keyframe on all of them.

4. Insert a keyframe in Arm1, as well, and drag an instance of Stunky_arm3.png to the Stage. Shrink and position it on the other side of Stunky, because physically this will be Stunky's left arm. Move the transformation point of this arm to the shoulder. Create a classic tween. Go 15 frames out and place a keyframe. Rotate the arm up, as though the hand is reaching to grab the door's handle. Extend the frames of Stunky, the door, and the castle background, so that the scene is still complete, as shown in Figure 9.29.

5. Insert a blank keyframe after the last one in the Arm1 layer. You will probably need to extend the viewable frames for the other scene elements here, too. In the blank keyframe you put on the Arm1 layer, drag an instance of Stunky_arm3.png and resize it. Place the hand over the handle of the door, and the two should match up so that it looks just like Stunkula is gripping the door handle, as shown in Figure 9.30.

6. Insert a new blank keyframe after the last one in the Door layer. Go ahead and extend your frames, all except for Arm1, so you can see the world as it looks now. Drag an instance of Castle_door2.png to the Stage on the new frame of the Door layer. It might help to turn the Onion Skins function on to see where your last door image was, so that you can resize this door to fit neatly to size. The button that turns Onion Skins on for you is shown in Figure 9.31. Onion Skins shows you a ghost image on the Stage of all the

**Figure 9.29**
Make Stunky reach for the door handle.

frames surrounding the current chosen one. The number of frames shown at a given time with Onion Skins is set by the brackets above the Timeline layers, also shown in Figure 9.31.

7. Insert a new layer after the last one in the Background layer and drag an instance of Sun.png to the Stage. Fill the entire Stage. It might look better, like it's looking back at Stunky, if we flip the sun horizontally (Modify > Transform > Flip Horizontal on the main menu). Go out 15 frames and insert a blank keyframe on the Background layer. Go back to the last frame you had showing the castle background, copy that object, and paste it on the new blank keyframe.

**Figure 9.30**
The next arm you use will make it look like Stunky is gripping the door handle.

8. On the Door layer, go to the last visible frame and right after it place a blank keyframe. This sort of clears the art-board, so you can start with a blank slate, so to speak. Now go to the castle interior shot right after the sun on the Background layer. Find that frame number and on the Door layer, place a blank keyframe with an instance of Castle_door1.png. Flip it horizontally, and resize and position it so that it is flush with the open doorway, as though wide open on its hinges.

9. Create a new layer and call it "Stunky—death." Insert a blank keyframe on Stunky—death on the same frame number as the one you placed right after the sun on the Background layer. Now in the scene, assemble the following Stunky parts and place them as you see in Figure 9.32: Stunky_tail4.png, Stunky_body1.png, Stunky_arm2.png, Stunky_arm1.png, Stunky_eyes1.png, and Stunky_mouthOH.png.

10. Add a classic tween animation to the frame. Go out 20 frames and add a new keyframe. Deselect your tween symbol briefly and then reselect it. In the Properties panel, under Color Effects, add the Brightness setting and set it to 100%, making Stunky turn into a completely white silhouette. Add another keyframe 5 frames over to keep him that way a while.

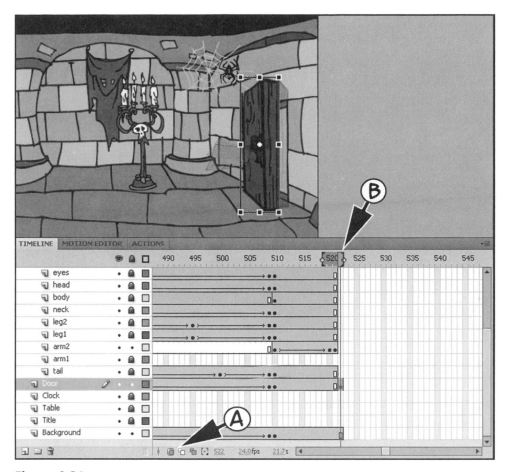

**Figure 9.31**
(A) The button that turns Onion Skins on/off, and (B) the brackets that set the number of frames Onion Skins will show you.

11. Extend the visibility of the Background and Door layers to the end of your movie.

12. Insert a blank keyframe in the next frame on the Stunky—death layer, and remove the tween. With your Brush tool, make a pile of gray ash in the air where the silhouette of Stunky is now. Add a shape tween. Go out 15 more frames and insert a blank keyframe and draw the pile of ash on the castle floor. Go out 35 more frames and insert another keyframe to keep it there a while.

13. We need to add a flash of light to cover the transition from Stunky to ash. So add a new layer above the others and call it "Whiteout." Insert

**Figure 9.32**
The parts after assembly on the Stunky—death layer. Yup, he's about to bite it!

a keyframe on the same frame number just 3 frames before Stunky's miraculous transformation to ash. Fill the Stage with a white rectangle. Use the Rectangle tool with the Fill color set to white, and align the rectangle to the Stage using the Align panel. Add a classic tween and in Properties add an Alpha Color Effect at 0%. Go to the exact frame number Stunky turns into ash and add a keyframe with an Alpha set to 100%. Go out 3 more frames and add a keyframe with the Alpha set to 0% again.

14. Extend the visibility of the Background and Door layers to the end of your movie, and then compare your work with Figure 9.33.

15. After the last visible frame of your Eyes layer, insert a blank keyframe to clear that slate, and then go out to where you have the ash pile sitting on the floor, being still. Go in a few frames and insert a blank keyframe on the Eyes layer there. Drag an instance of Stunky_eyes5.png to the Stage. Resize them and position them on top of the ash pile, and then convert them into a movie clip symbol called "mc_blinkingeyes2." Double-click to edit.

16. Squash them down to nothing in Frame 1 of Layer 1, add a classic tween, and on Frame 5 insert a keyframe where they are normal-sized. Copy Frame 1 to Frame 7 and Frame 5 to Frame 10. Add a new layer above Layer 1, and insert a keyframe on Frame 10 of it with the action "stop();" on that

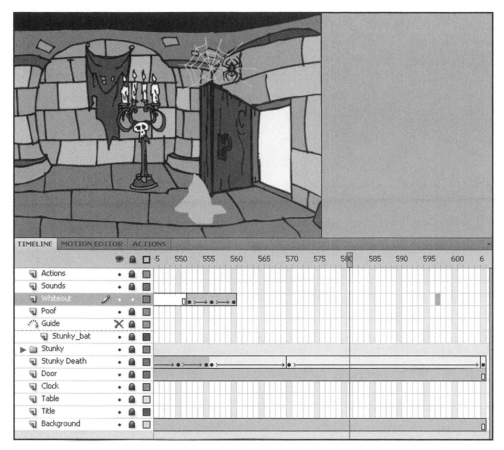

**Figure 9.33**
Stunky just became a pile of ash.

frame. Return to your project, extend the frames of the Eyes layer out to the end of your movie, and save your work.

## Add Credits

After the cartoon is through, we will want to boast. If you had friends contribute artwork, coding, voiceovers, or music, now is the best time to acknowledge their efforts.

1. Insert a blank keyframe on the last visible frame of the Title layer, which should be Frame 2. Then scroll all the way out to the end of your movie, or if you're like me, take the shortcut by going to Control > Go To End on the main menu. Insert a blank keyframe on the Title layer right after the last frame number of your movie. This will be your credits screen.

2. On your Actions layer, insert a keyframe on the same frame as your credits screen and apply a "stop();" action to freeze the animation here.

3. Use the Text tool to type your credits. They can go all the way off the bottom of your screen, if you like, but if they do, you will have to turn them into a movie clip that slowly scrolls up the screen over a period of several frames, slow enough for viewers to read.

4. On your Sounds layer, insert a keyframe on the same frame as your credits screen and drag an instance of Djring_insano.mp3 to the Stage.

5. You need to add a few more sounds to make this Flash movie better. First, scroll all the way back to Frame 1. The Sounds layer already has a blank keyframe here. Click on it, and then drag Djring_doves.mp3 to the Stage. Make another blank keyframe on Frame 2. On the play button script, add a "stopAllSounds();" action to the instructions just after the "gotoAndPlay(2);" action.

6. Add a blank keyframe on Frame 76 of the Sounds layer and drag Magic.wav from your Library to the Stage. Add another blank keyframe on Frame 78 and drag Bats.wav to the Stage. On Frame 130, put another instance of Grow.wav. On Frame 130 of the Actions layer, place a blank keyframe and the action "stopAllSounds();" onto it. On the frame number where Stunky starts opening the door, add the Wood_door.wav sound to the Stage, and on the frame number where Stunky begins to turn all white, add the Destroyed.wav sound to the Stage. Last but not least, add the Oh-drat.wav sound to the Stage on the frame number where Stunky's eyes start blinking on the ash pile.

7. Somewhere, add a button that says "Play Again?" and takes you back to Frame 2 of the movie (see Figure 9.34). The Play Again button should be scripted exactly like the Play button from the start, so that it stops all sounds, including the music playing through the credits, before jumping to Frame 2. I cheated and made a duplicate of my Play button, called it "btn_playagain," and changed what the text said.

8. You're done! Save your movie one last time and then test it out by going to Control > Test Movie on the main menu. Watch your show. If you see any trouble areas, be sure to go back to that section and evaluate what went wrong. This is by no means a perfect digital animation project. You could

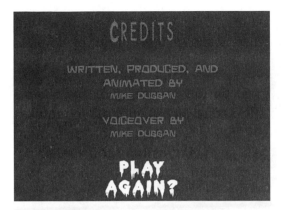

**Figure 9.34**
One example of a credits screen.

use better artwork and sound effects, and add more details to your own animation to make it so much better! But pat yourself on the back for a well-done job.

## Add a Preloader

Whew! We have come a long way, and if you take a look at the file size of our short animation, it is a hefty one. My .SWF file ended up being 550 kilobytes by this point. You can use Eltima's Flash Optimizer (found on the accompanying CD-ROM) to shrink the size of your Flash file somewhat, but it will still be quite large. Upload and download speeds for this cartoon will be more than just a few seconds, even over broadband. So, what do we do? We give the viewer something to look at while the file is loading, that's what we do!

Most Web surfers these days are used to seeing a preloader of some kind, whether it's a whirling disc of light or the simple phrase "Loading. . ." Adding a preloader to your Flash movie will be quick and painless. You can add this kind of screen to any Flash media you propose to make. It only enhances the look.

1. Create a new scene. To do so, go to Window > Other Panels > Scene (Shift + F2) on the main menu to bring up the Scene panel. Click the little Add Scene button. It's the one on the far bottom left. Your new scene, by default, will be named Scene 2, as we already have our current scene, Scene 1. Double-click the name Scene 2 in the Scene panel and rename it "Preloader." Move the Preloader scene up above Scene 1 in the stacking order, so that the movie will play the Preloader scene first.

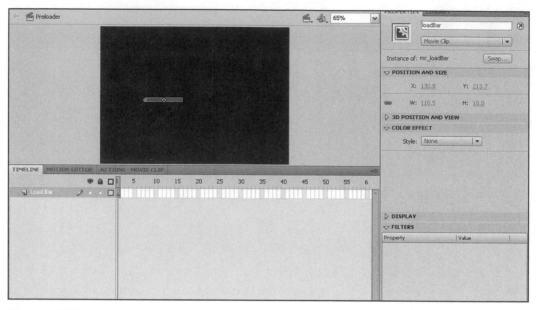

**Figure 9.35**
One example of a load bar.

2. Notice that you are currently in the Preloader scene in your Flash window. Great! Let's get started building it. Okay, the first thing we will need to start with is the load bar. Name the current layer "Load Bar." Use the Rectangle tool to create your rectangle. I made a 100 × 10 red rectangle. Be sure your rectangle has no Stroke color. If you forget to disable the Stroke before making your shape, you can always double-click on the outline after you make your shape and use the Delete key to remove it.

3. Select your rectangle shape and convert it to a new movie clip named "mc_loadBar" and set its registration point to the left center. With your new movie clip selected, go to the Properties panel and give your movie clip the instance name "loadBar." Check Figure 9.35 for visual aid. You might want to also put your mc_loadBar somewhere on the Stage you think looks best.

4. Create a new layer named "Border." Inside this layer you will use the Line tool to draw a border around your mc_loadBar movie clip. Be sure this layer is above the Load Bar layer, so you can see the outline clearly. I made my border image dark gray.

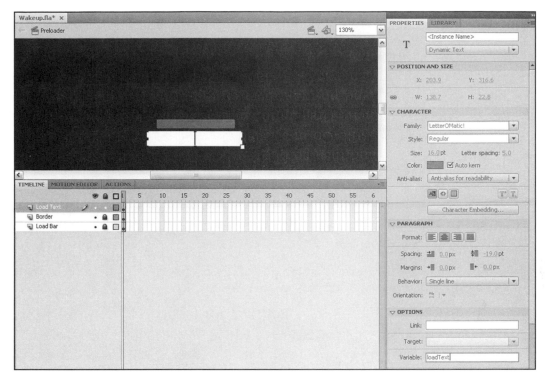

**Figure 9.36**
Add a dynamic text box that will show how much has loaded.

5. Now that you are finished setting up your load bar, it is time to get started on your percentage text area. Create a new layer called "Load Text." Use the Text tool to create a text box the size you want. It really only has to be one line long, and not even that long across. Just long enough to fit a maximum of 4 characters in this case. I changed my font to one that's more legible and to a size of 16 pt. At the top of the Properties panel be sure the drop-down box is set to Dynamic Text. At the bottom of the Properties panel, in the Options section, give the text box the Variable name "loadText." See Figure 9.36 to see what I mean.

6. Believe it or not, you are finished building the preloader. Now all you have to do is add the appropriate scripting to make it work! Create a new layer named "Actions" and insert a blank keyframe on Frame 2 and Frame 3. Be sure that all your frames below that span the three frames so your preloader doesn't strobe. To do this, right-click on the third frame in each layer and choose to "Insert Frame."

7. Click on the empty keyframe in Frame 1 of the Actions layer. Open the Actions panel. Add the following code:

```
bytes_loaded = Math.round(this.getBytesLoaded());
bytes_total = Math.round(this.getBytesTotal());
getPercent = bytes_loaded/bytes_total;
this.loadBar._width = getPercent*100;
this.loadText = Math.round(getPercent*100)+"%";
if (bytes_loaded == bytes_total) {
        this.gotoAndPlay(3);
}
```

8. Add this code to Frame 2 of the Actions layer:

```
this.gotoAndPlay(1);
```

Here now! Let me tell you what you've just done.

The line "bytes_loaded = Math.round(this.getBytesLoaded());" declares the variable "bytes_loaded" which uses a feature in Flash called getBytesLoaded and determines how many bytes of your movie have been loaded thus far by the viewer. The "Math.round()" in the code tells Flash to round the number off so it becomes a whole number rather than an eight decimal places number, because no one wants to read a percentage that is eight decimal digits!

The part that starts "getPercent" to take the variables "bytes_loaded" and "bytes_total" and divide them so you can determine how much has been loaded thus far in your movie. I declared it in a variable because you will be using it twice in the script, so instead of typing it twice, a variable saves time.

The line "this.loadBar._width = getPercent*100;" takes the value produced by the "getPercent" variable and multiplies it by 100. The 100 is purely arbitrary, because you can multiply the results by whatever you like. The number you place there determines the ending width of your mc_loadBar movie clip. Since you drew the border for your clip on the Stage already, I recommend using the width of your movie clip on the Stage. You can select your clip and open the Properties panel to see what the width is.

What the final conditional on Frame 1 (the part that starts "if (bytes_loaded == bytes_total)") says is that if the number produced in the variable "bytes_loaded" is finally equal to the number produced from the variable "bytes_total," then the movie should gotoAndPlay the third frame on the Timeline, which is empty and has no scripting to stop it, so it will carry right on to Scene 1 of your movie.

The ActionScript you placed on Frame 2 is there because if all the bytes are not loaded in your movie in Frame 1, it will automatically move on to Frame 2. Since you can't let it pass Frame 2 yet because the movie isn't finished loading, you must send it back to Frame 1. This will keep looping around over and over until both the "bytes_loaded" and the "bytes_total" variables are equal in numbers. Then the conditional statement declared at the end of the actions in Frame 1 will send the movie directly to Frame 3, and your movie or game or whatever will start from there.

You can create a preloader just like this one for anything you decide to make in Flash, although it is truly optional.

## What's Next?

Now you have learned all about making Flash animations, and you are ready to start making games with Flash. First, I will show you a brief behind-the-scenes look at what it takes to make successful electronic games, and then how to code your own using the Flash software.

## Review

At the end of reading this chapter, you should know:

- How to draft a storyboard for your Flash animations

- How to create title and credits screens with MP3s included

- How to create movie clips and buttons and manage imported media in your Flash Library

- When and how to use motion tweens, shape tweens, and guided motion tweens for your project

- How to craft a fluppet for animation purposes

- How to do lip synching in Flash by studying waveforms

- How to create a preloader in Flash to make your movies and games appear more professional

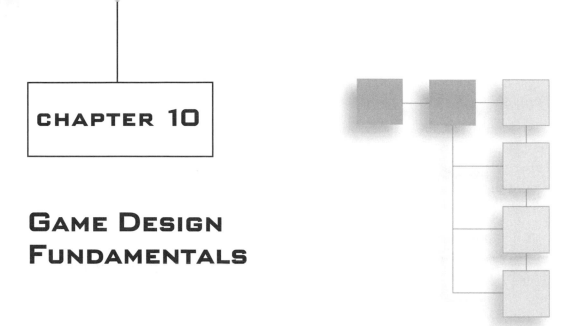

# CHAPTER 10

# GAME DESIGN FUNDAMENTALS

In this chapter you will learn:

- What it's like to be a game designer

- How to brainstorm killer game ideas

- What goes into making a great game

- The terminology used in game development

- What game genres and playing perspectives exist

Learn to put the "fun" back in fundamentals... or something like that. This chapter will show you how to make games. It does not include program code or resource files or an actual tutorial, not really (that's for later in this book). This chapter shows you what goes into making a great video game, the production process, types of games you can make, and some basic tricks of the trade that you can use in making your own video games once you have gotten your feet wet learning the physical process. In other words, this chapter shares with you the academics behind making fun Wii games.

## What Are Games?

Assumptions are terrible things to make. That's why we should start with some basic terminology. Some terms you probably already know, and others may seem totally new to you.

A *game* is, by definition, any activity conducted in a pretend reality that has a core component of play.

*Play* is any grouping of recreational human activities, often centered on having fun (well, duh!). The pretend reality of most games is based on the mental capacity to create a conceptual state self-contained within its own set of rules, where the pretender can create, discard, or transform the components at will. Sounds really complicated, but actually, play is meant to be fun!

## Huizinga's Magic Circle

This pretend reality is referred to by experts as Huizinga's Magic Circle, which was established by Johan Huizinga in 1971. *Huizinga's Magic Circle* is a concept stating that artificial effects appear to have importance and are bound by a set of made-up rules while inside their circle of use. For instance, the game of football is about guys tossing a pigskin ball back and forth to each other, but inside Huizinga's Magic Circle, the players abide clearly outlined rules to reach a victory for one team or the other. Consequently, the concepts of winning and losing are not essential to all games, but they do make a game more exciting, competitive, and positioned within a clear frame of reference.

As shown in Figure 10.1, the marketable resources in the *World of WarCraft* have so much value inside the "magic circle" of that game that players sell them online for real cash.

## Core Mechanics

Electronic games have one immense drawback to traditional board or card games: electronic games, most of the rules are hidden. The game still has its own rules, termed *core mechanics*, but they are rules that are rarely written down for the player to consult before jumping into play. Instead, video games allow players to learn the rules of the game as they play.

Harder games, or ones with entirely new/unheard-of rules, often offer players training levels to learn the core mechanics pretty early in the game. These are levels where players are taught the core mechanics by moderated experimentation. Given this route for learning rules, players with more practice playing a specific game will be better informed and can optimize their choices.

Hiding the rules offers video games one huge advantage over traditional games: because the computer sets the boundary of the "magic circle," the player no

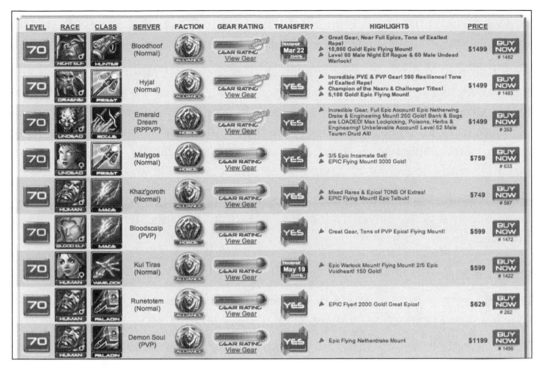

**Figure 10.1**
A screenshot of a market account for *World of WarCraft* items.

longer has to think of the game as a game! This level of immersion is found lacking in most traditional games.

Most of a game's core mechanics dwell on player interaction and randomization.

### Player Interaction

*Player interaction* involves a complex human-computer interface where the player gives her input to the game engine, and the engine responds proportionally. In other words, the player has to tell the game what she wants to do so the game can react accordingly. This interaction can reside on mouse and keyboard or game controller, but whatever the controller or source of input, it directs the course of action in a game.

Games are not at all like traditional stories. Stories are typically a series of facts that occur in time-sequenced order suggestive of a cause-and-effect relationship. When it comes to a game, the truth of the pudding is in the details, and the audience cannot understand the story from a typical causal relationship but are free to make choices and come at the options from various angles. A story is relatively static, while a game, on the other hand, is dynamic. It moves!

Interaction is important on several levels, but the most important one that you have to focus on is that interaction changes the nature of a game's challenges from being nearly technical dilemmas to being deeply emotional and inter-personal ones. In technical challenges, a gamer uses logic to solve each puzzle. In an emotional challenge, a gamer must approach each puzzle with surprise, tre-pidation, and the feeling of having something personal at stake.

There is some major significance in providing a dynamic game, one that does not lie cold, but sets the player up for challenge after challenge and keeps the player involved.

### Randomization

Almost every game out there has some *randomization*, which is a method by which a computerized system can change the way in which the game is played.

This encourages replayability in games, because the experience of playing the game is never the same twice. *Replayability* is the game designer's "sweet spot." In other words, it's what every game developer hopes for and once a developer has it firmly grasped in his game, he will have a warm feeling that only comes from repeat players. Replayability in a game means the player doesn't play the game only once through but wants to play the game repeatedly, either motivated by the need to excel or by the sheer excitement that comes from experiencing a compelling narrative.

Randomization in classic *Dungeons and Dragons* games involved the rolling of dice (shown in Figure 10.2), which can be simulated electronically (see *Knights of the Old Republic*) by random number generators. However, in the digital world, randomization can go much farther, often where whole game maps change each and every time the game is played, such as in the *Diablo* game from Blizzard Entertainment.

### Gameplay

*Gameplay* is defined by game designer Dino Dini as "interaction that entertains" and by game designer Sid Meier as "a series of interesting choices." Gameplay comes first, because it's the primary source of entertainment in all video games, the storyline falling in second. When designing a game, gameplay must be the first element you consider.

**Figure 10.2**
Pencil-and-paper games often used multi-sided dice for randomizing answers.

Gameplay differs from game to game, based on the player actions, options, and challenges. The challenges are central to the game, often varying by genre, and the options are the interactive abilities open to the player in order to overcome challenges. The player actions are steps players take to achieve their goals throughout the game.

Most gameplay in the *Grand Theft Auto* series, shown in Figure 10.3, can be condensed to, "Take missions to gain respect, steal automobiles to complete missions, make money by completing missions, and gain respect by making as much money as possible." The speed at which these actions are taken makes up the *game pace*, also referred to as *game flow*.

Industry celebrity Michael E. Moore wrote there were specific gameplay elements, including the following, inherent in all games, and that you could rate a game's entertainment value based on percentages of each:

- Combat

- Construction/destruction

- Driving/piloting vehicle(s)

- Exploitation

- Exploration

**Figure 10.3**
The *Grand Theft Auto* series of games.

- Physical dexterity

- Puzzle solving

- Storytelling

If you want to rate your game, or any game for that matter, by means of the above elements, just divide 100% among the individual traits the game displays.

One of the thorniest facets of successful game creation is making sure that the game has balanced play. If the player learns that his crossbow beats all the monsters in the game, possibly by some programming fluke, she'll never try another weapon during the course of play, not even when you attempt to give her a weapon she'll need to complete a quest later on in the game!

Players try to find the laziest and most efficient way to beat any game, because they understand that games have an underlying competitive challenge, even when the only competition a player faces in a game is the computer brain itself. So be on the lookout for minor imbalances in gameplay and the core mechanics and repair those imbalances so the player cannot cheat.

When you think you've found all the discrepancies, have a friend or two play it with fresh eyes and see what they discover. They might find a loophole or problem you missed. Don't feel bad if they find one, because even the large commercial game developers can be hit unexpectedly by a bug or problem within the game's programming.

### Gameplay Versus Graphics

There has long been a debate over which is more important, gameplay or graphics, in video games. In truth, both are of equal value and should be treated as such (see Figure 10.4).

In the early days of arcade games, the weakness of the display hardware seriously hampered the aesthetics, resulting in ugly and oversimplified graphics. With the growth of modern display technology, graphics have taken on a much greater role, one that some designers see as a handicap. In the 1990s, there was a major push by Hollywood film producers to take over the game industry, and to a certain extent because of this thrusting interest, game companies became focused more on outward appearances of the games they made.

Part of your job description as game designer is to give players aesthetic entertainment. Any ugly or awkward game with poor artistic style, clumsy animation,

**Figure 10.4**
As shown in this screenshot from Bethesda Softworks' *Bioshock,* awesome graphics and fun gameplay *can* coincide.

and sloppy artwork won't cut it anymore. But the appeal for games lies just as heavily in consistently fun and innovative gameplay as it does in beautiful artwork.

On the flip side, however, you don't have to be a great artist to make fun games. There are countless amateur stick-figure games proving this out there. The goal is to make a fun game, and if your game is enjoyable, the graphics become window dressing. So if you aren't confident in your artistic abilities, you can (a) take art classes and get better, (b) bribe your nearest artsy friend into helping you, or (c) do your best and move on.

## Release Your Inner Game Designer

The video game industry hasn't been around that long. It spawned from hacking communities in the early 1960s, and most industry veterans haven't even reached retirement age yet.

These days, being a game designer is akin to what being a rock star was in the '80s. Game designers are seen as young influential guys and gals riding the cutting edge of tech savvy, creating immersive entertainment for the masses. Game designers literally make fun, so why shouldn't their jobs be just as fun, right?

Not only does the job role as game designer have the perk of seeming fun, but there's money to be made at it. In 2007, this relatively new field brooked $18.85 billion in America alone, and sales of video games topped sales of CDs and DVDs combined, making more money per capita than either motion pictures or music. In fact, data from the market analyst NPD Group and announced by the Entertainment Software Association (ESA) reveals that first-day sales of Bungie's title *Halo 3* (shown in Figure 10.5) outsold first-day sales of author J.K. Rowling's long-awaited book *Harry Potter and the Deathly Hallows*.

## Get Educated

Electronic games are spanning the earth, and this global expansion has ushered in a need for skilled programmers and talented game artists. Most tech schools have started offering degree programs in game design to help fill this need, creating a brand new foundation in game education.

If you decide game design will be your career goal, get through high school with good grades, especially in art, math, and science (specific classes you should take include drawing, design, computer science, physics, and geometry). Then jump into a college that focuses on the STEM literacies.

**Figure 10.5**
An ad for Bungie's *Halo 3* game.

*STEM literacies* stands for science, technology, engineering, and mathematics. Most technical colleges teach game software development or game art. Perhaps there is one near you.

Here are a few:

- 3D Training Institute
- Academy of Art University
- American Sentinel University
- Collins College
- Daniel Webster College
- DeVry University
- DigiPen Institute of Technology
- Digital Media Arts College
- Emagination Game Design
- Ex'pression College for Digital Arts
- Full Sail Real World Education
- Global Institute of Technology

- iD Tech Camps

- International Academy of Design and Technology

- ITT Technical Institute

- Media Design School

- Pacific Audio Visual Institute

- Sanford-Brown College—St. Charles

- Seneca College's Animation Arts Centre

- The Academy of Game Entertainment Technology

- The Art Institute Online

- The Florida Interactive Entertainment Academy

- The Game Institute

- The Guildhall at SMU

- The School of Communicating Arts

- University of Advancing Technology

- Vancouver Institute for Media Arts

- Westwood College of Technology

- Westwood Online College

## Where Do You Get Those Killer Ideas?

A great game doesn't just happen. It takes someone to invent the idea, hash it out as a game concept, and put it to paper. The paper is called the game design document or game bible.

Game ideas can come from anywhere, including other games, TV shows, movies, and alternative media. But you can't outright steal another person's intellectual property. You can't make a game based on *Pirates of the Caribbean* without stepping on toes at Disney, but you could make a fun cheerful game about pirates, such as Twintale Entertainment's *Pirate Tales* game, as seen in Figure 10.6.

**Figure 10.6**
The *Pirate Tales* game from Twintale Entertainment.

You can find game ideas almost anywhere but only if you're looking for them. Creativity is an active, not a passive, process. Be ready for it when you are struck by the video game muse.

I bet you have plenty of game ideas. A lot of times these ideas will come from playing other video games. You start by thinking, "I wonder if they did it this way..." or "I could make this totally better if only...." Write your ideas down. Get a notebook and start jotting down an idea the second you have it, because otherwise you might forget and lose the killer idea that could make a name for yourself as a game designer. Personally, I keep several notebooks full of game ideas. They lie around, waiting for the free time to make them happen.

If my bet was wrong, and you don't have plenty of game ideas of your own, all hope is not lost. There are several ways to think of game ideas or find fresh angles to old ones. You could brainstorm ideas with friends, do some library or Internet research, or play other games to get ideas.

### Brainstorm with Your Buds

First, chat with your friends. In this cheap and efficient idea-scouring way, you can hash out ideas for games over pizza while talking about games that interest you. I have heard several game ideas start this way. Say your friend is complaining about a motion picture he saw recently, and you tell him you think it would make a much better game. Instant inspiration. Pretty soon you are both brainstorming ideas to complete a video game based on the premise.

Tracy Fullerton is the assistant professor at USC's School of Cinematic Arts, Interactive Media department, and co-director of the Electronic Arts Game Innovations Lab. She says, "Some of the best brainstormers are Imagineers [the kind folks who work at Disney Imagineering—see Figure 10.7]. They often have very large brainstorming sessions, with people from very different backgrounds, and they have physical toys to keep people loose. And somehow, tossing toys around gets the creative ideas flowing, and I find that very successful."

This process sounds wild and crazy, but it's actually encouraged in lots of companies that focus on creative entertainment. The more invigorating executives can make the work environment, the more productive their staff will be. This is one reason why you see so many toys surrounding game designers' work stations.

### Do Your Research

Next, you could search the library or Internet for ideas. Completely dry on fresh ideas? Google keywords and phrases like "game ideas," and you will be surprised at how many sites you hit on the Web where people are posting their own random game concepts.

**Figure 10.7**
A Disney Imagineer puts the finishing touches on the Stitch animatronic that is featured at Tomorrowland in the Magic Kingdom at Walt Disney World.

Don't just steal someone else's ideas, however. That's *plagiarism*. Ideas for games should come from within you. It is perfectly legit to have an inspiration when looking at the sorts of games other people would like to see made; it's just that your inspiration should be yours and yours alone. Plus, some of the top game producers browse sites like these to see what their target market wants, and they might recognize an idea you say you've had that you've actually stolen.

### Play More Games

The last trick for coming up with killer game ideas I can never repeat enough: play games! This advice sounds perfectly obvious, but that doesn't make it any less true. Great games beget other great games. You can make a list of the details you like about games you play most and what you could've done better. If you have ever played a game, I bet you dimes-to-donuts you at some time have thought, "This bites! Why did the designers make the game like this?" or "Why did they put this in the game? It totally sucks." When you do start making critical remarks like this, write them down and consider what would *you* do differently if you had to make the game over? Every game that exists out there could be made better. Think about how you can make a game better, and you will have the kernel of a killer game idea.

### The Frankenstein Method

Or you could try the Frankenstein method of Hollywood. The *Frankenstein method* involves taking the best bits from disparate sources and merging them together into a single concept. For example, take *Gran Turismo*, a car racing game, and *Elder Scrolls IV: Oblivion*, a fantasy role-playing game, and create a new-fangled game idea out of the two. How many racing games on the present market do you see that incorporate magic fantasy elements? Why couldn't they? Imagine a "race against the Ring Wraiths" kind of game. Take several video games you like and pick out details about them to thrust together and see what comes out of the mix-up.

### Don't Second-Guess Yourself

Never doubt your own abilities. One of the most oft-spouted self-defeatist arguments you hear is, "Every idea has been done to death! I could never make something new or exciting." Sure, every idea has been done to death (a fact supported by many critics), but you can make it better! Twist that idea in your own unique fashion, and you will be pleasantly surprised when people take a shine to it. Don't doubt yourself.

## Write It Down!

When that little light bulb comes on, you finally have a killer game idea. Write it down right away (like in Figure 10.8). Then start fleshing your idea out with more supporting details before attempting to write a game design document. There is no greater test for a killer game idea than trying to put it into articulate words on paper. Usually ideas in and of themselves are sublingual, full of images, emotions, and vague details. Trying to put your idea onto paper and then reading it aloud to hear how it sounds helps you to focus and reveals weak spots that might have made it past your original mental process as you wrote the idea down. You might find there are words you used that don't work as efficiently as what some others would.

After you have written your killer game idea down on paper, share it with your friends or family. Ask them to describe your idea back to you after they hear it, based on their own comprehension, and listen to them carefully. Don't ask for their opinion or let them cut you down just yet, as this is just an idea for a game right now and not a real game project. Especially ignore biased or hasty generalizations such as, "This won't ever work because racing games suck."

The more you practice coming up with game ideas, the easier they will come for you. You may notice yourself watching a new movie or reading a good book and

**Figure 10.8**
The more ideas you have, the more you're going to want to keep pencil and paper handy.

going, "Hey! I bet I could make a great game out of this." Best of all, with the training this book offers, you'll know you can!

### Writing a Game Concept

Expressly you should write a game concept encapsulating your killer game idea. A *game concept* is a short description of a game detailed enough to start discussing it as a potential project. The concept forms a general idea of how you intend to entertain someone through gameplay, and, more importantly, why you believe it will be a rich, compelling experience.

First, take stock of who your audience will be. In a commercial environment, publishers define this audience as their *target market*. In a play-centric design, you put the players first and design the game around their expectations. You could design a game for yourself and hope that there is more than one person out there like yourself who will find your game as appealing as you do, but it has been proven that you will make more return on your initial investment of both time and money if you make a game for a specific group of gamers instead. So look around at types of gamers you see and who you think would like your game.

Try for inclusiveness and *not* universality. What I mean is, don't make a game that will appeal to everyone; just make a game that will appeal to the largest segment of gamers in your target market.

Keep in mind that there are *core gamers*, who routinely play lots of games and play for the thrill of beating games, and there are *casual gamers*, who play for the sheer satisfaction of the experience and are less intense about the games they play. If you were to put a secret reward in your game, often called an Easter egg, it might escape most gamers' notice but not the core gamers. Try to design your game for both types of gamers.

Next, write the game concept out on paper. As a minimum, your game concept should include:

- A *high concept statement* that is a two-to-three sentence description of your game. Remember those blurbs of upcoming movies seen in the *TV Guide*? Keep your statement short and sweet.

- Who the player will be in the game, if they have a character they can see onscreen, and what role they're fulfilling.

- What the game world is like, if there is one.

- The game genre or a clarification of why its gameplay doesn't fit any known genre.

- The projected gameplay mode, including camera perspective, interaction, and gamer challenges.

- Who the target audience of the game will be, including their demographic (age, gender, how much money they bring in, and more).

- The type of machine and input devices the game will run on.

- Property licenses the game will exploit, if any.

- A short summary of how the game will progress from level to level, including a synopsis of the storyline.

## Get Your Game Idea Out There

In the popular electronic games industry, the role of game designer is a difficult one to achieve, partly because many people think they "have what it takes." It is not easy to go from killer game idea to reality, however. There are several people who believe that if they just talk convincingly and wave their hands around in the air in front of some aging cigar-chomping executive, they will see big money come from their big ideas. This is simply not true. Big ideas *don't* become big money without a lot of elbow grease.

### Publishers

Since a game publisher invests between thousands and millions of dollars toward developing a single game title, it is easy to see why they choose their game designers carefully: One or two risky game concepts could end up costing them millions of dollars in lost revenue. Some companies have been known to go bankrupt because of this. Now game publishers are much more selective. They choose developers with a long roster of triple-A game titles in their portfolio and a finger on the pulse of what is "hip." The downside to this trend is that they also choose games they figure will be big hits, often sequels to games that made bank or licenses tied to popular movies.

When we talk about a *triple-A (AAA) game title*, this description refers to an individual title's success or anticipated success if it is still under development. Triple-A titles are defined by the cost spent and the return on investment. Most triple-A title games cost between $10 and $12 million to make and become a smash hit, selling well over a million copies.

Publishers will usually only work with developers that have cranked out multiple triple-A titles. They do not have the petty cash to invest in smaller, less lucrative design houses.

I'm not telling you this to alarm you. If you love playing games and have read other books and informational periodicals like *Game Developer* or *Game Informer*, then you probably have a fairly decent idea what would or would not make it in the cutthroat market. You just need the mad skills and prototype development to make it happen. That is what this book can lend you.

You could become an independent game designer and, working in your bedroom or garage and on your own time, you could make the next hot game title. All you need is determination and practice and the right software. You can't expect to sell as many copies of your game as Electronic Arts or Ubisoft (shown in Figure 10.9), but you have one giant advantage they don't: You *don't* have their costs!

### Indie Game Movement

Just as game designers are the rock stars of today, the game industry is following the coattails of the music industry fairly closely.

Music is big business. Typically record companies compete for listing in the Top 40, and music artists whine when they're not getting the respect they think that they ought to be getting. However, in the music industry there are still some artists that are not afraid to experiment and create really edgy tunes outside the

**Figure 10.9**
Ubisoft: makers of *Assassin's Creed*, *Tomb Raider*, *Prince of Persia*, and more.

mainstream. From garage bands and unlicensed artists comes the wild side of independent music. Indie musicians are sonic artists who aren't afraid to take risks. They settle for lesser gigs so they can play the music they want to without the heavy influence of record companies.

In precisely the same way, indie game designers are also rebels who thumb their noses at the big industry giants. If you want to see real innovation in the game industry, you have to peer at the margins, at the indie game designers.

Imagine you had an idea for a great motion picture rather than a game. How would you make your movie idea a reality? Well, you could go to film school, become a film director, and work through several small film projects bankrolled by small-time producers until you have made a name for yourself and have enough clout to work on your own ideas. Or you could become a screenwriter, churning out screenplays and sending them to Hollywood where they could rise to the top of slush piles and eventually have one turned into a movie. These are all what are called "insider" ways to make your film dream come true.

However, this millennium is the age of do-it-yourself. You could take some petty cash, buy some costumes and props, talk your friends into playing the leads, and with a nominal purchase of a digital camera and software like Final Cut Pro or Adobe After Effects for video editing, you could make your movie yourself. It might take you a few months and $5,000 of your own savings, but your idea would be out there. You could then put it on the Web, enter it in indie film competitions, and get your show noticed. Or you could sell the DVD online, along with any secondary merchandise you can make up, partly to fund your next filmmaking project and partly to pay your coffers back for doing this one. This is what is referred to as the "outsider" way to make a film.

The exact same thing is true of games. If you have an idea for a great game, or even just an idea for a game you and your friends would like to play, you could make it happen.

You could do it the "insider" way: You could enroll in game school and learn computer programming, game art, and animation, start out at a game house working as a beta tester for a few years until you have enough clout to join the game design team, make several triple-A titles, and when you've developed enough repertoire launch your own game idea.

The do-it-yourself way is so much faster, in contrast: You could devote a little time to learning the software, talk some friends into helping you design the art and audio assets, and with the right game development software you could make your game yourself, without ever leaving home. It might take seven weeks or 12 months, but then you'd have your idea out there. You could distribute it on the World Wide Web, burn it to CD-ROM and sell copies at conferences or online, enter it into indie game contests, and generally get your video game noticed.

Don't think it can happen? Several developers, including Manifesto Games' very own Greg Costikyan, got together in the summer of 2000 and wrote the Scratchware Manifesto, which is a statement of purpose calling for game designers to stop paying attention to last year's A-lists and start developing novel experiences right now. *Scratchware*, a term coined at the time of the writing of the Scratchware Manifesto, is any game that is completely original, has great gameplay and replayability, runs well with few glitches, costs consumers less than $25 to purchase, and was created by fewer than three people.

Because of this underground movement, electronic games are getting easier to make. Independent games, or "indies," refer to games created independently of the financial backing of a publishing company. These games typically have a small, practically non-existent budget and are often available online for around $12 a download. Indie games are created by a small team of friends, often between one and 10 people. Usually one person is the concept and 2D artist, one is the character animator and 3D artist, one is pretty good at programming, one is a writer and does all the documentation and Web content, another is a musician, and so on.

Indie games are often developed in people's spare time and spare space (bedrooms, garages, basements, and such) and with software development kits that ease the game production process. The amazing thing about indie games is the money-making potential in them, and it is growing monthly. Every single game sold at retail in the last year sold at least 4,000 copies or more, even the bad games. That may not seem like much, but if you are charging $12 for your game, that means you have the potential to make $48,000 for one year's earnings for doing something you love doing.

## Game Developers

Most games are created through a working partnership of publishers and developers. Publishers are those wonderful companies that market your games and distribute them to the rest of the world. Developers are those people who actually make the games. You are learning, through the course of this book, to be part of the development team. There are four basic developer types to consider:

- **First-party developers**: Work in-house with a game publisher and make proprietary games for them. Nintendo is a good example of a first-party developer as well as a publisher; they make a lot of their own goods, so to speak.

- **Second-party developers**: Have signed contracts with a publisher to make games that will only be published by that publisher and a no-compete agreement that disallows them from selling their ideas to other publishers. In other words, they sign away exclusive publishing rights on their game titles.

- **Third-party developers**: The most common form of developer going. Are not possessed by a publisher and only sign contracts with publishers on a per-game basis. For instance, Rockstar's *Grand Theft Auto: San Andreas* appears on many different platforms, including PlayStation, Xbox, and PC. Most developers prefer being third-party because it means their games will be spread over a wider target market.

- **Independent developers**: The people who used to be known as "game sages" or "garage gamers" but today have broader titles and better acceptance. These developers, which includes you after you learn how to make your games, do not have huge overheads or extraneous responsibilities but do find it harder to be taken seriously by publishers and are often found devoting a lot of their spare time to self-promotion and self-distribution for that very fact.

### *Game Design Job Titles*

Developers are often comprised of teams composed of 1 to 100 individual designers, including texture artists, prop artists, technical artists, interface designers, level designers, animators, character modelers, graphics engineers, analysts, concept artists, cut-scene producers, storyboard artists, audio engineers, content editors, sound designers, music composers, motion-capture technicians, pipeline engineers, riggers, programmers, network or service technicians, content integrators, beta testers, quality assurance testers, and so much more.

A single triple-A game title, like Bungie's *Halo 3*, may have from 50 to 200 talented individuals on the project team and generally costs the same as a

Hollywood blockbuster to make. Because it costs so much to develop a triple-A title, most development teams are funded by a big-time publisher such as Microsoft, Nintendo, Activision, or Electronic Arts. Though this funding assists in reducing the enormous costs of building a game from scratch, the publisher often gains exclusive publishing rights to the finished game and the game must be set to make money even before its release date, often a daunting challenge for a new game developer.

Game designers fall into several skill-based job classifications. The broadest categories of game designers are as follows:

- **Artists**: Create the game's major thematic style through the development of concept artwork, 2D characters, 3D polygonal models (see Figure 10.10), and other visual assets, including props, weapons, vehicles, and monsters.

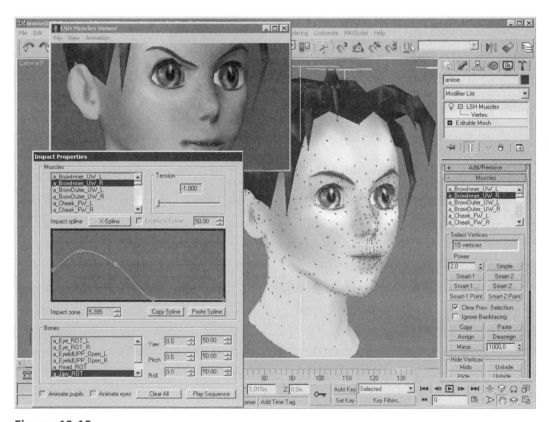

**Figure 10.10**
Game artists use powerful modeling software such as Autodesk's 3ds Max, shown here, to build and render polygonal models.

- **Leaders**: Communicate between the team members and make sure everyone is doing what they should be doing and that development milestones are reached on time.

- **Level Artists**: Take the design documents and art bibles and use apparatus therein to construct the individual maps, levels, and environments players will play through during the course of the game.

- **Programmers**: Make the most, because they have to script the program code that lets the computer know what to do and how to react to the game's players.

- **Sound Artists**: Set up Foley sound effects, musical scores, ambient sounds, and voiceover narratives to make the game sound so sweet to listen to.

- **User Interface (UI) Artists**: Design the look and feel of the game's shell interface, including the menu screens and in-game options lists. UI artists must test usability against aesthetics to maintain thematic style and gameplay.

- **Writers**: Not only have to write the storyline for the game, but they also script the dialogue and events that take place within the game, and write the game's manual.

Consider the above umbrella categories, as the descriptions listed are vague enough that several roles follow under each one. There are few standards in the industry as of yet when it comes to proper job titles, so one game company may call the level artists world builders while another may call them terrain editors, when they are talking about the same job role.

This book should help you in becoming an amateur artist, level artist, programmer, or leader. You have to learn to crawl before you can fly, as the old adage goes, and the exercises herein will benefit you in crawling by testing your mettle, so to speak.

The following are rudimentary skills useful to almost all game designers: (a) a huge imagination, (b) technical awareness, especially computer knowledge, (c) analytical skill (the ability to recognize the good from the bad), (d) math, artistic, communication, and research skills, (e) mental focus and self-discipline to get things done, and (f) the capability to adapt fast and compromise on major issues.

Noah Falstein, president of The Inspiracy and well-known icon of the games business, says, "Game designers are universally fascinated by what makes people tick, what makes *everything* tick. For the most part, they are somewhat intro-verted, although there are some who are extroverts. But that degree of intro-version is necessary to sit and noodle out how a design is going to work. In game design that introversion and extroversion tends to balance a bit. The personality of game designers is remarkably consistent, and this is an interesting point, specifically with full-time lead-designer types. There's a sense of kinship we have for each other in the industry."

### Game Developer Work Environment

Each job title has significant responsibilities, and depending on the size of the project and length of the deadline, the more team members are brought in to complete the title. The future of game development is moving more and more toward subcontracting labor, because many developers are seeing a loss of profits having 15 full-time artists doing concept artwork, when they twiddle their thumbs while programmers perfect the game engine for three months before the artists are needed again, and meanwhile the artists pull paychecks for play-testing and doing menial jobs around the office.

Some of the more forward-looking developers are starting to hire contract artists per job, even telecommuting designers over the Internet, and this leaves the artists to do more to progress their portfolios. Indie game designers will have a heads-up on this new work force as more work is done out of the home on a per-contract basis.

Let's take a look at one game development company, Foundation 9. Of its more than 450 employees before its merger with Amaze Entertainment, Foundation 9 had approximately 20% designers, 30% programmers, 35% artists, and 15% producers, administrators, and executives. Many of its employees "cross-pollinated"; in other words, some programmers became designers, and some designers became producers. The average development cycle at Foundation 9 was 14 months, and project budgets ranged from $1.5 million to $12 million per title. They never took breaks, either, apparently, as Foundation 9 shipped between 20 and 30 games every single year.

Typically a game development house (see Figure 10.11) is a casual work envir-onment. For instance, without breaking any non-disclosure agreements, I *will* say that when I visited Blizzard Entertainment in Irvine, California, most of the artists were sitting on bean bag chairs, sipping Starbucks coffee, and doodling

**Figure 10.11**
Employees working at Chronic Logic's Santa Cruz, CA, game studio.

their ideas on white boards. They also had an extensive game library, where they spent their time "chilling" in between business meetings and sitting in their cubicles getting work done.

However, don't expect that becoming a game designer means you just get to play games all day. Far from it! Hardly anyone gets paid overtime in the industry, and work days of 9 to 12 hours are not unheard of. Around crunch time (when designers are coming down to the end of their deadlines and finding themselves hurrying to get the project wrapped up) especially, anywhere from 80- to 140-hour work weeks are common. If you take 140 and divide it by 7 days per work week, that is assuming you work weekends, too, that averages out to 20-hour work days. For this reason alone, it is estimated that over one-third of all game designers burn out before finishing their first game.

Don't let these numbers scare you, though. Just be sure you like making games before you decide to make it a career. Making some games of your own, following this book, will help you make up your mind.

I know I listed for you earlier several game design schools, and to become more proficient at the technology used in game development, you should try to get into one; but honestly you don't *have* to have a formal education to become a computer-age rock star. In fact, most employers, recruiters, and headhunters will be looking at your *portfolio*, or a list of what you've done successfully in the past, as an indication of whether you'd fit within their company. Thus, it is imperative you start right away making games. If you have a few games of your own to show inside your portfolio, you have a much better chance of attracting the eye of a game design house.

### What's Up, Docs?

No artist can work in a vacuum, they always say. Well, the same is true in game design. No one who's considered a professional in the industry would condone going right from the idea stage to coding without the proper pencil-to-paper design work up front. It's a whole lot easier to build a game when you have a blueprint to go by, and that's the *numero uno* reason design documents are important to write.

Presumably a game development team uses the *game design document* to steer every step of game creation and to stay in touch on what each member is doing or needs to do. Most design documents not only list product goals but also a development schedule. The producer, or project manager, works closely with the lead programmer, artist, and designer to apply a timeline that lists all tasks that need to be completed and realistic steps of production that can be accomplished on that timeline. These steps are called *milestones*.

However, in real life this is what daily team meetings and lines of communication are for. The design document, however, does create a nice paper trail for the production, and it nails down potential problem areas before the team gets to them. It also sets the tone for the finished project.

Once upon a time, a single game design doc was written for each project, called the *game script*, but it was huge and unmanageable, one of the reasons it was eventually sliced into separate category-specific docs. Now the game script is used for a complete overview and for one purpose not covered by other docs: to target key rules and core mechanics of gameplay.

No two game design docs are alike, and some vary based on the intention of purpose. Here are some examples:

- A *high concept document* highlights the key elements of the game in bite-size chunks for the purposes of grabbing producer or investor interest. It is not used to develop from, because it does not give enough information about the game.

- A *game treatment document* is almost like a brochure, summing up the core ideas behind the game but with more technical gameplay details than the high concept will have.

- A *character design document* specifically targets one character, often the avatar of the game, and describes that character's appearance and *moveset*, or the list of animations documenting the character's movements.

- The *world design document* describes the background information and the sorts of things that the make-believe world will contain in a general overview. Most world design docs include a map of the world used, along with a list of objects and ambient sounds and their appropriate locations.

- *Story and level progression documents* record the storyline and the way that the levels will progress from one to the next. If you're creating a small game that won't have levels (like a Poker game) or use a game genre without a story (like a puzzle game) then this type of doc would be superfluous. Otherwise, you should write one out and in it indicate just how the player will experience and interact with the story, including the gameplay options and the narrative devices used.

- Another type of design doc, the *technical design document*, is created by the lead programmer on the project, using the game script as a springboard to describe to the technical staff how the game should be built or implemented in the software.

Although the majority of companies still use pencil-to-paper documentation, many are changing with the times and utilizing documentation organized in a Wiki format live online with major topics like design, art, code, and so forth. This makes the design document more fluid and flexible while remaining informative. If you are interested in creating a Wiki style of game design document for your game, you might try the free Wiki services of PBwiki online at http://pbwiki.com. Wikis can provide free, secure means for the entire development team and producers to stay on top of the development process and access anywhere in the world.

### Game Design Life Cycle

A game design life cycle is what professionals in the industry call the *development cycle*, from instance of conception to the release of a modern electronic game. It consists of a preproduction, production, and postproduction stage.

**Preproduction**  A game is thought out before it ever reaches development. The preproduction period is often useful for game design teams to find materials and funding, as it shows publishers and/or investors commitment and creative concept. In the preproduction step, a core team member hatches an idea, the game design document is written, art direction is finalized, technology and tool kits are selected, and a playable demo or "proof of concept" is created. This phase for the game is often called the *beta stage*, until the funding has been obtained and producers say "Go!"—at which time the game is given what's called the *green light*.

**Production**  The production time is where the game actually gets made. The team is scaled up to full size, the producer sets the production schedule and deadlines, programmers finalize the code, artists create all the in-game art assets, level designers create the game environments, sound engineers and composers work on sound effects, musical score, and narrative voice-overs, a playable game is tested by play-testers multiple times to work out bugs, and approval is finally met, followed by the game's release.

Production does involve a unique type of testing crucial to this phase, called *rapid iterative development*. Designers test ideas daily, see what's working and what's not, and abandon hurdles that are too difficult to get over. If the lead designer wants to see giant bumblebee enemies in one section of the game, the programmers will see if they can program flight abilities for the enemies. If the programmers can't get the bumblebee enemies to fly right, the team will discuss compromises. Also, programming is often a series of iterative stages. In the above example, the engineers will first try to get the bumblebees into the air and then see if they can get them to move around, and there will always be instances where they have to test, then revise, then test again.

The game, once approved by the producer and before hitting store shelves, has been said to hit gold. The *gold master* is the final edition of the game with all the bugs removed (hopefully). The phrase most likely resulted from the music industry and refers to the master discs sent to the manufacturer. These discs had to be first-rate and of more undeviating quality because they were used as the basis for the mass-produced retail copies, so they were made of gold. After the gold master is concluded and tested, it is sent to the CD duplicator to be reproduced for mass distribution.

**Postproduction**  And finally there is the postproduction phase, where the game is advertised, usually before Christmas, units are sold to retail outlets, and distributed to stores everywhere. Any foreign support necessary is finalized, language localization is accomplished, and the game is moved internationally, if possible. Technical support begins, and planning is put in motion for doing sequels, bug patches, or expansions.

Most of the postproduction phase of a game deals chiefly with marketing and distribution of the game. Because the game has to start making money before it's even released, the public relations person at a game publisher or developer must make sure people know about the game early on. Game magazines feature previews of early prototypes of the game or interviews with the game's creators. Web sites and forums are also great places to lead on curious target audiences.

Think about it for a minute. Most large retail outlets, chief among them being Wal-Mart, K-Mart, and Target stores, allocate a restricted amount of shelf space for games. Most of the stores stock between 200 and 300 titles at a single time. In a representative year, some 1,500 titles might get released. The retailer is thus pressured by supply and demand to get rid of titles that don't sell immediately. As a result, the typical shelf life of a game can be anywhere from 2 weeks to 6 months. Most games make their best money in the initial 60 to 90 days post-release. Many may quickly wind up in the bargain bin or returned to the manufacturer if sales don't carry on strong.

This is why adequate promotion and distribution of a game is imperative to the success of a game, and some may argue that it's even as important as the content of the game!

### Rating Games

American senator Charles Schumer has been quoted as saying that video games aimed at today's youth "desensitize them to death and destruction." Yet you can ask anyone in the military if real combat is anything like video games, and they will tell you they are worlds apart. Dire denouncement by the public against games has become a political token, and one that few people react to any more. For years it has been the same. Kids embrace some activity, be it dancing, comic books, or listening to rock-and-roll, and adults react negatively, and sudden outrage and panic ensue. Even with that said, games are not anarchic in nature, as they have rules promoting proper censure.

It is often during the production stage that most teams seek an ESRB rating. The ESRB (or Entertainment Software Rating Board) is an American independent game software ethics committee similar in function to the film industry's ratings board. Just as movies are given ratings for content, like PG-13 for a show that a teenager only 13 or older should view without the accompaniment of a parent, games also have ratings. They are E for Everyone, T for Teen, M for Mature (17 and older), and AO for Adults Only. There are several other designations. See Figure 10.12.

You may have not even realized that an AO rating exists, but this is because very few department stores or retail chains purchase units with that designation. For that purpose, AO games do not sell well, so developers don't normally make them.

There are no federal mandates saying your game, before it is published, has to even have an ESRB rating; the rating is still optional. But you need to know most distributors most likely won't buy games without an ESRB rating because it could cost them a lot of money and bad publicity in the end if they did and something went wrong.

The process of getting an ESRB rating is short and sweet, but it costs $25,000 every time you go through it. You send in a check or money order for that sum

**Figure 10.12**
The most oft-witnessed American ESRB ratings.

along with a questionnaire covering the contents of your game, as well as a demo tape of the most questionable content liable to be found in your game. The ESRB appoints three individuals who have no connection to the game industry, and who preferably don't play those sorts of games, to sit in a closed panel and review the questionnaire and demo tape for viability. These individuals are not experts in the game industry, nor are they trained at spotting questionable content. A lot of them have kids of their own, but they also have day jobs as construction workers, teachers, and civil service agents. This is meant to provide a purely "outside-interest" reaction that is sure to be objective. Based on those three peoples' unbiased suggestions, the ESRB then awards a rating for the game.

Many developers today have to keep pushing the limit to keep their game beneath the M for Mature rating and acceptable levels of content. For instance, when creating the game *Punisher*, the developer Volition Inc. had to send the ESRB review copies and $25K up to seven times before their content finally squeaked under the AO rating and merited an M for Mature. That's a lot of money to spend just to get by for having so much violence and language in your game!

The recent controversy over video game violence and the ESRB's overall effectiveness are nothing new. The first public harping took place in 1976 over Exidy Games' *Death Race*, in which players ran over stick figures representing pedestrians in order to win points (shown in Figure 10.13). The game, inspired by the 1975 cult film *Death Race 2000* starring David Carradine and Sly Stallone, was

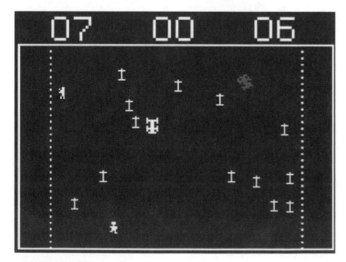

**Figure 10.13**
*Death Race* from Exidy Games.

protested until *60 Minutes* ran a story on it, beginning the national controversy over video game content. It's hard to tell from looking at a screenshot what could have possibly been so controversial when compared to the gruesome zombie-mow-down of *Dead Rising* for the Xbox 360 today.

Violence is not the only topic for concern when it comes to "questionable content." Drugs, sex, alcohol, swearing, and general bad behavior are all subject to scrutiny. The game developers have reasons for inclusion of "questionable content," including artistic license, cathartic release, and player acceptance, but the most prevalent reason is because these games sell lots of copies.

Game developers were fairly pleased when a federal court hearing set a precedent that games are to be considered the same as artistic media, and as such, they should be protected under the same rights as freedom of speech. Rockstar (creator of the *Grand Theft Auto* series) and other questionable developers are protesting that their games are pure art and not to be taken seriously.

The controversy continues today, and some legislators are pushing to have the ESRB removed and games placed in a government-sanctioned censorship review board to protect parental ratings of the entertainment products. The ESRB has countered, saying they are doing all they can, and that the ratings are effective as far as ratings go, that the problem lies with parents not knowing what their children are playing and with stores and retail outlets not enforcing the ratings.

For more information about the ESRB and the American ratings system in place for games, go to their Web site http://www.esrb.org.

## The Four Fs of Great Game Design

Game industries employ thousands of testers and market researchers and spend practically millions of U.S. dollars a year to determine what makes a great game. I have a specific formula of what makes a great game.

There are Four Fs of Great Game Design (4FOGGD) that must always be present for any game to be great. The Four Fs cannot exist without one another. They are listed here in their order of priority. When I speak of priority, I mean that if ever a conflict of interests should come up during development, you should always abide by what takes priority in the list.

FUN – FAIRNESS – FEEDBACK – FEASIBILITY

## Fun

### Tip

"Saying that a game needs to be fun is kind of like saying that a movie needs good dialogue and direction. Sure, you could have a great movie without a spoken line, but don't kid yourself: it will be an anomaly."

—Damion Schubert, BioWare Austin

Games are intended to be fun, by their very definition. Fun is a word synonymous with games. Fun is a short and simple word, easy to spell, and it is innate. Even the smallest child will begin inventing his/her own personal game if bored, and the purpose behind this natural instinct is to escape ennui by having a little fun.

The complexity and character of people's games evolve with their age and mental understanding. A game that outreaches a participant's age or understanding will quickly tire the participant and leave her bored. A boring game is no fun at all, as boredom is the antithesis to fun.

Give your players a fun, fresh, and original experience, one that is sure to encourage replaying and word-of-mouth advertisement, and you've done your first duty as a game designer. If your game is the slightest bit offbeat, offers cathartic release, or is irreverent and funny, it will get played.

## Fairness

Frustration can be a healthy motivator in games, challenging core gamers to achieve greater heights for themselves, but frustration can also lead to anger. Angry or frustrated players of electronic games are prone to throwing their game controllers or beating their computer keyboards while uttering epithets, none of which is conducive to a great game. Playing fair with your player equals better rewards in the end.

Do not force gamers to repeat complicated moves in the game or learn their lesson by seeing their character die over and over again. Don't kill their characters off suddenly or inexplicably without giving them a heads-up as to why. Avoid meaningless repetition or wrist-slapping like this. Help the gamer out without removing the challenges altogether.

As Duane Alan Hahn, game aficionado, says, "Play is supposed to be the opposite of work, but most video games are just jobs with a little bit of fun thrown in. These games can leave players feeling abused, frustrated, and overly aggressive. . . . Your game can either irritate or alleviate. Which would you rather do?"

Look at Nintendo's *Super Mario Kart*, as seen in Figure 10.14. There is a subtle shifting of balance in that game so that it appears challenging enough to keep the player's interest. The computer-controlled racers speed up when they lag behind your racer, and they slow down when you are way out ahead of you so that you, the gamer, always think there is a way to beat the game. A designer could program those other racers to be so fast and smart they'd beat you every single time, but where would the fun in that be? So treat your gamers fairly.

## Feedback

If the player does something right, give the player a reward. Give that player a Twinkie! (See Figure 10.15.) If the gamer does something downright stupid,

**Figure 10.14**
The racing game *Super Mario Kart* from Nintendo.

**Figure 10.15**
Yum. . . Hostess Twinkies.

show him that it was wrong to try that particular action: punish them. Video games are really all about pushing a player's buttons. A game world is little better than a Skinner Box, and if you know anything about psychology you will do just fine in the game industry. However, there are two critical rules of thumb to your punishments and rewards.

First, you should have your punishments and rewards fit the actions and environment, and always be consistent with your use of them. If the player always gets a higher score for grabbing purple jellyfish, and he grabs a purple jellyfish and his score is suddenly lowered, that gamer will become irate and wonder what sort of mean trick you're playing on him (see Fun, above).

Secondly, you should make your punishments and rewards come immediately so the player can get the gist of causal relationships. For instance, if your gamer has his character walk on lava, the lava should immediately burn or hurt the player's character. Similarly, jumping off a precipice and falling five stories should hurt. And beating up the bully should get the player character a kiss from the beautiful damsel he was attempting to rescue.

A player is eager to know that they do something right or wrong so they can adjust their play style and master the game. They listen for the bells and whistles to instruct them in how to play better. You can use this knowledge to your advantage by creating a better game.

## Feasibility

Encourage player immersion whenever and wherever in your game you can. To this end, avoid inconsistencies and a little terror called feature creep. *Feature creep* comes when a game designer gets too close to his project and begins adding "neat features" that really add nothing to the game or do not fit with the original game concept. For instance, if a somber horror game about mutants suddenly introduces to the gamer a switch that, if she pulls it, drops a bunch of gaily colored soda pop machines out of the ceiling to squash the mutants, the game has choked (and so might the gamer!). This fun little feature has destroyed the original game concept and the player's anticipations of the game being a serious horror game.

Keep your games simple. "I would say simplicity is a key factor in any good game design," Thorolfur Beck, founder of game development company CCP, comments. "Simplicity in interface, game systems, etc. . . Simplicity does not have to mean few possibilities (just look at chess), but creating a real good, well-balanced, simple game system is a much harder task than creating a very complex one."

Players are notorious for loading up a game and playing it. They hate to be bothered reading the game manual or having to look up a walk-through guide online. If the player consistently feels lost and frustrated, you have failed to make a great game. As Atari veteran Mark Cerny puts it, "Keep the rules of the game simple. Ideally, first-time players should understand and enjoy the game without instructions."

## Most Popular Game Genres

Game media, being fairly recent, did not spring up in a vacuum. It originated on the backs of other media, and so it borrows on their categorization by genre typing.

In books, movies, and television, genres are distinguished from each other by their subject matter, such as science fiction, fantasy, horror, Western, mystery, comedy, and romance. Subject matter is vital to games because the fiction genres appeal to different players. If someone likes horror movies, they might like horror games, and if they like horror games, they might want to play all the horror games they can get their grubby hands on. On the other hand, it is the types of challenges that games offer that distinguish their genre; game genres are just as much defined by their gameplay type.

The following are roughly the most popular game genres.

## Action Games

*Action games* are games where the player's reflexes and hand-eye coordination make a difference in whether she wins or loses. The most popular action games include:

- **Shooters**: Games in which the characters are equipped with firearms and focus on fast-paced movement, shooting targets, and blowing up nearly everything in sight. These games particularly measure a gamer's speed, precision, timing, and aim. The player moves her character through each game level, shooting at enemies and other targets, while avoiding being hurt herself. Examples include *Quake*, *Doom*, *Hexen*, *Wolfenstein*, *Duke Nukem*, *Serious Sam*, *Medal of Honor*, *Call of Duty*, *Half-Life*, and *F.E.A.R.*, to name just a few.

- **Platformers**: Allow the player's character to explore the upper reaches of a playfield by jumping on moving platforms and climbing ropes and ladders, all the while avoiding or knocking away enemies in a fast-paced animated world where one wrong step could spell disaster. These games used to be called sidescrollers, because the background would scroll from one side to another as the player moved her character along to get from Point A to Point B. Occasionally platformers will incorporate some shooter action gameplay to increase the challenge. The most well-known examples of these games are *Metroid*, *Crash Brandicoot*, *Sonic the Hedgehog*, and *Super Mario Bros.* 1996 brought us the more popular variant today called 3D platformer: games like *Super Mario Sunshine*, *Spyro the Dragon*, *Jak and Daxter*, *Ratchet and Clank*, *Malice*, *Tak 2: the Staff of Dreams*, *God of War*, and the latest sequels to *Prince of Persia*.

- **Racing Games**: Feature fast vehicles along twisting tracks or difficult terrain in a race to the finish line. Some have mayhem and combat, with the vehicle being a weapon in and of itself. Examples include *Super Mario Kart*, *Gran Turismo*, *San Francisco Rush*, *Crazy Taxi*, *Midnight Club: Street Racing*, and *Need for Speed*.

- **Sports Games**: Feature rules and team meets just like the real-world counterpart sports. Great sports games have realistic motion-captured animation, moves that follow realistic physics, game rules following official athletic guidelines, referees, cheering crowds, announcers, and those little touches that make the sport more realistic. Some primary cases in point include *John Madden Football*, Tony Hawk's *Pro Skater*, *SSX*, *Mario Tennis*, and Wii Sports.

- **Fighting Games**: are Duke-'em-out games that focus on competing against opponents in virtual arena combat. The controls are often limited to a number of combination moves. Some games that resemble fighting games feature an open arena, like half a city block, where the gamer must mow down countless oncoming enemies before moving on to the next area, such as Gungrave; this is a game design technique called the blood lock. Great fighting games include *Mortal Kombat*, *Street Fighter*, *Soul Caliber*, *Tekken*, *Double Dragon*, *DOA*, *Rumble Roses*, and (to a certain extent) games like *Devil May Cry* and *Onimusha*.

- **Stealth Games**: are Games that reward players for sneaking into and out of places without being seen and striking enemies silently. Though these games do have combat in them, the major focus is on avoiding direct confrontation. This is one genre that moves slower than most, because the gamer must have a bit of patience hiding in darkness and stealthily sneaking up on guards. Great stealth games should have lots of contrasting light-and-dark areas the player can use strategically to hide in, sneak attacks, such as tranq darts or garroting, and lots of wandering guards to avoid and include games such as *Hitman, Thief, Metal Gear Solid, Splinter Cell,* and *Sly Cooper.*

## Adventure Games

*Adventure games* traditionally combine puzzle-solving with storytelling. What pulls the game together is an extended, often twisting narrative, calling for the player to visit different locations and encounter many different characters. Often the player's path is blocked and she must gather and manipulate certain items to solve some puzzle and unblock the path.

*Zork* was one of the first interactive fiction games ever played on a computer. The name *Zork* is hacker jargon for an unfinished program, but by the time Infocom's *Zork* (see Figure 10.16) was released and going to be named *Dungeon* in 1979, the nickname *Zork* had already stuck. For many, the name *Zork* conjures up dim images of a computer game prehistory, before graphical adventures had become the norm. *Zork* was also one of the greatest adventure games of all time and set several precedents for the genre.

Adventure games primarily center on story, exploration, and mental challenges. Most, if not all, adventure games don't even have violence in them. Many have players solve mysteries through gathering up specific clues, as in Toshimitsu Takagi's 2004 game *Crimson Room.*

Examples of this genre include *Colossal Cave, Secret of Monkey Island, Myst, Siberia, Clue: Fatal Illusion, Still Life, Legend of the Broken Sword, Gabriel Knight, Grim Fandango,* and *Maniac Mansion.*

### Action-Adventure Hybrids

An offshoot of the adventure game is the popular action-adventure hybrid. A combination of shoot-'em-up, fighting, platformer, and puzzle-solving adventure game, *action-adventure games* originated first with the *Tomb Raider* series but now form a vast contingent of some of the best-selling games released every year.

## Role-Playing Games

*Role-playing games* (RPGs) got their start in pencil-and-paper in the 1970s with the late great Gary Gygax' *Dungeons and Dragons.*

**Figure 10.16**
Infocom's *Zork I* game.

I was introduced to tabletop RPGs in my teens, and they got me interested in computer games as the technology for them improved. Today's more complex computer role-playing games like *Neverwinter Nights*, *World of WarCraft*, *EverQuest*, and *Elder Scrolls IV: Oblivion* offer players pretend worlds with an amazing level of immersion. A player like Sally creates and enhances her own character from templates or from scratch. This character usually has a number of different game statistics used to resolve game actions, including statistics for health (expressed as hit points), physical attack strength, physical defense ability, and many more (such as intelligence, charisma, dexterity, and so on).

Most RPGs cover a core story arc that gives Sally a goal to achieve, but others are open-ended and allow Sally to go where she pleases and accept or deny quests offered her. The main goal of most RPGs is for Sally to gain enough experience or treasure for completing missions and beating monsters to make her character stronger. Along the way she'll travel to many locations and meet many *non-player characters* (NPCs), which are characters not controlled by the player but by an artificial intelligence programmed into the game itself.

## Strategy Games

*Strategy games* envelop a great deal of mental-challenge-based games, where the player builds an empire, fortress, realm, world, or other construct, manages the resources therein, and prepares against inevitable problems like decay, hardship, economic depravity, revolution, or foreign invaders.

Many strategy games, like Microsoft's *Age of Empires* game released in 1997, are *isometric perspective* games. This means that even though they are 2D they give the illusion of being 3D. Several of these games will have a military unit component and feature a dark screen that is opened up as the player travels the terrain, called the *fog of war* (which offers uncertainty as to the enemy's location and actions).

Examples include *Command and Conquer*, *Heroes of Might and Magic*, *World of WarCraft*, *Colossus*, *Warhammer*, and *StarCraft*.

### Consumer Games

A newer strategy game offshoot, pioneered by Gamelab's *Diner Dash* in 2004 (see Figure 10.17), features a customer-service core play, where the player is in charge

**Figure 10.17**
*Diner Dash* from Gamelab started a whole feed-'em-up game genre.

of an eatery and must please customers in order to make the biggest profits. This style of strategy game teaches players money sense, management, and prioritization skills.

### God Games

A related type of strategy game is the *Construction and Management Simulation*, or CMS. A CMS game is very much like a sandbox with lots of neat building and management tools, where the player virtually gets to play God and design his or her own little world. Popular CMS games include *The Sims*, *Rollercoaster Tycoon*, *GhostMaster*, and *Spore*.

## Other Known Genres

Besides the game genres already mentioned, there are many more:

- **Advertainment Games**—advertise a particular brand or service and are generally developed as part of a public relations' campaign.

- **Artificial Life Games**—make players care for a creature or virtual pet. Viacom's *Neopets* is one of the best known artificial life games on the market.

- **Casual Games**—include such traditional games as Chess, Poker, Texas Hold'em, Solitaire, mah-jongg, and trivia.

- **Puzzle Games**—never have much of a story but instead focus on mental challenges. Popular puzzle games include *Bejeweled* and *Tetris*.

- **Serious Games/Edutainment Games**—facilitate schools by teaching subjects in the guise of having fun, or they can help companies instruct their employees.

## Playing Perspective

There is another principle to consider when designing a game, called playing perspective. This is also known as the point of view, or POV, just as in the development of fiction stories. In film, cinematographers have to arrange the composition of all their camera shots to tell the story, but games utilize fixed or active cameras, thought of as floating eyes, to witness all the action in the games. The position of these cameras, fixed or not, defines the POV of the game. The following are the most popular playing perspectives seen in games today.

## First-Person View

Just as fiction has a first-person perspective, the "I," "me," and "our" voice, told from the perspective of the narrator, so to do games have a first-person perspective. The approved choice of 3D shooters, *first-person* perspective enhances the sensory immersion of a game by putting the player in the shoes of the character she is playing; she sees through the eyes of her character, and usually the only part of the player's character that can be seen is the hand holding the gun out in front of her.

It is important to remember when designing a first-person game that the player will start to think of herself as the avatar character, so cut-scenes that suddenly show her the character or asides where a particularly grating voiceover belonging to her character will take away the player's suspension of disbelief and (worst-case scenario) cause frustration.

*Suspension of disbelief*, first postulated by poet Samuel Taylor Coleridge, is that magical realm where the audience goes along with fantastical fiction elements as long as it is not brought back down to reality by some flaw in the writing. This concept is best demonstrated by watching a stage magician performing: You want to believe him, that he's doing magic, but your suspension of disbelief gets worn out if he constantly goofs or shows you how he's doing his tricks.

The first-person perspective worked suitably well in the Humphrey Bogart film *Dark Passage*, where the first part of the film is seen from Bogart's viewpoint until the bandages are removed from his head and the camera cuts to the third-person perspective for the first time.

## Third-Person View

Just as in fiction writing, where the third-person (or omniscient) style is typified by the "he," "she," "they," and "it" voice, games, too, have a third-person perspective. The *third-person* perspective is much more cinematic and immediate (see Figure 10.18). The gamer can see her character on the screen watch every move she makes. This leads to a greater identification with the player character but less immersion overall.

The worst restriction to this viewpoint is that the character is *always* on screen, and often seen from behind, so the character must look exceptional or gamers are going to complain about always looking at an ugly butt. Mario from *Mario 64* and Lara Croft from the *Tomb Raider* series were used in this perspective and rose

**Figure 10.18**
A third-person view used in Ubisoft's *Prince of Persia 2008* game.

to "movie star" fame because they literally became game icons and representatives of their gameplay.

Film cinematography features an *over-the-shoulder*, or OTS, camera view, which has recently seen its way into video games as a variation of the third-person perspective. One surprisingly well-done example of this was Capcom's *Resident Evil 4* and *5*.

## Top-Down (Aerial) View

The *top-down* or *aerial view* is a view looking straight down at the playing field. This perspective is most often seen in games like *Solitaire*, the early *Ultima*, or *Zelda: Link to the Past*. It limits the horizon for the player, so she has a harder time seeing what obstacles might be coming up, but it does add greater detail to what is on the surrounding map. *Grand Theft Auto*, before its 3D days, began as a vintage 8-bit top-down game.

## Isometric View

*Isometric* is the favored tilted "three-quarter" view hovering off to one side of certain RPGs as *Diablo*, *Baldur's Gate*, *Bard's Tale*, and *Planescape: Torment*.

This perspective is often used to give a fair impersonation of 3D even when the characters and environments are really 2D. Isometric games for this reason are popular in RTS and RPG but rarely seen in action shooters because of the limitations to aim and visibility.

As opposed to the old sidescroller games, isometric games offer player movement in eight directions: north, northwest, west, southwest, south, southeast, east, and northeast to be exact.

## Side View

The *side view* perspective reflects the traditional view of SEGA and Nintendo's sidescrolling games as popularized in *Sonic the Hedgehog*, *Super Mario Bros.*, and *Earthworm Jim*. Though largely unused in newer games, thought of as too "retro," this view *can* be mimicked quite well even when working in 3D if you set up satellite cameras from the side and provide a fenced-in path terrain.

## Adventure Scenes

Adventure games are well known for having 3D characters exploring pre-rendered 2D backdrops using an invisible box model, with each scene thus becoming a diorama. Or sometimes there isn't a player character at all, just a diorama to explore.

The player navigates and clicks through each *adventure scene*, sometimes having to backtrack many times or click throughout a scene to find elements to interact with, and if the designer is not careful this can quickly degenerate into "hunt-the-pixel" frustrations. This type of perspective is fixed and unmovable. Whenever the player moves to an exact location on screen, say a door leading to a hallway, another scene is drawn, say the interior of that hallway.

## Closed-Circuit Cameras

This perspective style was first pioneered by *Alone in the Dark* and became the basis for the *Resident Evil* cameras. The style was later copied by *Silent Hill* and countless other survival horror games in succession, because it made for better trepidation.

In this *closed-circuit camera* view, fixed cameras pan to follow the 3D player models wandering through pre-rendered settings. When a player character gets too far away from one camera, another one will "switch on" and pick up the action, so that the player character is always on display. Unfortunately, this perspective style has gotten a lot of flak: Players have griped that this style, while able to maintain a suspenseful mood, can be downright frustrating when trying to shoot enemies around corners or see if you are about to walk up on a potential hazard. This complaint is one of the reasons that *Resident Evil*, starting with *RE4*, switched to using over-the-shoulder third-person perspective.

## What's Next?

You have enough know-how under your belt to begin dreaming up a game idea and nailing it in a game design document, so let's start there.

## Review

At the end of reading this chapter, you should know:

- The ins and outs of being a game designer and working for a developer

- The pros and cons of becoming an indie developer

- How games are made

- What terminology to use when talking about games and game development

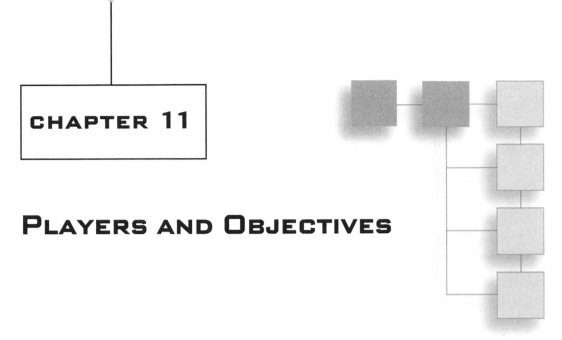

# CHAPTER 11

# PLAYERS AND OBJECTIVES

In this chapter you will learn:

- How to put the player in control

- How to entertain the player through game narrative

- Why most gamers play games

- What player immersion is and how to obtain it

- How to look out for and use emergent gameplay

- What types of game challenges exist and how to use them

To sum up: You know the logical process that goes into making games; you know they must be fun and fair; you know you should provide feedback and make your game feasible to the player; and you know the most popular game types. But what really separates a game from other media, such as listening to music, watching a movie, or reading an engrossing book, is an element only games have: *interactivity.*

## Interactive Entertainment

All games are interactive. That's part of their playability. Games are not passive entertainment forms, such as watching a football game on television. Games are active: They put you into the football field and place a ball of pigskin in your hands! They expect you to react.

Games are not at all like traditional stories. Stories are typically a series of facts that occur in time-sequenced order suggestive of a cause-and-effect relationship. In other words, a story plods from step to step to step in a linear fashion. A story is a great way to represent reality as a cause equaling an effect.

In the movie *Indiana Jones and the Kingdom of the Crystal Skull* (if you've never seen it, you really should!), we see the heroic archaeologist Indiana Jones as good and the Nazis as misled bad guys. Even a three-year-old can understand the story. The facts, architecture, and background are nearly inconsequential to the audience attempting to understand the story. When it comes to a game, however, the truth of the pudding is in these details, because the audience cannot understand the story from a typical causal relationship but is free to make choices and comes at the options from every angle.

This freedom interactivity leads to immersion, which sells games. Indeed, a game that has a lot of immersion is a game that players will want to play over and over again to explore new opportunities and avenues for expression. A story is relatively static, while a game, on the other hand, is dynamic and constantly in motion!

Have you ever played an obnoxious game that appeared to be one long cinematic scene after another with short pauses in between where you got to explore the environment as your character before hitting just another cinematic scene? These games behave more like abstract film projects than fun games, and that's because games are meant to be interactive!

Players don't want to be told a story; they want to tell or discover the story themselves. Listening to long-winded exposition, forced to watch long animated sequences, and even talking with characters should *always* be secondary to exploration, combat, manipulation, and problem-solving. In other words, story is supplementary to interactivity.

Interaction is important on several levels, but the most important one that you have to focus on is that interaction changes the nature of a game's challenges from being merely technical dilemmas to being deeply emotional and interpersonal ones. In technically static challenges, a gamer uses logic to solve each puzzle. In an emotionally dynamic challenge, a gamer approaches each puzzle with surprise, trepidation about the outcome, and the feeling of having a personal stake in the matter.

**Tip**

"It's like these developers are trying to invent chess and have created a superb, glossy-looking board and a whole new set of exciting pieces and then sit back and say, 'Look! Look at this new board game we've made! Look at these shiny pieces and this state-of-the-art board! What a great game this is!' But they haven't thought about how the game is played. They haven't thought about what pieces can move in what directions. They haven't thought about how these pieces then interact with each other. They haven't developed a set of rules. In short, they haven't thought about the actual game itself. . .."

—Neil West, "The Way Games Ought to Be" (*Next Generation Magazine*, October 1997)

There is major significance to you, the designer, in providing a dynamic game, one that does not lie cold, but sets the player up for challenge after challenge and keeps the player involved. To do the latter, there are several steps to follow:

- Empower the player

- Keep the player entertained

- Provide reactive environments

- Immerse the player

- Prep for emergent gameplay

## Empower the Player

**Tip**

"Our species can only survive if we have obstacles to overcome. You take away all obstacles. Without them to strengthen us, we will weaken and die."

—Captain Kirk, *Star Trek* ("Metamorphosis")

Putting the controls in the player's hands can sound scary for any designer at first. You are abdicating some of your control to allow the player to interact with, and possibly lose at the game you've provided. However, without elevating your player to status of co-creator of your game, you will never make a great fun game, because games are all about interactivity.

Let's call our game player Sally. When Sally picks up her game controller or takes over her keyboard and mouse, she wants to be able to explore make-believe worlds, encounter responsive creatures, and interact with her game environment in ways she can't get out of watching a show or reading printed words. If you fail to empower Sally with interactive control, you fail as a game designer.

### Teach Players to Play

First, you have to teach Sally how to play your game.

Every game is slightly different in the way that it is played. Games of the same genre are generally more similar in their gameplay, and thus players can figure them out quicker than games of different genres.

Tom Smith, once creative manager at THQ and now senior producer at Disney Mobile, says, "Communication is hard because players are not here to learn; they're here to play. But if they don't learn, they will never know how to play."

Things to think about when teaching a player how to play your game include:

- Who is the player in your game?

- What can the player do in your game? What are the controls?

- Why should the player do anything in your game? What are the goals and rewards?

Probably the easiest and most efficient way of telling the player how to play the game is to have a short briefing before the game starts. This briefing can be so short it takes up a single screen with a picture of the controls used in the game. This requires players to have excellent memories, or for the controls to be so simple that they are virtually intuitive. Or you could weave the instruction into the first level of gameplay, where short pop-up messages give the player hints about how to play the game, like, "Press A to jump over hedge." There are some games that use these pop-up messages as gates, blocking the player from moving on in the game until the player shows he understands the control system. Like in *Conker's Bad Fur Day* for the Nintendo 64, the player is told how to use her squirrel tail as a propeller to jump farther and is immediately given a challenge that forces the player to demonstrate she knows how to do it, or else she can't escape the waterfall's edge. Forcing the player to show they "get it" is a neat way of reinforcing your message, but it can also make players feel like they aren't in control, robbing them of their enjoyment, and on rare occasions it can reveal weaknesses in the game interface.

Of course, most shipped games come with short manuals that, when read, can help the player learn how to play the game, but most gamers these days skip the manuals and dive right into playing the game, often assuming the designers have made some leeway in the learning curve.

However you decide to instruct your player in the game's controls, strive to make the game fun (don't make the rules tedious to learn!), fair (don't teach after your player fails, or forget to mention an important control), with proper feedback (let the player know when they've "got it"), and feasible (arbitrary or rarely-encountered controls shouldn't be thrown in willy-nilly).

Show the player the ropes and then step back and let him make the big choices governing the game's direction.

### Give Players Important Choices to Make

Part of empowerment is giving the player choices. This involves two main things to be present in your game for it to work:

- Difficult, not easy, decisions that have to be made by the gamer

- Tangible consequences in the game for decisions the gamer makes

Tabletop role-playing games like *Dungeons and Dragons* (shown in Figure 11.1) are predecessors to their video game variants, but a huge difference between the

**Figure 11.1**
The classic tabletop RPGs used to keep kids busy for hours.

two kinds of games lies in the type of decisions gamers have before them. Tabletop games run on the imagination of the players, including the Game Master, in ad hoc fashion, starting with one suggested possibility and continuing open-ended. Video games do not have that luxury. In video games, the narrative has to be completely decided on and programmed before letting the player toy with it, so there are fewer chances for leaving anything open-ended.

Yet there is a joint partnership between you, the game designer, and your future gamer. You essentially must pass off partial control of your game and its contingent story to the person who plays your game. Doing this is exciting. It is even more exciting when you are watching your testers for the first time playing through your game missions and seeing how they make different decisions than you would to come to the same resolution.

When creating decisions for the player to make, you must remember a couple of rules that can save your game:

- First of all, no one likes being "led by the nose," or feeling like they have no control over what happens to them or their avatar.

- The choices the player is given should be reasonable ones. Don't ask her to go in a door marked "Great Stuff Inside" and then have a brick wall on the other side of it. Likewise, don't ask her to choose between getting a magnificent sword and a pile of junk, because she'll pick the sword every time.

- The choices the player is given should be real ones. Don't invent arbitrary decisions, like where you ask the player if she wants to go through Door A or Door B, and both doors lead to the same room. To the player, this is as bad as cheating. Another type of hollow decision is one that is too obvious. If you ask the player whether she wants to pick up a pile of gold or not, and there are no repercussions for her if she does except that she gets richer, she will pick up the pile of gold and be shaking her head at the stupidity of a game designer who would create such a hollow choice.

- The choice a player must make must never be an uninformed one. In other words, you must give the player enough knowledge to make a proper decision when faced with it. If you leave out the fact that if she keeps the Sword of Eons, she will have to slaughter her only surviving sibling, you are sure to see a player throw a tantrum.

The best choices of all to present your gamer with are difficult ones, especially if there is a perceptible tension surrounding the outcome of the decision. The most common decision that players can make in a game is, "Oh, no! I am coming around another corner, and I have only two bullets left. Should I wait to reload?" If you do your job as game creator right, this in itself can be fraught with thrills.

Here is an example. Say that the player has one golden arrow, which she is led to believe might be the very last one, because golden arrows are extremely rare. The golden arrow, she has been told, is the only weapon that can hurt Baron Bone-daddy. Now imagine you have scripted a scene where the player's ally gets hit with a poison gas cloud of a death mushroom and lies dying. The player is informed that the only antidote for the poison is a golden arrow melted down and mixed with bitter root and sea water. The player is now faced with a dilemma: she can choose to save her friend and lose the only weapon she has to kill Baron Bonedaddy, or she can kill Baron Bonedaddy and lose her BFF. This can be an extremely tense decision if you script it right, with tangible results either way.

As long as you carry out the Four Fs of Great Game Design, you won't have any problem empowering the player and providing a game experience that Sally will remember.

## Keep the Player Entertained

**Tip**

"Fairy tales do not tell children the dragons exist. Children already know that dragons exist. Fairy tales tell children the dragons can be killed."

—G.K. Chesterton

A motion picture is about a decent fellow having stones thrown at him, and we, the audience, wait with baited breath to see what he will do. Video games, on the other hand, are unique, because we cannot sit on our laurels and watch the action: We are that guy, and we decide what the guy will do when the stones are launched at him.

### Interactive Storytelling

In literature, this sort of interactive fiction has been portrayed in classic *Choose-Your-Own Adventure* or *Fighting Fantasy* game books (see Figure 11.2). If you don't know what one is, for an example you should look at some of Joe Dever's game books, which can be found online at http://projectaon.org.

**Figure 11.2**
Book cover of *Grey Star the Wizard.*

Basically, a game book starts each page describing what you, the reader and also the player, see: "The castle gates look rusted with age and pelting acid rains, and the stones show signs of weathering and pitting. A guard mans the gates, but a little ways down the trail to your left you see what looks like a side door, hidden against the castle wall by an overgrown oak tree." Then the game book gives you your choices: "If you wish to walk up to and ask the guard entrance to the castle, turn to Page 24. If you wish to go down the path to your left and see if you can get in the side door, turn to Page 31." You don't read the books cover-to-cover but follow the twists in the story based on your decisions.

Writing a game narrative is a lot like these early game book examples.

### Writing Game Scripts

A *game script* is what developers used to call the huge unwieldy game design document that the team had to build a game around, but it later got chopped into multiple types of documentation to cover every departmental aspect of design. Today, when you hear someone in the industry mention "game scripts," they are usually referring to the story and/or level progression documents, which are similar to a movie's screenplay.

A game script must be versatile to account for the different story paths resulting from the player's decisions. The paths in a game script are always going to reflect the game's interactivity as the paths are chosen by the players themselves.

You can write these multiple paths into a comprehensive storyline on paper using a charting method like a flowchart with nodes representing deviations in the player's path. Creating a flowchart helps you illustrate the game in a way that you and the rest of the team will have no room for doubt, so that if there ever is a question about what kind of contingency was planned, you simply refer back to your flowchart.

Some designers prefer making a walkthrough instead. A walkthrough appears as a text translation of a flowchart. It is not a chart, but it describes the major twists and turns in your game and where scripted events take place.

Here is a sample walkthrough style game script excerpted from David Kennerly's "Tree of Life" scenario:

EXT. CORRUPTED TREE OF LIFE - DAY (INTRO)

FADE IN:

Underneath an imposing BLACK CLOUD is an even more imposing sight: The CORRUPTED TREE OF LIFE. The great oak's limbs span about a hundred feet in diameter. The trunk itself is thirty feet in diameter. It's withered, leafless, and spotted black. Some of its limbs are cracked or broken. It resembles a tree of death more than a tree of life.

MAIR, 30s, female AVIAN sheriff with a hawkish face, is visible beyond one of the massive ROOTS by the tree's TRUNK. Sleek feathers coat her athletic body, since avians are a species of bird-like humans.

MAIR

Look at what you've done to the Tree of Life ---
Suddenly, from the root, CORRUPTED VINE 1 coils around her leg. It TRIPS her. She leaps to her feet and raises her SPEAR but behind her, CORRUPTED VINE 2 wraps around her neck and CHOKES her. She struggles and screeches.
Corrupted vine 1 rises and sways like a cobra, left of Mair, who is still being choked. Then CORRUPTED VINE 3 rises and sways on the right.

RESCUE MAIR (INTERACTIVE)

A vine attempts to trip, and hurt, the player.

THE FIRST TIME that a player JUMPS OVER a trip, the vine sweeps underneath in slow motion.

If the player has been tripped, then its next attack is a choke. While being choked, the player cannot act, except to STRUGGLE, and is slowly suffocated. Struggling for a few seconds releases the choke.

If a player is far away, a vine BURROWS underground, at a rate faster than a player can run. After catching up, the burrowing vine emerges behind the player. While burrowing, the vine causes a small RIPPLE, which trips any character that it passes.

[SELECT SCENE]

Mair dies.

Any player dies.

The first corrupted vine dies.

Any corrupted vine dies.

All corrupted vines die.

Repeat scene "Rescue Mair."

MAIR DIES

Mair gasps. The corrupted vine, having drained her life, lets her go. Her blackened body falls limp to the ground.

GAME OVER.

ANY PLAYER DIES

[Player] gasps. The corrupted vine, having drained her life, lets her go. Her blackened body falls limp to the ground.

GAME OVER.

THE FIRST CORRUPTED VINE DIES

BLACK SMOKE begins to rise from the corpse. The smoke touches and withers adjacent shrubs and grass.

[Player] looks at her weapon.

A wisp of black smoke rises from the weapon.

ANY CORRUPTED VINE DIES (INTERACTIVE)
A small cloud of black smoke rises from the vine's corpse. After a few seconds, the cloud fades away.

If a player touches the black cloud, she gains a DEMON BLOOD item. Using this item causes black smoke to rise from her weapon. On the player's next hit, the black cloud envelops the opponent, which drains life, and then fades away.

[Repeat scene "Rescue Mair."]

ALL CORRUPTED VINES DIE

[Player] hacks the final vine that binds Mair. Black ooze spills from the stump. Mair stabs the stump with her spear.

For more examples on creating a game script, including a template you can use, visit http://finegamedesign.com.

### Game Narration

The important thing to remember is to not become fixated on the narrative or descriptive details and forget about interactive gameplay, because story and the foregoing artwork is no replacement for fun gameplay. You can take the story out of a game, and it is still a game; after all, *Tetris* doesn't have a plot to speak of, but it is a classic video game (shown in Figure 11.3). And you can replace the fancy

**Figure 11.3**
*Tetris*, created by Alexey Pajitnov in 1984, is one of the most popular puzzle video games.

graphics with stick figures and still have a strong game. It is the gameplay, and the decisions the player faces in the game, that have main priority.

There are three ways story is told through most games that weds narrative with gameplay. These are backstory, cut-scenes, and in-game artifacts.

- *Backstory* is the history of all events that have led up to the current action of the game. This can be as far-reaching as the creation myth of the world composing the game's setting, or the abduction of a perilous princess from her tower the night before the player's character wakes up and starts his quest. Backstory is sometimes shown in a cut-scene before the game starts or through in-game artifacts, such as journals. It can also be information passed along through dialogue with non-player characters.

- *Cut-scenes* are the short in-game movies, often displaying CG art, that serve as the vehicle for exposition you find in other media. Cut-scenes often reveal clues, reward the player, give the player a break to stop and breathe before continuing the action, and continue the game narrative. A string of cut-scenes with high polish are called *cinematics* and can ride the line between acceptable game narrative and machinima. (*Machinima*, exhibited in Figure 11.4, are short film projects created using 3D characters and environments found in game technology. They are motion pictures, rather than games, even though they may feature popular game icons.)

- *In-game artifacts* are those objects discovered during playing the game that enhance or reveal story elements. They include dialogue with non-player characters, or NPCs, reading journals and letters, and stumbling upon

**Figure 11.4**
In machinima, the actors are virtual avatars or player characters from popular video games.

significant weapons, items, or landmarks. These items of information help divulge backstory and current events of the game narrative.

So remember:

- Keep the gameplay and mechanics in mind at all times

- Ensure the writing relates to the gameplay

- Use narrative tools, such as setting and journals, to tell the story

- Accept that most of the actual story will have to be revealed in backstory

The number one no-no in developing game scripts is to have a predictable story. Symptoms include a player figuring out plot twists or finding out who the murderer is before she is ever expected to. If these symptoms rear their ugly head, then you have just lost the player. She might become so bored playing your game as to never pick up the controller again.

So if you're going to have a story to your game, make sure to place some well-crafted twists and turns designed to surprise and delight throughout your game. Never let your game get dull.

**Note**

Where is the writer in a game studio? Sometimes the actual writing is outsourced when needed to develop the game story for a particular project. Often due to the importance of gameplay and stable mechanics and great-looking graphics over narrative, traditional writers are not always in high demand in the game industry. This is unfortunate and might change as more developers attempt to integrate storytelling with gameplay for a more cohesive game experience.

Right now, it is not all that unusual for a game designer or director to write the story themselves, or for the members of the design team to write the story and dialogue for their respective game levels or missions. There are only a few writers, such as Douglas Adams or Clive Barker, who have forayed into the game industry and come back with a gem.

### String of Pearls Method of Scripting

Jane Jensen, creator of the *Gabriel Knight* adventure game series, shown in Figure 11.5, developed a method early in her career to help herself in writing game scripts. This method usually pertains to puzzles and quest-driven games but works pretty well with other game types. It is called the String of Pearls Method, and if you want to you can incorporate it into your game scripts.

**Figure 11.5**
*Gabriel Knight* was a mystery graphical adventure game series started in 1993 by Jane Jensen.

The String of Pearls Method is easy:

- Picture each major plot point as a pearl on a string. Each plot point opens at one side of the pearl, coming from the string.

- The player is let loose after some basic cut-scenes or instruction and explores the pearl. She uses what she knows, what you the designer have told her, and there may be as many as 3 or 15 little scenes or side quests the player can trigger. Let the player trigger these in any order she chooses; this is vital because the game ceases being static and takes on the illusion of a free-roaming game.

- Then, once the player has triggered all these scenes, the game registers the fact and comes back to a central story point.

- There is often a cut-scene, and the next pearl on the string starts.

Here is an example of a game scenario based on Jane Jensen's String of Pearls Method. It could come from any typical survival horror game.

The hero, a mercenary named Janice, is trapped in downtown L.A. surrounded by zombies. She has a Jeep Grand Cherokee in the garage to escape in, but the Jeep is out of fuel and Janice can't find the ignition key. We have started a pearl, and the player knows her goal: to assemble the components needed in order to continue the adventure.

The hero's companion, Blake, thinks he left the keys in another part of the level. They split up, Janice going to look for fuel and Blake going back for the keys. The

**Figure 11.6**
*Land of the Dead* is a free Web-based game made by RobotInk (http://www.robotink.com) to advertise the George Romero movie of the same name.

player finds a fuel station a few blocks away, but the pumps are turned off and the electronic door to get inside and turn them on is out of order. She can easily see why, too: The electric control panel is missing a fuse. The player will move on with her search.

She soon stumbles into a room upstairs of the filling station and finds some ammo. . . along with several zombies that have to be put down! See Figure 11.6. Just as she's leaving, her partner Blake radios her, needing some real help. Blake found the keys to the Jeep but is now completely surrounded by zombies, without a weapon to stave them off, and he is begging Janice to come to his rescue. The player races to rescue her companion, and tension mounts!

After Blake has been saved (notice the girl character has to save the guy for a change, which is good because it breaks an old mold), the player returns to the filling station with a working fuse she finds while rescuing Blake. She uses the fuse on the electric control panel to open the door, but the door only opens a little way, something jamming it from the inside. Janice can fit under the door, but Blake must stay behind.

The door suddenly shuts, and the player finds she is locked in the fuel station! Imagine she also felt sorry for her companion and gave him her gun before entering the building, so now she is trapped and defenseless, looking for a way to turn the gas pumps on all alone in a dark storehouse filled with zombies!

Finally, after a lot of hard work on the player's part, she gets the Jeep and goes back to the filling station to fuel up and takes off just in the nick of time. The pearl closes and a new one will open, as the player discovers that the Jeep gets a flat tire while driving through a zombie-infested forest outside of L.A.

This example shows how the String of Pearls Method, along with a very simple component-gathering puzzle, can turn a plodding horror shooter game around for a much more suspenseful and entertaining spin.

## Provide Reactive Environments

The environment in video games must be somewhat reactive. Having *reactive environments* means that the game world responds to the player in logical and meaningful ways that help immerse the player in that game world.

This can mean that if the player sees a guy standing around as if he's waiting for something, the player's character should be able to walk up to and talk to the guy to find out some information about the place the player's character has found herself in. Or if there appears to be a weak spot in a wall, a strong enough force from the player's character should be able to knock a hole through it. Or if the player sees a neat looking door and wants to open it, she should be able to do so, or you should let her know, "This door is locked. To open it, you must find a key." This empowers the player to explore the game's environment and to treat it as if it were its own real self-contained world.

One of the most common complaints about early video games, especially 3D shooters, was the lack of reactive environments. Players' characters were given powerful firearms such as shotguns and could freely explore mazelike level maps, but they were restricted to only shooting bad guys in those maps. If players shot at computer monitors or TV screens, nothing would happen. Eventually enough complaints made developers rethink their game levels and how they could make environments respond to player actions, so that when a player shot a computer monitor or TV screen it would cause an explosion. This took more time coding and prepping the environments, but it paid off in the end, because that's what players wanted. Nowadays it is uncommon to find a 3D shooter where you aren't capable of putting holes through or blowing up just about anything you find in the game's environments. See Figure 11.7.

When in doubt about whether to make the game background more interactive, always opt for the "yes" answer, although it usually means more work for you.

**Figure 11.7**
One problem that shooter games used to have in them was having a character with unlimited firepower and flimsy, locked wooden doors she couldn't get past. . .. What was that about? *Swat 4*, by Irrational Games, gets it right!

## Immerse the Player

Have you ever played a game that you focused on so hard that when your friend called or your parents interrupted your concentration, you realized with shock you'd been playing for hours straight? Have you ever been playing a game so intently that you didn't want to stop? If the answer to either of these was "yes," then it's because you've discovered another key element of popular games: *immersion*.

When you hear the word immersion, you might immediately think of slipping into a hot tub and letting the warm bubbly water cover you. That's one form of immersion, and the slow sinking goodness of climbing into a Jacuzzi is more similar to game immersion than you might think.

Immersion makes gamers want to spend more time playing a game. It creates addictive gameplay by submerging players in the entertainment form. With immersion, you get so engrossed in a game that you forget it's a game! You lose track of the outside world. You also believe the intrinsic game rules more stringently than if you were not so immersed, a trick called the *suspension of disbelief* (covered in Chapter 10, "Game Design Fundamentals").

### Depths of Immersion

The following are the different depths of immersion the gamer (again, we'll use Sally) feels when playing a game:

- **Curiosity**: Sally feels a slight but fleeting interest in the game.

- **Sympathy**: Sally is paying attention to the game but is still not personally motivated; she can put the game down if she wants.

- **Identification**: Sally identifies with her character and suddenly has a vested interest in the game's outcome.

- **Empathy:** Even though the characters are make-believe, Sally shares a strong emotional connection with one or more of them and wants to see the best ending to the game.

- **Transportation**: This is the "plenary state" or dream-like trance that you enter into whenever you are really intent in playing a game. The game becomes more real to Sally than the room where she's playing it.

Perhaps to better understand how to make a game more immersive, it is first imperative to appreciate why players play games to begin with. What are a player's motivations?

### Discover the Player's Motivation

Tim Schafer, designer of such games as *Grim Fandango*, *Psychonauts*, and *Brutal Legend* (shown in Figure 11.8), once noted that all games, in his view, are about wish fulfillment. Whenever a player plays a game, she is put into a fictional scenario that she cannot experience in real life, and she can delight in the wonder, newness, and thrill of it all, at least for the duration of the game.

But wish fulfillment is an over-generalization of why players play games. There are many more factors that motivate people to play games. Let us take a look,

**Figure 11.8**
*Brutal Legend* is Tim Schafer's latest game, this time a third-person sandbox game with voiceover by actor Jack Black.

briefly, at a few. As you read through these motivating factors, consider what motivates you to play the games you like!

- **Escapism**: One of the top motivating factors reported by gamers is escapism. After a long day of real life, it is nice for them to escape from the mundane world and enter an imaginative, sometimes "limitless" universe, where their character might either have superhuman powers or be in the habit of breaking the law without facing ramifications. This is known as *cathartic release* by doctors, and it has been shown to improve behavior in even the most stable citizen. *Grand Theft Auto*, a game often subject to debates, allows players to mug old ladies, run over pedestrians with their car, steal automobiles, and more things that society deems inappropriate for citizens to do, even if some citizens harbor secret wishes to do them. The taboo is often okay in video games, for reasons of cathartic release. Are you ever motivated by escaping boredom, by entering an artificial reality?

- **Competition**: Lots of people play multiplayer online games, or MMOs, in order to compete with other players, either indirectly by gaining more tributes than other players or directly in player-versus-player, or PVP, confrontations. South Korea, the most wired nation in the world today, is the hub of game competition. The World Cyber Games, a sort of Olympic event for video game competitors, got its start in South Korea, and today it still converges for world finals in their part of the world. Players are bigger than life there, appearing on billboards and committing to celebrity ad campaigns to further their sponsorship. Do you find that the spirit of competition motivates you to play games?

- **Social Interaction**: All multiplayer games contain strong elements of social interaction, whether they are online, LAN-based, or multiplayer console games. Players can chat with other gamers over the Internet, even talk to other gamers by using headsets, and communication runs the gamut from taunts to strategy discussion. Some gamers band together in guilds, clans, or other social groups, often to team up together or to manage simulated worlds and societies. These games have also sparked a micro-economy of gamers buying and selling in-game merchandise in the real world for real coin. Do you ever play games that allow you to connect socially with others?

- **Creative Expression**: These games allow players to exhibit some form of creative expression. Games like *Def Jam* and *Dance Dance Revolution* allow gamers to express themselves musically, while games like *Dungeon Keeper* and *The Sims* allow gamers to build original environments to be utilized as game environments. Then there are countless role-playing games, sports games, and fighting games today that allow players to customize their characters in unique ways. All of these focus on creative expression factors. Some researchers go so far as to say there are two types of creative expression, which tie in with Sigmund Freud's *eros* and *thanatos* concepts: creative power and destructive power. Some games offer more creative power, such as *Sim City*, where you have to build and maintain a city, while others offer more destructive power, such as *Serious Sam*, where you blow up whole cities. Are you ever motivated to play a game that allows you to express yourself in some way?

- **Addiction**: A motivating factor that is difficult to clearly define is addiction, an intangible factor that results in an almost constant urge to play a game or type of game, without a rational explanation. Addiction works on a basic psychological level, consisting more of a feeling than a thought. Many people have criticized games for being addictive substances and game designers as being little better than peddlers of a narcotic agent, yet this case scenario has always been overruled by psychologists who point that the same traits of game addicts exist in bookworms, who cannot put down a new book. Have you ever found yourself playing a game for no apparent reason? Was it difficult for you to tear yourself away, even if you wanted to?

- **Therapy**: For some players of some games, the games can be a form of therapy. I do not mean cathartic release, as that is a part of escapism. Some doctors are beginning to prescribe games to their patients in order to relax them emotionally and to engage in eye-hand coordination for physical therapy. Patients after surgery to their fingers and hands are often encouraged to play console games like the Nintendo Wii, because it provides physical therapy for their recuperating digits, while at the same time removing the patient from his misery by providing escapism. A particular game called *Re-Mission*, created by Pam Omidyar and the HopeLab, focuses on a real-time cancer simulation, where the player controls Roxxi, a powered-up nano-bot destroying cancer cells in the human body. See Figure 11.9. *Re-Mission* has shown a small but marked improvement in the psychological well-being of cancer patients who have given it a go, proof of mind over matter perhaps. Do you ever find it relaxing and unwinding to play a game? Can playing a game sometimes be good therapy for you?

**Figure 11.9**
HopeLab's game *Re-Mission* has gotten a lot of publicity for its therapeutic qualities.

### Use Emotioneering

One of the premier ways to inspire immersion in players, to gently sink them into your game world, is by getting them to care. Once a player cares about her character, the outcome of the game, or the game's story and/or environment, then you can get that player to make hard decisions and manipulate her through the challenges you have set up for her.

You will learn that making players care about what happens in a game is not always an easy task. A radical new way game developers are approaching their trade is through *emotioneering*, whereby they use gamer emotions as buttons to press to make the experience more fraught, immersive, and riveting.

Fashion design guru Marc Eckō (shown in Figure 11.10) broke onto the video game world in 2006 with *Getting Up: Contents Under Pressure*, a game about a graffiti artist. Eckō called games "emotional entertainment products" because he considered games to be a form of entertainment unique in that it's the only form of entertainment that forces players to interact with it on a closely personal and emotional level. Emotions can be used to make players care about the games they play.

Eckō is not the only game creator out there who shares this viewpoint. Screenwriter David Freeman started the Freeman Group, which studies the many ways writers can put emotions into games. Freeman pioneered *emotioneering*, a cluster of techniques seeking to evoke in gamers a breadth and depth of rich emotions.

**Figure 11.10**
Marc Eckō's *Getting Up: Contents Under Pressure* has the player play at being an oppressed graffiti artist.

These emotions not only create stronger immersion, but they also generate control points for the designer to maneuver the player through the game.

Game developers consistently exercise a psychological gambit called the *emotion gap*. This is where the game developer makes use of a gamer's expectations and acts upon them to heighten suspense, make the gamer jump, or further enmesh the gamer in the game's mood. It is also useful for tugging the player around on a leash or getting her to be more interactive with the game environment.

For example, say that the developer wants to include a pit trap to block off parts of the dungeon he doesn't want his player going. He has designed it so that when the player comes near one of these areas, a short cut-scene starts, probably of an unwitting jungle rat running across a floor tile and the tile giving way, with the rat falling helplessly onto sharp spikes below. The floor tile that gave way beneath the rat has several cracks through it that other tiles do not, a dead giveaway (pardon the pun) of a pit trap lurking beneath. If the player ignores the designer's warning, she gets her character killed.

Later in the game, the designer will have the player chased by a monster and come across an entire labyrinth where half the hallway floors are covered in cracked tiles. It does not matter if there are pit traps in the floors or not, because by this point the player will make the logical association in her mind and start sweating at this point! This is one of the many ways to improve substance in your game by using the gamer's emotions against her. You sneaky devil, you. You didn't know psychology was such a useful tool in your design kit, now did you?

Flaws are another way that you can help the player grow fonder of and identify with the game's characters or settings. As Takayoshi Sato, art director of *Virtual Heroes* and the genius behind the *Silent Hill* and *Silent Hill 2* cinematics, says, "Finding flaws in your characters can bring them away from a false perfection, and creates great intimacy. Asymmetry is the typical method. The human face is not symmetrical—making the eyebrows unbalanced, or making one cheek sag compared to the other side, or even adding a distortion of the entire skull—these little things bring surprising intimacy." People and places are not 100% perfect, so neither should their virtual counterparts be.

Games can play with people's minds, manipulating the tenets of psychology to further gameplay or story progression. However, there are vast boundaries of psychology that have never been tapped in games.

Some dungeon and stealth games have emulated feelings of claustrophobia in gamers. Some cliff-top platformers have come near to arousing acrophobia—or fear of heights—in gamers, but only when the sensation of height was an exaggerated one. Other fears, such as the fear of the unknown, dread, and phobias of certain creatures like spiders, snakes, or clowns, have only been grazed by designers without any intent to push the boundaries. Most of the time, game developers will tell you that these sorts of immersive sensory tricks are only possible if the interface is just right: If the player is sitting in a darkened room at night with surround sound speakers and a bass that rumbles the house when playing games. Gamers approve of these set-ups, but few have the sort of income to afford them.

Most of the emotioneering tricks are subtle triggers you can plant in your game's story, including:

- Keeping the plot twists coming. Remember: "Out of the frying pan, into the fire."

- Having the other characters recognize or refer to one another as if they were real people.

- Giving the player ambivalent feelings toward an ally or enemy character, like loving and hating them at the same time.

- Forcing the player to do something evil or otherwise violate their character's integrity.

- Having the player discover she's been tricked or betrayed by an ally.

- Setting up incongruous events (like when the main character of Nintendo's *Chrono Cross* suddenly switches places with the main villain and has to gain new allies after losing all his friends).

### Set Up Conflict

One of the ways that games keep players involved is through the nature of *conflict*, which can be very emotional for the player.

Chris Crawford once said, "Conflict is an intrinsic element of all games. It can be direct or indirect, violent or nonviolent, but it is always present in every game." He goes on to describe why: "Conflict implies danger, danger means risk or harm, and harm is undesirable." Every human being and other animals are afraid of having harm come to them. No one likes to get hurt. Even human beings who are long-time sufferers, the so-called victims of learned helplessness, are not really all that keen on being hurt; they get used to greater rewards coming from being hurt a little, not a lot.

This element of conflict is simple. In gambling halls and casinos across America, the way people can get hurt by playing the games is that they can lose all their money at the craps tables or slot machines. But it is the essence of conflict that drives them to take the chance and win big or lose it all. The same is true for video games.

Conflict in established storytelling is straightforward. The audience is introduced to a character, made to feel something about that character, and then shown a dilemma that character faces. Whether or not the character survives the dilemma or triumphs in the end is the suspense-building conflict the writers weave into the story. The writers know they have to keep the reader or viewer on the edge of his seat in anticipation of the outcome.

Video games are not static. A game's audience includes the players of the game, and the player is often given control of a central figure in the game story. This puts the audience in direct control, and gives them an abiding interest in, the main character's future. The audience has a more intimate experience with the character of the game story, because that character is, in essence, them. The player's choices directly affect the outcome of the story, too, which adds an especially juicy wrinkle to this form of entertainment.

But how do you create tension? What could threaten the player enough to inspire conflict within the game? Surely there will be objectives for the player to succeed at in the game, but what threats will the player face?

Most video games feature "life points" where, after getting hit enough times, the player's onscreen avatar will eventually expire. This is why so many games are slammed by the media for having too much violence, because the threat of danger is represented as bodily harm coming to characters in the game.

It is very important to know the difference between conflict and violence, because they are not one and the same.

ESRB (Entertainment Software Rating Board), the gaming rating board (refer to Chapter 10, "Game Design Fundamentals"), has eight different rating definitions for violence. They are:

- **Animated Blood**: Discolored and/or unrealistic depictions of blood.

- **Blood**: Depictions of blood.

- **Blood and Gore**: Depictions of blood and/or mutilation of body parts.

- **Cartoon Violence**: Violent actions involving cartoon-like situations and characters; may include violence where a character is unharmed after the action has been inflicted.

- **Fantasy Violence**: Violent actions of a fantasy nature, involving human or non-human characters in situations easily distinguishable from real life.

- **Intense Violence**: Graphic and realistic-looking depictions of physical conflict; may involve extreme and/or realistic blood, gore, weapons, and depictions of human injury and death.

- **Mild Violence**: Mild scenes depicting characters in unsafe and/or violent situations.

- **Violence**: Scenes involving aggressive conflict.

Note that violence is "aggressive conflict," as opposed to being conflict in itself. Violence, therefore, is one type of conflict that can be represented in games but doesn't necessarily have to be.

When asked if a game could be non-violent, Warren Spector (shown in Figure 11.11), creator of games like *Thief: Deadly Shadows* and *Deus Ex: The*

**Figure 11.11**
Warren Spector is a game industry veteran who has created several triple-A titles.

*Invisible War,* said that it was frankly impossible. In his opinion, conflict implies the risk of winning or losing, and in video games it is often how many times your character gets fragged that decides the conflict.

In the day and age of coin-op arcades, the loss of their quarters was enough to make players wag their heads in shame if they lost. Today's players are forced back to previously saved checkpoints or made to lose treasure or experience points they have gained as their punishment for losing. The penalty has to appear large enough to threaten players to seek greater rewards within the game, and one way to do that is through violence or implied violence.

What are some other ways to threaten players that do not include violence? If you think about it, games have a penalty/reward system built into them, where the player can get hurt (penalty) or gain something (reward). The simplest game is one where a player gains ambiguous Score Points for doing good in the game and loses the same Score Points for not doing so good. That being said, what you rate as "good" or "not so good" are dependent on you, the designer, as long as you are sure to impart that difference to your player. Therefore, you could have a completely non-violent game that does not upset anybody and still have a fun game.

## Prep for Emergent Gameplay

There is another form of interactive play and a way that a player's emotions can be infused in the game. This technique, called *emergent gameplay,* is created almost by accident, or is a side effect you might say, of free-roaming or "sandbox" games like *Grand Theft Auto* or *World of WarCraft*, in which the player creates her own stories.

Give the player breathing room and enough random elements with which to interact and then let her shape the game herself. This is called *collaboration*, or where you are the co-author of the game, and the player creates the other half by his or her actions. Occasionally players will design their own fun that was not intended or anticipated by the game's designers.

For instance, in early trial builds of Lionhead Studios' game *Fable* (seen in Figure 11.12), which, at that time, was going under the code name *Project Ego*, players discovered that their avatar could marry women characters in the game and earn a small dowry by doing so. They also learned that if they killed the women's fathers, their avatar would inherit the family fortune. So several players during beta testing made a game of marrying women and offing the women's fathers to gain money, something that surprised, enlightened, and kind of delighted the game's designers.

The designers were surprised and enlightened because it showed them a loophole, or cheat, the players could use to make money in the game that they weren't supposed to (the inheritance part of the programming was removed from later builds), but it also delighted the designers, because they knew they were making a game that would inspire emergent gameplay, something a lot of designers like to witness.

**Figure 11.12**
Romance is certainly not dead in Lionhead Studios' game *Fable*.

## Game Challenges

**Tip**

"The very best games are the ones where you have to figure out what the object is. The trick is to provide direction subtle enough that it's not perceived immediately. Theme parks have that, too. When you enter Disneyland, you don't know the Sleeping Beauty Castle is your objective, but there's no doubt when you're in Town Square that you should be walking up Main Street USA. Just like in a great game, you always have an idea that you need to go this way or that way. Eventually you catch on to the themed worlds and the central hub."

—Danny Hills

A real game wouldn't be a game if it didn't offer the player a challenge. The types of challenges games offer vary widely, from the accumulation of resources to puzzles to self-preservation. Many challenges are staples of the game genres they belong in; others fit with the gameplay and are thus included.

The most important thing you can remember about challenges is that they are met with bravado. All the cheats that you see online for games have been discovered and used by gamers who have learned the one almighty truth when it comes to winning video games: "Don't play the game, play against the game's underlying programming!"

Dennis Wixon who worked with Microsoft Games Studios in Redmond, Washington, says about challenges, "You're always trying to get the right level of challenge. You can't be too simple or it's not fun. [Nolan] Bushnell's famous quote is something along the lines of, 'A game should be easy to pick up and impossible to master.' We want that sweet spot where there's always another threshold to cross. In *Halo 1*, as we improved targeting, we found it was too intelligent and too simple. It was pretty straightforward for the Bungie team to fix that...."

Andrew Glassner calls this process the *game loop*, a cycle of repetitive steps the player takes to win at any given game challenge:

1. Player observes the situation.

2. Player sets goals to overcome the challenge.

3. Player researches or prepares.

4. Player commits to plan and executes decisions.

5. Player stops and compares the results of his actions to his original intention.

6. Player evaluates the results.

7. Player returns to step 1.

## Types of Game Challenges

Most of the time, challenges take the form of obstacles that must be overcome. Either the player's character faces hordes of hungry zombies shuffling along a grainy windswept city street, or the player's character is trapped within a ski lodge during a blizzard while a serial killer erases all of the player's in-game allies one by one. These game obstacles, and the resulting types of game challenges, can be classified into these categories:

- Lock mechanisms

- Mazes

- Monsters

- Traps

- Quests

- Puzzles

### Lock Mechanisms

Some of these challenges habitually appear as lock mechanisms, and players are used to them (and the standard manner in which the lock mechanisms must be unlocked). *Lock mechanisms* by their very nature fence the player in, preventing access to some area or reward in the game until that moment when the player beats the challenge and unlocks the next area or recovers the reward.

The simplest and most prosaic lock mechanism is a common lock: a locked door, a jammed gateway, or elevator without power stand in the way of the player getting to level three or three hundred. The player knows when encountering any aperture that is locked that she must find the "key" to unlocking it.

Other lock mechanisms are more subtle. For instance, an overbearing guard standing at attention at the gate the player wants passage through might just be overcome if the player bribes him with a peanut butter and banana sandwich.

And let's not forget blood locks. *Blood locks* are where the player is locked in a single locale (usually a room or arena) with lots of foes to defeat, and the exit

**Figure 11.13**
LucasArts' game *Zombies Ate My Neighbors* has recently been released as a retro Wii game.

from the locale will not appear until the player destroys all oncoming enemies. Blood locks can be seen in most third-person fighting and shooter games, such as Midway's *Gauntlet: Dark Legacy*. An imaginative twist on this is the '80s game from LucasArts, *Zombies Ate My Neighbors*, where the lock's goal is not to defeat all the zombies (and other monsters) that keep popping up, but to save the neighbors. See Figure 11.13.

Whatever the lock mechanism you might use, it will be a powerful vital tool in your arsenal of gameplay devices, and it should be scripted with intelligence and creativity to work right.

### Mazes

Below-average gamers can get lost in standard game levels, so making the level more difficult to get through by adding in lots of twists, turns, and deadends might quickly make for a player headache. On the other hand, if you use an in-game map or set up a trail of breadcrumbs and some clever surprises along the way, a maze can become a wonderfully entertaining way to break the monotony of locked doors.

A maze can be one of the simplest ways to make a game more fun, as long as you don't leave the player completely in the dark on where to go. Besides, no one likes a straight-and-narrow game environment with nothing in it but blank space, so tinker with your game maps and make them thrilling to explore.

### Monsters

Fighting games have progressive matches where the player must beat a tough opponent. Shooters have hordes of stinking zombies, war-time combatants, shielded androids, or other dehumanized monsters running at the player, which she must mow down with her firepower. Role-playing games have dungeons littered with monsters to tackle, and tackling them wins the player treasure or experience points.

Battles with monsters typify the combat system of these game genres. There is always something to be gained by overcoming the monsters in games, no matter how unlikely it might seem. Even killer crows tend to drop boxes of gold.

Monsters should never get short shrift. They scare and titillate us on an instinctive level, and they make for fearsome foes, even if they are normal-looking humans in tanker gear. Either the monsters block the door to escape or they carry the key to the next level. Many games will ramp up the difficulty by using an evolution of ever-tougher monsters for us to fight. And the toughest of all are the "boss monsters" that guard the gates on the hero's journey (or at least the end of the level).

One monster is usually not enough for a single locale, excepting Piggsy in Rockstar's game *Manhunt* in the "Deliverance" level. Usually, each monster is of a "type" and each "type" has several variations, making up a slew of dangerous baddies.

You might notice, if you have ever played Midway's *Gauntlet: Dark Legacy*, that the game features several monster types: foot soldiers, kamikaze creatures with explosive barrels strapped to their backs, archers slinging arrows, magic-casting sorcerers, and so on. Then, in each game region, *Gauntlet* will feature these same types given unique traits to that region. So, for instance, the monsters will all be in various decomposing states of the undead in the "Forsaken Province" region, or they will all look like wrapped-up Egyptian mummies in the "Desert Land." In some games, the only way to tell types apart is the color of the monster.

### Traps

Traps, as shown in Figure 11.14, are a hodgepodge of suspense, scenery, and intrigue. Good traps can have whole stories behind them. Give some thought to each and every trap you place. Here are some things to keep in mind when creating traps for your game....

**Figure 11.14**
Since the days of classic *Prince of Persia*, spike traps have been featured as a common obstacle in video games.

A trap in a high cleric's abbey may appear and work very differently from a trap set in a demon warlord's dungeon. Traps reflect the places and people who built them, even if they do share a common goal: to stop trespassers or thieves. Use style to cater your traps to the game's locale. Consider adjusting traps according to their immediate surroundings, including terrain, special features of the land, and weather conditions.

Traps do not need to be lethal. Some may be designed to wound, harm, or hold a trespasser. Others may raise an alarm, scare off, or deter would-be invaders in other ways. Some traps may not have actually been designed to be traps in the first place, but through age and disuse or negative natural conditions accident-prone areas may have developed. A typical example of such is a rickety bridge that, over the years, has planks that have started to rot and rope that has started to fray: A once-solid bridge may end up a death trap for our hero!

Traps must have two elements in order to work properly: a trigger, or means by which the trap monitors conditions and knows when to spring, and a response, or a way to deliver the trap's full effect. When creating traps, consider that players can evade traps in one of three ways:

- They could bypass the trigger, leaving the trap intact for later.

- They could prevent the response, basically disabling the effectiveness of the trap.

■ They could sever the connection between the trigger and the response, so the trap can spring but nothing happens.

Traps, like monsters, have become a staple of popular games ever since the days of pen-and-paper games like *Dungeons and Dragons*. One of the earliest video games to showcase traps was Atari's *Pitfall!* in 1982. In it, the player character Pitfall Harry must leap or swing over tar pits, quicksand, water holes, rolling logs, crocodiles, and more.

In 2005 a game from Tecmo, called *Trapt*, had the player using magic to set up and spring vicious traps on bad guys chasing after and trying to harm the player's character, a young helpless girl named Princess Allura. The player of this game earned additional points, leading to the ability to build bigger, more deadly traps later on, for mauling enemies in clever ways or doubling traps.

## Quests

*Quests* are special sets of challenges that take place in both stories and games, thus linking narrative and play. Quest games, including the *King's Quest* series, have quests that make up activities in which the players must overcome specific challenges in order to reach a goal. When players successfully surmount the challenges of the quest and achieve the quest's main goal, the player's actions bring about or unlock a series of events comprising the game story.

Game writers often cite Joseph Campbell's monomyth or "hero's journey" as a pattern for their quest games. In the "hero's journey" there are several legendary steps, which you can imagine as a staircase, where the first step starts with the hero in his own world confronted with a terrible evil threat requiring him to go where he's never gone before or do things he's never done before. This mythic story structure forms the basis for the majority of our ancient legends and our current Hollywood story compositions. For a look at this pattern, you should peer at *Star Wars* and *The Lord of the Rings*. You can read more about the monomyth in Chapter 6, "Character and Story."

As Jesper Juul explained in *Half-Real: Video Games between Real Rules and Fictional Worlds*, "Quests in games can actually provide an interesting type of bridge between game rules and game fiction in that the games can contain predefined sequences of events that the player then has to actualize or effect." You don't have to write a quest game to use quests to improve your games.

Many of your standard action or shoot-'em-up games, including 2K Games' *BioShock*, have implemented quests to reveal narrative and create further depth of player experience.

Quests, also called *missions* in game-speak, would be very dull if they were uneventful. If you told the player, "Go to Ornery Cave and bring back the Scepter of Sam," and the player went to the cave, conveniently marked for her on her map, and returned with the scepter, it would be very boring indeed. Instead, you have the player go to the cave and fight or sneak her way past a gaggle of killer geese to get inside. Then when she does get the scepter, the walls begin to close in. When the player barely escapes Ornery Cave alive, she is beset by highwaymen intent on robbing her of the scepter. Eventually the player finishes her mission with a sense of fulfillment and pride. That is the manner in which plot must be kept in pace with tension; anything less will end with the player scratching her head, wondering what the point to your game is supposed to be.

### Puzzles

The most noted use of puzzles in video games, aside from actual puzzle games like *Bejeweled* and *Tetris*, are the use of objects to further the story. If the player does not know what key will unlock a specific lock mechanism to continue her quest in the game, she will have to find it.

Sometimes this is through the obvious use of in-game objects. For instance, say that the player's character can see a key lodged in the keyhole on the other side. If the player can find something small, like an ice pick, she can push the key out, and if she has something thin and flat, like a newspaper, she can pull the key through the bottom of the door. Then she can unlock the door.

Unfortunately, some puzzles require unusual use of in-game objects to fix a situation. One of the most notorious was in one of LucasArts' *Secret of Monkey Island* games, where the designers expected the gamer to pair a monkey with a wrench to create a spanner to throw into the works and stop a machine from working. (Get it, a monkey wrench? No, neither did most of the players out there.)

Some puzzles are cryptographic or clue-driven in nature, where the player must supply a crucial bit of info, such as a password, key code, whodunit, etc., to pass by a guard, a locked door, open a wall safe, or close the case. To figure out what the code/password/other is, the player must search for clues. These clues are often left lying around in convenient journals, computer e-mail messages, tape recordings, or by talking to people. The player may have to figure out what something cryptic means in order to identify a clue, such as a cryptogram (a short, encrypted text message) or rebus (a word puzzle that uses pictures or parts of pictures to represent words).

## What's Next?

Now that you understand the player's motivation and psyche and know how to entertain her better, let's look at game worlds and what goes into making them.

## Review

At the end of reading this chapter, you should know:

- The best ways to offer player interaction and decision-making

- How to write a game script and use game narrative to entertain the player

- The most common reasons why players play video games

- How to fully immerse players in your game world

- All about emergent gameplay and why it can be useful

- The types of game challenges and how to use them in your game

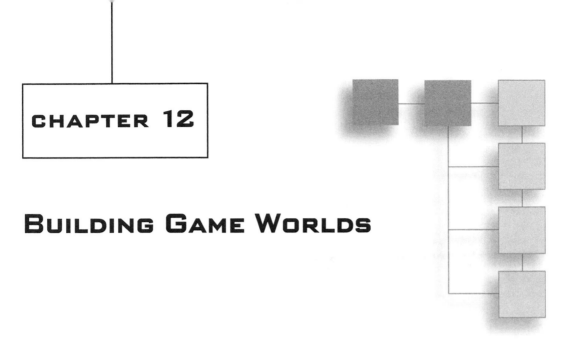

# CHAPTER 12

# BUILDING GAME WORLDS

In this chapter you will learn:

- About World Immersion

- About level design

- How the gamer interacts with the game through its interface

Without an appropriate playground in virtual space, a game could never take place. The player would be just so many random pieces without a place to be. Gameplay also has to have a background for reference, a playground for the player to explore, find resources, and beat combatants in.

One of the key features players look at when playing games is the artwork. Simply stunning vistas, crumbling mountain ruins, and rusty futuristic metalwork can always astound a gamer, but making those places explorable and interactive helps further game immersion, putting the player into the game like nothing else can. This is the connection between playing a video game and being at an amusement park, like Disney World.

**Figure 12.1**
Danny Hillis invented the Clock of the Long Now, a timepiece that is supposed to last 10,000 years, and left a posh job at Disney to bring technological innovations to the entertainment industry.

## World Immersion

Themepark imaginer Danny Hillis (as seen in Figure 12.1) designed ride technology for Disney, but now he also makes computer games. He says, "Parks take you out of the everyday and re-create that sense of wonder from childhood, the time when nothing made sense, when you didn't know what would happen next and didn't need to. They're wonderful, thrilling, and unpredictable—but safe. That's how I felt the first time I played *The Legend of Zelda*. It was a new thing."

I often tell my students that designing a game is a lot like being a host at a haunted house theme park (shown in Figure 12.2), or a really good travel agent. You are removing the players from their reality construct and plunking them down somewhere completely new and scary.

You are also designing for them a weekend getaway, a retreat, and if you don't start thinking about it that way, you will end up creating for them a sloppy awful place they'll never want to come back to.

Consider, when designing your game maps, what the visual and emotional impact is of every part of your world. Put yourself in your player's shoes all the time, and just have fun. If you're not having fun, the player won't have any fun. This will guarantee game immersion on a deeply psychological level.

**Figure 12.2**
The House of Torment in Austin, Texas, is sure to scare would-be visitors.

## Level by Level

Inside this game world there are several scenes, or chapters, we call *levels*. Each level is its own distinctive region with its own set of objectives that the player must reach before he can travel to the next level. To continue the analogy of the haunted house, levels are like each of the rooms visitors go into to get scared.

*Level design* is formally defined as the creation of environments, scenes, scenarios, or missions in an electronic game world. Being a level artist is like being part architect, part interior designer, part illusionist, and part tour guide.

Most 3D level artists use level design tools, or level editors, such as Valve Hammer Editor (Valve Software), Unreal Editor (Epic Games, shown in Figure 12.3), or the Torque World Editor (GarageGames). Or they use 3D graphics editing software like 3ds Max, Maya, or SoftImage XSI (Autodesk). 2D level artists, on the other hand, use editors like Game Maker (YoYo Games) or Flash (Adobe).

## Elements of Levels

Almost every game level is composed of the following:

- Basic geometry or architecture (you know. . . the stuff player characters walk and jump on)

- Details such as textures or sprite decals

- Stage props such as models of furniture, trees, rocks, and so on

- Lighting

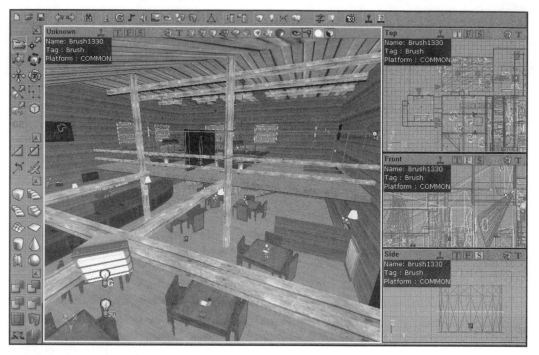

**Figure 12.3**
3D level artists use level editors like the Unreal Editor from Epic Games.

- In-game artifacts, or the items that can be picked up or interacted with, such as power-ups

- Non-player characters, allies, or pedestrians

- Enemies, monsters, or other obstacles

- Goals

- History

- Environmental teasers

- Gimmicks

- Artistic or cultural style

### Goals

Each level should have a clear set of objectives called *goals* that the player understands and operates from. Otherwise, the player will assume he is supposed to move around, shooting or eating everything in sight, finding all the gold, puzzle-solving, or collecting points until a signal appears to tell him the level is complete or that a new level is loading.

Some game designers put "briefings" at the beginning of their game levels in the form of a cut-scene or tutorial.

**Goal Trackers**    A designer might also place *goal trackers*, or in-game objects, that update the player on the status of accomplishing her goal. Goal trackers are expected to change during the course of the game to show the player how close she is to getting to the goal. For instance, an arrow might point the way to where the player needs to go, or a progress report might show the player how "hot" or "cold" she is getting.

**Training Levels**    The best games start the player out slowly, letting the player "get her feet wet," learning the game rules and the expected rewards/punishments, before ramping up the difficulty.

Some games start the player off with *training levels*, where the player suffers no adverse repercussions such as life-or-death consequences for her actions, and where she is led by hand along the way. Training levels also help players learn how to play the game before they get started.

Most games today allow the player the option of training levels while letting the action of the game start right away, so players that feel unsure can learn while players ready to tackle the fun stuff can jump right in.

### History

A rich immersive world needs to have a tradition or history about it. Think about what came before. Realize that for there to be a tree growing in a battlefield, that tree had to start out as a seedling. Consider who built the imaginary cities in your levels, who has lived in the ancient ruins before, who set the traps, and where the monsters came from. Levels should not just exist in limbo but should have a history surrounding them.

If possible, the information you learn about the history should figure into gameplay, but although this is ideal, it is not a fixed rule.

You might not even share the world history with your players, but it will help you to crystallize details about the setting and figure out how everything ties in together.

### Environmental Teasers

One of the most difficult but definitely one of the most rewarding level elements is the environmental teaser. *Environmental teasers* give the player an illusion of world depth, or that there is an entire world just outside the area the player is looking at right now or currently exploring (see Figure 12.4). Even indoor levels are better if they have some windows or skylights or cracks in the walls that give the player a glimpse of the outdoors, the current time of day, or the weather conditions. You will succeed in making your player more curious about, and inspired by, the little details you put into your game world, and the player will explore more of the game world, if you use environmental teasers.

Common environmental teasers include:

- A few awesome background shots in the distance

- Architectural details that sweep out past the playing area

- Apertures in the walls that share glimpses of another area outside

- Swooping camera shots that zoom in on the main character while giving a brief glance at the outside terrain

- Sound effects of things going on just outside the playable area

**Figure 12.4**
Blue Omega's shooter game *Damnation* featured levels like the one above, rich and immersive with lots of places to explore.

### Gimmicks

A lot of games, from the early years of SEGA and Nintendo onward, contain gimmick areas. In marketing, a *gimmick* is a quirky feature that distinguishes a product, establishing familiarity with the person who might buy the product. A lot of games have whole levels that are gimmicks in and of themselves. Gimmick levels are immediately memorable for players, similar to the use of mythic symbols in stories. Gimmicks can become so tacky, though, that they become clichés, so be careful that if you use gimmick levels they don't become too dull.

Some of the most common gimmick levels found in games include:

- A sewer level full of noxious fluid, low lighting, and nasty surprises

- An underwater level where the player swims with the fishes

- A lava level where one wrong step hurts

- A graveyard level where the dead start coming back to life

- An icy realm where slick surfaces, snowfalls, and prickly icicles form obstacles

- A wind-tunnel level where the player might get blown away

- A high up-in-the-clouds level where a fall would be disastrous

- A mine cart ride where gaps in the track are decidedly fatal

Look at the games you like to play, and I'm sure you will see obvious gimmicks, although they are more notable in platformers and action games.

Regardless of whether you use a gimmick in your game or not, be sure that the area you choose to represent your game is tied neatly to the game's narrative. Don't throw a graveyard level crawling with undead monsters into an otherwise level-headed science fiction game on Mars unless you are absolutely sure you can get it to fit or explain it with the story.

According to industry veterans, you should brainstorm these gimmicks and write them down on paper, then keep only the best 8 out of 10.

Try to make your gimmick levels fresh, so they don't become hashed-out or parodied clichés. For instance, if you plan to stick a cemetery full of undead in your game, consider what is making the undead crawl out of their graves. Are they hungry for brains? Are they dissatisfied with the building construction next door, or with the necromancer who has taken up residency in their crypts?

If you plan to drop your player into a level filled with dangerous goop (a twist on the lava level idea), where one wrong step makes the avatar messy or toast, consider first what makes the goop so deadly, where it comes from, and why it is in this level to begin with. If the goop is supposed to be lava, why doesn't the player's character spontaneously combust this close to it or choke to death on the sulfurous fumes? If the goop is green toxic sludge, who created the nasty chemical and who dumped it here?

When you ask these questions (who, what, when, where, why, and how) you will discover a wealth of fresh gimmick ideas that may be untapped by previous level designers.

### Artistic Style

Most level designers copy real-world concepts of architecture and nature. Many actually go location scouting, taking digital photographs of the areas or drawing quick sketches in their notebooks. They incorporate their photos or their sketches into their environments they build in 2D or 3D.

The most difficult design component of working on levels in 3D, as opposed to 2D, by the way, is that the level must look good from any angle, because the player will be able to explore the level and by so doing will see the realm in all three dimensions and from many possible angles. Not only 3D level artists, but also architects and interior designers have to keep this in mind.

Think of places where you would like to vacation. These places are fun, they are outside the ordinary, breathtaking even, and each of them has that special *feng shui*. You ought to learn to integrate *feng shui* into your level designer. We'll get back to that in a moment, but one of the ways you do this is through proper use of artistic style.

The level artist's style will carry throughout the level and create a rhythm or mood that pulls it all together. The style influences everything, including the way characters will dress, the game interface, the architecture and way structures look, the level exteriors, and the rules of the game. American artists tend to be rather conservative in nature, but many of them have been influenced by global trends, such as the Japanese style of animation called *manga*, to create cutting-edge games that push the boundaries.

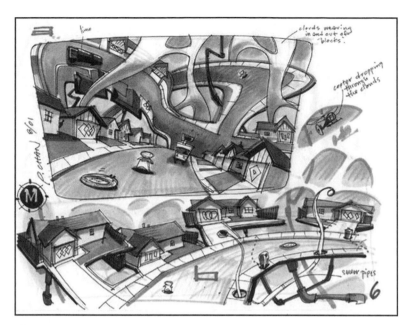

**Figure 12.5**
Original concept art for the Milkman level in Tim Schafer's and Double Fine's *Psychonauts* game.

Tim Schafer's game *Psychonauts* is well known for its Milkman level (revealed in Figure 12.5), which actually recreates an M.C. Escher masterpiece in a third-person action game. It is unique because the laws of physics no longer apply. One moment you might be standing upside-down, above the area you were on just moments ago!

### Cultural Style

Culture can definitely influence level art style. Dusty Western shooter game levels are affected by the pioneer days of America's Wild West and may feature dust-swept towns, rowdy saloons, iron-horse engines, clapboard wagons, and ranch-style farmhouses. Games like Beep Industries' *Voodoo Vince* and Acclaim Entertainment's *Shadow Man* (shown in Figure 12.6) utilize the romance and superstitions surrounding New Orleans in Louisiana. Their voodoo atmosphere evince a spectacular cultural style all its own.

The same can be true of made-up fantasy cultures. Each culture in a fantasy role-playing game like Blizzard Entertainment's *World of WarCraft* or Ankama Games' *Dofus* should be as distinct from the next as possible, and the application of their cultural style can change the look and feel of a game level, one from the next.

**Figure 12.6**
Acclaim Entertainment's game *Shadow Man* had voodoo action going on in it.

I will give an example. The Norse folk of yore believed that elves fell into two categories: Light Elves, of tree and lake, and Dark Elves, of tunnel and shadow. Popular fantasy fiction has applied this folklore to manufacture two distinguishable cultures, one of the green nature-loving elves, who play music while tripping lightly through oaken groves, and another race of elves, which live in the Underworld and worship powers of darkness and cruelty. Each culture has a shared lineage, but neither would look like or behave like the other.

Light Elves have flaxen gold hair, while Dark Elves appear as polished jet with snow-white hair. Light Elves dress in tanned leathers and bark, green leaves and vine-whirled patterns, and they would probably live in trees, while Dark Elves dress all in black, so as to blend into shadow better, and live in caves. This split between two similar but different societies would form naturally distinct cultures, each with its own unique style. You could liven up a normally dull fantasy role-playing game by embellishing the two cultures even more and adding little details to their game levels. For instance, Light Elves might carve oak leaf patterns on the wood timbers of their tree-house homes, while Dark Elves might trace the silver filigree likeness of spider webs and poisonous snakes on the cold stone of their dwellings.

### Be Aware of Software Limitations

Most video games are inherently visual, so players will always count on experiencing your game through its graphics. Most video games are auditory, in other words, they have awesome sound effects and voiceovers by paid actors. *Haptic systems* are interactive devices where you can feel, or get direct sensation from, your video game. When I describe haptic systems, I am usually referring to the rumble function of console game controllers that vibrate whenever a player's character's health sinks too low or their avatar gets slammed by an oncoming bus.

Some science fiction writers extrapolate that eventually we all will be plugged into a matrix and get direct virtual play shot straight to our brains. The television show *Star Trek: The Next Generation* featured a place called a *holodeck*, where a room creates a nearly real 3D imagination environment that is as small as a private eye's smoke-filled office or as grand as the peaks of Mount Vesuvius, and you can dictate what sorts of enjoyment or escapism you want to experience. These wild-seeming imaginings are not that far off. Today, however, we must make do with our computer screens and input devices, which are supremely limited.

We simple human beings have 250 million receptor cells in our eyes, 120 to 140 degrees of visual field scope, a depth that discerns hue, saturation, light, and darkness, and fully stereoscopic and constantly shifting visual focus. Viewing a computer monitor hampers our visual field. For instance, a monitor only has a 45-to-60-degree angle of visibility, a low light intensity range of about 255, and flickers at 50 to 100 Hz. Absolute darkness on a computer monitor is impossible. The monitor is also fixed and cannot shift its focus as rapidly or in as stereoscopic a way as humans can. 3D video cards are trying to raise the standard for a computer, but there will always be some limitations. And that is just a look at the visual handicaps.

Let us look at the auditory ones. Humans can detect fully 3D sounds, react to minute echo clues, can speak or even sing any time at will, and are not normally followed around by a music soundtrack, with the exception of people who walk around with iPod buds glued to their ears. In opposition, a computer has only limited reflection of 3D sounds along separate channels, cannot accurately simulate echo sounds yet, does not allow gamers to speak or sing at will into virtual reality (and even if they can, it is never guaranteed there will be appropriate feedback), and often force onto gamers music soundtracks meant to heighten emotions.

University-funded game development tcams are experimenting right now with games designed for the sight-handicapped, or the blind, that focus on sounds alone and have no real graphics to them. They use a state-of-the-art Doppler system built into 3D game engines.

I won't even go into touch or olfactory receptors that we humans have that are vastly underutilized by games today, but maybe one of these days you will see a game that allows you to smell flower-strewn fields or gross you out with the stench of death as you enter a slaughterhouse. Or they might allow you to pick up and feel objects that aren't even there, with special gloves. Who knows?

There is one thing games are good at, and that is messing with people's minds. For reference on how to use a gamer's brain against him through emotioneering, read Chapter 11, "Players and Objectives."

### Build a Vacation or Amusement Park

Again, one of my rules of thumb when developing levels for a game is to consider the game world as a giant amusement park, vacation resort, or haunted house, and the player as a client, tourist, or visitor. Players play games, watch movies, and read books about far-off locales, pretty or scary landscapes, and places the players themselves wish they could visit. This is one of the main components of escapism, and one of the leading motivations for gamers to play video games.

If you have a game that is decent to play, has a great story, and unique characters, it might still suffer on the player market. You might not know why, but it might be because the levels are plain and uninteresting. Get it in your head quickly that, as a game designer, you are delivering a whole package: Treat your players as tourists and be their tour guide, setting them up for thrills in lush and exciting game worlds!

## Level Architecture

*Level architecture*, which creates space and defines the virtual reality, plays an important role in game development, because it provides a point of reference for the player and sets the stage for the game action.

Level architecture serves a multifold purpose. Here are the top reasons why you use level architecture:

■ To set the stage

■ To create game flow

- To set the mood or theme

- To fence the player in

**Tip**

"Most often, when you think of game art, it is the characters and creatures that come to mind—even though it is the environments those creatures inhabit that really creates the illusion of a world. ... You want your game to be convincingly real to truly inspire mood and drama—and yet you have to be inventive without straining credulity. It's a matter of combining and synthesizing, keeping the aspirations in your head, but looking for new ways to fit it all together."

—Marc Taro Holmes, Obsidian Entertainment

### Set the Stage

Impressiveness and decoration are frequently the only ways that real-life architecture influences game architecture. Buildings created in this virtual space do not have to suffer with usability concerns. Windows and doors can look like real windows and doors, but the level artist doesn't have to worry himself with making them sized correctly so people can use them. Although you want to make places look like they could exist, they don't have weight, they don't really exist, and so you do not have to confine yourself to physical limitations when building them. Game levels can twist and wind and ignore the laws of physics or gravity. Such building details as protection from the weather are irrelevant because weather, if it is shown in the game at all, is purely cosmetic.

Game scenes, whether 2D or 3D, are little better than a theatrical stage with cardboard props (like in Figure 12.7). A lot of times, games will have buildings that are merely "false fronts" and have no real depth to them, or tree lines with nothing beyond them but the illusion of a bigger world out there. You might have witnessed these first-hand in games where your character falls outside the actual level and is floating in empty space.

Level architecture, therefore, is more about gameplay than it is about perfect simulation of the real world. Compare level architecture to movie sets in that they both support the narrative by putting certain details in graphic context for the viewer or gamer. They do this by mimicking real-world buildings and objects, but they do so only as necessary to the story.

### Create Game Flow

The most important function of level architecture in games is to support the gameplay. When working off a game outline, a game can be long or short,

**Figure 12.7**
This painted backdrop to a stage play is not that much different than game levels.

depending on the built-in challenges and resources. It can also be based on the detail of level architecture. A game where each level is the size a small dormitory will be vastly different from a game where each level is the size of Las Vegas, obviously. The pacing of the game's action, what is called *game flow* by industry professionals, can be short and sweet or long and meditative and is often dictated by the size and complexity of the game's levels and their content.

### Set the Mood or Theme

The secondary function of level architecture is to support the mood or theme of the game. The reason that mood or theme gets a backseat to game flow is because there should be a careful balance between each, and if there is any dispute, game flow must take priority. It is far too easy to create a beautiful game level but not think to make it serviceable to the player. Kevin Saunders of Obsidian Entertainment says, "If a level plays well, you'll find a way to make it pretty, but the reverse isn't necessarily true."

As mentioned, places in game levels are analogous to movie sets: they are collections of false fronts and "dress up" the scene rather than serve the virtual people so-called "living" there. There are no right and wrong ways to engineer game levels, and sometimes doors and houses can be made to fit humans and sometimes can be eight or ten times larger, as if for giants. When it comes down to it, it is all up to you. Sometimes irregular and asymmetrical level engineering is curiouser and more enjoyable to look at than stodgy "realistic" engineering. Just remember that game levels have to set the stage for the action later on.

People respond emotionally and reactively to familiar locations and styles of architecture. A creepy candle-lit castle has a vastly different atmosphere than a bright, cheerful glen with birds chirping in the trees. Game architecture, when used appropriately, sets up game atmosphere, and game atmosphere becomes the background for gameplay and reflects the mood and emotional string-pulling that you, the game designer, are trying to accomplish.

Look at fantasy role-playing games such as Blizzard's *Diablo* game (shown in Figure 12.8). In these game types, the player character often starts out in a homey inn or tavern filled with boisterous non-player characters, and before long she is trekking through some nearby dungeon, which is cold and foul, with water dripping from slimy stone walls and gloomy music sets the ambience. Dungeons do not have too many characters in them, only cretinous beasts to defeat. Even the least experienced player can gather that one area is for recuperation and equipment management, while the other is for exciting if somewhat terrifying action.

Level design can entertain and set the atmosphere for a game, immersing the gamer in the world, making her feel like she's actually hiking through steep mountain trails or hacking up monsters in dank dungeons. Make your scenes as realistic or quirky as you want, given the limitations of the software you use, and make them appropriate to the story and characters your player meets. If you do that, you have the underpinnings of a truly great game!

### Fence the Player In

Architecture also serves to hide the fact that the player character is actually inside a big invisible box she cannot escape. The box must have virtual constraints as to how far, and where, a game character can explore. Without a proper frame of

**Figure 12.8**
Blizzard's RPG *Diablo* featured awful, dank dungeons slimy with mood.

reference, the player would not be able to get around in the virtual world you are creating. Without appropriate level architecture, the player character could even wander outside the bounds of the game field!

Keeping players from wandering off the game field you have constructed or going places you don't want them to go is called "*fencing the player in*" by game developers. Your fences may be frustrating for the player as a general rule of thumb, because nobody likes being told they cannot go somewhere nor do something they want to do, so you have to make your fences patently obvious. The player has to understand that the fences are part of the level and not merely thrown in to frustrate them. Most games don't advertise their game world boundaries, but there has not been a game yet built that didn't have some kind of boundary. Essentially, the level architecture puts these boundaries into graphic context.

## Level Layout

The level layout can also influence the game flow.

Let's go back to *feng shui*, which I mentioned earlier. *Feng shui* is a concept used by some Asian and American architects and contractors to create an atmosphere within a building. This atmosphere follows the flow of invisible energy called *chi* through the building. Interior designers and artists think along these same lines, considering where a visitor's or viewer's eye will go when looking at a room or painting. Think of the chi within your game world. You have to decide where the gamer looks and where you want her to look next.

Games that do not take this into consideration are often easy to spot, because gamers complain about constantly getting lost or not knowing where to head next. The level layout should always make the player's goal apparently obvious, unless you expect her to get lost intentionally, as in a maze game.

There are roughly four ways a game can be laid out:

- Linear

- Non-linear

- Hub-based

- Death-match

What is the difference between linear, non-linear, or hub-based games? It's simple: the game might, or might not, support backtracking, or there might be a central location the player keeps coming back to. These are the sorts of considerations taken into account when the game scripts are constructed.

### Linear Layout

Linear games do not have to be sidescrolling platformers, although that's where they originated. A *linear layout* is where the player never has to stop or backtrack but steadily proceeds from Point A, the start, to Point B, the end, while overcoming any obstacle in between.

The pro to making linear levels is that they are fairly straightforward. Players don't have to wander around, wondering what to do, because they know where they are heading at all times. The con is that you have your work cut out for you: You have to build more levels to satisfy the player's speed and the story's faster pacing. You also have to make each of these levels look good and carry immediate emotional weight, because most of the time players will not bother to slow down to enjoy the scenery.

### Non-Linear Layout

Non-linear game levels not only allow backtracking, they demand it. Sometimes a player can be kept in a single level for hours on end while she seeks to solve a single challenge. This is a primary component of adventure games or game narratives written using the String of Pearls Method described in Chapter 11, "Players and Objectives." There do not need be as many levels overall, because the player sees more out of each one. After the player finishes everything he has to do in one level, he is then transported to another level of the game, but oftentimes he returns to that level later on. Sometimes a doorway between two or more levels is not opened until an event is triggered afterward in the game, making passage easier and backtracking less redundant (this cleverly avoids rising player frustration).

The main problem with building non-linear levels is that it is too easy to lose the player, who might not see his goals clearly, or he gets lost in large levels where his direction is not prominently marked. On the other hand, non-linear levels allow for emergent gameplay and further exploration. Since players will see more of each level, it's important to make each level very distinct and decorate them with lots of eye-catching details.

### Hub-Based Layout

*Hub-based* layouts have one pretzel-like level forming the hub, or the place the player comes back to after exploring other levels, which branch out from the hub like spokes on a wheel. Usually there are blocked doors or rooms within the central level that let out into all the other sublevels, and each and every one of the sublevels has specific goals to be met before returning to the hub. Often the blocked doors or rooms open up only after the player completes an objective or gains enough keys.

Games like Midway's *Gauntlet: Dark Legacy*, Nintendo's *Super Mario 64*, and Team Silent's *Silent Hill 4: The Room* have popularized hub-based games. For instance, in the *Silent Hill* game, shown in Figure 12.9, the player starts out and returns to The Room in the title of the game, and after each obstacle is overcome, a new hole in a wall or way out of The Room shows up to allow the player to exit into even more difficult levels. This is repeated until every opening has been unblocked, and the player opens the final exit and faces the boss of the game.

### Death-Match Layout

There is a fourth type of game layout called a *death-match* level, which serves the primary purpose of being self-contained, often circular. A death-match level goes nowhere, but it sets the stage for an arena-type competition. This is common to

**Figure 12.9**
In *Silent Hill 4: The Room*, the player character was trapped within a single dust-hazed room until mysterious holes appeared. These holes do not lead to escape, however!

online player-versus-player, or PVP, games, such as *Unreal Tournament* and *Halo*. Death-match levels belong in only specific types of action games, such as fighting or shooter games, although you could stretch to call *Tetris* a death-match layout in a way.

**N o t e**

A *tile*, also known as a cell, is a rectangular or square area of a game map. In isometric worlds such as *Diablo* or *Baldur's Gate*, tiles are almost always diamond-shaped. A tile can be just about any size, but most often they are designed to be just slightly larger than the player character's feet that are touching the ground. Tile-based worlds, or TBWs, are common in strategy and role-playing games, and can be designed using Adobe Flash.

## Pacing and Balance of Resources

Proper pacing in a game is even more important than how the game looks. Pacing is imperative, a real sink-or-swim mark for the game creator. A balance between player resources and game challenges is one of the keys to pacing the game.

If the player has too many resources in a game level, such as health or ammo, then the challenges will seem too easy, or the importance of gaining resources will seem needless. If you have too many challenges (see Chapter 11, "Players and Objectives"), or those challenges seem repetitious, without resources or places for the player to stop and take a breath, you will merely frustrate the player and lose potential future players when they hear, "That game's too hard!" Balance is imperative for fairness.

Alternate between forcing the player to struggle to stay alive and reflectively exploring or solving puzzles; this increases the playability of the game.

## Industry Insiders' Dos and Don'ts

From leading industry designers today, here is a compilation of things to keep in mind at all times when designing game levels:

- Avoid areas that look important but aren't really.

- Don't put all your monsters or power-ups in one area; proper distribution is important.

- Don't forget to give your player enough power-ups to survive.

- Don't design levels that are so hard they become "choke points" that players can't get past.

- Don't design levels so confusing that players resort to looking at a walk-through guide online.

- Don't forget to accommodate the different types of players, casual and hardcore.

- Don't reveal all your best eye candy in the first level.

- Don't keep fiddling with your level; design it once and move on.

- Don't forget to test your level as you build.

- Don't arbitrarily frustrate players; provide them opportunities to skip or avoid the difficult parts if they want.

## The Game Interface

### Tip

"The interface is one of the least understood yet most critical elements in the game. The interface is the connection between the player and the game world."

—Richard Wainess, M.S.Ed. (Senior Lecturer, University of Southern California)

The gamer interacts with the game through its interface. The *interface* is the way the computer program interprets what the player wants (input) and displays important information or options back to the player (output). A game-specific interface is the connection between the player and the game itself.

## History of Game Interfaces

Game interfaces have changed greatly. Back in the day of retro arcade games, the visual and manual interfaces were never the same. Before a player put quarters into the machine, a screen would display the game title, and another screen would show how the game should be played. The manual interface itself consisted of different combinations of button presses or joystick pulls. *Centipede* was one of the few arcade games that featured a trackball, which was more durable than the joystick.

Other interfaces, often related to the arcade simulation games, mimicked real-life objects, such as rifles, steering wheels, and periscopes. These were some of the earliest input devices, apart from keyboards and mice.

Nowadays input devices range from the consoles, which all feature similar toggles and buttons and are made to fit into a player's two hands, to the Nintendo Wii Remote and Nunchuk device or game mats used for dance or rhythm games. Almost all games are shipped with a *game manual* or instruction guide for how to play the game, and include in-game instructions and reminders for how the game is played or what the objectives and options are.

While much or most of what makes a great game so good is intuitive, it is vital to remember that gameplay starts with the interface.

## Common Game Interfaces

Many different game interfaces are becoming standards of the gaming media. They are:

- Manual interfaces or input devices

- Feedback interfaces

- Graphical user interfaces

### Manual Interfaces

First, there are the *manual interfaces*, the hardware-based input devices like the keyboard/mouse or console controller, which have preprogrammed options allowing the player to budge her character around onscreen and execute specific actions therein. These interfaces are closely linked to the game's hardware platform.

**Note**

> The motion-sensing EyeToy manual interface allows players to control actions in the game through bodily movement. What type of game, besides the ones you might have seen advertised for the EyeToy, might be ideal for this kind of interface?
>
> Along a related line, what kind of input devices could be used in an unusual way? For instance, the Nintendo Wii console theme skateboard deck is currently used for the Tony Hawk skating game, where players can control their characters' actions through their physical use of the skateboard-shaped controller. But the skateboard could also be used as a snowboard in a Winter X-Games electronic game or where the player character is a superhero like Marvel Comics' Silver Surfer.

### Feedback Interfaces

There are *feedback interfaces*, such as the vibrations from rumble functions on console controllers or noises and lights coming from the game. Dedicated computer gamers prefer Dolby surround sound speakers with heavy bass and even go so far as to purchase gaming motion chairs (shown in Figure 12.10), which have built-in subwoofers to provide bass as well as a rumbling sensation to enhance the user's experience as she plays a video game.

### Graphical User Interfaces

**Tip**

> "All the components of an interface are equally important. It is like a symphony orchestra. If the performance is to be effective, all instruments must be in tune and all notes must be played correctly. If the interface is to be successful, all components must work together."
>
> —Jan McWilliams (Artist/Educator, Director of Interactive Design, Art Institute of California, L.A.)

There are also onscreen information panels that make up the visual part, the graphical user interface. A *graphical user interface*, often abbreviated GUI and pronounced "gooey," is the vehicle that allows for interacting with the game that employs graphical images and widgets in addition to text messages to represent vital information and options to the player. Most of the time, but not always, the obtainable actions the player can take are performed through the manipulation of graphical elements or through keyboard commands.

In the GUI alone, there are varied types of interfaces. There are menu screens, loading screens, character screens, options screens, save/load screens, and much more. Each can appear distinct and characteristic.

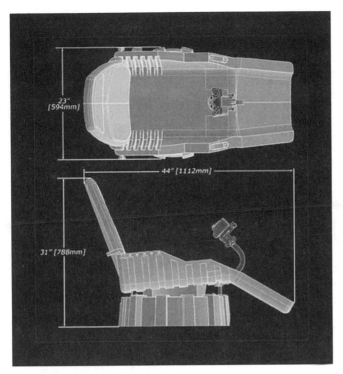

**Figure 12.10**
Something of a novelty, gaming motion chairs can make a game experience more immersive as an entertainment form.

**Heads-Up Display**    Perhaps the most important GUI a design team must create is the *heads-up display*, or HUD. The HUD shows the player at a glance the most vital information the player must know from the game.

*Common HUD Information*    Most often this information includes the player character's health, which is often a number or a life bar that decreases or changes color whenever the player character gets hurt, ability, magic or *mana*, and firepower or ammunition.

**Health.** The *health bar* indicator is used in many games. This indicator consists of a horizontal or vertical bar colored in full red or blue. If the player character is at full power, the bar will be full of color, but as power depletes, the color drains from right to left or up to down, like a thermometer, until it reaches zero, at which time the player character's life is over.

Now and then the health bar's color fluctuates to symbolize the percentage of bar left, starting out green (for healthy) and resulting in red (near death).

Some games use "dials," a variant of the health bar like you might see in *Mario 64*, or bubbles, like you see in *Diablo* and *Dungeon Siege*.

Other quantifiable attributes, such as a character's life power, willpower, stamina, magic ability, or *mana*, may also be revealed in a bar, dial, or bubble, like health would be. If more than one bar, dial, or bubble are used, or they are shown in pairs, it is customary for the health bar to appear red and the other bar to appear blue, to keep them separate in the player's mind. See Figure 12.11.

**Score.** A lot of game HUDs show the player's *score*, or a numeric indicator that measures the player's success in the game. A high-score meter might keep track of past scores and gives players a standard by which to measure themselves.

Some games only show the player's current score at the end of beating a level successfully, at which point the game might reveal whether the player not only attained a particular numeric score but also a grade. For example, in the *Devil May Cry*, *Advance Wars*, and *Bullet Witch* games, players discover at the end of each mission whether they received a traditional letter grade, such as an A, B, or C, or a "superior" grade designated by an S.

**Figure 12.11**
An example of using red and blue bars to measure a character's health and magic. (Image from *Priston Tale 2* used courtesy of Key to Play.)

**Map or Radar.** For players to get a larger view of their game world and find their way around in it, a *map* or *radar* is sometimes necessary. Either a map or radar can be displayed as part of the HUD interface located at the bottom left or right of the screen. Radars show blips of goals, items, or enemies in the surrounding terrain, whereas maps show macro views of the game area and the cardinal direction the player character is presently heading.

**Firepower.** Games with violence in them more often than not have player characters finding or equipping themselves with melee or ranged weaponry. Ranged weaponry, including such varied metal weaponry as pistols, revolvers, shotguns, laser guns, and rocket launchers, require ammunition. HUDs will often showcase the weapon the player character is currently armed with, and if that weapon is a ranged weapon, how much ammo is left in it. This adds the gameplay complexity of having to watch how many more shots you can take in a fight and having to search for more ammo to reload your weapon.

Melee weapons do not have ammo, but games like Capcom's *Dead Rising* have started implementing melee weapon health, where the melee weapons eventually break after several uses.

If the game supports a magical attack system, the offensive magical spells can be armed just like a weapon would, and the magic ability or *mana* quantity can act as ammo to fuel the attack. Some magical spells can also be defensive in nature.

**Inventory.** The *inventory* is also an important game interface component. It helps players keep track of the items that are available to their characters, especially in games that involve collecting and gathering items, such as adventure games and RPGs (*Priston Tale 2*, shown in Figure 12.12, is one example). The ability to manage the items in this inventory and keep track of what items are available to the player character greatly helps the player make certain decisions during the game.

The inventory will often take up quite a bit of screen real estate, so it is not a permanent fixture to the HUD but accessed through a menu or manual interface.

**Character.** A *character* interface can occasionally be a highly complex series of screens that allow players to create and customize their player characters. Everything from personal appearance, accessories, ethnicity, class, and even biographies can be selected and managed through this interface. This type of interface is most popular among games that involve character advancement, such as RPGs.

Image courtesy of Key to Play.

**Figure 12.12**
In this screenshot from *Priston Tale 2*, you can see an inventory interface at the bottom.

Characters in these types of games often have skills or attributes that are either intrinsic to the character selected or that can be attained during the game. These skills/attributes are usually reflected by numeric integers and will rise and fall based on player choice and experience won during the course of the game.

As this interface takes up a lot of onscreen real estate, like the inventory, it is usually hidden until the player accesses it through a menu or manual interface.

*HUD Layout*   The HUD can be simple and straightforward in its layout, like the sheer blue interface of NCsoft's *City of Heroes*, or it can be complex and representative of the game world's artistic and cultural styles, like the rusted metal and grunge look of Black Isle Studios' *Planescape: Torment*.

Some games have a large HUD that covers up an eighth of the entire screen size, but most developers frown on this waste of screen real estate. In fact, the next generation of games is stretching for a nearly transparent interface, including almost invisible or nonexistent HUD panels.

**Figure 12.13**
Checking your ammo and reloading become pseudorealistic in Bethesda Softworks' and Headfirst Games' horror game *Call of Cthulhu: Dark Corners of the Earth.*

Bethesda Softworks and Headfirst Games created the horror game *Call of Cthulhu: Dark Corners of the Earth* to have a nonexistent interface. Their original plan was to take the interface out completely, to have the player so immersed in the narrative that the interface became purely intuitive. This involved having the player character stop and physically look to see how many shells were left in a gun they were carrying (see Figure 12.13), and being able to tell how wounded they were by how much the character wobbled and breathed heavily. This ploy did not suit 100% of the beta testers, so some conventional compromises had to be made before the game was shipped to stores. The game does feature one of the most developed and important feedback systems used in first-person shooters to date.

**Note**

Did you know that high-definition television screens are changing the way console game interfaces are designed? HDTVs are the latest hardware, and now all cable television in America is expected to be HD-ready. The picture is digitally clearer than any television set before. The downside is that logos or persistent static images can produce a permanent "ghost" of the image on the screen.

Persistent static images include heads-up display panels common to most first-person shooters. With this in mind, games being ported to consoles are designed with fluctuating, animated, or hidden interface elements. This desire to avoid burnt images on HDTV screens reinforces the industry push for transparent or nearly invisible GUIs.

You don't have to worry for now, though, because most gamers spend less time playing their games than it takes for an image to create a permanent "ghost" on the screen, thereby damaging it. But it is something to note.

## Planning the Game Interface

Interface design is traditionally thought of as a user interface design. The user is someone who is making use out of a certain technology, such as a mobile phone, laptop computer, or Web site. The user of a game-specific user interface is the player.

Creating a detailed plan for your user interface in the game graphics section of your game design documents can really help drive the design of the interface. Figuring out the little details of the game's look, such as in-game menu screens and the heads-up display, will force you to make many gameplay decisions early on. It may even settle decisions for the direction the game's construction might take.

Developers can change the way an entire game is played and appreciated based on their growing understanding of the scope of a game, which is exemplified in the user interface.

When it comes to the interface, remember the immortal words of T.V.'s Judge Judy: "Keep it simple, stupid!" This is the KISS principle, and it applies to game interfaces best. A great game that makes it to the top of the charts and wags the tongues is when it is simple, neat, clean, and straightforward, when lots of different kinds of people can play it without getting lost or confused, and when it runs smoothly and still has room for upward mobility.

When you catch yourself thinking of how to design an interface so that it's cool, complex, cutting-edge, and flashy, put yourself in the player's shoes for a moment and see if your great idea will really help the player play the game without getting frustrated. The interface should always be aesthetic, or look good, and be functional. In design, this is called "form and function."

Keep your design interface tidy. Hide any and all unnecessary tools or icons. Reduce the screen windows, inventory windows, and character sheets. Clean up the clutter, because screen real estate is virtually a priceless commodity. Make your interface as transparent and intuitive as possible. The best interface is the one that a player hardly notices, that never pulls the player out of his fantasy world.

This concept of quick and intuitive interface design is referred to by those in the industry as scanability. *Scanability* means the controls must be clear. You want the player to find the most important information, such as health, magic, ammo, and so on, first, and the less important information, like journal notes, maps, and such, second. You want the player to swim through the interface without having to stop and think about how it operates. The player should understand what to do at a glance and should be able to jump right in without having to spend a good hour pouring over your carefully crafted game manual.

In designer Donald A. Norman's book, *The Design of Everyday Things*, he says, "Design must convey the essence of a device's operation; the way it works, the possible actions that can be taken, and, through feedback, just what it is doing at any particular moment."

Occasionally this means that you have to pay attention to and not deviate so much from game genre conventions. For instance, players who play first-person shooters are used to being able to see how much health and ammo they have, and players who play third-person or isometric RPGs are used to melee attacks and collecting loot from vanquished enemies. You start taking these interface elements away, and your player is liable to gripe about their absence.

If there's a certain established way in which a game type is played, and it works and you like it, why change it at all? As physicist Albert Einstein once said, "Make things as simple as possible, but no simpler."

### Building the Interface

Once you have the priorities and initial planning of your interface set out before you, you can give serious consideration to the look of your visual interface components. Design a prototype of the interface fairly early on and, as designer Bob Bates says, "Keep noodling with it."

**Make Thumbnails**  Start with making thumbnails, just some small sketches about a few inches wide. Generate several thumbnails, scribbling variations upon a theme, for each interface element. Once you run through your standard stock of ideas, your brainstorming will force you to be more creative and think "outside the box."

**Interface Mock-Ups**  When you have plenty of thumbnails ready, pick the very best, the cream of the crop, as the old saying goes, and work them into serviceable mock-ups. A *mock-up* is sample art that is not the final product but a definitive visualization of the look and feel of the finished piece. It's kind of like a visual rough draft.

The mock-up should look practically finished, and it should include button schemes and logo images. The mock-up is a trial stage for designing the finished piece, so do your best and keep in mind that you will be making edits later. The mock-up is also crucial for generating the color scheme you want to go with and seeing how the artistic style, cultural style, mood, and theme of the game world plays into the interface.

**Color Scheme and Texture**  Color is a vital ingredient in video games. What color are each of the buttons and elements of your game going to be? Keep your colors consistent with the theme. Colors have a dynamic effect on people's moods and the way they react intuitively to objects. The same can be true of texture. Having bright-red rusty elements immediately cause the player to react apprehensively or be afraid of getting hurt or dirty, while having soft blue fur elements make the player feel relaxed and comforted. These intuitive effects can be manipulated by a game developer to set the mood or theme of the game.

**Typeface**   Planning what fonts to use in your game interface can also appeal to the player's mood and play up the theme of the game. A comic book style font family is excellent for a superhero or funny game, but a typeface font that looks like it is dripping blood would better fit a horror game. Looking at a font list that shows you the typeface used will give you an immediate sense about the fonts you might want to use. Typefaces are covered in more detail in Chapter 7, "Building Scenes in Flash."

**Putting It All Together**   Once you have settled on a mock-up you like, you can finalize the piece and pick it apart to see how you will include it in your game. Some custom interface pieces are easy to make in Flash, such as buttons, and input fields can display current game scores.

## What's Next?

Now that you are prepared a little bit better for designing games for the Nintendo Wii, it's time to look at the Adobe Flash software application you will use to make your very own Wii games.

## Review

At the end of reading this chapter, you should know:

- How successful World Immersion in your games makes for better game play

- How appropriate level design can benefit your games

- How the interface allows gamers to interact with the game

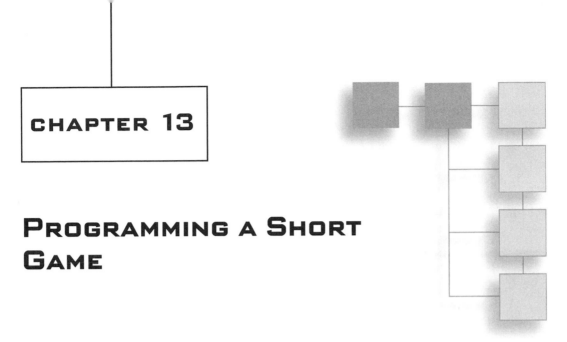

# CHAPTER 13

# PROGRAMMING A SHORT GAME

In this chapter you will learn:

- To make a tunnel maze game using Flash

- To make a dress-up doll game using Flash

- To make a shooting gallery game using Flash

- To make a Fantasy Machine using Flash

- To put together frames, buttons, and movie clips to form games in the Flash environment

- Some handy tips for making more games with Flash

Finally, you've made it! It has taken a while to get here, I know, but first understanding the Flash program and how games work had to take precedence. Now you are ready to jump in, figuratively speaking, and start designing Flash games. Then we will look at how you have to set them up to work with the WiiCade API that allows you to port these Flash games to the Wii.

Upon embarking, we will start with some basic games that do not require much programming. The initial game I will show you how to make has very basic scripting involved. The games will get harder after that.

Do not fall for the false assumption that the bigger, more complicated a game's programming is, the better the game will be. Clunky heavy-ended games often fail on the trial floor when simpler, cleverer games outrace them in terms of player endearment. The first game, a tunnel maze game, shows you how to make an outstanding game in its own right when you put some creative engineering behind it.

At the end of each experimental session, I will give you some suggestions on what you can do to make your game better, but really this is a conceptual part of game development that only you have control over. You can follow these practical tutorials, but in the end it is really what *you* decide to do with what you learn that will determine your future as a game designer.

At any time you can preview each of these games on the accompanying CD-ROM in the Exercises folder. The .SWF and .FLA files are all there, along with some of the materials that went into making them.

## Make a Tunnel Maze Game

I think it helps to know where you are going before you start on a new tutorial, don't you? Well, as the title to this section makes clear, we are going to make a tunnel maze game (shown in Figure 13.1). Essentially, a tunnel maze is a twisting or turning maze the player has to navigate, from a start point to an end point. Similar to any action game, the player must avoid obstacles along the course to her goal. In this case, the obstacles she faces are the walls of the tunnel itself.

**Figure 13.1**
What the finished tunnel maze game ought to look like.

Whenever the player touches the edges of the tunnel, she is forced to start the game over.

## Create a Start Screen

First things first... a proper game has a start, or welcome, screen as part of its shell interface. This is the first screen the player sees after the game loads.

1. Open a new Flash file (ActionScript 2.0). The Publish Settings must be set to ActionScript 2.0, because this works best with the API we will export the game to the Wii for. The Properties panel will show you this information after you have created the new Flash file.

2. I prefer to work within the Essentials workspace, but with the Library panel open and docked with the Properties panel. To do this, go to Window > Workspace, Essentials on the main Menu Bar (if you are not already in the Essentials workspace). Then, if your Library panel is not already open, go to Window > Library (or Ctrl + L on Windows, Command + L on Macs) to open it. If it opens as a floating panel, click-drag it to the Properties panel (in the Essentials workspace, this is found on the right) and let go when you see the blue border surround that other panel, docking Library with Properties.

3. Select Frame 1 on Layer 1 in the Timeline.

4. Go to the main Menu Bar and go Window > Common Libraries > Buttons to bring up the Buttons Library. Scroll down to Classic Buttons and find the subfolder Arcade Buttons, Playback. Select the gel Right button, which is round and green (shown in Figure 13.2).

5. Click and drag the gel Right button from the Library preview window to the Stage. It will appear on Frame 1 of Layer 1, as that was the area selected. Position it in the bottom left of the screen and resize it as necessary (using the Free Transform tool), but don't make it too big. The exact size and position of your Play button depends on the tunnel maze you create next, because wherever the Play button is will be where the player starts.

6. On Frame 1, if you like, you can add text or graphics. This is kind of the start, or intro, screen to the tunnel maze game. So you can add text at the top of the screen that says, "Tunnel Maze Game by—" and then your name, or at least add some instructions like, "Guide your way through the maze

**Figure 13.2**
The gel Right button as shown in the Buttons Library.

without touching the walls!" The Play button, by itself, is pretty self-explanatory, being one of those universal GUI elements, but you might want to reinforce it by adding some text above or to the side of the button saying, "Click button to play."

7. Select the gel Right button we are using for our start game button, and add a script to this button. If your Actions panel is not already visible, bring it up. Go to the main menu and then Window > Actions (hotkey F9). The Actions panel will probably appear as a floating panel. This one is easier to dock going horizontally, so dock it with the Timeline, as shown in Figure 13.3.

8. Note that to add a script to a button, you *must* have the button selected before you start typing! If you try adding a button script to a non-selected entity, such as Frame 1 by itself, you will receive errors. You can tell if you have your button selected by looking beneath the white scripting area, where you will see a tab telling you what is currently selected. If it says "gel Right" you are good.

9. Flash offers you several functions within the Actions panel to help you with scripting. You can use these, or if you know the scripting language by heart, you can simply type in the panel. I will show you how to add a script through the buttons on the left of the Actions panel, first. Go to Global Functions and expand both the Movie Clip Control and Timeline Control, as these are the two areas we will be working in.

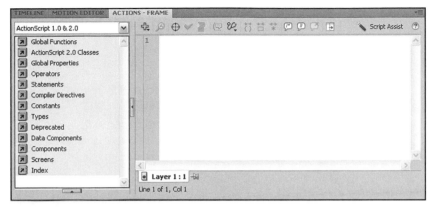

**Figure 13.3**
In the Essentials workspace, it is often easier to dock the Actions panel going horizontally, as with the Timeline panel.

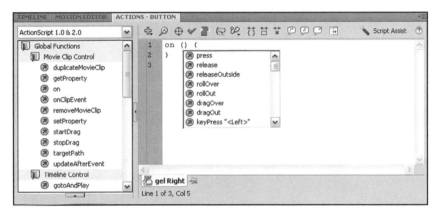

**Figure 13.4**
Adding the "on (release)" part of the script to a button.

10. Double-click "on" under Movie Clip Control, and you will get a screen that looks like Figure 13.4. The pop-up tips help guide you through the scripting phase. Here, you will want to pick "release" as this means when the button is pressed and the mouse is released.

11. Move your cursor between the open brackets to the right of the script. This is where we will actually put our function's instructions. In almost any scripting language, you will find functions that read like:

```
do.this (now) {
    my.operation;

}
```

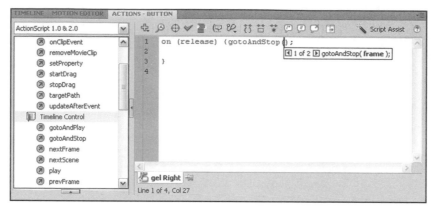

**Figure 13.5**
Telling the script what frame you want it to go to when this button is pressed.

12. In the blank space where "my.operation" is, you will choose "gotoAndStop" from the Timeline Control in the Global Functions on the left. Your screen should appear like the one in Figure 13.5. All you have to do is type in the number 2, which tells the computer you want the script to carry the player to Frame 2 when they click the Play button.

13. Click the Auto Format button to help the computer read your script better. This button looks like lines of text staggered, and it is just above the white scripting area, about the middle of all the other buttons. (You should be able to mouse over it and a tool-tip will pop up to tell you what the button's name is.)

14. Proofread your script to make sure there are no errors. It should now read like:

```
on (release) {
    gotoAndStop(2);

}
```

## Quick Tips: Programming

To get a computer to do something, well, anything really, you have to come down (or up) to its level.

A computer cannot process information in human language. It can only communicate in *binary machine code*. This numeral code, really just a positional notation with a radix of 2, is a bunch of 1s and 0s forming a pattern of switch-on and switch-off. A line of machine code looks something like 10100101100. This is not only the language of machines, starting with electronic switch-boarding, but it is the way computers get things done.

A computer cannot, insofar, read a human being's mind and extrapolate what to do. To have a little chat with a computer, you are going to have to use a translation device of some kind. This is where scripting language comes in.

*Scripting languages* bridge the gulf between coders and computers. The scripting language follows a specific syntax, or code language, but the syntax is nothing without a compiler. *Compilers* chop up syntax into understandable portions and then convert them to binary. In this fashion, the coder can tell a computer what to do when.

Any coder worth his salt knows that to tell a computer to do anything is like talking to an alien species. You are learning a foreign language (at least, foreign to us!) in order to communicate the most basic of logic. It would be like teaching a Neanderthal just woken up out of a block of ice how to start and drive an automobile.

So a programmer comes up with an algorithm. An *algorithm* includes the solution to a given problem (like how to teach the Neanderthal) and the steps by which the machine can solve it. To create an algorithm, the coder must identify what the problem is, define a solution, turn the solution into an algorithm, program the algorithm, and finally, check to see if the algorithm works.

Solutions to algorithms are called *functions*, and functions have fairly common flavors: sequential, conditional, and looping. Let's take a brief look at them.

- **Sequential**: *Sequential functions* move along at a set course, step by step, without break. You do not expect any random factors or deviations from norm when using sequences of functions.

- **Conditional**: *Conditional functions* follow the logic of British mathematician George Boole, or what we call Boolean logic. Conditional functions, also called selective logic statements, are most often identified by the start of them, which goes "if...then/else" or just "if." You use them to check if some criteria is met before executing an operation. For instance, a wandering monster probably needs a conditional function to check for the proximity of our wayward hero before knowing to attack him.

- **Looping**: *Looping functions* are logic functions you want to continue into perpetuity or until some measure has been met. They are most often noted by their syntax start of "while." For instance, most enemies have a while statement somewhere in their overall function that says while(alive), because if they aren't alive they wouldn't be able to do their other operations.

Besides functions, most scripting languages, including ActionScript 2.0, share other elements.

*Variables* are usually placeholders of fixed-point integers. Common variables include X speed, Y speed, score, life, and ammo. You define your variables before the functions that use them.

*Strings* are placeholders of fixed text strings written within quotation marks, often intended for in-game text and dialogue.

*Arrays* are a systematic arrangement of information, usually in rows or columns, used in programming. Arrays help to store information the same way variables or strings do, and have a lot of manipulation potential.

You might hear the word "OOP" a lot in conjunction with ActionScript. This is because ActionScript is an *object-oriented programming language*, or a scripting language that focuses on the handling of virtual objects. Rather than using linear subroutines, OOP uses reusable code modules that interact dynamically in the programming. Each reusable object can be viewed as an independent machine with a distinct role or responsibility and is capable of receiving data, processing data, or sending data. OOP-related objects are virtual and should not be confused with the onscreen visual objects of games.

To learn more about ActionScript 2.0 syntax, and programming with it, you might pick up a slightly outdated copy of *Essential ActionScript 2.0* by Colin Moock or use Ultrashock.com's tutorials online at http://www.ultrashock.com/tutorials/flashmx2004/as2-01.php.

## Create a Maze

With the start screen out of the way, we need to build the screen where the actual gameplay takes place.

1. Now right-click on Frame 2 on the Timeline and choose to Insert Blank Keyframe. A new, blank screen will accompany you as Flash takes you to Frame 2. This will be our actual game screen.

2. Select the Rectangle tool from the Toolbox. You will pick one color for your Fill, and None for your Stroke (you don't want to add a Stroke here). I have chosen a dark ruddy brown for my Fill color.

3. Draw a rectangle that fills your Stage. You don't have to make it perfect, because after you are done you can use the Align panel to stretch and move the rectangle. If you want to use the Align panel, and it is not already visible to you, go to the main menu and choose Window > Align (Ctrl + K on Windows, Command + K on Macs), and the Align panel should appear as a floating panel. You don't have to dock it, unless you want to keep using it; I usually use it once and then close it when I am through. Make sure your rectangle is selected with the Selection tool and that the Adjust to Stage button is highlighted in your Align panel. Then click the Match Width and Height button to stretch your rectangle to the Stage's dimensions, and click both Align Left Edge and Align Top Edge to move your rectangle to fit exactly inside the Stage. You're done aligning!

4. Select the Eraser tool from the Toolbox. You can use the default Eraser shape and size. Draw your tunnel through the brown rectangle now. You can make it very simple, or you can make it a long intricate maze. As you can see in Figure 13.6, I made a generic zigzagging line with a few smaller, branching

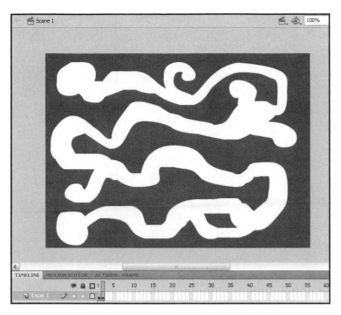

**Figure 13.6**
Your maze can literally look like anything, but this is the maze I created as part of this demonstration.

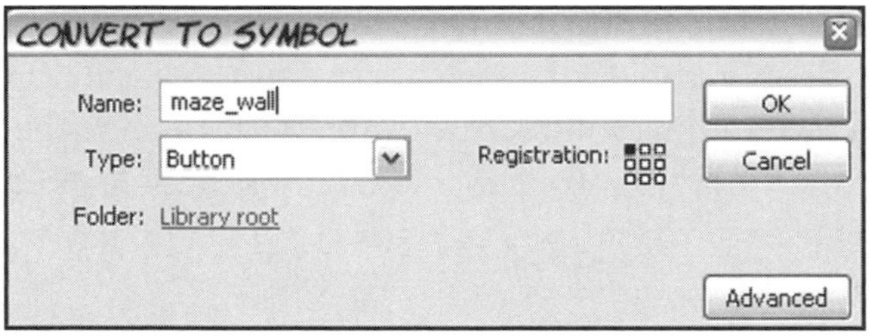

**Figure 13.7**
Turn your maze into a button symbol called "maze_wall."

tunnels. You start out with a wide area around where the player starts, which is where you placed the Play button on Frame 1, and end with a wide area around where the player ends, which is where we will place a finish button.

5. When you have finished with your maze, right-click anywhere off the Stage on Frame 2 and choose Select All. This will highlight, or select, the entire maze you just finished crafting. Right-click on the maze and choose Convert to Symbol from the pop-up options list. You want to make your maze into a button symbol, so choose Button from the Type drop-down list, and name your new symbol "maze_wall." See Figure 13.7.

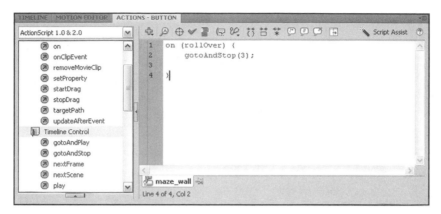

**Figure 13.8**
Add this rollover function to your maze_wall button.

6. Now it is time to add a script to your new button. With your maze_wall button selected, go to the Actions panel and double-click the "on" button found on the left, under Global Functions, Movie Clip Control. Choose as your "on" parameter "rollOver" and in the operation add "gotoAndStop" from the Global Functions, Timeline Control options on the left. As to what frame to take the player to, pick Frame 3, since we haven't put anything on that frame yet. After you finish adding your script to the button, click the Auto Format button above the white scripting area (again, it's the staggered text lines button) to make the text formatted for Flash to read it. Then compare your script to Figure 13.8.

## Create a Lose Screen

If your player hits the side walls of the maze, she should be slapped on the wrist to know she did wrong. For this reason, we will create a lose screen.

1. Right-click on Frame 3 on the Timeline and choose to Insert Blank Keyframe. A new, blank screen will accompany you as Flash takes you to Frame 3. This will be the player's lose screen that she will see when she goofs. Go ahead and add some text here using your Type tool. It can say anything you like, such as "Oops! You crashed." Just put something that gives the player enough feedback to show her she messed up but not too negative that, if she comes back to this frame more than once, she won't get frustrated or mad at you, the game's designer.

**Tip**

One way to perform this sort of positive-negative feedback successfully is the way Don Bluth did when making his game *Dragon's Lair*. If the player messed up, he showed her a screen where the intrepid player character, Dirk the Daring, made a funny face before being reduced to a skeleton; it made the player laugh as much at Dirk as she did herself, and she got the point that she had to try harder without feeling like her wrist was slapped.

2. Go to the Buttons Library. Scroll down to Classic Buttons and find the subfolder Arcade Buttons, Playback. Select the gel Left button, which is round and green and points back.

3. Click and drag the gel Left button from the Library preview window to the Stage. It will appear on Frame 3 of Layer 1, as that was the area selected. Position it in the bottom left of the screen and resize it as necessary (using the Free Transform tool), making sure you place it exactly where the first Play button was at, because this button will take the players back to the maze where they start over again.

4. If you want to make sure your back button is placed the same as the initial Play button, you can switch to Frame 1 and use the Selection tool to select the gel Right button and take note of the X and Y position values in the Properties panel (shown in Figure 13.9). Switch back to Frame 3 and select the gel Left button and compare or alter its X and Y position values accordingly.

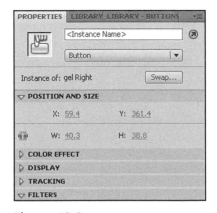

**Figure 13.9**
Make sure the X and Y positions (or where the object is placed on the Stage) are the same as the start button.

**Figure 13.10**
The player's lose screen.

5. The back button, by itself, is pretty self-explanatory, being one of those universal GUI elements, but you might want to reinforce it by adding some text above or to the side of the button saying, "Try again?" Your lose screen does not have to look anything like mine, but you can see what I did in Figure 13.10.

6. Select the gel Left button, our back button, and add a script to it in the Actions panel that takes the player back to Frame 2, so she can try the game again. You can add this script by double-clicking on the left of the Actions panel, under Global Functions, as I have previously shown you, or you can simply type it in accordingly; but if you decide to type it in, double-check your spelling for errors before you hit the Auto Format button. The script should read as follows:

```
on (release) {
    gotoAndStop(2);

}
```

## Add Movie Stop Actions

It's high time to add actions to your frames. We do this to stop action on each frame. Although our button scripts tell the Flash player to stop when it goes to a frame, we still should add a stop action on each frame; after all, redundancy can protect us from errors.

1. Go to Frame 1 and create a new layer by right-clicking on Layer 1 and choosing to Insert Layer from the pop-up list. A new layer, called Layer 2 by default, will be added above your Layer 1.

2. Now that we have more than one layer in our stack, it's best to name our layers. Double-click on the layer title of Layer 1 and when you see it blink and become highlighted, change the name to "Content" simply by typing the new name and pressing Enter (or Mac users press Return) when you're done.

3. Do the same to Layer 2, calling it "Actions," as this is the layer you will add your frame actions to.

4. Our Actions layer does not have any keyframes, besides the default one on Frame 1. We need to change that. Right-click on Frame 2 and choose to Insert Blank Keyframe from the pop-up list, and do the same with Frame 3. Compare your work to Figure 13.11.

5. Go to Frame 1 of the Actions layer, and with that frame selected, switch to the Actions panel. On the left-hand side of the Actions panel, under Global Functions, Timeline Control, double-click on "stop" to add the short script "stop();" to the white scripting area on the right. This will stop the movie from playing any farther than this frame.

6. Highlight "stop();" in the white scripting area and press Ctrl + C (Command + C for Mac users) to copy this snippet to the Clipboard. Back in the Timeline panel, go to Frame 2, then with Frame 2 of the Actions layer selected, return to the Actions panel and click anywhere in the blank white scripting area. Press Ctrl + V (Command + V for Mac users) to paste your snippet from the Clipboard to the scripting area. Return to the Timeline panel and do the same for Frame 3.

You should see lowercase letter As appear in each of the frames on the Timeline when you finish. These lowercase letter As reveal that the frame indicated has an action applied to it.

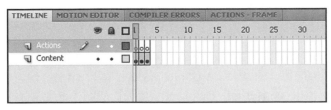

**Figure 13.11**
Add a new layer you name Actions and place blank keyframes on Frames 1, 2, and 3.

## Test Your Game

Now is a great time to test your work so far!

1. On the main menu, go to Save to open the Save As dialog box. Find someplace on your computer to put all your Flash game files. You might want to create a new folder and call it (simply) Flash Games. Save your current Flash file as Tunnelmaze.fla, and click OK when you're done.

2. Go to the main menu and choose Control > Test Movie. The shortcut for this is Ctrl + Enter (Win) or Command + Return (Mac). What Test Movie does is (a) publish the current file as a .SWF file and (b) open the .SWF file in the Flash Player so you can preview it. Play your game and see what it does. You should be able to click the Play button and move your cursor through the maze. If your cursor touches the walls of the maze, you should immediately go to the player lose screen, where you can click the back button to try again.

After playing this for a while, you will probably wonder what the objective is to the game. You can move your cursor successfully through the maze, but there's no reward when you get to the end.

## Create a Win Screen

We have to make a reward now, so close your Flash movie and return to the Flash program, where our game file is still open.

1. Go to Frame 2. On the Content layer, you will want to create two text objects. First, using the Text tool, add some text at the player start that says, "Start." This is superfluous, really, but it may help some players to realize that what they are looking at is a maze and they are at the start of it.

2. Position the Start text where the player will start. Look at Figure 13.12. I have used a comic font and the Free Transform tool to slightly rotate the text, making it more appealing, and with the Free Transform tool still active, use the arrow keys to move the object into best position.

3. Holding down the Alt (Win) or Option (Mac) key while click-dragging the Start text object to the end of the maze, you create a duplicate of the Start text object. Double-click on the center of the Start text object to edit what the text says. Type Finish for this object, then pick the Selection tool (hotkey is the letter V) to exit the text editing phase.

**Figure 13.12**
Add your first text object to your maze to signify where the player starts.

4. You now have two text objects: Start and Finish. We want to turn Finish into a button, so that it will interact with the player's actions. To do so, select the Finish object, right-click somewhere on it, and choose Convert to Symbol from the pop-up options list. This will need to be a button symbol, so change to Button under Type if it is not already there, and name this button "Finish."

5. The Finish button needs to take the player to a win screen when they reach it. With the Finish button selected, go to the Actions panel. You need to add the following script to this button:

```
on (rollOver) {
    gotoAndStop(4);

}
```

6. Switch back to the Timeline panel and right-click on the Content layer on Frame 4 and choose to Insert Blank Keyframe. A new, blank screen will accompany you as Flash takes you to Frame 4. This will be the player's win screen that she will see when she wins the game by getting to the end of your maze.

7. Go ahead and add some text here using your Text tool. It can say anything you like, such as "Yay! You made it." You may also plan to put your credits here, telling the player who made the game and did the graphics and sound

work on it. Whatever you decide, make it look fun and eye-pleasing, because this is the player's reward for surviving your maze.

8. Right-click on Frame 4 on the Actions layer and choose to Insert Blank Keyframe. In the Actions panel for Frame 4, you will add another "stop();" action to stop the movie here. Again, this may be redundant, but it protects you against errors later.

9. Save your game and test it again. Now you should be able to navigate through the maze from Start to Finish, and when your cursor touches Finish, the win screen should become visible.

Congratulations! You have just completed your first Flash game. It may be short, but it has infinite possibilities, and now you know how to design a game using Flash and ActionScript 2.0.

### Tunnel Maze Game: What Else?

Your maze game only has one tunnel maze to it right now, but you can change that. You can add multiple levels, each progressively harder. Each one could be a different color, or contain dissimilar artwork, to give your game more variety.

To do so:

1. You would add a button on the win screen that takes you to the next level, which would be on Frame 5, and the button would say "Ready for next level?"

2. On Frame 5, you would make another maze, just like you did on Frame 2, except you would name the maze button something different, such as "maze_wall2."

3. The new maze button would take the player to a fresh lose screen on Frame 6, which would contain a "Try again?" button that takes her back to Frame 5.

4. Your Finish button would be labeled something like "Finish2" and take the player to a new win screen on Frame 7.

5. And so on . . .

You could also add a player score, which increases with each new level passed. This does not have to be dynamic, either. Just add a text object in the upper-left or upper-right corner of the Stage, and on the first maze make it say "0." After the player has passed the first maze have it say "1." After she beats the second maze, have it say "2," and so forth.

We also did not cover adding sound effects or music to your game. You could add more attraction and interest to your game by dropping music in for each maze level and adding appealing sound effects to your buttons. Never forget that this is an aural as well as a visual experience.

The last thing I might do to make the tunnel maze game better is to add a character that the player is moving around in the tunnel. This is the same technique used to make the crosshairs in the shooting gallery exercise demonstrated later.

1. Draw any image you like (a top-down view of an intrepid archaeologist or a side view of a submarine, for instance).

2. After importing the image to the project Library, convert it to a movie clip symbol, say, named "Player." While in the Convert to Symbol dialog box, set the Registration point to the center before clicking OK.

3. Then add the following code to your new Player symbol:

```
onClipEvent (enterFrame) {
    mouse.hide();
    this._x = _root._xmouse;
    this._y = _root._ymouse;
}
```

When the game starts up, your mouse cursor will be followed by your player character's image!

When you're ready, share your game!

## Make a Dress-Up Game

In the mid-to-late 1990s, sites on the World Wide Web began creating interactive virtual dress-up games. *Dress-up games* are games in which a person can drag and drop clothes onto a paper doll-like image on the screen. As with paper dolls, these virtual dolls can be based on actual people, celebrities, or cartoon characters.

Several Web sites provide a directory of dress-up games and are updated regularly to list the new games that appear online. There are now also many online dress-up arcade sites specializing in interactive Flash-based dress-up games, such as 1dressup.com (http://www.1dressup.com). You can see a dress-up game found on 1dressup.com in Figure 13.13.

The same game mechanic behind these dress-up games can be used to build jigsaw puzzle games, click-together Rube Goldberg invention games, or even scene creator games.

Have you ever thought of making your own dress-up game? It's not that hard to do in Flash, and it makes a great project for the Nintendo Wii!

**Figure 13.13**
*Rocky Roxy Dress Up,* one of the many dress-up games on 1dressup.com.

## Create a Doll

First, you must have a doll on which to put clothes and accessories. This doll can be anything you like it to be, from a photo of a famous celebrity to a cartoon character you have drawn yourself. Whatever it is, you must import your image into Flash and use it as the basis for your dress up game.

I am going to use an image I have created and colored. You can use it, too, for the purpose of this exercise, if you like. You will find it on the companion CD-ROM in the Exercises folder, and it is named dressupgirl.png (see Figure 13.14).

1. Open a new Flash file (ActionScript 2.0).

2. I will be working within the Essentials workspace, with the Library panel docked with the Properties panel.

3. Select Frame 1 on Layer 1 in the Timeline and add a title, such as "Dress Up Game." You can also change the background color to any color you like. You do so by going to the Properties panel when nothing is selected and under Document Properties, click the color tab beside Stage, or go to the main Menu Bar and choose Modify > Document and click the Background color tab in the Document Properties dialog box that comes up. Either way, a color swatch panel will appear with several hex colors from which to choose. I chose #FFCDFF for my Stage color, but you may pick any hex color you feel complements your setup best. This can also be changed at any time

**Figure 13.14**
Dressupgirl.png.

during development, as it is not set in stone. If you are unsure what hex color to use, and you don't like the sample color palette shown in the color swatch panel, you can preview other hex colors online at http://www .visibone.com/colorlab.

4. Go to the main Menu Bar and go Window > Common Libraries > Buttons to bring up the Buttons Library. Scroll down to Classic Buttons and find the subfolder Arcade Buttons, Push Buttons. Select push button—green (shown in Figure 13.15).

5. Click and drag the push button—green button from the Library preview window to the Stage. It will appear on Frame 1 of Layer 1, as that was the area selected. Position it in the bottom center of the screen and resize it as necessary (using the Free Transform tool).

6. The button, by itself, is sort of innocuous, so you might want to reinforce its meaning by adding some text above or to the side of the button stating, "Click to play." Compare your work to Figure 13.16.

7. Select the push button—green button we are using for our start game button, and add a script to this button. If your Actions panel is not already

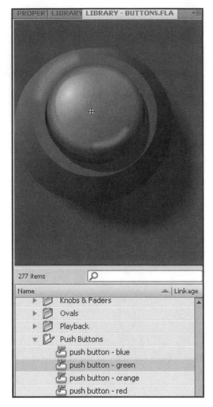

**Figure 13.15**
The push button—green button as shown in the Buttons Library.

**Figure 13.16**
One example of a start screen.

visible, bring it up by going to the main menu and selecting Window > Actions (hotkey F9).

8. Double-click "on" under Global Functions, Movie Clip Control, and select "release" as this means when the button is pressed and the mouse is released.

9. Move your cursor between the open brackets to the right of the script. Choose "gotoAndStop" from Global Functions, Timeline Control on the left. Type in the number 2, which tells the computer you want the script to carry the player to Frame 2 when they click the green button.

10. Click the Auto Format button to help the computer read your script better. At the moment, it should read:

```
on (release) {
    gotoAndStop(2);

}
```

11. Right-click on Frame 2 of Layer 1 on the Timeline and choose to Insert Blank Keyframe. A new empty keyframe will be created and you will be taken there directly.

12. Rename Layer 1 by double-clicking on the Layer 1 title, highlighting the previous name, then typing "Content—BG." This will be our main content layer for the background.

13. Insert a new layer above the Content—BG layer, and name it "Actions."

14. Right-click on Frame 2 of the Actions layer and choose to Insert Blank Keyframe. Then, on both Frame 1 and Frame 2 of the Actions layer on the Timeline, you will need to add "stop();" actions so the movie freezes on those frames. Do this by selecting the frames, one at a time, and in the Actions panel, either typing "stop();" or double-clicking on "stop" under Global Functions, Timeline Control on the left.

15. On Frame 2 of your Content—BG layer, you will create a dressing room. You can be simple or fancy with these, and you can import artwork and really dress them up. As this will be a static background, you could add richer details and small self-contained animations to make the frame more attractive. However, you do not want it to be so busy it takes precedence

**Figure 13.17**
One example of a dressing room.

over your dress-up doll. The easiest way to do this is to fashion a window frame out of two boxes. You can see the frame I created in Figure 13.17. I used the Rectangle tool with Rectangle Options (in the Properties panel) set to 7.0; this gives my rectangles rounded, or beveled, corners. The box on the left will be the area that I place clothes to put on the dress-up doll, and the box on the right will be the area that I put the dress-up doll.

16. The last thing to do, after setting up our start screen and dressing room, is to place our dress-up doll in the dressing room. As mentioned before, you can use dressupgirl.png (found on the companion CD-ROM in the Exercises folder). Go to File > Import > Import to Library, and find where the image is that you want to use. When you have the image, click OK to import the artwork. It will be dropped into your project's Library.

17. Go to the Library panel and find your new image. See what it looks like against your chosen background color in the Library preview window. Then select Frame 2 on the Content—BG layer and click-drag your dress-up doll to the Stage. Once she's there, you can use Free Transform to resize her as needed. I made my girl about 221.1 (width) by 354.1 (height). You can see and edit these numbers in the Properties panel. Position her so that she is clearly visible and looks attractive in the dressing room you've made.

18. When you are through arranging the dress-up doll, lock the Content—BG layer by clicking on the lock/unlock icon beside the layer name (revealed in

**Figure 13.18**
Lock the Content—BG layer.

Figure 13.18), because we do not want to accidentally disturb any of the objects we have placed on this layer.

## Making Clothes for the Doll

You have a pretty neat setup for a game, and your doll is all set to be dressed. Now you have to come up with the components used to dress your doll. I will show you how to generate one shirt and one pair of pants, and you can do the rest. For this, I have supplied two images on the companion CD-ROM: dressupshirt.png and dressuppants.png.

1. Insert a new layer and name it Content—Items. Make sure this layer is above Content—BG in the layer stacking order.

2. Import your shirt and pants image to the project Library. Get a foretaste of each of them in your Library's preview window.

3. Drag and drop your shirt image to the dressing room on the Stage, positioning the object over the top of the frame area you have designated for clothes. You might need to resize it to fit over the top of your dress-up doll. It has to cover her completely, with no skin showing from underneath, so resize your image as required. I made mine 116.0 (width) by 129.6 (height) to fit my girl.

4. Right-click on the shirt image and choose to Convert to Symbol from the pop-up options list. Make this a button symbol and name it "btn_shirt," as shown in Figure 13.19. At the top of the Properties panel, name the instance of your btn_shirt button "Shirt."

5. With the btn_shirt symbol instance on the Stage selected, go to the Actions panel. Make sure the tab below the white scripting area, signifying what object the actions will be applied to, says "btn_shirt." If not, you do not have

**Figure 13.19**
Convert the shirt image to a button symbol.

> the btn_shirt selected properly. Once you have the btn_shirt selected, add
> the following code to it:

```
on (press) {
    startDrag("Shirt");
    dragging = true;
}
on (release, releaseOutside) {
    stopDrag();
    dragging = false;
}
```

6. Click the Auto Format button at the top of the Actions panel to make your lines of code easier to see. Proofread carefully.

7. Save your game file as Dressupgame.fla. Then test it by going to Control > Test Movie on the main Menu Bar. Watch as your .FLA file is published as a .SWF file and opened in the Flash Player. Click the Play button to enter the dressing room. Here, you should be able to click and drag your shirt on top of the dress-up doll, as exposed (or rather, covered up) in Figure 13.20. When you let go, the shirt should stay where you put it. If you have any glitches, close the Flash Player and review your code.

8. When done playing with your doll, close Flash Player and return to your Flash project. You still need to add the pants. Follow steps 3 through 7. Now, I had to shift my pants image to 139.0 (width) by 202.6 (height) and rotate it to the right just slightly, which I had to zoom in to be able to do. Just work at it until all the underlying girl is covered. Name your pants object "btn_pants" and the just Stage instance of it "Pants." When you add your action code, change "Shirt" to "Pants."

9. Before you finish with your pants symbol, right-click on the instance of it on the Stage and choose Arrange > Send to Back. The reason you do this is

**Figure 13.20**
Test play your dress-up game.

because, since the pants were created last, they would appear above the shirt symbol, if the two were placed on the girl at the same time, and you want the shirt to appear above or overlapping the pants, instead. As you add more items to the scene, you will have to experiment with the Arrange options of each until you get them where you want them in the stacking order.

There you go! You should now be able to put a shirt and pants on your first dress-up doll. The next thing to do is to add more clothes to dress your doll. Go wild with designing this dress-up game and truly express yourself.

### Dress-Up Game: What Else?

Your dress-up game only has one dressing room to it right now, but you can change that. You can add more dolls. Instead of one Play button on the start screen, have a button for each available doll, then add more frames like Frame 2, including different dressing rooms and artwork. Use the exact same code snippets I've shown you to build whole wardrobes and really expand your dress-up game.

Another thing you can do is add a button that allows players to print their finished dress-up doll. Drag a button symbol to the Stage (for convenience and consistency, you could use the same push button—green symbol you used for the start screen). Put some text next to it to inform the player what this button does: "Print."

Then add the following action to that button:

```
on (release) {
    printAsBitmap(this, "bmax");
}
```

Or, as stated at the beginning of this exercise, you can use what you have learned here to make jigsaw puzzle games, where players have to put jigsaw puzzle pieces together to "see" a whole picture.

## Make a Shooting Gallery

A shooting gallery, as opposed to a first-person shooter, does not have the player actually move his character. Instead, the player character assumedly stands in one spot while taking pot-shots at any targets or on-rushing enemies.

A *shooting gallery*, also called a gun game, is a video game genre in which the primary design element is aiming and shooting with a gun-shaped controller. Shooting galleries revolve around the protagonist shooting targets, either antagonists or inanimate objects. They generally feature action or horror themes, and some may employ a humorous, parody treatment of these conventions.

Shooting galleries that do have more than one background setting typically feature "on-rails" movement, which gives the player control only over aiming, while the protagonist's other movements, including walking, are determined by the game. Games featuring this device are sometimes called *rail shooters*, though this term is also applied to games of other genres in which "on-rails" movement is a feature.

Mechanical games using gun-shaped controllers existed all the way back in the 1930s, though they operated differently to those used in the video games you see today. It wasn't until the 1980s that popular shooting galleries such as *Duck Hunt* emerged. The genre was most popular in the early 1990s but is less popular today.

Some of the most noted shooting galleries include *The House of the Dead*, *Virtua Cop*, *Time Crisis*, and *Mad Dog McCree*.

You may not have a gun-shaped controller, even one for the Wii (see Figure 13.21), but Flash makes making shooting galleries a snap, and the Nintendo Wii Remote makes it a blast to play them!

## Create the Crosshairs

Similar to Sega's *The House of the Dead* rail-shooter game (in Figure 13.22), the shooting gallery we create will be a zombie shooting gallery. The environment will be creepy and the targets will all be slobbering zombies. But before we start blasting, we must first have a gun to shoot with, or at least the illusion of one.

**Figure 13.21**
The Nintendo Wii Magnum Gun controller.

**Figure 13.22**
*The House of the Dead*, a rail-shooter game series developed by Sega, has seen recent release for the Nintendo Wii.

To create a firm illusion of aiming with a gun, we will develop crosshairs that will show onscreen and follow the player's movement.

1. Open a new Flash file (ActionScript 2.0).

2. I will be working within the Essentials workspace, with the Library panel docked with the Properties panel.

3. Change the background color to any color you like by going to the main Menu Bar and choosing Modify, Document and clicking the Background color tab in the Document Properties dialog box that comes up. In the color swatch panel that appears, pick a hex color for your background. I chose dark blue, or #000066, for my Stage color.

4. Select Frame 1 on Layer 1 in the Timeline and add a title, such as "Zombie Shooting Gallery." It is best to make your text bright against the dark background color, so I have used bright yellow, or #FFFF00. I used a font called Rocky AOE, but I noticed that the line spacing between "Zombie" and "Shooting Gallery" was too wide, so in the Properties panel, with the entire text highlighted, I went underneath the Paragraph settings and altered line spacing (the second Spacing value) to – 12.0. This looked much better, as you can see in Figure 13.23.

5. Go to the main Menu Bar and go Window > Common Libraries > Buttons to bring up the Buttons Library. Scroll down to Classic Buttons and find the subfolder Arcade Buttons. Select arcade button—red (shown in Figure 13.23). Drag and drop it on the Stage. Use the Free Transform tool to enlarge the button.

6. You might wonder how I get the titles and buttons to be centered on my Stage. I'll tell you. I select an object and use the Align panel's Distribute

**Figure 13.23**
Start screen for the shooting gallery game.

Horizontal Center button to align the object to the Stage accordingly. This is a fast and professional-looking way to put objects in their place.

7. Add a line of text beneath the red button that says, "Start."

8. Right-click on Layer 1 Frame 2 and choose to Insert Blank Keyframe.

9. Insert a new layer above Layer 1 and name it "Actions." Rename Layer 1 "Player." On the Actions layer, right-click on Frame 2 and Insert Blank Keyframe. On both Frame 1 and 2 of the Actions layer, place a "stop();" function.

10. Save your file as Shootinggallery.fla and go to Control > Test Movie to see it in action. So far you should see the start screen, and when you press the red button you go to a blank screen. Now close the Flash Player and return to your project.

11. On Frame 2 of the Player layer, use your Oval tool to draw a perfect circle. Before drawing, set your Stroke color to the same bright color you used for the title (in my case, #FFFF00) and set your Fill color to None (the red slash mark). Sct your Stroke weight to 4.0. Then draw it. You can draw a perfect circle by holding down the Shift key when click-dragging to create the oval. You should have a yellow circular outline, as seen in Figure 13.24.

12. Use the Line tool to draw two crossing lines in the circle, as shown in Figure 13.25.

13. Select the crosshairs by dragging a marquee selection over them with the Selection tool, right-clicking on them, and selecting Convert to Symbol. Make them a movie clip symbol called "crosshairs." Set the Registration point to the center before clicking OK. Look at Figure 13.26.

**Figure 13.24**
A perfect circle is the start of the crosshairs.

**Figure 13.25**
Complete the crosshairs as such.

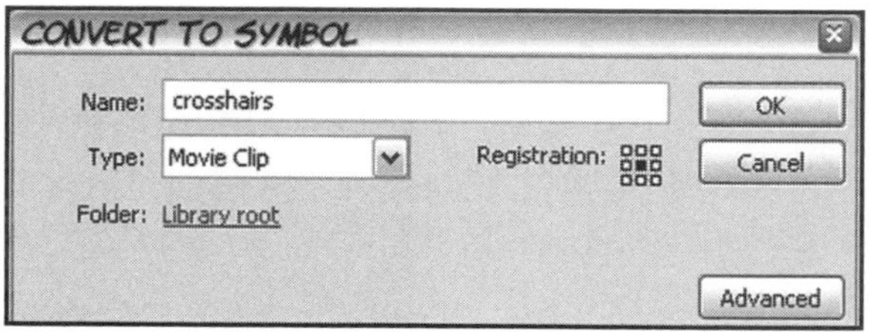

**Figure 13.26**
Convert your crosshairs to a movie clip symbol.

14. To make the crosshairs follow the mouse pointer, add the following script to the crosshairs symbol in the Actions panel:

```
onClipEvent (enterFrame) {
    mouse.hide();
    this._x = _root._xmouse;
    this._y = _root._ymouse;
}
```

15. Test your game as you have it so far. The crosshairs should appear on the screen and move when you shift your mouse around.

## Create the Environment

The environment is really there to add atmosphere and provide the player with a frame of reference for this kind of game. It can also gain you more exciting play by offering another obstacle.

In this case, I will show you how the zombies can "surprise" the player by popping up randomly from behind different objects in the scene. I will use wooden fences for this game, but in your game you can get more creative with the types of objects you use for cover. Whatever you use, however, be sure that they fit with the environment.

1. Insert a new layer underneath the Player layer in the layer stacking order. Name your new layer "Cover." Lock your other layers, but keep your Cover layer unlocked so you can edit it. Insert a blank keyframe on Frame 2 of the Cover layer.

2. On Frame 2 of the Cover layer, draw a rectangle with a black Stroke color, Stroke weight 2.0, and a brown Fill color. Open the Align panel (Window > Align on the main menu) and use the Match Width and Align to Vertical Center buttons to resize and position the rectangle.

3. Use the Line tool (Stroke set to 2.0 weight and a black Stroke color) to draw vertical lines alternating along the rectangle to separate the boards in your fence, as shown in Figure 13.27. When done, use the Selection tool to draw a marquee selection around the whole fence, right-click on it, and Convert to Symbol. Make it a movie clip symbol called "fence."

4. With the fence symbol still chosen, go Ctrl + C (Win) or Command + C (Mac). Right-click off the Stage and select Paste In Place from the pop-up options list.

5. Move the duplicate fence symbol up the screen to a new place with the Shift + Arrow Up key. With it still selected, go to the main Menu Bar and go Modify > Transform > Flip Horizontal. This will make it look a little different from the first fence.

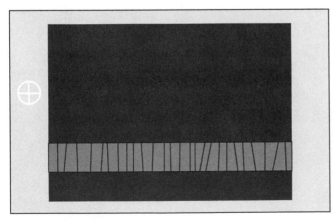

**Figure 13.27**
Draw a fence using the Flash tools.

## Create the Targets

I have provided a zombie image for your use, termed Zombie.png. It is shown in Figure 13.28 and can be found on the companion CD-ROM in the Exercises folder.

1. Insert a new layer beneath the Player and Cover layers. Rename the new layer "Enemy." Lock all other layers except Enemy.

2. Go to File > Import > Import to Library and find the Zombie.png file. Import the zombie image to your project's Library. When it's in the Library, use the preview window to see the zombie against your background color. With the Enemy layer selected, drag and drop your zombie image to the Stage. Use the Free Transform tool to resize it as needed.

3. Right-click on the zombie image and Convert to Symbol. Make it a movie clip symbol called "mc_zombie."

4. Double-click on the mc_zombie movie clip symbol to edit it within its own Timeline. Right-click on Frame 1 of Layer 1 and select Create Classic Tween from the pop-up options list. Right-click on Frame 15 of Layer 1 and select Insert Keyframe from the pop-up options list.

5. Return to Frame 1, select your zombie image on the Stage, and using the Free Transform tool, shrink the zombie vertically by holding down the Alt key

**Figure 13.28**
Zombie.png.

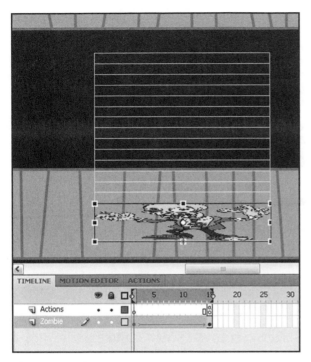

**Figure 13.29**
Scrunch the zombie down in Frame 1 and make it look normal in Frame 15.

while pulling down the top border (see Figure 13.29). Scrub through the 15-frame tweened animation, and it should look like the zombie is "popping up." This will create the tweened animation we want for the zombie image.

6. Edit your mc_zombie symbol some more. First, go out to Frame 35 and insert a new keyframe, then do the same on Frame 45. Go to Frame 1, right-click on it, and choose to Copy Frames. Then you need to right-click on Frame 45 and choose to Paste Frames. This takes what the zombie looks like on Frame 1 and puts it on Frame 45, creating a looping cycle. The zombie will go up and down. Lastly, you should create a "dummy" frame in front of the first frame, for the sake of the button we will turn this into later. So right-click on Frame 2 and Insert Keyframe. Right-click on Frame 15 and Copy Frames. Right-click on Frame 1 and Paste Frames. Deselect everything by clicking somewhere off Stage, and then select your zombie on the Stage on the new Frame 1. In the Properties panel, under Color Effect, choose Alpha for Style and move the slider to 0%. This makes your Frame 1 full-size yet invisible. See Figure 13.30.

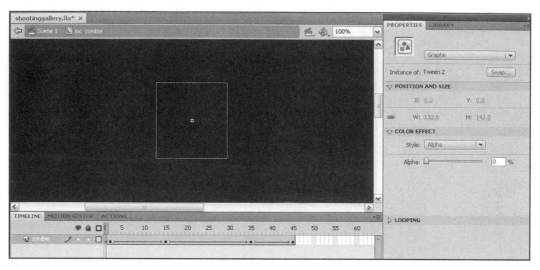

**Figure 13.30**
Edit the mc_zombie symbol.

7. Double-click anywhere off the Stage to return to Scene 1 and exit the movie clip symbol editing mode. Your zombie movie clip will appear as it would in the first frame of its animation, which should be a full-sized blue bounding box. Click and drag it behind one of the fences.

8. Try out your game. Save and test your movie to see the zombie pop up from behind the fence. If your zombie is placed wrong, or you cannot see him very well, simply go back to the Flash project and reposition him.

9. Close the Flash Player and return to your Flash project. With the mc_zombie symbol instance selected on Stage, go to Modify > Convert to Symbol (hotkey F8) and make it a button symbol named "btn_zombie."

10. Using the Actions panel, attach the following ActionScript to the btn_zombie symbol that is on Stage:

```
on (press) {
    nextFrame();

}
```

11. Unlock all layers. You need to expand the gameplay to a new frame. Each time you extend the game screen to a new frame, you will need to do the following: (a) right-click on the new frame (in this case, Frame 3) on the

Back and Player layers and choose to Insert Frame; (b) right-click on the new frame on the Enemy layer and choose to Insert Blank Keyframe; and (c) right-click on the new frame on the Actions layer and choose to Insert Blank Keyframe and add the action "stop();" to it. Look at Figure 13.31.

12. Copy and paste a duplicate of your btn_zombie from Frame 2 to Frame 3 of the Enemy layer. Then move your btn_zombie to a new location, still behind one of the fences. To make it look separate from the first zombie image, you can use the Free Transform tool or go to Modify > Transform > Flip Horizontal on the main menu.

13. Expand your gameplay to a new frame, following the instructions in step 5. Copy and paste another duplicate of btn_zombie from Frame 3 to Frame 4, and then move your btn_zombie to somewhere new.

14. You could continue this in perpetuity, adding new frames to expand the gameplay and adding more zombies for each new frame. Eventually, though, the game has to stop. For now, we'll stop it on Frame 5 by including a win

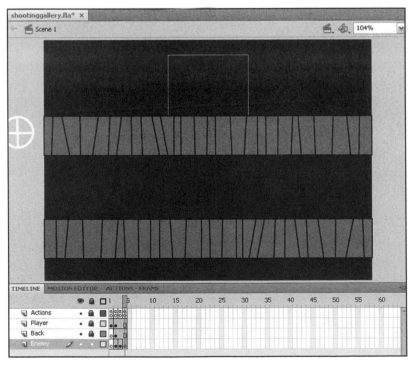

**Figure 13.31**
Expanded gameplay.

**Figure 13.32**
One example of a win screen.

screen. Add a new blank keyframe on the Back layer and the Actions layer, where you should put a "stop();" action. Add some text to the screen on the Back layer that says something like "Congratulations! You beat them all!" Compare your work to Figure 13.32.

15. Save your game and test it out by going to Control > Test Movie on the main menu. Click the button to start play. Whenever you shoot a zombie, he will disappear and another will pop up elsewhere, until you get to the win screen. If you find any glitches, go back through this exercise and check your code for errors, because it should work just fine.

### Shooting Gallery: What Else?

Your shooting gallery only has one environment right now and only one kind of target, but you can change that. You can put in more frames between the last shooting frame and the win screen, extending the length of the gameplay as far as you want, whether it's for 5 frames or 150, and on those frames you can insert more opponents popping up from behind cover. You can also add new cover objects, like trees, rocks, or houses, the enemies can pop out from behind, and come up with creative enemies whose appearances are different from one another, such as mutant dogs, Frankenstein monsters, bloodthirsty vampires, and more.

Another important element you might add to your shooting gallery game is a player score, showing how many targets the player has eliminated. This can be a static factor you don't even have to program. Put a text object in the upper-right corner of the screen that is bright and noticeable, and enter "0" for it on Frame 2. On each passing frame the player has beaten, add +1 to this score, so that by Frame 5 the player's score should say "3." On the final win screen, then, you can show the player a tally.

You can also have a Next Level button on the win screen that takes the player from Scene 1 in your game to Scene 2, where you could have a totally different look and set of monsters.

By the way, how you built this shooting gallery game is essentially the same way you would build a trivia quiz game. For each frame of gameplay, you would design a question with four possible right answers, each of which would be a clickable button. When the player clicks on a wrong answer, the button's scripting would take her to a lose screen with a button to retry the question. When the player clicks on a right answer, the button's scripting would take her to a brief win screen and on to the next question in the series. Graphics, sound, and animation could all come into play to make the trivia quiz game even more exciting.

For an example of a trivia quiz game made in this manner, take a look on the Web at *The Impossible Quiz*: http://www.cubefield2.com/the-impossible-quiz.html.

## Make a Fantasy Machine

Rick Dyer was inspired by the text game *Adventure* to create his classic arcade game *Dragon's Lair*, which was developed by former Disney animator Don Bluth and his studio on a shoestring budget of less than $1 million.

*Adventure* originally inspired Dyer to build an invention he dubbed "The Fantasy Machine." The Fantasy Machine, a more interactive variation of Choose-Your-Own Adventure or Fighting Fantasy game books, went through many incarnations from a rudimentary computer using paper tape with illustrations and text on it (a prototype of which is shown in Figure 13.33) to a system that manipulated a videodisc. The game it played was a graphic adventure game called *The Secrets of the Lost Woods*. Attempts to market The Fantasy Machine repetitively failed, so it never saw the light of day.

Afterward Dyer elected to take a limited but previously undeveloped location from *The Secrets of the Lost Woods* known as The Dragon's Lair and turn it into a laserdisc game by itself. *Dragon's Lair* (see Figure 13.34) was made by Bluth and published by Cinematronics in June 1983. Reportedly, the game became a sensation when it appeared, and was played so heavily that many arcade machines broke from overuse. Lately *Dragon's Lair* has been repackaged in many alternative formats, including a DVD game and a "retro" game for the iPhone.

*Dragon's Lair* was billed as an "action interactive movie." This game type came about with the invention of laserdiscs and laserdisc players, the first nonlinear or random access video play devices. The fact that a laserdisc player could jump to

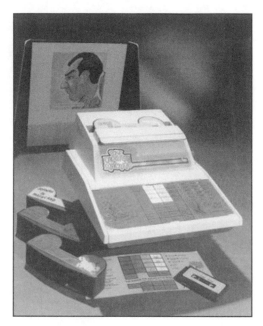

**Figure 13.33**
One of Rick Dyer's Fantasy Machine prototypes.

**Figure 13.34**
Promotional poster for *Dragon's Lair.*

and play any chapter directly, rather than plug along in a linear path from start to finish like videotape would, meant that games with branching plotlines could be built from out-of-order video chapters in much the same way as Choose-Your-Own Adventure books could be constructed from out-of-order pages.

The games following in *Dragon's Lair*'s wake, before the action interactive movies lost their flair, included *Dragon's Lair II*, *Space Ace*, *Braindead 13*, *Cliff Hanger*, and *Star Wars: Rebel Assault*.

These kinds of games are wonderfully easy and artistically expressive to create in Flash for the Nintendo Wii. They are entertaining, because they have branching storylines, animated graphics, and fun gameplay. I can show you how to get started, but to make a really great Fantasy Machine, you will need to keep working on it and adding more branches to it. The better you get at art and story writing, the better your Fantasy Machine will become.

The Fantasy Machine I make will be practically blank, an empty canvas upon which you can express yourself. Feel free to make up your own story and characters when designing your own.

## Create the Basic Layout

Before you get started making a Fantasy Machine, it's best to have a roadmap. You must know where you are going before you start heading there. This is not unlike the Boy Scout motto, "Always be prepared," but it goes further than that. If you are going to slap together a game with branching pathways, you have to have some inkling where those paths will take the player.

You can do this with a flowchart, which is like a diagram of directed outcomes. For the Fantasy Machine I will show you how to make, I am using a flowchart similar to Figure 13.35. I can then start to build a Flash game around this.

1. Open a new Flash file (ActionScript 2.0).

2. I will be working within the Essentials workspace, with the Library panel docked with the Properties panel.

3. Create four layers named as follows, in descending stack order:
   - Actions
   - Labels
   - Nav
   - Rooms

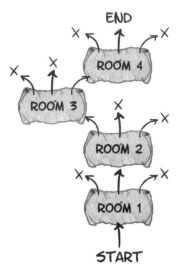

**Figure 13.35**
Flowchart for the following Fantasy Machine.

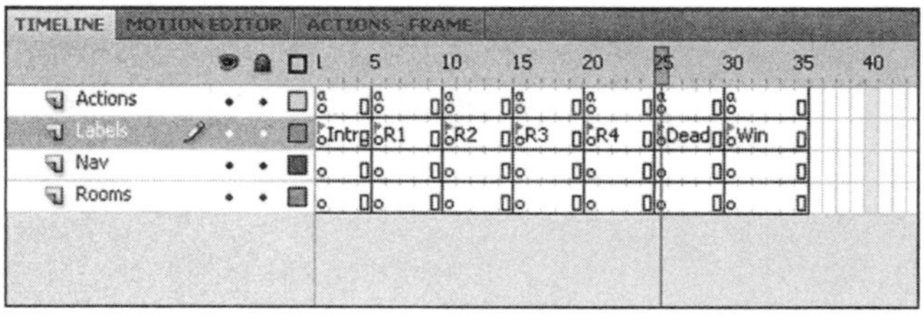

**Figure 13.36**
The layers for your Fantasy Machine.

4. On the Actions layer, set "stop();" actions in blank keyframes on Frame 1, 5, 10, 15, 20, 25, and 30.

5. On the Labels layer, you should add labels. Rather than call specific frames, it may be simpler to use labels to code the game navigation. First, insert blank keyframes on Frame 5, 10, 15, 20, 25, and 30. Then, with each of those frames selected, go to the Properties panel on the right. Notice that there's a place under Label for Name. Name Frame 1 "Intro," 5 "R1," Frame 10 "R2," Frame 15 "R3," Frame 20 "R4," Frame 25 "Dead," and Frame 30 "Win."

6. On the Nav and Rooms layers, insert blank keyframes on the same frames: 5, 10, 15, 20, 25, and 30.

7. On all layers extend the frames out to 35 by right-clicking on Frame 35 of each and selecting to Insert Frame. Compare your work to Figure 13.36.

8. Select Frame 1 on the Rooms layer in the Timeline and add a title to the Stage, such as "The Fantasy Machine by . . ." and your name. You can add some other graphics, if you like, and even a story, but for now, at the bottom, type some instructions: "Find your way out of the Wizard's Tower, and watch your step!"

9. On the rest of the keyframes in your Rooms layer you will add a text title for each, just to help you navigate them for now. Starting with Frame 5, you should type "Room 1," Frame 10 "Room 2," Frame 15 "Room 3," and Frame 20 "Room 4." On Frame 25 put a funny message like, "Yikes! Wrong turn. You're dead. Try again?' And on Frame 30 you should type, "Yay! You've made it out of the Wizard's Tower!"

## Create a Navigation

You have all your rooms put together. They're blank for now, although you can add graphics and animation and sound to them later on as you will. But the rooms, by themselves, don't really do anything. You have to be able to navigate through the Wizard's Tower in hopes of escaping (or whatever story you come up with).

I am going to use a graphical user interface, or GUI, to help the player navigate through the rooms. Some similar games make these buttons invisible so that the player has to pixel hunt to move around the scenes. You are free to do that, too.

I've discovered that it can be very frustrating for the user, however, and frustration kills the fun factor of any game. I just think it's easier in the long run to have a clearly visible navigation scheme, but it's up to you. If you want these buttons to be invisible, you probably want to make them larger, rectangular, and covering visible exit areas of your room. You will also have to set their Color Effect (Properties panel) to Alpha at 0%, so they are invisible. Either way, the coding would be the same.

1. Now it's time to add a GUI for navigation on the Nav layer, starting with Frame 5 (leave the Intro section of the Nav layer blank). If it's not already available, go to Window > Common Libraries > Buttons on the main menu to bring up the Buttons Library. Drag and drop the circle button—next, from under Classic Buttons, Circle Buttons to the Stage. Position it at the bottom of the Stage, just slightly right of the center, and enlarge it using the Free Transform tool and holding down the Shift key to keep it uniform.

2. Holding down the Alt (Win) or Option (Mac) keys while dragging, make a duplicate of the circle button—next. Do this twice to make a total of three buttons: one in the center, one left of center, and one right of center. Select the leftmost button and go to Modify > Transform > Flip Horizontal on the main menu to make the arrow point to the left instead of the right. Select the centermost button and go to Modify > Transform > Rotate 90° CCW on the main menu so that the arrow points up.

3. Pick the Rectangle tool from your toolbox. Set the Rectangle Options bevel corners to 75.00, the Stroke weight to 5.0, the Stroke color to black, and the Fill to white. Draw a rectangle that surrounds and encapsulates the arrow buttons. Compare your work to Figure 13.37.

4. With the Selection tool, select the buttons and the rectangle by dragging a marquee all the way around them. When they are completely selected, use Ctrl + C (Win) or Command + C (Mac) to copy them. One at a time, go to Frames 10, 15, and 20, right-click off the Stage somewhere, and choose to Paste In Place.

5. On Frame 5, select the up arrow button you've made, and add this action to it:

```
on (release) {
    gotoAndStop("R2");

}
```

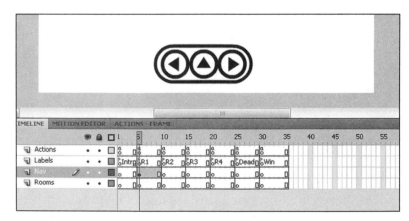

**Figure 13.37**
Put together a navigation bar.

6. The other two buttons will need this action applied to them:

```
on (release) {
    gotoAndStop("Dead");

}
```

7. Repeat this step on Room 2 on the Nav layer, picking the left arrow to go to "R3" and the others to send the player to her death.

8. Repeat this step on Room 3. Send the player to her death on every choice except the right arrow, which will take her to "R4."

9. On Room 4, make the up arrow take the player out of the tower, to "Win." The other buttons will take her to "Dead."

10. Go to Frame 1 (Intro) on the Rooms layer. You need to put a Play button here. Drag and drop an instance of the circle with arrow button from the Classic Buttons, Circle Buttons Library to your Stage. Use the Free Transform tool to enlarge it and use the Align panel's Distribute to Horizontal Center option to center your button. Look at Figure 13.38. Then add this action to the button:

```
on (release) {
    gotoAndStop("R1");

}
```

**Figure 13.38**
Make a Play button on the welcome screen.

**Figure 13.39**
Make a back button on the game over screen.

11. Copy the button, go to Frame 25 (Dead), and Paste In Place. Make the button smaller, use Modify > Transform > Flip Horizontal to make it look like a back button, and edit its action so that, instead of taking the player to R1, it takes the player to Intro (see Figure 13.39).

12. Save your file as "Fantasymach.fla," and test your movie to try it out. If you forgot the correct pathway to make it out of the Wizard's Tower, it's up, left, right, and up. Try the wrong way a few times to test out the death scenario. After all, you can always try again, can't you? If you find any glitches, or a button isn't working the way you want, go back to your project file and find the source of the problem.

### Fantasy Machine: What Else?

You have a decent start for a game, but what will make it special and unique is you. Use your imagination and artistic/writing talents to take your Fantasy Machine to the next level.

Add artwork where there are only blank rooms now. Give the navigation some cause; for instance, show doorways or trails leading off in those directions onscreen. Add animated characters or items out of movie clips to make your scenes more distinctive.

You could even make some of the props or characters into buttons, that, when you click on them, word balloons pop up to help tell the story. Remember, you aren't just creating a click-and-go game. You are creating a branching storyline game with depth and mood and theme. Plus, if your game is very long (longer than our four-room-long one), the player may need some clues to help him out.

To add clues, follow these steps:

1. Start by creating the graphic for the character or prop and import it to your Library before placing it on your Stage.

2. Convert it to a button symbol.

3. Double-click on it to enter the button symbol editing mode. Buttons have very distinct timelines all their own, with an up, over, down, and hit state. The up state is what a button looks like when you aren't doing anything with it. The over state is what a button looks like when you mouse over it, and the down state is what a button looks like when clicked. The hit state is supposed to be where you define the targetable button area, but you can ignore it and the button will default to the size of the initial graphic.

4. To add a word balloon, add a keyframe on the over state and import a word balloon graphic and type some text next to your button image.

5. Double-click off the Stage somewhere to exit the editing mode and return to your original scene.

6. Now, when you mouse over the button, the word balloon will appear to "pop up." You can test this without even testing the movie. Go to Control > Enable Simple Buttons on the main menu. This places a check mark next to Enable Simple Buttons in that drop-down list, showing that you have turned that function on. With this function on, you can treat buttons on your Stage just as they would be treated in the published game, with the exception of the coding you attach to them. When you are through testing your buttons, go back to Control > Enable Simple Buttons to turn off that function.

You should also, along with graphics and animations, add sound to your rooms. Let me give you some examples. Say that my Room 2 is a dank dungeon with animated rat eyes blinking in the shadowy recesses and rusty chains hanging from the vaulted ceiling. I might add a looping sound of a slow water drip to this room. Another room, Room 4, might appear to be a mad scientist's lab, complete with a table laden down with beakers of obnoxious chemicals, an animated Jacob's ladder crawling up between two electrodes in the background, and blinking computer lights across several terminals. This room deserves some electric sparks and maybe some computer beeps or bubbling liquid noises.

You could also have more than one death scene. Be inventive. *Braindead 13* from ReadySoft showed Lance, a young computer hacker the player controls, getting shot, stabbed, flambeaued, grilled, hacked, melted, and so many more deaths it was almost fun taking a wrong turn!

Not every wrong turn has to lead to certain death, either. I did that for simplicity here, but you could have buttons that take the player back to earlier rooms, like a twisting maze, or down multiple branching pathways that meet up again later. Think of how Choose-Your-Own Adventure or Fighting Fantasy game books are plotted.

## More Games

Of course, these are by no means the only game gems you can create using Flash. Flash is so versatile, especially when you learn to use the ActionScript better, that you can create virtually any game imaginable.

The games in this chapter are what I refer to as "beginner-level" games to design. For more tutorials, you can look online. There are several free Flash tutorials that will show you how to make brick-breaker games, *Dance Dance Revolution* clones, platformers, and more. However, many of the tutorials will stray heavier on the programming side and are thus more difficult to attempt unless you're already an adept Flash user.

Be sure, too, when you are seeking out Flash tutorials to look only for tutorials involving ActionScript 2.0. Most of them do, but some may not.

Here is a list of Flash tutorial sites you might surf:

- **Deziner Folio**: http://www.dezinerfolio.com/2008/02/06/20-free-tutorials-to-create-your-own-flash-game—*and*—http://www.dezinerfolio.com/2008/10/31/20-free-tutorials-to-create-your-own-flash-game-2

- **Flash Game Design**: http://www.flash-game-design.com

- **Flashkit**: http://www.flashkit.com

- **Mr. Sun Studios**: http://www.mrsunstudios.com/tutorials

- **Tutorialized**: http://www.tutorialized.com/tutorials/Flash/Games/1

## What's Next?

Now that you know all about making games in Flash, it is time to make them ready to play on the Nintendo Wii. In the next, and final, chapter, I will show you how to prepare your games for the Wii using the WiiCade API and how to showcase your finished games.

## Review

At the end of reading this chapter, you should know:

- How to make a tunnel maze game using Flash

- How to make a dress-up doll game using Flash

- How to make a shooting gallery game using Flash

- How to make a Fantasy Machine using Flash

- How to put together frames, buttons, and movie clips to make games in the Flash environment

- Some helpful information about making other kinds of games with Flash

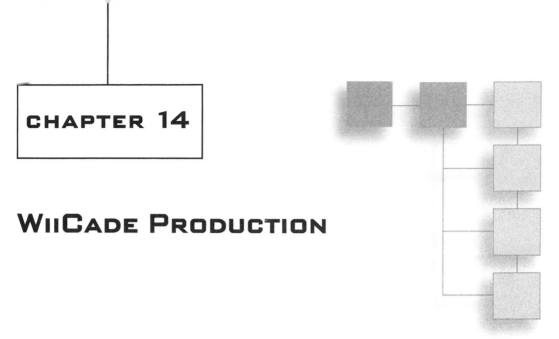

# CHAPTER 14

# WiiCade Production

In this chapter you will learn:

- What the WiiNode network can do for you

- To set up a WiiNode ID so you can upload Flash files to WiiCade

- How to upload Flash files to WiiCade

- To integrate the WiiCade API for button functionality of the Wii

- Where to find other Wii Flash game sites

- To build Web sites to publish your Flash files with

- To submit your sites to search engines

WiiCade, as mentioned before, allows your Flash files to interact with the Wii console system. After you read this chapter, you will understand what I mean when I say that, and you will know how best to distribute your Flash files when you have finished designing them.

First, I will show you what WiiMedia, WiiCade, and the WiiNode network have in common, and how they can help you make great content for the Wii. Then I will discuss the API integration and finally show you how to publish your Flash to the Web yourself.

**Figure 14.1**
WiiMedia.

# WiiMedia

Wii Media (http://www.wiimedia.com) is the largest Wii community on the Internet. Shown in Figure 14.1, it is now easier to find your friends, share saved games, customize your Wii system, and read the latest news on Nintendo products, all through WiiMedia.

WiiMedia started on December 9th, 2006 and has all the best innovative features at the same place where Wii users can interact with others easily and efficiently. Today, WiiMedia has over 14,550 members sharing more than 146 saved games from 852 available Wii and Virtual Console games.

Why is this important to you (besides the fact that if you're a Wii rocker WiiMedia might be a great community in and of itself)? It's important, because WiiMedia is the birthplace of WiiCade, which can help you get your Flash games and animation to the masses!

# WiiCade

**Tip**

When Nintendo Wii was let loose on the Internet via the Opera browser, it allowed Wii rockers to surf the Internet to their heart's content without ever leaving the console. The Wii Remote acted just like a mouse would, making it possible to click anywhere on the screen and navigate through Web links.

It also allowed for users to play online Flash games through popular Flash game sites such as:

- **Addicting Games**: http://www.addictinggames.com

- **Andkon Arcade**: http://www.andkon.com/arcade

- **Armor Games**: http://www.armorgames.com

- **Newgrounds**: http://www.newgrounds.com

- **U Got Games**: http://www.ugotgames.com

Any Flash game can potentially be played using the Wiimote. The Wiimote acts just like a mouse, with all the point-and-click functionality. There are several quality Flash games that work really well with the Wii.

Unfortunately, games that require more than just point-and-click mouse control have a greater difficulty of being played with the mouse/Wiimote, and for this WiiCade, as seen in Figure 14.2, has developed an API so that keyboard commands can be translated for use with the Wiimote.

WiiCade (http://www.wiicade.com) originally launched November 19th, 2006, the same day the Nintendo Wii was released. The WiiCade team had originally banked on the idea the Opera browser would come out when the Wii did, but this was not the case. However, WiiCade launched without problems and immediately started a strong Wii fan base.

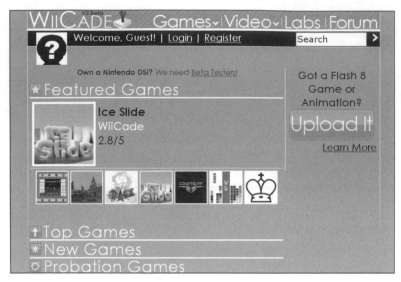

**Figure 14.2**
WiiCade.

While the Wii is a Nintendo product, WiiCade is not in any way endorsed by Nintendo and is entirely fan made and run.

The original team at WiiCade consisted of John Eysman, David Stubbs, and Aaron Worrall. Later, a man by the name of Jerason Banes came aboard as the fourth member of the WiiCade team, and he was the one who introduced the landmark WiiCade API that revolutionized independent Wii Flash games forever.

With the extended functionality offered by the API, as well as the intuitive site around which it revolves, WiiCade continues to make a strong impact on the Wii fan base.

## Upload Your Flash to WiiCade

Here are a couple of things you should check before you can upload your Flash to WiiCade:

■ Your game or animation must be Flash Lite 3.1–compatible (which you can set up by going to File > Publish Settings and looking under the Flash tab for the options to publish your .SWF file for the Flash Lite type compatibility; see Figure 14.3).

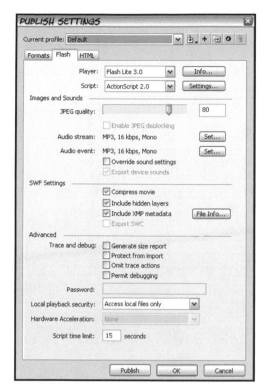

**Figure 14.3**
Flash Publish Settings.

- Your game must NOT require any essential keyboard controls without the use of the WiiCade Remote API. If you have an ActionScript that has an "on key press" code snippet of any kind, you *must* use the WiiCade API (see later in this chapter)!

- You must be the rightful owner of the game or animation, or you must have the explicit permission by the owner, to upload the file.

- Your game or animation must NOT contain any pornographic or otherwise inappropriate content.

- Your game or animation must NOT contain any characters, places, or objects currently owned by Nintendo (or for that matter, any other game company). This could brook lawsuit, and we don't want that!

- You understand that your game or animation will go through a one-week probation period where it must sustain a rating of at least 2.5/5 to remain on the site.

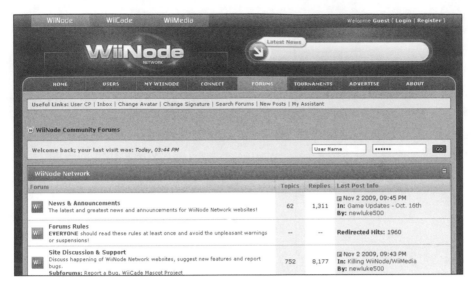

**Figure 14.4**
WiiNode.

If you meet all of these requirements, then you're ready to upload your game or animation!

Just go to the WiiCade Web site at http://www.wiicade.com, and click on the big Upload It button. You will need a WiiNode ID to log in and upload your file. WiiNode, as seen in Figure 14.4, is a network WiiCade is a part of.

### Get a WiiNode ID

It is free and easy to register for a WiiNode ID. The WiiNode ID will give you access to all the WiiNode network Web sites, helps you manage all your Wii-related data easily, lets you interact with other Wii owners, keeps track of your arcade game scores, and gives you your own profile page.

WiiMedia approached WiiCade with a partnership/affiliation offer, with the intent that they would create a one-stop network of sites for anyone interested in downloading/uploading game saves, playing/creating Flash games, reading Nintendo product reviews, and more. Consider WiiNode like Microsoft's .NET Passport system, where it's a global log-in that keeps all your information in one central place so you don't have to worry about remembering all your credentials. You can use this log-in on any WiiNode network Web sites, including WiiMedia, WiiCade, and the WiiNode forums.

Go to http://www.wiinode.com/auth/register to register for your WiiNode ID. Fill out the form. Note that the Personal Data section is completely optional, if you don't want to give away your personal information (which would be smart to conceal).

If you own a Wii console and plan to use your WiiNode ID for the stuff mentioned above on top of uploading games, be prepared to enter your Wii console's number, the 16-digit code unique to your Wii console. This number can be found in the Wii Address Book. If you don't own a Wii console, or you'd prefer not to use your WiiNode ID for the other purposes, then you can skip the Wii Settings section of the registration form.

You will receive your validation e-mail within moments. After validating your e-mail, you will now have a WiiNode ID you can use to upload files to WiiCade.

### Upload Your File to WiiCade

Go back to WiiCade and click the Upload It button again, and you should log in using your new WiiNode ID. See Figure 14.5. Once logged in, you will be returned to WiiCade, but you should see your user name up near the top. Simply click Upload It one final time to be taken to the WiiCade Upload page (shown in Figure 14.6).

**Basic Information**    There are two types of content WiiCade allows to be uploaded: games and animations. Select the kind of file you are uploading, whether it's a game or an animation. You will need to type in the name of

**Figure 14.5**
WiiNode log-in.

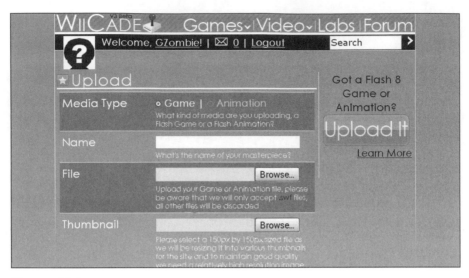

**Figure 14.6**
WiiCade's file upload page.

your file, too. Browse to find the correct .SWF file you have made. If you try uploading any file besides a .SWF file, then it will automatically be discarded.

**Thumbnail**   You will need to select a graphic that is 150 pixels by 150 pixels. This image will be resized into various thumbnail sizes for the WiiCade site. To maintain quality you will need a relatively high-resolution image for WiiCade to work with.

Accepted graphic file formats include .JPG, .BMP, .PNG, and .GIF. Most users take a screenshot from their computer of the game or animation in action, then, in an art application like Adobe Photoshop, they cut and resize a small part of the screenshot to 150 pixels by 150 pixels. Or, you can draw an image, scan it in, and size it within an art application.

Remember that the thumbnail will give first-time visitors the first impression of your game or animation, so make it attractive.

**Description**   Input a short summary, blurb, or high concept for your game or animation in the Description field. You want to give a viewer an immediate indication as to what your game or animation is about. Leave out superfluous details or misleading words. Don't say that, "This is the best game EVER!" or "Play my game or else!" Be witty and clever, attract an audience, but don't act stupid or people will only be turned off.

**Category** For a game, you have a drop-down list of category options, including:

- **Action**: Any action genre games that do not include platformers or shooters.

- **Platform**: Run-and-jump platformers.

- **Puzzle**: Classic puzzle-type games.

- **Shooter**: Games that feature shooting stuff or blowing up stuff.

- **Various**: If your game doesn't fit into any of the other genres, choose this.

At the time of this writing, the animation part was still forthcoming, so the categories for them could be anything.

**Sandbox** Would you like to upload your file to the Sandbox? The Sandbox is an area where only you may see the file that you have uploaded. It is used for testing your game before you release it to the public. You may want to use the Sandbox to test out WiiCade API integration, among other things.

**API Integration** Have you integrated a WiiCade-specific API into your game? If so, select which API you have used with your .SWF file, whether it's the WiiMote API 1.0, Wii Remote API 2.0, Multiplayer, or JavaScript. If you haven't used the WiiCade API, because your game does not contain any ActionScript other than mouse-clicking, then select "None."

**Tags** There are separate tags you can flag your content for, including disturbing themes, violence, sexually suggestive content, or coarse language. If your .SWF file contains any of these, you need to tag them here.

### Wait Out Probation

Your Flash file will be put on probation. Visitors can still access your game or animation, but it stays on probation for one whole week, and during that time it must maintain a rating of at least a 2.5 (out of 5). This means your Flash must appeal to 50% of the Wii fan base or better.

Don't sweat it! Unless your Flash is exceptionally dull, dreary, disgusting, or worse, you will get that popularity vote. After probation, your file will go into WiiCade's database for good.

**Figure 14.7**
The screen from Example1.fla.

## WiiCade API Integration

The WiiCade API is available for download from WiiCade Labs (http://labs
.wiicade.com) and is also on the companion CD-ROM for this book. There is a
server and client side of the API.

To see how the API works, open up Example1.fla from the Examples subfolder
of the API folder found on the disc. You should see the same screen shown in
Figure 14.7.

Look in the Actions panel for the script placed on Frame 1. It reads:

```
/*
 * This example shows off the functionality of the API by displaying which buttons
 * are currently pressed. Use the 'Test Movie' functionality to test this on your
 * Desktop Computer.
 */

//Here we tell flash about the WiiMote API.
import com.wiicade.*;

//This function gets called on every frame of the movie. The if statements
//check to see if any of the Remote buttons have been pressed.
onEnterFrame = function()
```

```
{
    var remote = Wii.getPrimaryRemote();

    if(remote.isDown(WiiRemote.BUTTON_LEFT)) buttonleft._visible = true;
    else buttonleft._visible = false;
    if(remote.isDown(WiiRemote.BUTTON_RIGHT)) buttonright._visible = true;
    else buttonright._visible = false;
    if(remote.isDown(WiiRemote.BUTTON_UP)) buttonup._visible = true;
    else buttonup._visible = false;
    if(remote.isDown(WiiRemote.BUTTON_DOWN)) buttondown._visible = true;
    else buttondown._visible = false;
    if(remote.isDown(WiiRemote.BUTTON_1)) button1._visible = true;
    else button1._visible = false;
    if(remote.isDown(WiiRemote.BUTTON_2)) button2._visible = true;
    else button2._visible = false;
    if(remote.isDown(WiiRemote.BUTTON_A)) buttona._visible = true;
    else buttona._visible = false;
    if(remote.isDown(WiiRemote.BUTTON_B)) buttonb._visible = true;
    else buttonb._visible = false;
    if(remote.isDown(WiiRemote.BUTTON_PLUS)) buttonplus._visible = true;
    else buttonplus._visible = false;
    if(remote.isDown(WiiRemote.BUTTON_MINUS)) buttonminus._visible = true;
    else buttonminus._visible = false;
}
```

The first part of this, "import com.wiicade.*;" tells the Flash Player to go out and bring in the WiiCade API. "var remote = Wii.getPrimaryRemote();" lets the program know which remote control to set the script to read. Use this function to retrieve a Wii Remote object containing information about the primary remote. This function is useful in single-player games where the user expects the remote that's turned on to be able to interact with the Flash movie.

Out of the four remotes available through the use of this API, only one remote is allowed to directly interact with the Web content. This remote is the "Primary" remote. While this remote is usually the first remote (it's set to ID 0), it is possible for other remotes to be the primary remote if the first remote is turned off.

If you decide to use the WiiCade API to script your game, make sure the Com folder (found in the Exercises\API folder on the accompanying CD-ROM) is in the same folder as your game file. Then attach the script "import com.wiicade.*;" on Line 1 of Frame 1 of your game. Use "var remote = Wii.getPrimaryRemote();" near the start to call that remote. Then, in place of using key presses on your keyboard, you can use the following button classes to script actions in your game:

- BUTTON_LEFT

- BUTTON_RIGHT

- BUTTON_UP

- BUTTON_DOWN

- BUTTON_1

- BUTTON_2

- BUTTON_A

- BUTTON_B

- BUTTON_PLUS

- BUTTON_MINUS

Of course, unless you hook a Wiimote up to your desktop computer, it will be difficult to test your movie. What you can do is upload your file to WiiCade's Sandbox to test it out privately after implementing a bit of code.

Here is an example of using the Wii Remote options through use of the API. This excerpt has been copied from the Deimos.as file found in WiiCade's Deimos—Example folder.

```
        if(remote.isDown(WiiRemote.BUTTON_LEFT))
        {
            lateralvelocity -= 0.04;
            fuel -= BURN_RATE;

if(!softThrustSoundStarted)
{
softThrustSoundStarted = true;
playSound("thrust-soft.wav", true);
}
        }
        else if(remote.isDown(WiiRemote.BUTTON_RIGHT))
        {
            lateralvelocity += 0.04;
```

```
      fuel -= BURN_RATE;

 if(!softThrustSoundStarted)
 {
 softThrustSoundStarted = true;
 playSound("thrust-soft.wav", true);
 }
      }
```

This snippet of code is controlling the movements of the player's rocket ship.

First, the code uses conditional logic to check to see if the player is pressing the left button on the Wiimote and gives the operations that will govern what happens to the player's rocket ship if she is (move craft to the left of the screen, burn rocket fuel, and play rocket thrust noise).

It also checks to see if the player is pressing the right button on the Wiimote and gives all the operations for it if she is (move craft to the right of the screen, burn rocket fuel, and play rocket thrust noise).

When you upload your .SWF file to WiiCade, and you have used the WiiCade API, be sure to check the option that you are using WiiCade's Wiimote API, because you will not be given the chance to upload the Com folder yourself. WiiCade uses that information about API integration to add the appropriate WiiCade API to your game.

### Multiplayer API

The WiiCade Multiplayer API is a software interface that provides Flash and JavaScript programs with the ability to communicate over the Internet. This allows developers to create rich multiplayer titles filled with players from around the world!

The software, at the time of this writing, was currently still in its beta testing phase, so I don't know that much about it. Check at WiiCade Labs (http://labs.wiicade.com) for more information.

Features of the multiplayer API will include:

- Server-side language similar to ActionScript 1.0 and JavaScript

- Automatic handling of connecting and messaging

- Built-in support for lobbies and rooms

- Easy to use messaging format

- Support for games and applications on both the PC and Wii

## WiiNode Forums

If you have started getting your feet wet with Flash ActionScript and you are having any difficulties getting your WiiCade API to integrate correctly, or you just want to toss off some questions about how all this is supposed to work, with your WiiNode ID you can log in to the WiiNode forums and participate in ongoing discussions.

WiiNode forums can be found at http://www.wiinode.com/forums.

There are lots of community members, including the original team at WiiCade, on the forums, who can help further your understanding of programming for the Wii or any other query you might have.

## Other Wii Flash Game Sites

One of the terrific things about the WiiCade API is that it works anywhere, not just on WiiCade! As long as you include the API files with your Flash, the API will enable Wii users to play your more complicated Flash media.

There are other sites besides WiiCade where you can upload your Flash games for Wii users. These are great in many respects, because Wii fans are already giving them quite a bit of attention, and your game will get played.

They include:

- **Flash Warrior:** http://www.flashwarrior.com

- **MiiBoard:** http://miiboard.com/arcade.php

- **Orisinal Games:** http://www.ferryhalim.com/orisinal

- **Wii Arcade:** http://www.wiiarcade.com

- **WiiPlayable:** http://www.wiiplayable.com

- **Wiiscape:** http://www.eiksoft.com/wii/index.htm

# Publish Your Flash Yourself

These days, the easiest way to self-publish is to build a Web site and put your art on it, and get people to come to your Web site to see it—something that anybody can do for little or no cost. There's no question that the Internet has profoundly changed our society. These days, people from all over the world chat over the World Wide Web, instantaneously sharing information in ways humans never considered possible before the birth of the Web. In this day and age, "I found it online," has become a household refrain.

## The World Wide Web

The *Internet* is a global network of computers that enables people from around the world to share information. Many people use the terms interchangeably, but the Internet and the World Wide Web, often referred to as simply the Web, are not one and the same.

The *World Wide Web* (WWW) is a subset of the Internet that supports Web pages, or specially formatted documents created using languages such as *Hypertext Markup Language*, or HTML.

*Hypertext* allows you to click on words in a document that are linked to related words, graphics, and other elements in the same or in another document.

Put another way, you might think of the Internet as the connection between various computers worldwide, and the World Wide Web as the content that resides on those computers that is transmitted via these connections.

In order to maintain your Flash online, you'll of course need a computer, and you'll need a connection to the Internet. That means that you'll need an Internet service provider, or ISP. These providers offer connections of various types, including the following:

- Dial-up, using a telephone line and modem (generally horrifically slow)

- Digital Subscriber Line (DSL), using a telephone line and a DSL modem

- Cable, available anywhere cable TV is offered

- Fixed wireless, using either satellite or microwave technologies

- Mobile wireless, using cell phone or wireless fidelity (Wi-Fi) technologies

Often your personal circumstances will dictate which option is best for you.

If you don't have your own personal computer with access to the Internet, the next best choice is to use Internet connections provided for public access in places like libraries, colleges, and schools. Although certain restrictions may apply in such places, computers in these places are typically available for your use. Even if you do have your own computer with Internet access, it's nice to know these public computers exist. For example, you might use them to update your Web pages if your home machine is out of commission.

## Web Speak

Just as terms like the Internet and the World Wide Web run together after a while, so, too, do terms like Web pages and Web sites. Take a look at the following distinctions:

- **Web sites**: A *Web site* is a location out on the Web. It is kind of like a neighborhood full of homes. For instance, http://www.msn.com is a Web site.

- **Web pages**: A Web site consists of two or more Web pages. A *Web page* is a single HTML document found on the Web, residing at a Web site. It is like one of the homes on a neighborhood block.

- **Home pages**: A *home page* is the first Web page you see when you enter a Web site, and it is often referred to as the index page.

## Browsers

A Web browser is a software program that is used to locate and display Web pages. More than likely you've used Web browsers without knowing what they were before, such as Internet Explorer, Mozilla Firefox, and Netscape Navigator. The Wii console system uses the Opera browser.

All these browsers can display graphics in addition to text. Additionally, they can display sound and video, although many require special plug-ins in order for these features to work correctly. For instance, your audience will need to have an Adobe Flash Player plug-in installed on their home computer to see your Flash animations. Many people already have a Flash Player, but some don't. For this reason, you should place a link on your Web page that enables site visitors to install Adobe Flash Player if needed. The link at the time of this writing is http://www.adobe.com/products/flashplayer.

## Hosting Servers

It all seems very simple. You click, and a new page appears on your screen. But where do these pages live while they're not being looked at? Where are Web pages stored?

Web sites and their pages are stored on special computers called servers. A server is a computer that is hooked up to the Internet 24/7 and might have one or more Web sites stored on it at any given time. The number of sites and pages that can reside on a single server depends on the server's memory capacity. When you enter a Web page address in the Address bar of your browser, the server responds by sending a copy of that page to your browser.

To publish your Web site, you don't need to set up your own personal server (although, if the spirit took you, you could). You can borrow someone else's server to put your files on. This type of server is called a *Web host*. There are countless choices in finding Web hosts: some are free, and others cost. Following is a list of free Web host services:

- **110 MB**: http://110mb.com

- **AtSpace**: http://www.atspace.com

- **Byet Internet Services**: http://www.byethost.com

- **FreeHostia**: http://freehostia.com/free_hosting.html

- **FreeWebs**: http://freewebs.com

- **Jumpline**: http://www.jumpline.com

- **Tripod**: http://www.tripod.com

When choosing free hosting, go with a reputable host. Some free hosting sites add bulky code to your page, which increases the loading time or speed at which your page displays. Others place advertisements on your page or even program code that can download scripts to your visitor's computer, infecting them with spyware. Avoid these types of hosts if you can.

Companies with dedicated servers cost you more, but as in everything in life, you get out what you put in. The top Web hosts with dedicated servers you can pay for at the time of this writing are listed here:

- **BlueHost**: http://bluehost.com

- **Dot5 Hosting**: http://www.dot5hosting.com

- **GoDaddy**: http://www.godaddy.com

- **HostMonster**: http://www.hostmonster.com

- **HostPapa**: http://hostpapa.com

- **StartLogic**: http://www.startlogic.com

## Build Your Site

Think of your Web site as a neighborhood. In that neighborhood, you'll need to put stuff, such as houses, trees, and sidewalks. Just as a city planner would, you will want to have a clear concept of what kind of stuff you want to include in your site before you start building it.

I will give you a brief primer for Web development. If you decide you really want to publish your Flash on the Web, however, there are whole books devoted to that topic you should really read.

A few I'd suggest from Cengage Learning include the following:

- *Web Design for Teens*, by Maneesh Sethi

- *Principles of Web Design, 4th Edition*, by Joel Sklar

- *Web Design BASICS*, by Todd Stubbs and Karl Barksdale

- *PHP for Teens*, by Maneesh Sethi

### Prep Your Text

Before you build your site or update it with new material, take time to write all your text beforehand. Your best bet is to use a word-processing program like Microsoft Word. It enables you to check your spelling, and it even makes suggestions relating to grammar and usage. You can right-click words to view your options, including other spellings, word choices, and synonyms. This both simplifies the process of writing and double-checking your work and speeds it up. In addition, writing things out beforehand helps you ensure that you're conveying the message you want to convey on your Web page without being distracted by any coding or technical aspects that are sure to crop up later.

## Prep Your Images and Animations

Note that images and Flash files must be small enough for transmission over the Internet. When I say "small," I am referring, of course, to the size of the file, not the dimensions of the file itself.

Unlike images you prepare for print, which must have a resolution of 150 to 300 dots per inch (dpi), an image bound for the Web needs to have a resolution of 72 dpi with a file size equivalent to 200 kilobytes (KB) or less. In order to achieve this file size, you will likely need to compress your images. This reduces redundancy in image data, often without a noticeable loss in image quality. Compressing your images not only makes it more convenient for you to upload them to the Web, it also benefits your visitors because it enables your site to load more quickly, displaying your graphics almost as soon as the text appears. Use an art or photo-editing software application such as Adobe Photoshop to compress your images.

There are three image types widely supported on the World Wide Web:

- **JPEG**: JPEG (pronounced *jay-peg*), short for Joint Photographic Experts Group, is among the most common image compression format available.

- **GIF**: The Graphics Interchange Format (GIF) is an eight-bit-per-pixel bit-map format that supports alpha transparencies. You can pronounce GIF with a hard or soft "G" sound.

- **PNG**: Short for Portable Network Graphics, the PNG (pronounced "ping") format is a bitmapped image system with 24-bit RGB colors and improvements over the GIF format. PNG is great for creating low-sized files with excellent quality.

The differences between these three image types are marginal.

When publishing your Flash files, the program itself has built-in optimization settings (found under File > Publish Settings). If you stuck with vector art and reused symbols, then file size shouldn't be that big of an issue.

However, if you are concerned about compression, some software programs, like Eltima's Flash Optimizer (http://www.show-kit.com/flash-optimizer), promise to reduce the size of your Flash movie files by 50 percent or more, which could definitely be a boon if you are worried about the large file size or download times. You can see a screenshot of the Flash Optimizer program at work in Figure 14.8. A free-trial version of the Flash Optimizer is included on the companion CD-ROM for this book.

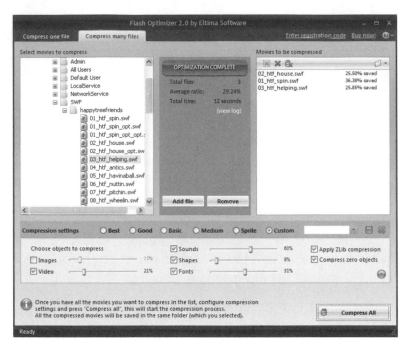

**Figure 14.8**
A screen from the Flash Optimizer program.

### *Put It Together*

Adobe Dreamweaver is the premiere Web site construction kit for professionals. It allows pros to work in either a WYSIWYG (what-you-see-is-what-you-get) or code environment—or in both simultaneously. Dreamweaver comes with several built-in site templates. All you need to do is add your content and create your custom logo. In addition, there are many free templates available online. Note that Dreamweaver can be fairly complicated, and as such, you will probably need to read a book that focuses on teaching you its inner workings, such as Sherry Bishop's *Adobe Dreamweaver CS4 Revealed*. Also, you can learn more about Dreamweaver and how to use it from Adobe's site at http://www.adobe.com/products/dreamweaver.

Another site creation tool is Microsoft Expression. Expression's goal is to overtake Dreamweaver and to overcome the limitations of its predecessor, FrontPage, with a more viable alternative. Expression is most compatible with Windows XP and Vista. You can learn more about Microsoft Expression at http://www.microsoft.com/expression.

A third alternative, especially if you don't have the budget required to own Dreamweaver or Expression, is Nvu (pronounced "N-view"), which is available

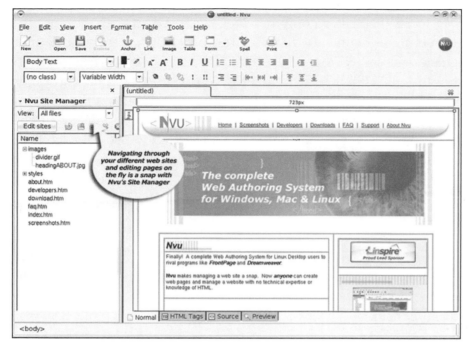

**Figure 14.9**
A screen from the Nvu Web-authoring program.

online at http://www.nvu.com. Nvu is an open-source Web-authoring application for Windows, Mac, and Linux users. This free program provides a great WYSIWIG editing environment and built-in file transfer system to satisfy most designers' needs. If you've always wanted to get your feet wet building Web sites, but don't have much in the way of disposable income, consider Nvu.

Nvu, shown in Figure 14.9, is also on the companion CD-ROM for you if you want to install and try it out.

You are not required by any law to use a Web-authoring program like these at all. If you prefer, you can hand-code it using HTML. HTML is a simple markup language that tells the browser how to display code on the page. It's so simple, in fact, that anyone can learn to do it. There are numerous HTML tutorials online that can get you up to snuff in hand-coding in no time. To find them, search Google for "HTML tutorial."

Note, too, that you don't need special software to hand-code Web pages in HTML. I usually use a text editor such as Notepad (Win) or BBEdit (Mac) to type my code and then save my file with the .HTML extension. When you open it later, it will launch in your default browser to preview.

*Cascading style sheets* (CSS) is a computer language used to describe the presentation of structured documents that declares how a document written in a markup language such as HTML or XHTML (Extensible Hypertext Markup Language) should look. CSS is used to identify colors, fonts, layout, and other notable aspects of Web document staging. It is designed to facilitate the division of content and presentation of that content so that you can actually swap out different looks without having to alter the content at all. CSS can thus be kept separate from the HTML or XHTML coding.

Once you have your pages created, upload them to your hosting server by way of file transfer protocol (FTP) or other upload option. This is usually dependent on which host you go with.

Whatever you do, don't lose your FTP, log-in, or password information on any of the sites or servers you decide to use. If you lose this information, you might have problems retrieving access to your site. Write them down in a notebook, so that you don't lose them.

### Blog and Community Profiles

Do you keep a blog or community profile, such as a MySpace or Facebook page? These are other reputable ways to get your Flash noticed.

You don't have to learn anything about HTML, and the blog or community service editors are nowhere near as complicated as Dreamweaver can appear. You can also host Flash videos, including your animations and games, on many of these types of sites. You don't have to get a hosting server or domain name, which will save you money in the long run. The biggest downside is getting your content noticed by search engines in order to corral people to your work.

Nonetheless, this is one viable way to start distributing your Wii Flash files online, and it doesn't require you to pick up a markup language or pay for hosting services.

### Submit to Search Engines

Now that you have some cyber real estate and you're confident in your overall design abilities, it's time to open the doors wide and let Wii users in.

If you aren't using sites like WiiCade that Wii fans are already going to, your first step is to submit your site to search engines so that it can be indexed with them and people can find you.

Pages are published to the World Wide Web by their domain owners or contributors, and just as easily, they can be changed or taken off the site. Thus, a page may be there one week and gone the next. This makes the Web an ever-shifting environment. Humans can compile directories of Web links that point to subjects of interest, but if these same people don't check up on their links on a regular basis, they may quickly become dead ends. This is why we've developed other methods for searching the Web for the content we want: search engines.

A *search engine* is a program that searches the Web for specified keywords and phrases and returns a list of documents in which those keywords or phrases are found. Popular search engines include Google, MSN, Yahoo!, AOL, Alta Vista, Dogpile, and AskJeeves.

A search engine is composed of three parts: a spider or crawler, which "crawls" through all the Web sites for keyword traces; an index of sites containing those keywords; and a search algorithm that makes it all happen. How the results are arranged and ranked varies by engine, although most try to put what they determine to be the most relevant and authentic results near the top of their list.

Because everybody wants to be noticed on the Web, it is very hard and sometimes expensive to get included in search engines by demand. Often, however, if your site is active for any time at all, search engines will include it for free. If you are intent on promoting yourself right away, there are some search engines you can submit to right away. Each is different and will require a different method for URL submission.

What follows is a list of those search engines you can submit your site to right now:

- **AltaVista**: Visit http://addurl.altavista.com/sites/addurl/newurl, click on Submit a Site, and follow the onscreen instructions.

- **Google**: Visit http://www.google.com/addurl.html and follow the onscreen instructions.

- **Open Directory Project**: A bunch of search engines use Dmoz.org for their search material, and you can submit to Dmoz.org, too. Go to http://www.dmoz.org/add.html and follow the onscreen instructions.

- **Yahoo!:** Visit http://search.yahoo.com/info/submit.html and follow the onscreen instructions.

To learn more about search engine submission, the dos and don'ts, go to http://searchenginewatch.com/webmasters.

## What's Next?

Hopefully this book has taught you a lot. You have gone through an arduous process. If you skimmed most of this book, it is probably a good time to go back and read the chapters that have interested you the most or read about specific areas your skills might be weak in.

Overall, this book has hopefully shown you (a) how to draw, (b) how to animate your drawings, (c) how to make up stories and games, and (d) how to put all those skills together into Flash animations and games you can put on the Web for users of the Wii console system to play.

Now it is up to you to carry what you have learned to the next level. One way to do that is to continue the exercises where I left off. Build them into full, engaging, and appealing Flash masterpieces. Play around with the software programs on the companion disc, such as Nvu, Flash, Flash Optimizer, Audacity, and Any Audio Converter. Practice and improve your skills in art, animation, and game design. This can remain a hobby for you, or you can turn it into your main career goal.

Whatever you do with what I have taught you, I hope you have a fun time doing it! And certainly, "we" would like to play!

## Review

At the end of reading this chapter, you should know:

- What the WiiNode network is and what it can do for you

- How to set up a WiiNode ID

- How to upload Flash files to WiiCade once you have a WiiNode ID

- How to integrate the WiiCade API for button functionality of the Wii

- Where to find other Wii Flash game sites

- How to build Web sites you can put your Flash on

- How to submit your sites to search engines

# INDEX

# License Agreement/Notice of Limited Warranty

By opening the sealed disc container in this book, you agree to the following terms and conditions. If, upon reading the following license agreement and notice of limited warranty, you cannot agree to the terms and conditions set forth, return the unused book with unopened disc to the place where you purchased it for a refund.

## License

The enclosed software is copyrighted by the copyright holder(s) indicated on the software disc. You are licensed to copy the software onto a single computer for use by a single user and to a backup disc. You may not reproduce, make copies, or distribute copies or rent or lease the software in whole or in part, except with written permission of the copyright holder(s). You may transfer the enclosed disc only together with this license, and only if you destroy all other copies of the software and the transferee agrees to the terms of the license. You may not decompile, reverse assemble, or reverse engineer the software.

## Notice of Limited Warranty

The enclosed disc is warranted by Course Technology to be free of physical defects in materials and workmanship for a period of sixty (60) days from end user's purchase of the book/disc combination. During the sixty-day term of the limited warranty, Course Technology will provide a replacement disc upon the return of a defective disc.

## Limited Liability

THE SOLE REMEDY FOR BREACH OF THIS LIMITED WARRANTY SHALL CONSIST ENTIRELY OF REPLACEMENT OF THE DEFECTIVE DISC. IN NO EVENT SHALL COURSE TECHNOLOGY OR THE AUTHOR BE LIABLE FOR ANY OTHER DAMAGES, INCLUDING LOSS OR CORRUPTION OF DATA, CHANGES IN THE FUNCTIONAL CHARACTERISTICS OF THE HARDWARE OR OPERATING SYSTEM, DELETERIOUS INTERACTION WITH OTHER SOFTWARE, OR ANY OTHER SPECIAL, INCIDENTAL, OR CONSEQUENTIAL DAMAGES THAT MAY ARISE, EVEN IF COURSE TECHNOLOGY AND/OR THE AUTHOR HAS PREVIOUSLY BEEN NOTIFIED THAT THE POSSIBILITY OF SUCH DAMAGES EXISTS.

## Disclaimer of Warranties

COURSE TECHNOLOGY AND THE AUTHOR SPECIFICALLY DISCLAIM ANY AND ALL OTHER WARRANTIES, EITHER EXPRESS OR IMPLIED, INCLUDING WARRANTIES OF MERCHANTABILITY, SUITABILITY TO A PARTICULAR TASK OR PURPOSE, OR FREEDOM FROM ERRORS. SOME STATES DO NOT ALLOW FOR EXCLUSION OF IMPLIED WARRANTIES OR LIMITATION OF INCIDENTAL OR CONSEQUENTIAL DAMAGES, SO THESE LIMITATIONS MIGHT NOT APPLY TO YOU.

## Other

This Agreement is governed by the laws of the State of Massachusetts without regard to choice of law principles. The United Convention of Contracts for the International Sale of Goods is specifically disclaimed. This Agreement constitutes the entire agreement between you and Course Technology regarding use of the software.